MW01691291

The Moneyers of England, 973–1086

Labour organisation in Late Anglo-Saxon and Early Anglo-Norman English mints

Jeremy Piercy

BAR BRITISH SERIES 650 | 2019

BAR
PUBLISHING

Published in 2019 by
BAR Publishing, Oxford

BAR British Series 650

The Moneyers of England, 973–1086

ISBN 978 1 4073 5374 6 paperback
ISBN 978 1 4073 5623 5 e-format

DOI https://doi.org/10.30861/9781407353746

COVER IMAGE *Moneyers working in a mint. Bern, Burgerbibliothek, Mss.h.h.I.16, p. 222 – Diebold Schilling,* Spiezer Chronik *(www.e-codices.ch).*

BAR
PUBLISHING

BAR titles are available from:

BAR Publishing
122 Banbury Rd, Oxford, OX2 7BP, UK
EMAIL info@barpublishing.com
PHONE +44 (0)1865 310431
FAX +44 (0)1865 316916
www.barpublishing.com

For Arthur Maynard Poole (1912–2001) and Blanche Wilson Poole (1912–1994).

Some of my fondest childhood memories are from time spent at my great-grandparents' house. My great-grandparents always had a kind word for everyone and never wavered in their love and support for their neighbours, their family, and each other. They were inspirational in so many different ways. Perhaps being regaled with tales of how far a nickel used to go at the mill store or the county fair (a popcorn to share and all the rides you could handle) while watching baseball or working in their garden prompted my fascination with coinage and what you can do with it. This book is dedicated to the loving memory of my Grandma and Grandpa Poole.

Acknowledgements

This book would not have been possible without the assistance and support of several people. Martin Allen and Rory Naismith have been exceedingly kind with their time and attention, both reading and providing feedback on the manuscript and guidance towards its publication. Bill Aird and Rick Sowerby also read multiple versions of this work and provided detailed feedback and direction throughout this research. Katharine Keats-Rohan gave me great advice on the prosopographical aspects of this work and several members of the British Numismatic Society, notably Stewart Lyon, and Hugh Pagan, along with Martin Allen, spoke with me about my research, enhancing the numismatic arguments of the text. Several others have taken the time to speak with me on various aspects of the project, reading drafts of my work, attending conference presentations, and inviting me to speak. While they are too numerous to address individually, I would like to specifically thank Chris Lewis, who took the time to read my work and offer comments, as well as Stephen Baxter, Tom Brown, Adam Fox, and James Fraser, who have all offered input and guidance on different aspects of my writing. The editorial team at BAR has been very helpful and extremely patient.

Most importantly, I would like to thank my wife, Katie. Her support of this endeavour has never wavered. She has been my constant companion and inspiration on this adventure. Her work as editor, commentator, and counsellor has been invaluable. While this work, and any mistakes contained herein, is my own, none of this would have been possible without her love and encouragement.

Photographic Credits

Related Titles

Urban-Rural Connections in Domesday Book and Late Anglo-Saxon Royal Administration
Jeremy Haslam

Oxford, BAR Publishing, 2012 BAR British Series **571**

Royal Authority in Anglo-Saxon England
Edited by Gale R. Owen-Crocker and Brian W. Schneider

Oxford, BAR Publishing, 2013 BAR British Series **584**

The Place-Name Evidence for a Routeway Network in Early Medieval England
Ann Cole

Oxford, BAR Publishing, 2013 BAR British Series **589**

The Anglo-Saxons: The World through their Eyes
Edited by Gale R. Owen-Crocker and Brian W. Schneider

Oxford, BAR Publishing, 2014 BAR British Series **595**

Social Dynamics in South-West England AD 350-1150: An Exploration of Maritime Oriented Identity
Imogen Tompsett

Oxford, BAR Publishing, 2014 BAR British Series **599**

The Significance of the Place-Name Element *funta in the Early Middle Ages
Jillian Hawkins

Oxford, BAR Publishing, 2015 BAR British Series **614**

The Place-name Kingston and Royal Power in Middle Anglo-Saxon England
Patterns, possibilities and purpose
Jill Bourne

Oxford, BAR Publishing, 2017 BAR British Series **630**

Coinage in the Northumbrian Landscape and Economy, c.575–c.867
Tony Abramson

Oxford, BAR Publishing, 2018 BAR British Series **641**

Contents

List of Figures ix
List of Tables x
List of Maps xiii
Foreword xiv
List of Abbreviations xv
Glossary xvi
Abstract xvii

1. Introduction 1
Who were the Moneyers and what was their status? 1
Political and Economic Development in Anglo-Saxon England 6
Minting and Coinage in Anglo-Saxon England 16

2. Methodology 19
Problems with the Current Resources on the Moneyers 19
A Preparatory to a Prosopography 19
Die-Links 23
Charters 25
Uses of the Database in Historical Analysis 27
The Coverage of the Database 29
Data Entry 30
Moneyer Name 30
Mint 32
Range of Active Dates 32
The Organisation of the Database 35
The Moneyers of England Database, 973–1086 35

3. Onomastic Patterns in the Late Anglo-Saxon Moneyers 39
Introduction 39
Inheritance in Late Anglo-Saxon England 39
Moneyer Groups as Families 40
Onomastic Trends in the MED 44
Case Study 1: The [Brun-] Name Sequence 48
Case Study 2: The [Os-] Name Sequence 48
Case Study 3: The [Deor-] Name Sequence 49
Case Study 4: The [Eald-] Name Sequence 49
Case Study 5: The [Gold-] Name Sequence 49
Case Study 6: The [Theod-] Name Sequence 50
The Primary Name Sequences of London 50
Name Sequence Variation in the London and Southwark Mints 50
The [Ælf-] Name Sequence in London 52
The [Æthel-] Name Sequence in London 53
The [Beorht-] Name Sequence in London 54
The [Ead-] Name Sequence in London 55
The [God-] Name Sequence in London 57
The [Leof-] Name Sequence in London 58
The [Wulf-] Name Sequence in London 59
The Southwark Mint 61
Conclusion 61

4. The Moneyers and Mints of Late Anglo-Saxon England 63
Mint Classification and Name Sequence Organisation 63

5. Moneyer Grouping Patterns in Anglo-Saxon Mints 111
Moneyers Operating in Groups within the London Mint 111
The 'Stair-Step' Pattern of Moneyer Grouping 119

6. Organisational Structure of Late Anglo-Saxon Mints 127
Introduction 127
Moneyer Rotation Cycles 127
Theories and Possible Causes of this Rotation Cycle 132
Major Mints Summary 136
Minor Mints Summary 139

7. Conclusions, Limitations, and Future Implications 145
Introduction 145
Findings 145
Limitations of the Research 147
Future Implications 148
Final Thoughts 149

Bibliography 151
Primary Sources 151
Unpublished Material 151
Printed Material 151
Websites and Online Resources 151
Secondary Sources 152

Appendix 1 161

Supplementary data on moneyers and their coins, including Appendix 1 in graphical format, are available to download from: www.barpublishing.com/additional-downloads.html

List of Figures

Figure 1.1. Copper alloy *nummus* of Diocletian 10
Figure 1.2. Circumscription type coin of Æthelstan 11
Figure 2.1. First Hand type coin of Æthelred II 31
Figure 2.2. Coins of Edgar (1), Edward (2), and Æthelred II (3) 34
Figure 3.1. Instances and percentages of moneyers with the top seven protothemes as compared with all other moneyers' in the *MED* 46
Figure 3.2. The seven most frequently occurring name elements as a percentage of all protothemes and the number of moneyers with those top name elements 47
Figure 3.3. Number and percentage of moneyers from the top seven name sequences, the next largest sequences with ten or more iterations, and all other sequences 47
Figure 3.4. Total number and percentage of protothemes with ten or more iterations and all other name elements 47
Figure 3.5. Occurrences of the most common Name Sequences over time in London 51
Figure 5.1. Moneyer groupings of the [Ælf-] sequence in London 112
Figure 5.2. Moneyer groupings of the [Æthel-] sequence in London 113
Figure 5.3. Moneyer groupings of the [Beorht-] sequence in London 114
Figure 5.4. Moneyer groupings of the [Ead-] sequence in London 115
Figure 5.5. Moneyer groupings in the [God-] sequence in London 116
Figure 5.6. Moneyer groupings in the [Leof-] sequence in London 117
Figure 5.7. Moneyer groupings in the [Wulf-] sequence in London 118
Figure 5.8. Operational years of London moneyers from the seven largest name sequences 119
Figure 5.9. Operational years of all moneyers in London 120
Figure 5.10. Operational years of all moneyers in York 121
Figure 5.11. Operational years of all moneyers in Lincoln 122
Figure 5.12. Operational years of all moneyers in Winchester 123
Figure 6.1. The Moneyer Rotation Pattern 127
Figure 6.2. Operational years of London moneyers in the [Ælf-] name sequence 128
Figure 6.3. Operational years of London moneyers in the [Ead-] name sequence 129
Figure 6.4. Operational years of London moneyers in the [Leof-] name sequence 130
Figure 6.5. Operational years of London moneyers in the [Wulf-] name sequence 131
Figure 6.6. Moneyers of London in the Rotation Pattern 134
Figure 6.7. Some London [Ead-] moneyers in the Rotation Pattern 134
Figure 6.8. Some London [Ælf-] moneyers in the Rotation Cycle 135
Figure 6.9. Some London moneyers in the Rotation Pattern 135

List of Tables

Table 2.1. Example from the Index of Names ('Cild') 21
Table 2.2. Example from the Index of Fused Names ('Ada') 23
Table 2.3. *Ministri* Witnesses and Corresponding Moneyers on Charters of Hunewine and Dodda 26
Table 2.4. Comparison of Moneyer Origins for Lund 29
Table 2.5. Epigraphy variations of London on late Anglo-Saxon coins 32
Table 2.6. Coin Types by Date 33
Table 3.1. Moneyers of the [Brun-] sequence in London 48
Table 3.2. Moneyers of the [Os-] sequence in London 49
Table 3.3. Moneyers of the [Deor-] sequence in London 49
Table 3.4. Moneyers of the [Eald-] sequence in London 49
Table 3.5. Moneyers of the [Gold-] sequence in London 50
Table 3.6. Moneyers of the [Theod-] sequence in London 50
Table 3.7. Moneyers of the [Ælf-] sequence in London 52
Table 3.8. Moneyers of the [Æthel-] sequence in London 54
Table 3.9. Moneyers of the [Beorht-] sequence in London 55
Table 3.10. Moneyers of the [Ead-] sequence in London 56
Table 3.11. Moneyers of the [God-] sequence in London 57
Table 3.12. Moneyers of the [Leof-] sequence in London 59
Table 3.13. Moneyers of the [Wulf-] sequence in London 60
Table 4.1. Name Sequences of the London Mint 65
Table 4.2. Name Sequences of York Mint 70
Table 4.3. Name Sequences of Lincoln Mint 73
Table 4.4. Name Sequences of the Winchester Mint 75
Table 4.5. Name Sequences of the Exeter Mint 77
Table 4.6. Name Sequences of the Thetford Mint 78
Table 4.7. Name Sequences of the Stamford Mint 80
Table 4.8. Name Sequences of the Chester Mint 81
Table 4.9. Name Sequences of the Canterbury Mint 82
Table 4.10. Name Sequences of the Norwich Mint 84
Table 4.11. Name Sequences of the Oxford Mint 85
Table 4.12. Name Sequences of the Southwark Mint 86
Table 4.13. Name Sequences of the Cambridge Mint 86
Table 4.14. Name Sequences of the Shrewsbury Mint 87
Table 4.15. Name Sequences of the Gloucester Mint 88
Table 4.16. Name Sequences of the Wallingford Mint 89

Table 4.17. Name Sequences of the Worcester Mint 90
Table 4.18. Name Sequences of the Lewes Mint 90
Table 4.19. Name Sequences of the Bedford Mint 91
Table 4.20. Name Sequences of the Colchester Mint 92
Table 4.21. Name Sequences of the Ipswich Mint 93
Table 4.22. Name Sequences of the Dover Mint 93
Table 4.23. Name Sequences of the Hereford Mint 94
Table 4.24. Name Sequences of the Wilton Mint 95
Table 4.25. Name Sequences of the Northampton Mint 95
Table 4.26. Name Sequences of the Leicester Mint 96
Table 4.27. Name Sequences of the Warwick Mint 96
Table 4.28. Name Sequences of the Hertford Mint 97
Table 4.29. Name Sequences of the Ilchester Mint 98
Table 4.30. Name Sequences of the Bristol Mint 98
Table 4.31. Name Sequences of the Shaftesbury Mint 99
Table 4.32. Name Sequences of the Derby Mint 99
Table 4.33. Name Sequences of the Chichester Mint 100
Table 4.34. Name Sequences of the Huntingdon Mint 100
Table 4.35. Name Sequences of the Rochester Mint 100
Table 4.36. Name Sequences of the Bath Mint 101
Table 4.37. Name Sequences of the Cricklade Mint 101
Table 4.38. Name Sequences of the Hastings Mint 102
Table 4.39. Name Sequences of the Nottingham Mint 102
Table 4.40. Name Sequences of the Salisbury Mint 102
Table 4.41. Name Sequences of the Wareham Mint 103
Table 4.42. Name Sequences of the Maldon Mint 103
Table 4.43. Name Sequences of the Malmesbury Mint 103
Table 4.44. Name Sequences of the Totnes Mint 104
Table 4.45. Name Sequences of the Barnstaple Mint 104
Table 4.46. Name Sequences of the Dorchester Mint 104
Table 4.47. Name Sequences of the Romney Mint 104
Table 4.48. Name Sequences of the Stafford Mint 105
Table 4.49. Name Sequences of the Tamworth Mint 105
Table 4.50. Name Sequences of the Lympne Mint 105
Table 4.51. Name Sequences of the Steyning Mint 105
Table 4.52. Name Sequences of the Taunton Mint 106
Table 4.53. Name Sequences of the Bridport Mint 106
Table 4.54. Name Sequences of the Lydford Mint 106
Table 4.55. Name Sequences of the Southampton Mint 106
Table 4.56. Name Sequences of the Guildford Mint 106

Table 4.57. Name Sequences of the Buckingham Mint....107
Table 4.58. Name Sequences of the Winchcombe Mint....107
Table 4.59. Name Sequences of the Axbridge Mint....107
Table 4.60. Name Sequences of the Langport Mint....107
Table 4.61. Name Sequences of the Sudbury Mint....107
Table 4.62. Name Sequences of the Aylesbury Mint....108
Table 4.63. Name Sequences of the Sandwich Mint....108
Table 4.64. Name Sequences of the Watchet Mint....108
Table 4.65. Name Sequences of the Gothaburh Mint....108
Table 4.66. Name Sequences of the Warminster Mint....108
Table 4.67. Name Sequences of the Cadbury Mint....108
Table 4.68. Name Sequences of the Crewkerne Mint....108
Table 4.69. Name Sequences of the Bedwin Mint....108
Table 4.70. Name Sequences of the Bruton Mint....108
Table 4.71. Name Sequences of the Cissbury Mint....109
Table 4.72. Name Sequences of the Bury St Edmunds Mint....109
Table 4.73. Name Sequences of the Newport Pagnell Mint....109
Table 4.74. Name Sequences of the Torksey Mint....109
Table 4.75. Name Sequences of the Berkeley Mint....109
Table 4.76. Name Sequences of the Dernt Mint....109
Table 4.77. Name Sequences of the Marlborough Mint....109
Table 5.1. Groups of Moneyers in the [Ælf-] sequence of London....112
Table 5.2. Groups of Moneyers in the [Æthel-] sequence of London....113
Table 5.3. Groups of Moneyers in the [Beorht-] sequence of London....114
Table 5.4. Groups of Moneyers in the [Ead-] sequence of London....115
Table 5.5. Groups of Moneyers in the [God-] sequence of London....116
Table 5.6. Groups of Moneyers in the [Leof-] sequence of London....117
Table 5.7. Groups of Moneyers in the [Wulf-] sequence of London....118
Table 5.8. Major and Minor Mints by Historic County....124
Table 6.1. Some London [Ead-] Moneyer Placements by Coinage Type....135
Table 6.2. Some London [Ælf-] Moneyer Placements by Coinage Type....135
Table 6.3. Some London Moneyer Placements by Coinage Type....136
Table 6.4. Grouping and Rotation Patterns in the Major Mints....137
Table 6.5. Grouping and Rotation Patterns in the Minor Mints....140
Table A1. Alphabetical List of Mints and Data....161
Table A2. Mints by Periods of Moneyer Activity....164

List of Maps

Map 1. Mints active in the reign of Edgar (from 973 to 975)....167

Map 2. Mints active in the reign of Edward the Martyr (975–978)....168

Map 3. Mints active in the reign of Æthelred II (978–1016)....169

Map 4. Mints active in the reign of Cnut (1016–1035/6)....170

Map 5. Mints active in the reign of Harold I (1035–1040)....171

Map 6. Mints active in the reign of Harthacnut (1040–1042)....172

Map 7. Mints active in the reign of Edward the Confessor (1042–1066)....173

Map 8. Mints active in the reign of Harold II (1066)....174

Map 9. Mints active in the reign of William I (1066–1087)....175

Foreword

This is a weighty volume dealing with a weighty subject: the moneyers of later Anglo-Saxon England. Jeremy Piercy has written a rigorous account of this small yet influential segment of the population, visible primarily through the corpus of surviving silver pennies. His work is an important resource for all those interested in Anglo-Saxon society, and not just because of the scale of the numismatic corpus: Jeremy also interrogates the material in bold, imaginative ways, identifying possible families of moneyers who dominated mint-towns for generations.

What he offers here is nothing less than a glimpse of the urban elite of the tenth and eleventh centuries. That glimpse is tantalising in its implications, and like all good scholarship invites more questions. How, for instance, did moneyers generate custom? On what basis did the mass of the population – which would, of course, have been for the most part peasants in the countryside – interact with the makers and exchangers of new coin at their mint-place of choice? And who, indeed, made that choice? Familial or social blocs of moneyers might be part of the answer, in that they could constitute part of larger constellations of patronage, extending upwards and downwards, and indeed sideways via horizontal ties. The way forward may lurk in large-scale comparison of the coinage with figures recorded in late Anglo-Saxon documents from areas rich in charters (such as Kent or the west midlands), or in Domesday Book.

Jeremy Piercy's study equips scholars with a model for how to deal with a challenging part of that evidence: the coinage. The results of this study will be a core pillar of future research, using the coinage to reveal how late Anglo-Saxon England really worked. Its great strength is that it envisages a coinage embedded organisationally in the world around it – not as a free-floating entity abstracted from economic and social realities of the day. This is exactly the approach that serious scholarship on the coinage needs to adopt more widely.

Rory Naismith

List of Abbreviations

ASC	*Anglo-Saxon Chronicle*
ASE	*Anglo-Saxon England*
BL	British Library
BM	British Museum
BMC	*British Museum Catalogue*
BNJ	*British Numismatic Journal*
BNS	British Numismatic Society
CH	*Coin Hoards*
CIL	*Corpus Inscriptionum Latinarum*
EcHR	*Economic History Review*
EHR	*English Historical Review*
EMC	Corpus of Early Medieval Coin Finds of the British Isles AD 410–1180
GDB	Great Domesday Book
HCR	Heberden Coin Room, Ashmolean Museum
MED	*Moneyers of England Database, 973–1086*
NC	*Numismatic Chronicle*
NCirc	*Spink Numismatic Circular*
PAS	The Portable Antiquities Scheme of the British Museum
PASE	Prosopography of Anglo-Saxon England
RNS	Royal Numismatic Society
S (with number of document)	Sawyer, *Anglo-Saxon Charters*
SCBI	Sylloge of Coins of the British Isles
TNJ	*The Numismatic Journal*

Glossary

deuterotheme	The second element in a dithematic name.
die	The primary tool used for the production of hammered coins. A die is either an 'anvil' or 'hammer' type. The anvil dies typically lasted longer than the hammer dies because the latter were struck directly which resulted in damage and mushrooming of the material. The anvil die usually has the obverse face of the coin because it was more detailed and needed to be better protected from the regular impact of the moneyer's hammer. This resulted in obverse/anvil dies lasting longer than reverse/hammer dies. The dies were square in shape and the hammer die interlocked into the anvil die to hold it in place. Very few dies from late Anglo-Saxon England have been discovered.
die axis	The alignment of the obverse and reverse sides of a coin. Most Anglo-Saxon coins have die axes of 0°, 90°, 180°, or 270°, making the most likely shape of the dies an interlocking square because of this regularity.
die-link	A die-link is the connection between two or more coins that have been produced from the same die. This identification is made through the markings and designs on the coins themselves.
dithematic names	Names that are made up of two distinct elements, a prototheme and a deuterotheme. Dithematic names are generally Germanic in origin.
fission	The act of separating two or more records within a database.
fusion	The act of combining two or more records within a database.
generation	A generation within a mint is all moneyers operating from a single name sequence during the same time period.
name element	One of the components of a dithematic name.
name sequence	A name sequence is the collection of all moneyers with the same prototheme within a single mint.
obverse	The front of a coin. For late Anglo-Saxon coins this side includes the portrayal and title of the monarch.
prototheme	The first element in a dithematic name.
reverse	The back of a coin. For late Anglo-Saxon coins this side includes the name of the moneyer, the mint, and imagery that helps identify the coin type.

Abstract

This book examines one labourer group within developing urban society in England during the tenth and eleventh centuries in order to address both its status and whether the internal workplace organisation of this group might reflect on the complexity of an Anglo-Saxon 'state'. In reviewing the minting operation of late Anglo-Saxon England, and the men in charge of those mints a better picture of the social history of pre-Conquest England is realised. These men, the moneyers responsible for producing the king's coinage, were likely part of the thegnly or burgess class and how they organised themselves might reflect broader trends in how those outside of the aristocracy acted in response to royal directives. In order to address this, a database combining information from multiple catalogues, coin cabinets, and online repositories was developed and is presented in the appendix as well as the downloadable supplemental materials. Titled the *Moneyers of England Database, 973–1086,* it consists of 3,646 periods of moneyer activity, derived from 28,576 individual coins produced at ninety-nine geographic locations.

Chapters three through six provide potential uses for the database through two different types of study. Chapters three and four argue that the mints were primarily controlled and operated by families. Pointing to the repetition of the protothemes amongst the moneyers on a large scale across nearly all the mint locations known from the 970s to 1086, the text argues that the mints were dominated by a few select families that maintained authority through wars and conquests. Chapters five and six present two new theories on late Anglo-Saxon mint organisation. The first theory is that groups of moneyers would begin and end activity within the mints together, most often within family units, but regularly in conjunction with other minting families in the same location. The second theory is that these groups would operate in rotation. The moneyers would operate for a set period of time, then withdraw in favour of another member of their dynastic group, before returning to activity at a later date. The book concludes that this was potentially, if not likely, in response to royal imposition on the mints restricting the number of coinages that a moneyer could be responsible for, and take profit on, consecutively.

The book is structured with a brief introduction and literature review, inclusive of discussion on the status of the moneyers and the concept of an Anglo-Saxon 'state', followed by a methodological section that outlines the creation of the *Moneyers of England Database, 973–1086*, as well as the limitations in the source material. This is followed by two analysis sections and the conclusion. The database is presented in the appendix along with nine maps and general information about the corpus. There are also four supplemental material downloads available with the book. The first is an organisation of the coinage record supporting the identification of the moneyers by mint. The second is the raw database information in a manipulatable format for independent research. A large format diagram of all 425 moneyers in operation in London between 973 and 1086 is the third supplement and the tabular and graphical results of the analyses found in the latter sections of the book are presented in full in the fourth.

1

Introduction

Who were the Moneyers and what was their status?

Godwinus Socche fuit tempore Regis Edwardi magister monetarius, et tenuit unam domum de feudo Episcopi Winton.[1]

Claiming that a single mention of a 'master-moneyer' from one line of the Winton Domesday, itself compiled a generation after the Norman Conquest, provides support for an extraordinary level of organisation within the mints of late Anglo-Saxon England is admittedly a difficult proposition. And yet, the line does exist. There must be a reason that of the nearly 20 moneyers noted in the *c.*1110 survey, only Godwine Socche, or possibly Godwine Ceoc, is labelled a 'master' moneyer.[2] Was this a true indicator of Godwine's status *TRE*, as noted within the survey, or had his status changed post-Conquest to include a differentiation from his fellow minters? Is this just a step in the long process of moneyers first appearing on coins in the time of Offa to their eventual disappearance from the coinage after the final consolidation of minting into the predecessor of the Royal Mint in 1278?[3] Who were the moneyers and how did they structure their mints at the end of the Anglo-Saxon era? In order to address these questions, a means of studying the moneyers as a collective group must first be established. But, before that, just what is already known about the moneyers?

This study aims to address some aspects of the status of the moneyers and how they structured their minting practice through the creation of a central point of reference and analysis of that material. Moneyers appear in miracle stories which occasionally provide a view of their life not readily apparent from the other extant sources. For example, a story in *Translatio et Miracula S. Swithuni* written by Lantfred after the saint's translation to Winchester in 971, describes a moneyer with great wealth, servants, treasure, and a large house.[4] The miracle story of Deorman of London in *De Miraculis Sancti Ædmundi* outlines that this man, whom Simon Yarrow equates to Deorman the moneyer, was a man of great wealth, 'who stood out among other businessmen, for the costly silk and splendid robes he wore'.[5] Another story, from Goscelin's *Miracles of St Augustine*, describes a group of men, a father and two sons, all moneyers, moving from Canterbury to Bath looking for work in the mints.[6] Two moneyers of similar name to those mentioned in the story, Æthelred and Sired, are documented on the coinages in Canterbury around this same time.[7] While it is not clear that these were the same individuals as those mentioned by Goscelin, the implication that families of moneyers existed is clear.

There are also several moneyer-related items from Domesday that shed light on who these men were in relation to the society around them. Certainly, they were not common workmen, but it is equally certain that they were not part of the aristocracy, at least not generally, because of the lack of written records of their lives.[8] In short, the moneyers were the men in control of the mints that produced the king's coinage and beyond the characterisations below, not a lot is known about them, the social circles that they moved in, or how they operated. They have always been something of a special case, in being neither peasant nor noble, they represent a junction between those two large social bodies.[9] Some of the

[1] H. Ellis, 1816, *Libri censualis vocati Domesday Book, additamenta ex codic antiquiss: Exon Domesday, Inquisitio Eliensis, Liber Winton, Boldon Book*, London, 533; M. Biddle, 1976, *Winchester in the Early Middle Ages, an edition and discussion of the Winton Domesday*, Oxford, translation at 36, discussion at 421–22.

[2] M. Biddle, 2012, *Winchester Studies 8: The Winchester Mint and Coins and Related Finds from the Excavations of 1961–71*, Oxford, 581–2, n. 2.

[3] G. C. Brooke, 1931, 'The Medieval Moneyers', *BNJ* 21, 59–66 at 66.

[4] Lantfred, Translatio Miracula S. Swithuni, in M. Lapidge, ed., 2003, *Winchester Studies 4: The Cult of St Swithun*, Oxford, 267–75.

[5] Abbot Samson, De Miraculis Sancti Ædmundi, in T. Arnold, ed., 2012, *Memorials of St. Edmund's Abbey*, Volume 1, London, 107–208 at 183. *Inter quos quidam praedives a urbis Londonie, Deormannus, affuit, qui prae ceteris negotiatoribus in caris speciebus et sericis et cycladibus splendidus et egregius mercator effulsit.* S. Yarrow, 2006, *Saints and their Communities: Miracle Stories in Twelfth-Century England*, Oxford, 58. Yarrow utilises Samson's *De Miraculis S. Ædmundi*, which was likely compiled at the end of the twelfth century. This makes provenance for the Deorman miracle story difficult, as the Deorman family was influential in London and beyond during the late 1100s. The contemporary local politics could have influenced the creation of this story. See also R. Pinner, 2015, *The Cult of St Edmund in Medieval East Anglia*, Woodbridge, 60.

[6] *Acta Sanctorum*, May, vi, 402. *Novit Cantuaria tres cives suos, quorum duo videntur germani, Wilfronius et Ælredus, tertius Ælredi silius Siredus, qui pari solertia et arte vitam alebant, et de inopia ad divitem sufficientiam excreverant.... In tali negotio venientes ad oppidum, quod a balneis calidis ibidem scaturientibus, Bathan Anglice nuncupatur, emptasque ex more copiosas arsuras, quas dicunt scopaturas, ad proximum flumen ferebant diluendas.* For discussion of the miracle story in detail see H. Tsurushima, 2012, 'The Moneyers of Kent in the Long Eleventh Century', in D. Roffe, ed., *The English and Their Legacy, 900–1200: Essays in Honour of Ann Williams*, Woodbridge, 33–59 at 37.

[7] Tsurushima, 2012, 37.

[8] While the 'special status' of moneyers is not in dispute, and is elaborated upon below, the lack of written records associated with their office and practice indicates that they likely moved in different social circles to ecclesiastic officials, royal agents, and the large land holding aristocracy, making their classification difficult, even if they shared some common privileges attributed to those other important groups. See: R. Naismith, 2017a, *Medieval European Coinage, Vol. 8: Britain and Ireland c. 400–1066*, Cambridge, 10–11.

[9] R. Ruding, 1840, *Annals of the Coinage of Britain and its Dependencies: from the earliest period of authentic history to the reign of Victoria*, Volume I, Third Edition, London, 48. See also R. Naismith, 2013b, 'London and its mint *c.* 880–1066: a preliminary survey', *BNJ* 83, 44–74 at 53–4.

earliest studies on the coinage of Anglo-Saxon England attempted to outline the unique position of the moneyer. In 1840, Ruding outlined the points in Domesday that framed the possible uniqueness of the moneyer office:[10]

- Some moneyers had tax-free housing.
- A moneyer may have been required to march with the sheriff or could pay a fee instead. It is not clear if military service was expected or if this was so that the sheriff had ready access to coin as needed.
- A moneyer was obligated to hammer coinage for the king upon his arrival at a mint, utilising the king's silver.
- Moneyers had sac and soc.
- When a moneyer died without a will their property devolved to the king.
- Moneyers paid rent to the king.
- Moneyers paid a fee at coinage renewals for the new dies from London. This fee was occasionally paid after the dies were received.

So, this states that moneyers were men of some authority within their local communities but were not by and large as important or as powerful as the local sheriff or reeve. According to Ruding, they were too numerous to be noble but could not be peasants or simple workmen because of the enormous responsibility they had and the trust that their name on the coinage was meant to instill into those taking the silver pennies from them.[11] Ruding's contemporary, Edward Hawkins, compiled a detailed list of the moneyers and descriptions of the different coinages produced in England in 1841, utilising Ruding's findings as a starting point in his own interpretation of the coinages.[12] Hawkins refers to Ruding's work as the history of the coinage, while his own work is the history of the coins themselves, making notes on hoard discoveries and coin types.[13] Perhaps, due to the marked increase in hoard discovery during industrialization, later historians and numismatists disputed some aspects of the certainty provided in the reasoning of Ruding.[14] In 1885, J. Drummond Robertson referred to Ruding's descriptions as too vague and sought to solidify the standing of later moneyers through the use of the Pipe Rolls, noting that several moneyers were also Bailiffs in Gloucester in the thirteenth century.[15] Drummond Robertson also noted that in the Registers of the Abbey of Gloucester these moneyers acted as witnesses in 'almost every document' and in a few occurred as principals.[16] Drummond Robertson speculated that the status of the moneyers may have been influenced by the French. He refers to Ernst Dumas' writing from 1868 that in 864 it was recorded that 'no one could be a master moneyer unless he were descended from the old coiners, who were men of gentle blood, and privileged to dine at the king's table'.[17] Dumas goes further in the lines following to state that this measure of control (from progenitor to descendant) in the position of moneyer is what allowed the moneyers of Rouen to maintain control of their craft and keep others out for nine centuries, with few exceptions.[18] Drummond Roberston's final characterisation of the moneyers disputes Ruding's findings, noting that Henry II, in utilising a French artist in his reorganisation of the coinage in 1180, established a 'superior rank of men holding the office' than would have existed at the time of Domesday.[19] If one takes Dumas' characterization of the Rouen moneyers at face value, however, it would seem that at the very least the Normans would have had knowledge of this sort of process when they reached English shores. Taking this reasoning a step further, it is also evident that Normans were present in London, with special privileges, during the latter years of the Anglo-Saxon kingdom and could have transferred minting knowledge in this period as well, long before Henry II's 1180 reform.[20] Another criticism of Ruding's outline of the moneyers is in the realisation that not all moneyers would have needed to travel to London in order to purchase a new die. Several studies suggest that the dies utilised in the hammering of coins were made regionally, thus making frequent travel to London unnecessary. For example, Peake suggested as early as 1893 that an original die was produced in London and that copies were made regionally.[21] Further discussion of the regional die hypothesis is in the section on die-links below. Other points of contention with regards to the utilisation of Ruding's classifications on the status of the moneyers have developed into debates within the numismatic field.

[10] Ruding, 1840, 49. While not explicitly stated, it would appear Ruding was using Ellis's 1816 *Boldon Book* for some of his research into Domesday as he references it specifically on page 1 in reference to the use of *pecunia* in the text.

[11] Ruding, 1840, 48.

[12] E. Hawkins, 1841, *The Silver Coins of England Arranged and Described with Remarks on British Money, Previous to the Saxon Dynasties*, London.

[13] Hawkins, 1841, 2.

[14] E. Hawkins, 1887, *The Silver Coins of England Arranged and Described with Remarks on British Money, Previous to the Saxon Dynasties,* Second Edition, London, iii–vi. The second edition of this book, published by the author's grandson, still lists it as the predominant 'handbook' on English silver coinage but acknowledges that a great deal of additional information had been uncovered through 'numerous disturbances of the soil caused by building and other operations'. This publication followed Hildebrand's, which, being published in Swedish, is acknowledged but noted as unhelpful for the current study.

[15] J. Drummond Robertson, 1885, 'The Status of the Anglo-Norman Moneyer', *NC* 5 (Third Series), 209–12 at 210.

[16] Drummond Robertson, 1885, 210.

[17] Drummond Robertson, 1885, 212.

[18] E. Dumas, 1868, *Notes sur l'émission en France des monnaies décimales de bronze (1852-1865)*, Paris, 39 n.1. Dumas does not provide a source for this information. Dès 861, les monnayeurs possédaient cet exorbitant privilége, que nul ne pouvait être reçu maître s'il ne descendait de la race des anciens monnayeurs, gentilshommes commensaux de la table du roi. C'est ce qui explique comment les monnayeurs de Rouen conservèrent cet état dans leurs familles, exclusivement à toutes autres, pendant plus de neuf siècles. Cette loi ne souffrit que des exceptions rares et dans des circonstances particulières. Full text available at the Hathi Trust Digital Library, https://babel.hathitrust.org, Accessed 11 October 2017.

[19] Drummond Robertson, 1885, 212.

[20] J. Green, 2017, *Forging the Kingdom: Power in English Society, 973–1189*, Cambridge, 200. Green notes that there were Normans in London with special legal privileges during the reign of Æthelred II. This, perhaps not coincidentally, is the period in which the coinage reforms of Edgar from the mid-970s solidified into periodic type changes, which would, more than anything else, make the late Anglo-Saxon coinage distinct.

[21] A. E. Packe, 1893, 'The Coinage of the Norman Kings', *NC* 13, 129–45 at 130; P. W. P. Carlyon-Britton, 1905a, 'A Numismatic History of the Reigns of William I and II (1066–1100)', *BNJ* 2, 87–184 at 91.

For example, taking Ruding's work a step further in 1901, Walter Andrew published a monumental article, 502 pages in length and taking up an entire volume of the *Numismatic Chronicle*, in which he outlined, using evidence from Domesday, two theories for mint operation.[22] His first theory was that the mints were allocated by the king for his direct service or farmed to a local lord.[23] His second theory, which proved to be the more controversial, was that those mints farmed to local lords could only be active when the lord was physically present in the relevant mint-place.[24] He developed these theories in light of the sporadic reporting of mint dues within Domesday and the then limited supply of Anglo-Saxon coinage finds for certain locales. His theories received harsh criticism, especially and most prominently in the form of a five-page rebuttal article published the following year in which C. G. Crump and C. Johnson state that Andrew's work contained no concrete historical evidence and was in effect 'bad history'.[25] The article concludes with an acknowledgement that Andrew was attempting to readdress Ruding's work in a modern context but that such work would be better served by being undertaken by a numismatist with 'a knowledge of history' instead.[26] The fallout of this harsh response to his work would cause an irreparable rift in the Royal Numismatic Society. Andrew resigned and within months the society had split into two distinct groups: the Royal Numismatic Society and the British Numismatic Society.[27] The details of this split stem most directly from the publication of Crump and Johnson's rebuttal to Andrew.[28] Carlyon-Britton and Lawrence, both prominent members of the Society, protested the editors' decision to publish the letter on the grounds that the paper had not been delivered to the Society at a regular meeting, that the writers were not members of the Society, and that they clearly stated that they had no knowledge of numismatics.[29] This was followed by several months of infighting over procedure and editorial misconduct. The editors also refused a rebuttal from Andrew to the Crump article. Following these incidences and some problems with Societal Council elections, Carlyon-Britton, Lawrence, and others established the British Numismatic Society in November 1903, electing Carlyon-Britton as its first President.[30]

Several decades later, D. M. Metcalf would outline Andrew's work as still the only firm attempt at solving the historical questions the coinage of Henry I raises about the moneyers (outside a two-page summary provided by Adolphus Ballard in 1904).[31] He also stated that Crump and Johnson failed to actually disprove the hypotheses Andrew put forth, but that subsequent research and coin finds over the intermittent 80 years had provided ample examples to dispute the theories put forth in 1901.[32] So, this intervening period saw the development of several theories on the status of the moneyer without any real movement beyond the original list developed from Domesday in 1840 by Ruding. A notable exception to this, and one stated by Mark Blackburn to have 'stultified further research for more than sixty years' was George Brooke's introduction to the British Museum Catalogue of the Norman kings' coins.[33] In Brooke's work he outlines the continuation of Anglo-Saxon minting practices after the Norman Conquest and goes into some detail on what was at the time known about the role of the moneyer.[34] The listing provided by Brooke is effectively Ruding's list with more detail, thus perpetuating the same characteristics outlined in the first half of the nineteenth century.[35] This acknowledgement of the continuation of Anglo-Saxon minting practices as continuing virtually unchanged through the Norman Conquest and the reigns of the first Norman kings is reiterated in recent scholarship. In the modern era, Ruding's list of moneyer characteristics has seen continued support generally, with the exceptions regarding its rigidity noted above, but with very little elucidation beyond the initial list. The idea of the moneyers as being part of a special, thegnly class, for example, has been espoused by several historians. As early as 1981, Loyn noted that the names found in coin epigraphy parallel name patterns associated with thegns.[36] In 1982, Pamela Nightingale produced a lineage of a twelfth century London moneyer, Deorman, and his family, highlighting the high social status he and his descendants held within the city.[37] Scholarship has continued to acknowledge the special status of the moneyers with some studies seeking to correlate the names on the coins with the written records of the time, thus providing further evidence of their status. In 1988, Ian Stewart set out to connect a moneyer to a

[22] W. J. Andrew, 1901, 'A Numismatic History of the Reign of Henry I. (1100–1135)', *NC* 1 (Fourth Series), 1901, 1–502.
[23] Andrew, 1901, 12, 16, 22, 27, and 29.
[24] Andrew, 1901, 230, 254 and 262.
[25] C. G. Crump and C. Johnson, 1902, 'Notes on "A Numismatic History of the Reign of Henry I" by W. J. Andrew', *NC* 2 (Fourth Series), 372–77 at 373.
[26] Crump, 1902, 376.
[27] R. A. G. Carson, 1976, 'A history of the Royal Numismatic Society', *NC* 16 (Seventh Series), xii–xv.
[28] Carson, 1976, xiii.
[29] Carson, 1976, xiii.
[30] Carson, 1976, xiv.

[31] D. M. Metcalf, 'The taxation of moneyers under Edward the Confessor and in 1086', in *Domesday Studies: Papers read at the Novocentenary Conference of the Royal Historical Society and the Institute of British Geographers, Winchester, Woodbridge, 1986*, 279–93 at 279–80.
[32] Metcalf, 1986, 281.
[33] M. A. S. Blackburn, 1990, 'Coinage and Currency Under Henry I: A Review', in M. Chibnall, ed., *Anglo-Norman Studies XIII. Proceedings of the Battle Conference*, 49–82 at 49.
[34] C. E. Brooke, 1916, *A Catalogue of English Coins in the British Museum: the Norman Kings*, 2 vols., London, xii.
[35] Brooke, 1916, cxli–cxlii. Brooke pointed out the specific instances of moneyers having the privileges in Domesday that Ruding outlined earlier. While Ruding noted that the moneyer at Oxford had a free house, Brooke also includes moneyers from Wallingford and York. Brooke also notes that the translation of *liber* by Ruding as 'free' may not be so clearcut and that this may simply indicate certain privileges associated with the house and not the house itself. Considering that the house at Wallingford was provided to the moneyer for as long as he worked at the mint, it would appear that the provision of a house 'free' was implicit.
[36] H. R. Loyn, 1991, *Anglo-Saxon England and the Norman Conquest*, Second Edition, London, 125.
[37] P. Nightingale, 1982, 'Some London Moneyers and Reflections on the Organization of English Mints in the Eleventh and Twelfth Centuries', *NC* 142, 34–50.

recorded thegn from a corresponding charter.[38] In his work, for the late Anglo-Saxon era he focused upon the moneyer Hunewine, a moneyer of Totnes, who had a long career and, according to Stewart, at some point was appointed a thegn, or *minister*, by Æthelred II.[39] David Roffe, in 2007, noted that the classifications given within Domesday, those outlined nearly two centuries before by Ruding, indicated that the moneyers held thegnly status.[40] Roffe does not refer to Ruding directly but does address the same points from Domesday, that some moneyers had sake and soke, were exempt from certain taxes, and in some instances were provided housing – all measures of thegnly status.[41] Roffe also notes that land owned by the moneyers of Nottingham was held in a separate fee by the crown and is evident in the annual Pipe Rolls in the late twelfth century, implying that this landholding status was already in place before the Pipe Rolls were recorded.[42] Biddle also pointed out that the Norman moneyers held burgess status and landholder rights, and that this status could have predated the Conquest.[43] In 2012, Martin Allen compiled a list of those moneyers that could be identified as aldermen or burgesses in the twelfth century, utilising Domesday, the Pipe Rolls, and the works of other scholars.[44]

We also know that the moneyers' forges were typically grouped and on the high street or in the commercial district close to the goldsmiths.[45] This seems reasonable in that there are some studies that suggest moneyers and goldsmiths were closely linked, and that some individuals potentially held both offices.[46] Moneyers, goldsmiths, and metal workers were also linked for more practical reasons, such as the need for centralized smelting facilities, which made access to fuel easier. Moneyers were also exchangers, taking in foreign currency and changing it for the king's silver, a practice that was regulated in 1103 by Henry I to restrict them from operating exchanges outside of their county, implying that the practice was widespread during the eleventh century.[47] Moneyers certainly maintained other offices after the Conquest.[48] From at least the early reign of Æthelred II the moneyers had workers operating under their supervision, thereby giving some credence to Godwine Ceoc's possible status as a 'master-moneyer'.[49] Moneyers seemed to operate their own mint-places as independent establishments.[50] This seems to have been regulated to some extent, even though the legislation supporting such regulation has not survived, because in the 1160s the moneyers of Winchester were fined for 'shared premises'.[51] Moneyers were also specialists in their craft. The moneyers were expert metallurgists and capable of manipulating the silver content of their coinages to exact detail. For example, in their study of debasement in the purity of silver coinage for the period 1009 to 1052, D. M. Metcalf and J. P. Northover found that moneyers were capable of maintaining specific percentages of silver content within the coinage alloys.[52] Metcalf and Northover stated that moneyers were able to bring a previously unexpected level of sophistication to the minting practice that goes beyond the skill of the sporadic individual because this expertise was evident in every mint across late Anglo-Saxon England.[53] The implication that the

[38] B. H. I. H. Stewart, 1988, '*Ministri* and *Monetarii*', in *Revue numismatique, 6e série - Tome 30, année*, 166–75.

[39] Stewart, 1988, 167. Stewart states that the unusual moneyer name Hunewine coincides with charters listing an individual of the same name at the same location in generally the same period of time. He makes the assumption that these two individuals are one and the same based on this information.

[40] D. Roffe, 2007, *Decoding Domesday*, Woodbridge, 121–22. Also: D. Roffe, 2012, 'Hidden Lives: English Lords in post-Conquest Lincolnshire and Beyond', in D. Roffe, ed., *The English and their Legacy, 900–1200: Essays in Honour of Ann Williams*, Woodbridge, 205–28 at 217–8. Roffe states that the moneyers may have served also as 'lawmen' or had similar status.

[41] Sake and soke refers to the right of the possessor to administer justice within a specific jurisdiction, most probably the relevant hundred. Sake and soke was common amongst the king's thegns and the moneyers having similar rights indicates similar status. For discussion on this and further definition see: J. Hudson, 2012, *The Oxford History of the Laws of England*, Volume 2, Oxford, 59–62.

[42] Roffe, 2007, 121 n. 66. Also: Nightingale, 1982, 38–9. Nightingale notes that Deorman held land as tenant-in-chief in Domesday.

[43] Biddle, 1976, 402, 421, 443–4.

[44] M. Allen, 2012a, *Mints and Money in Medieval England*, Cambridge, 5–8.

[45] Biddle, 1976, 400–5; Nightingale, 1982, 46.

[46] For discussion on the connections between moneyers and goldsmiths see D. J. Symons, 2006, 'The Moneyers of the Worcester Mint, 1066–1158: Some Thoughts and Comments', in B. Cook, ed., *Coinage and History in the North Sea World, c. AD 500–1250*, Leiden, 545–88 at 546–7.

[47] Symons, 2006, 547.

[48] Allen, 2012a, 8–9.

[49] IV Æthelred 9.1, in Felix Liebermann, 1883, 1905 (Reprint), *Die Gesetze der Angelsachsen. Herausgegeben im Auftrage der Savigny-Stiftung*, Volume 1, Halle, 234–6. *Et illi habeant suboperarios suos in suo crimine, quod purum faciant et recti ponderis, per eandem witam quam prediximus*. 'And they shall be responsible for the production by their employees of pure money of the proper weight, under pain of incurring the same fine as we have fixed above.' Translation from R. S. Kinsey, 1960, 'Anglo-Saxon Law and Practice Relating to Mints and Moneyers', BNJ 29, 12–50 at 20. The idea that Godwine Socche and Godwine Ceoc are one and the same is also stated in H. Ellis, 1837, 'Note on Ruding's Annals', *Transactions of the Numismatic Society, The Numismatic Journal*, Vol. 2, 252–5 at 253 in which he states that Godwine and Ceoca from Ruding's work were the same individual. Ruding had labelled Godwine and Ceoca as two separate moneyers of Edward the Confessor, whereas Ellis noted that they were likely one moneyer named either Godwine Socche or Godwine Ceoca. See also: H. Ellis, 1836, 'Letter from Sir H. Ellis', in *Proceedings of the Numismatic Society*, 1837–8, London, 97–9 and R. Ruding, 1817, *Annals of the Coinage of Britain and its Dependencies: from the earliest period of authentic history to the reign of Victoria*, Volume I, First Edition, 398.

[50] P. W. P. Carlyon-Britton, 1909, 'A Numismatic History of the Reigns of William I and II (1066–1100)', Part II, *BNJ* 6, 147–76 at 163–4. This position, that moneyers likely operated in their own establishment with workers operating for them has been reiterated in J. D. Brand, 1984, *Periodic Change of Type in the Anglo-Saxon and Norman Periods*, Rochester, 45–50; D. M. Metcalf, 1987, 'A penny life will give you all the facts', *NC* 147, 184–8 at 187–8; B. H. I. H. Stewart, 1992, 'The English and Norman mints, c.600–1158', in C. E. Challis, ed., *A new history of the Royal Mint*, Cambridge, 1–82 at 59; Allen, 2012a, 1; Naismith, 2017a, 11 and 240.

[51] M. Allen, 2012b, 'The mints and moneyers of England and Wales, 1066–1158', *BNJ* 82, 54–120 at 56–7.

[52] D. M. Metcalf and J. P. Northover, 2002, 'Sporadic debasement in the English coinage, c.1009–1052', *NC* 162, 217–36.

[53] Metcalf, 2002, 220–4. Metcalf and Northover hypothesize that some of the differentiation in purity found between the east and west mints in England were the result of political events and were planned. The invasion by King Swein of Denmark in 1013 and his recognition as king by most of the west and then Oxford and Winchester provide the backdrop for a largescale debasement of coinage from those areas. Metcalf and Northover provide several different explanations but conclude that the most likely result was either a command from Swein to debase the coins

moneyers, who were probably of a class at least similar, if not equivalent, to thegns, were also experts at their craft and that every instance of minting in the period exhibited this implies a comprehensive level of training and skill. Also, the manipulation of the silver content in the coins was widespread, with regional differentiation possibly impacted by political events, implying communication and organisation.

In the centuries to come the organisation of the moneyers would cement itself into a far-reaching, centralised conglomeration that would regulate the coinage for the entire country.[54] The governing regulations of the mint were not particularly clear even into the fourteenth and fifteenth centuries, but the idea that they had built upon a longstanding tradition of internal rules and regulations is clear. The moneyers created a self-sustaining structure that Grierson would label as an 'international corporation', although he was unable to precisely label the mechanics of that incorporation.[55] But, aside from the knowledge that the moneyers organised into some kind of collective enterprise that was evident in later centuries, and that some moneyers would also be in other prominent government roles during subsequent monarchies, how do we get from the vague 'international corporation' to the Royal Mint?[56] What we are left with, then, is the list compiled by Ruding in the first half of the nineteenth century being more or less the same set of characteristics we have of the moneyers in the present. While the specific aspects of those characteristics have been questioned and debated, sometimes with wide-ranging implications for the field of numismatics as a whole, the underlying points remain the same. Moneyers were of a certain class that included privileges and rights normally associated with the thegnly or burgess class, but because of a lack of documentation in the written record, the implication is that they were of a different sort of *minister* than the typical thegn.[57] Scholarly pursuits of the minting practice of the late Anglo-Saxon system continue to describe the moneyers in generally the same way: these men were important, they had some rights and privileges, they may have been thegns or royal agents of some sort, they operated alone, or at least individually controlled a mint-place, they may have operated within the confines of a family structure, and we know they existed because we find their names on the coinages that they produced. That is how they have been described to a greater or lesser degree in most work on the coinage for nearly two centuries.[58] Obviously, this is not an indication of poor scholarship, if anything, the level of clarity that has been achieved from so little documentary evidence is astounding, but the lack of source material is a limiting factor.[59] If a central point of reference for all of the known moneyers operating from Edgar's Reform to the Domesday survey were available, would the picture of late Anglo-Saxon minting, and the status of the moneyers, become clearer?

As noted earlier, this study aims to address some aspects of the status of the moneyers and how they structured their minting practice through the creation of a central point of reference. The database itself is presented as part of the download package accompanying this book. Chapters five and six outline how the database can be used to determine the structure that the moneyers of late Anglo-Saxon England created. This structure was likely in response to royal authority which sought to impose more direct control upon the minters' monopoly of the hammering of the king's coinage. This resulted in groups of minters operating together before allowing another member of their dynasty, in conjunction with other minting groups, to take over and carry forward for a set period of time. This temporary replacement resulted in a pattern of rotation through which the individual, within the realms of feasibility with regard to extant material evidence, can be witnessed to act as moneyer, withdraw from the role, and then take up the role again at a future time, generally for an additional one or two coinage issues.

The cultural and political interaction of Anglo-Saxon and early Anglo-Norman moneyers with the crown, with their respective communities, and with society at large illustrates the depth of the minting endeavour in the British Isles. The mint structure, being complex in and of itself provides an example of the level of sophistication the Anglo-Saxon state had achieved by the end of the tenth century and prior to the Norman Conquest of 1066. But, in order to establish the mints as an indicator for the advanced status of the Anglo-Saxon state, the development of that state, and how the coinage produced within the mints facilitated that development, must be addressed. In outlining the historiography of the centralization of authority within pre-Norman England and highlighting the importance of the mints as a symbol of this centralization, a better picture

in the mints under his control, even though the coins themselves were still minted in Æthelred II's name using old dies. The problem with this conclusion is that it is not clear who benefitted from the debasement. Another option is that the breakdown in royal authority following the invasion led to moneyers acting independently in the debasement. While not stated in the article, it is conceivable that had this occurred, the moneyers would have benefitted most directly in that they would have been able to take in a larger amount of silver than they were returning in exchange and conceivably keep the excess themselves.

[54] C. E. Challis, 1978, *The Tudor coinage*, Manchester, 20.

[55] P. Grierson, 1975, *Numismatics*, Oxford, 100.

[56] Challis, 1978, 4–5.

[57] Naismith, 2017a, 242.

[58] This type of description, at least in its purest form, can be found recently in Naismith, 2017a, 240–3. Naismith outlines the moneyers as being of a special class, likely not in the same circles as other high-ranking officials. He utilises Biddle's survey of the Winton Domesday, Nightingale's account of Deorman of London, and the laws of the late Anglo-Saxon kings to outline the general status of the moneyers. Naismith also highlights the importance of die-links as potential uses for expanding our knowledge of the moneyers but acknowledges the limits of this source. Discussion of die-linking can be found below. The use of moneyer names as a point of onomastic study is a significant exception to this general line of discourse. Moneyer names have become an important source for personal and place-name studies. The use of moneyer names as a point of linguistic extrapolation for the possible inhabitants of Anglo-Saxon towns is discussed in chapter one.

[59] Moneyer name studies have been used to great effect in determining when certain coin types were produced and the order of types generally. The use of moneyer names as a source for the ordering of coinage types is discussed in detail in below.

of the significance of the mints, and the men in charge of them, can be developed.

Political and Economic Development in Anglo-Saxon England

The progression of urban development in Anglo-Saxon England and the resultant royal administrative structures have been the subject of much debate, as detailed below. Through study of the mint structure and the moneyers, perhaps a clearer picture of the complexity of the Anglo-Saxon state, and the models that were incorporated into the Danish and Norman administrations can be developed. The idea of an 'Anglo-Saxon state' is the subject of several different viewpoints on the development of pre-Norman English government and society. Was the level of governance in late Anglo-Saxon England exceptional? Did the economic reforms of Edgar and Æthelred II lead to a system that points to a royal authority that constituted something beyond the idea of normative monarchial power for the period? Or is the mint system indicative of an even more complex system that incorporated ideas of nationhood and ideology beyond simply the economic structures? In order to address these questions, the concept of the 'state' in Anglo-Saxon England, and how it has developed in scholarship, needs to be reviewed.

The concept of an Anglo-Saxon 'state' is supported most predominantly by the development of the coinage system in England from the period of Edgar's reform in the early 970s. Sawyer saw the coinage as the opportunity for a greater understanding of Anglo-Saxon England as a whole.[60] In his groundbreaking work he noted that coin evidence complements the information found in Domesday and the *Anglo-Saxon Chronicle*.[61] Decades later, Sawyer points to the ongoing studies of the coinage as realisation of that opportunity, giving elucidation on many aspects of late Anglo-Saxon administration.[62] Spufford, in 1988, argued that the influx of silver from Germany through trade led directly to the increase in urban development and the accompanying minting activity[63] This supported Sawyer's earlier assertions that native silver could not have supported the increase in minting and coinage in the late tenth century.[64] These conclusions also support recent work that argues for a 'customer driven' increase in minting for the period rather than purely political motivations.[65] The movement of silver from the Continent to England precipitated expansion of urban communities and the facilitation of money within those communities acted as a means of advancing the visible authority of the crown. The minting system and coinage of late Anglo-Saxon England provide evidence of a sophisticated administrative mechanism. Molyneaux recently combined work on the ideological, administrative, and economic strengths of Anglo-Saxon England and argued that these led to the formation of a cohesive kingdom of England in the late Anglo-Saxon period that has essentially remained intact to the present day.[66] But, alternative viewpoints on whether this was a deliberate effort, or a result of circumstance, are evident. As the mints are a focal point of this debate, and indeed the primary point of evidence in support of the concept of the Anglo-Saxon 'state', it is important to frame how the concept of that 'state' has developed in relation to minting in the tenth and eleventh centuries.

The idea of the Anglo-Saxon 'state' is most predominant in the work of James Campbell with several later historians supporting or disputing his assertions. Through a combination of ideological, administrative, and economic strengths, late Anglo-Saxon society developed a cohesive and complex political state according to Campbell.[67] Campbell based his conclusions on several different factors. First, he pointed to the hidage system outlined in Domesday as evidence of a sophisticated governmental structure.[68] This conclusion was based in part on the work of W. J. Corbett, who in 1900 made correlations between the number of hundreds in the ninth or tenth century County Hidage and Domesday.[69] Other support for Campbell's position that there was a sophisticated and complex government in late Anglo-Saxon England comes from his conclusion that large-scale projects such as Offa's Dyke could not have been constructed without the means of organizing and supplying 'many thousands of diggers'.[70] The concept of a national identity is also important to Campbell's position. Drawing on Reynolds and Wormald, Campbell points out that the inhabitants of England identified themselves as 'English' rather than 'Anglo-Saxon' or 'Saxon'.[71] Campbell also points to contemporary post-Conquest historians for support of the idea of a national identity, noting that the English were seen as inhabiting a distinct and defined *patria* in historical

[60] P. H. Sawyer, 1965, 'The wealth of England in the eleventh century', *Transactions of the Royal Historical Society* (Fifth Series) 15, 145–64 at 148.
[61] Sawyer, 1965, 148–53.
[62] P. H. Sawyer, 1998, 214; idem, 2013, *The Wealth of Anglo-Saxon England*, Oxford.
[63] P. Spufford, 1988, *Money and its Use in Medieval Europe*, Cambridge, 74–9.
[64] Sawyer, 1965, 159.
[65] Naismith, 2017a, 13.

[66] G. Molyneaux, 2015, The Formation of the English Kingdom in the Tenth Century, Oxford, 1–9.
[67] J. Campbell, 1986, *Essays in Anglo-Saxon History*, London, 155–89; idem, 1987, 'Some agents and agencies of the late Anglo-Saxon state', in J. C. Holt, ed., *Domesday Studies: Papers Read at the Novocentenary Conference of the Royal Historical Society and the Institute of British Geographers, Winchester, 1986*, Woodbridge, 201–18.
[68] J. Campbell, 1995, 'The Late Anglo-Saxon State: A Maximal View', *Proceedings of the British Academy* 87, 39–65 at 40.
[69] Campbell, 1995, 41; W. J. Corbett, 1900, 'The Tribal Hidage', *Transactions of the Royal Historical Society* 14, 187–230. Campbell points to some problems in Corbett's work, notably the latter's attempt to correlate the Tribal Hidage of the seventh or eighth century with the County Hidage of the ninth or tenth with tenuous connections. Campbell states that this, along with the implication that acceptance of the work would mean acceptance of 'large scale royal action', is why Corbett's work has been largely left out of contemporary scholarship on late Anglo-Saxon England.
[70] Campbell, 1995, 44.
[71] S. Reynolds, 1984, *Kingdoms and Communities in Western Europe*, Oxford, 266; eadem, 1985, 'What do we mean by "Anglo-Saxon" and "Anglo-Saxons"?', *Journal of British Studies* 24, 395–414 at 398; P. Wormald, 1994, 'Engla Lond: The Making of an Allegiance', *Journal of Historical Sociology* 7, 1–24.

accounts of the late Anglo-Saxon period.[72] Along with the idea of a complicated system of governance, consisting of an organisation into vills, hundreds, and shires, Campbell points to how this system was utilised as a means of geld collection and public works as support for an Anglo-Saxon state.[73] He notes that the ability to maintain a widespread and uniform coinage is 'comparably [as] important' as a strong monarch's ability to maintain peace.[74] Campbell points to the coinage and minting system as evidence for the sophistication of the state and states that economic success goes hand in hand with the ability to successfully maintain roads and bridges, which must have been organised through the public execution of power.[75]

Campbell's ideas built on earlier work that pointed to the complexity of the Anglo-Saxon economy as evidence of an advanced administration, but which did not go so far as to attribute statehood to England for the period.[76] Administratively, the 'state' was purported to have an advanced structure that allowed for the authority of the king to be vested into offices rather than individuals, making it easier to replace non-compliant office-holders, like reeves and moneyers, binding them to the central authority of the crown.[77] For example, the position of Earl, itself a powerful position within the kingdom, was invested with authority by virtue of the office, not the individual holding the office, and was held to certain expectations in how they utilised their power.[78] The movement of earldoms from appointed ealdormen to hereditary office is discussed in more detail in chapter three. Although, in the case of the latter, there were, as discussed below, additional legal ramifications associated with noncompliance to royal authority.

This administration of royal authority as a model that relied heavily on direct support from the king indicated a move towards centralization in government and economic control. This move towards centralized economic control in particular illustrates the complexity of the late Anglo-Saxon governmental system. Domesday highlighted the sophisticated management and productivity of late Anglo-Saxon England, pointing to a system that was embedded into the social systems of the period.[79] Wickham states that the administrative systems of late Anglo-Saxon England were built on Merovingian models from the Continent and that the English were more successful in adapting these systems into a cohesive government than their Carolingian-descended counterparts.[80] The collection of large tribute payments, facilitated in no small part by the minting system, highlighted the strength of the Anglo-Saxon system.[81] This is illustrated in charters and writs, the law codes, and in the coinage. Each aspect of this shows how the royal government functioned. By the end of the tenth century, a unified kingdom of England existed that had a complex system of minting and administration that would be maintained more or less intact until at least the reign of Stephen two centuries later.[82] Elements of the mint structure were evident as early as the ninth century, but the reform coinage of Edgar in the late 970s incorporated these different elements into a single embodiment that would prove to be an effective means of monetary regulation more advanced than any other northern European currency for the period.[83] The periodic recoinage, discussed in detail below, served as a means of protecting the coinage from forgery and debasement, similar to practices in Byzantine mints.[84] This protectionist practice was not the only reason for the recoinages. They also served as a method of projecting royal authority and power to the population, as well as, according to Keynes, Naismith, and Molyneaux, a practice in protecting the moral and spiritual life of the populace.[85] According to Keynes and Naismith, Wulfstan associated the improvement of the coinage (*feos bot*) with avoidance of sin, peacefulness, and the moral fabric of society.[86] Molyneaux supports this and states that the symbolism on the coins, updated with the periodic recoinages, was an important part of Anglo-Saxon England's moral and spiritual life.[87] This made the recoinages an integral part of Anglo-Saxon 'statehood' by casting them as 'statements of authority, good governance and even morality, as well as a tool of royal finance'.[88] In understanding more about the men responsible for this activity, perhaps a better picture of the Anglo-Saxon 'state' can be developed.

But, there is debate on whether or not the so-called 'state' of the Anglo-Saxons was a planned enterprise or a matter of circumstance. Roach, in his recent work on kingship

---

[72] J. Campbell, 1984, 'Some Twelfth-Century Views of the Anglo-Saxon Past', *Peritia* 3, 131–50.
[73] Campbell, 1995, 52.
[74] Campbell, 1995, 53–4.
[75] Campbell, 1995, 54; idem, 2000, 7–8, 32–3, 160, and 181.
[76] H. R. Loyn, 1991, *Anglo–Saxon England and the Norman Conquest*, Second Edition, London, 125–32; idem, 1992, *Society and Peoples: Studies in the History of England and Wales, c. 600–1200*, London, 224–40.
[77] Wormald, 1994; S. Baxter and J. Blair, 2006, 'Land tenure and royal patronage in the early English kingdom: a model and a case study', *Anglo-Norman Studies* 28, 19–46; A. Williams, 2008, *The World before Domesday: the English Aristocracy 900–1066*, London.
[78] Wormald, 1994, 1–2. Wormald outlines the replacement of Tostig, Earl of Yorkshire, by his thegns in 1065 with eventual support from the king. Wormald also notes similar situations on the Continent with the aristocracy forcing reform or removal upon Emperor Henry IV.
[79] Roffe, 2007; Harvey, 2014; Loyn, 1991, 152–205; C. Wickham, 2009, *The Inheritance of Rome: a History of Europe from 400 to 1000*, London, 467–71.
[80] Wickham, 2009, 460–7.
[81] S. Keynes, 2013a, 'Church councils, royal assemblies, and Anglo-Saxon royal diplomas', in G. R. Owen-Crocker and B. W. Schneider, eds., *Kingship, Legislation and Power in Anglo-Saxon England*, Woodbridge, 1–182; P. Wormald, 1999, *The Making of English Law, King Alfred to the Twelfth Century, vol. I: Legislation and its Limits*, Oxford.
[82] Allen, 2012a, 1–40.
[83] R. Naismith, 2014a, 'Prelude to reform: tenth-century English coinage in perspective', in R. Naismith, M. Allen, and E. Screen, eds., *Early Medieval Monetary History: Studies in Memory of Mark Blackburn*, Aldershot, 39–83 at 81–2.
[84] E. Screen, 2007, 'Anglo-Saxon law and numismatics: a reassessment in the light of Patrick Wormald's *The Making of English Law*', *BNJ* 77, 150–72; M. F. Hendy, 1985, *Studies in the Byzantine Monetary Economy, c. 300–1450*, Cambridge, 320–8.
[85] S. D. Keynes and R. Naismith, 2011, 'The *Agnus Dei* pennies of King Æthelred the Unready', *ASE* 40, 175–223; Molyneaux, 2015.
[86] Keynes and Naismith, 2011, 197–8.
[87] Molyneaux, 2015, 187–94.
[88] Naismith, 2017a, 221.

in Anglo-Saxon England, points to the development of heregeld and many of the royal powers as reactionary and crisis-driven, in response to the threat of Viking attacks.[89] Roach also notes that royal action was limited in scope. Even though there were laws in place, the enforcement of those laws and the king's justice was selective at the local level and the king often had to operate against local elites.[90] Sometimes the king had to resort to violence to enforce his laws within his own lands. Reuter noted that the use of 'harrying' by the late Anglo-Saxon kings to maintain order 'suggests a lack of sophistication in a polity allegedly so advanced' and points to Campbell's own words as a measure of the status of the state in the period – 'Royal violence maintained peace'.[91] Wickham also points to the brutal retaliation of Harthacnut in Worcester following the death of two of his tax collectors in 1041 as evidence of limited royal authority without violence.[92] Even the displays of authority at the Witam were more symbolic in nature than realistic in power according to Roach.[93] It has also been argued that the centralization of authority within the personage of the king led to problems with the idea of 'statehood' because failure in the king led to political collapse.[94] But, the contrast of this is that when invasion occurred there was a quick and efficient transition in authority from the previous ruling power to the new invading force, supporting the power of the office over the individual in the overall governing apparatus, although Baxter notes that this was a limiting factor in the determination of Anglo-Saxon England as a state.[95] Institutional and territorial cohesion in the face of invasion, especially in the period 1013 to 1066, highlights the importance of this aspect of royal authority and the centralization of power.[96] The coinage of late Anglo-Saxon England provides evidence for various aspects of the complexity of the 'state'. Campbell uses it as evidence of the sophistication of the system.[97] Loyn and Sawyer use coins to point to the complexity of the economy, followed by Naismith and Molyneaux.[98] Keynes and Naismith use them to point to the moral fabric of the society and how they constitute expressions of royal authority more broadly.[99] Detractors of the 'state' model highlight the circumstances behind the development of these systems but generally not the systems themselves.[100] An exception to this is Bolton's assertions in 2004 and 2012 against a monetary economy in Anglo-Saxon England, which is supported somewhat by Allen's 2012 arguments against a complicated system of exchange before the Norman Conquest.[101]

Between Bolton's first assertion and his restatement of it, Baxter, in 2009, posits that there is a middle ground between the maximal and minimalist viewpoints, one in which a complex system was established in leaps of circumstance instead of gradual political progression, but that maintained cohesive systems through upheavals and invasions.[102] The formation of a centralized economic system in Anglo-Saxon England can be traced directly to the development of trade with Francia in the late seventh century.[103] According to Naismith this increase in trade with the Continent led to the widespread minting of silver coins in England around 700 and was followed by a substantial increase in the movement of trade goods from Frisia to eastern England.[104] These early steps in the development of the monetary economy were followed by moves from the monarchies in England to consolidate and unify their coinages. Between 700 and around 760 coins in England were not uniform and many different types of coins were being produced in about 30 locations.[105] While evidence of minting practices in England for the eighth century is sparse, Hendy's work on concurrent coinages in Francia indicates that coins were largely produced by moneyers working in mints independent of royal authority because of the transfer of authority from the Merovingians to the Arnulfings and that systematic land taxation had ceased by 751/2.[106] Hendy goes on to state, based on changes in the legal codes outlining the profits of the moneyers, that the moneyers were hammering coins for anyone that could provide bullion, including churches and private individuals, relying on their name and the occasional inclusion of their mint place as guarantee of the fineness of the money they provided.[107] With the increase in trade that accompanied the expansion of minting, it became necessary for the royal authorities to step in and regulate monetary production. Naismith outlines the progression of a unified coinage by pointing to the different aspects of coinage regulation in Anglo-Saxon England as developing nearly simultaneously with the coinage reforms instigated by Charlemagne on the Continent.[108] Monarch names

[89] L. Roach, 2013a, *Kingship and Consent in Anglo-Saxon England, 871–978: Assemblies and the State in the Early Middle Ages*, Cambridge, 216–7.
[90] Roach, 2013a, 122–46.
[91] T. Reuter, 1998, 'Debating the "feudal revolution"', in J. L. Nelson, ed., 2006, *Medieval Polities and Modern Mentalities*, Cambridge, 72–88 at 85 and 85 n. 44.
[92] Wickham, 2009, 464.
[93] Roach, 2013a, 218–27.
[94] Reuter, 1998, 290.
[95] S. Baxter, 2009, 'The limits of the late Anglo-Saxon state', in W. Pohl and V. Wieser, eds., *Der frühmittelalterliche Staat – europäische Perspektiven*, Vienna, 503–14.
[96] E. John, 1996, *Reassessing Anglo-Saxon England*, Manchester, 139–65; C. Insley, 2002, 'Where did all the charters go? Anglo-Saxon charters and the new politics of the eleventh century', *ANS* 24, 109–27.
[97] Campbell, 2000, 7–8, 32–3, 160, 181.
[98] Loyn, 1991, 125–32; idem, 1992, 224–40; Sawyer, 1965; idem, 2013; R. Naismith, 2016, 'The coinage of Æthelred II: a new evaluation', *English Studies* 97, 117–39; Molyneaux, 2015, 116–41.
[99] Keynes and Naismith, 2011.
[100] Roach, 2013a; Reuter 1998.
[101] J. Bolton, 2004, 'What is money? What is a money economy? When did a money economy emerge in medieval England?', in D. S. Wood, ed., *Medieval Money Matters*, Oxford, 1–15; idem, 2012, *Money in the Medieval English Economy, 973–1489*, Manchester; Allen, 2012a, 377–81.
[102] Baxter, 2009.
[103] R. Naismith, 2014b, 'The social significance of monetization in the early Middle Ages', *Past & Present* 223, 3–39 at 9.
[104] Naismith, 2014b, 12.
[105] R. Naismith, 2012b, 'Kings, crisis, and coinage reforms in the mid-eighth century', *Early Medieval Europe* 20, 291–332 at 295.
[106] M. F. Hendy, 1988, 'From Public to Private: The Western Barbarian Coinages as a Mirror of the Disintegration of Late Roman State Structures', *Viator* 19, 29–78 at 37–8.
[107] Hendy, 1988, 38.
[108] Naismith, 2017a, 9.

appeared on coins as early as the beginning of the seventh century in Kent and at the beginning of the eighth century in Northumbria.[109] But, there is no currently known evidence to support that these were centrally controlled or regulated. By the mid-700s, however, the English monarchies were taking steps to more directly control the production of money in order to help define their rule, their realm, and their authority. King Eadberht of Northumbria (737–758) developed a royal coinage in the 740s, this was followed by King Beonna in East Anglia (749–760) and Peppin III, King of the Franks (751–768), who both produced coins that included their names and titles.[110] These were followed by the reforms of Offa and Charlemagne on the Continent in the 790s.[111] Naismith, utilising Grierson's work on the coinage of Charlemagne and long held to be the standard for dating his reforms to post-793, argues that Offa acted first in the period 792–3, while more recent work by Garipzanov points to a potential redating of Charlemagne's reform to the same time period.[112] These reforms likely included regulations that compartmentalized the currencies and required that only those coins minted within the respective kingdoms were acceptable, thus limiting the usage of Continental coins in England and requiring coins brought into the kingdom to be reminted into the local currency.[113] While this study is not focused so much on the order of reforms so much as that they occurred at all, it is an important distinction to note that the reform of the Anglo-Saxon coinage, itself derivative of Merovingian influence that diverged from the subsequent Carolingian minting practices, may have been the impetus for Continental reform (and vice versa) through the interconnectedness of their respective trade network).

This interconnected trading sphere was also important to the development of urban centres in the early medieval period. During the eighth century, minting became heavily associated with the development of emporia, which typically developed near to fortresses as the concept of protection led to peaceable trade.[114] As emporia spread, so too did the mint structure, with the two becoming interlinked to the point that the presence of a mint was a significant indication of the importance of the emporia and subsequent town.[115] Those emporia that were successful and thrived would become more permanent, resulting in the development of towns, often around the original fortification.[116] In this way, minting was intrinsically linked to urban development.[117] The gradual move from fortresses to emporia to towns in Anglo-Saxon England during this period parallels the expansion of urban centres in the northern areas of the Continent.[118] Along with this expansion of urban centres, the economy of the North Sea greatly expanded during the same period, highlighted by the dispersion of goods such as the pottery from Ipswich, which illustrated the value of English goods, but also points to the need for access to mints in order to facilitate money changing.[119] This activity was followed in the tenth century by the widespread expansion of towns in northern Europe.[120] Johanek also notes the close relationship between the development of towns and the activity of mints.[121] Several scholars have noted that the presence of a mint specifically is a criterion for defining what constituted a 'town' in Anglo-Saxon England. Stenton provided an elaborate list in 1943 that included a market, a mint, fortifications, tenements, and open fields.[122] Loyn noted in 1961 that a town must have a market, a mint, and jurisdictional authority.[123] Haslam, two decades later, noted that the definitions set by Loyn and Stenton were exclusionary and limiting in that they could neglect towns in their infancy that have not yet fully developed all of the criteria, but he acknowledges that some aspects of their definitions are useful in research.[124]

In tracking the growth of minting, a better picture of urban expansion, and royal authority and administration, could be developed. Wareham argues that mint expansion corresponded with economic growth, town expansion, and royal need.[125] The expansion of minting in the late

[109] Naismith, 2012b, 299–300. For Kent: King Eadbald (616–40); For Northumbria: King Aldfrith (685–704).
[110] Naismith, 2017a, 8.
[111] Naismith, 2012a, *Money and Power in Anglo-Saxon England: the Southern English Kingdoms 757–865*, Cambridge, 175–8.
[112] I. Garipzanov, 2016, 'Regensburg, Wandalgarius and the *novi denarii*: Charlemagne's monetary reform revisited', *Early Medieval Europe* 24, 58–73 at 58; Naismith, 2012a, 176 n. 101.
[113] Naismith, 2014b, 14–15.
[114] N. Christie and H. Herold, eds., 2016, *Fortified Settlements in Early Medieval Europe: Defended Communities of the 8th–10th Centuries*, Oxford; J. Baker, S. Brookes, and A. Reynolds, eds., 2013, *Landscapes of Defense in Early Medieval Europe*, Turnhout.
[115] Naismith, 2017a, 12.
[116] G. Williams, 2013a, 'Military and Non-Military Functions of the Anglo-Saxon Burh, *c.* 878–978', in Baker, 2013, 129–64.
[117] Williams, 2013a, 136–8; J. Haslam, 2011, 'Daws Castle, Somerset, and Civil Defence Measures in Southern and Midland England in the Ninth to Eleventh Centuries' *Archaeological Journal* 168, 195–226 at 207.
[118] D. Russo, 1998, *Town Origins and Development in Early England, c.400–950 A.D.*, Westport, esp. Chpt. 5, 'The Age of Anglo-Saxon Emporia (c.650–850)', 137–68; G. G. Astill, 1991, 'Towns and town hierarchies in Anglo-Saxon England', *Oxford Journal of Archaeology* 10, 95–117; idem, 2006, 'Community, Identity and the later Anglo-Saxon Town: the case of southern England', in A. Reynolds, W. Davies, and G. Halsall, eds., *People and Space in the Middle Ages*, Turnhout, 233–54; A. Reynolds, 2013, 'Archaeological Correlates for Anglo-Saxon Military Activity in Comparative Perspective', in Baker, 2013, 1–38.
[119] Russo, 1998, 142–44; Naismith, 2017a, 107; D. Keene, 2004, 'Towns and the growth of trade', in D. E. Luscombe and J. S. C. Riley-Smith, eds., *The New Cambridge Medieval History*, vol. IV, Cambridge, 47–85.
[120] P. Johanek, 2000, 'Merchants, Markets and Towns', in T. Reuter, ed., *The New Cambridge Medieval History*, vol. III, Cambridge, 64–94 at 64; D. M. Palliser, ed., 2000, *The Cambridge Urban History of Britain*, Cambridge, esp. 'Part II: The Early Middle Ages 600–1300'.
[121] Johanek, 2000, 68 and 88–9.
[122] F. M. Stenton, 1971, *Anglo-Saxon England*, 3rd Edition, Oxford, 527–8. The 1943 first edition contained the same reference.
[123] H. R. Loyn, 1961a, 'The origin and early development of the Saxon borough with special reference to Cricklade', *Wiltshire Archaeological Magazine* 58, 7–15 at 9; idem, 1961b, 'Boroughs and Mints, A.D. 900–1066', in R. H. M. Dolley, ed., *Anglo-Saxon Coins: Studies Presented to F. M. Stenton on the Occasion of his 80th Birthday, 17 May 1960*, London, 122–135.
[124] J. Haslam, 1984, *Anglo-Saxon Towns in Southern England*, Chichester, xv–xvi.
[125] A. Wareham, 2012, 'Fiscal policies and the institution of a tax state in Anglo-Saxon England within a comparative context', *EcHR* 65, 910–931.

Anglo-Saxon period pointed to a complicated system of administration. From Edgar's reform of the coinage in the early 970s the number of mint places increased from around 40 to over 70 by the end of the millennium.[126] Dolley and Metcalf detail that this expansion produced a minting system that provided every town with access to a mint within 15 miles.[127] The expansion of minting led to an increase in the utilisation of money in everyday Anglo-Saxon life. Money was used to pay rents, taxes, and for trade.[128] According to Wareham, Edgar's reform marked a divergence between the internal structures of Anglo-Saxon England and the Continental powers that produced royal currencies.[129] Specifically, he states that the development of a unified coinage that incorporated processes for the production of lighter weight coins later in a minting sequence that were considered the same value as previous coins provided English merchants with an advantage over their Frankish counterparts, whose currency was still regulated solely by the intrinsic value of the precious metal utilised in its minting.[130] This regulated control of the coinage provided the monarchy with additional income as well. In developing a unified system of minting that was quickly spread throughout the kingdom for ready access at all levels of society, the Anglo-Saxons created the means of advanced economic manipulation and control, which points directly to a system of governance that was complex. And, in the centre of this growth and development is the corresponding increase in importance of London as the main hub of commerce and administration in Anglo-Saxon England.

London constituted the predominant urban establishment in this late Anglo-Saxon period, and indeed well beyond. Coin minting in London dates to at least the late third century. Indications of a moneyed economy in Roman London are evident in coin usage from the earliest archaeological records.[131] Copper alloy coins of the Roman Emperor Diocletian (284–305) surviving from this period and attributed to *Londinium* are well documented.[132] Copper coins of the Roman Empire were minted in London from this point until the end of the fifth century. The iconography of these coins is considered to have been the standardised methodology for this period: a profile of the ruler on the obverse, or front, of the coin with variations of symbols or images on the reverse allowing for differentiation in types, value, and age [Figure 1.1].[133]

Figure 1.1. Copper alloy *nummus* of Diocletian.

With the decline and withdrawal of the Roman Empire, a lack of coin finds in London indicate a diminishing of coinage production during the sixth and seventh centuries. Minting in London returned as early as 757 under Offa, whose reforms are discussed above.[134] Throughout the late Anglo-Saxon period, London became increasingly important and as its importance as an urban centre grew, so too did the level of minting.[135] The importance of the mints in town development and the accompanying economic growth highlights the importance of the moneyers within those same structures. With minting being a foundational aspect of urban development it stands to reason that the organisation and administration of the minting structures would also be of some importance in this process, which could explain why the moneyers were often, even before the tenth century, men of importance with favour from the king and high status in urban societies, often involved in the governance of the towns.[136] Likewise, the presence of moneyers, who could act as exchangers for traders and merchants coming to the markets, was a prerequisite for urban status.[137]

Regardless of the impetus for the creation of the systems of taxation and governance, the end result is that by the end of the Anglo-Saxon period a unified English kingdom with extensive legal structures, centralized royal authority, and a complex monetary system existed. Debate on whether or not the Anglo-Saxon 'state' constituted an exceptional political and social experiment designed to be such from the aspect of legal, moral, and economic pursuits or was a happenstance development in the face of diversity will likely never be fully settled, but both sides acknowledge that the systems put into place in the late tenth and early eleventh century laid the foundations for the modern English state. Integral to this was the mint system, operated by a group of men that have remained elusive in specificities about their lives beyond the general trends about their status outlined above. The creation of a central database that focusses specifically upon their placement

[126] Wareham, 2012, 922; R. H. M. Dolley and D. M. Metcalf, 1961, 'The reform of the English coinage under Eadgar', in R. H. M. Dolley, ed., *Anglo-Saxon Coins: Studies Presented to F. M. Stenton on the Occasion of his 80th Birthday, 17 May 1960*, London, 136–68.
[127] Dolley, 1961, 149.
[128] Wareham, 2012, 924; Dolley, 1961, 154; J. Campbell, 2000, *The Anglo-Saxon State*, London, 181.
[129] Wareham, 2012, 924.
[130] Wareham, 2012, 924.
[131] L. Wallace, 2015, *The Origin of Roman London*, Cambridge, 120.
[132] 'The Portable Antiquities Scheme'. The British Museum. Roman coins of Londinium. https://finds.org.uk/romancoins/mints/mint/id/130.
[133] 'The Portable Antiquities Scheme'. The British Museum. Coin NMS-835D2A discovered at Suffolk on 19 November 2014. https://finds.org.uk/database/artefacts/record/id/711383.

[134] 'The Portable Antiquities Scheme'. The British Museum. Coins of Offa of Mercia. <https://finds.org.uk/database/search/results/mint_id/131/ruler/152/page/1>; See: I. Blanchard, 2001, *Mining, Metallurgy and Minting in the Middle Ages, Volume 1: Asiatic supremacy, 425–1125*, Stuttgart, 174–5; Naismith, 2012a, 152–3.
[135] Campbell, 2000, 203–4; D. Keene, 2000, 'London from the post-Roman period to 1300', in Palliser, 2000, 187–216; idem, 1995, 'London in the Early Middle Ages 600–1300', *The London Journal* 20, 9–21.
[136] Naismith, 2012a, 150–3.
[137] Biddle, 1976, 100.

and minting operation is a step towards establishing more fully their place within these momentous developments.

Before addressing the database and to understand the position of the moneyer within the Anglo–Saxon system of coinage, the history of taxation policies, which led to wide scale minting, should be understood.[138] Scandinavian invasions had tapered off during the reign of Edward the Elder (899–924), leading to an extension of West Saxon political influence and an increase in the efficiency and collectability of the Danegeld throughout the countryside. Edward's son, Æthelstan, saw a continuation of this dominance. Upon the incorporation of Northumbria in 927, Æthelstan styled himself not just king of the West Saxons, but king of the English, having gained control over the entirety of England.[139] Following the battle of Brunanburh, Æthelstan's influence spread to Scotland, Strathclyde, and Ireland.[140] During his reign, the production of royal charters was centralised, perhaps by necessity due to the decreasing number of scribes in the late ninth century.[141] Following from this, the reign of Æthelstan witnessed the first consistent utilisation of mint names on the royal coinage.[142] The coins themselves would speak directly to the changing status of the monarchy during this period, with Æthelstan's title becoming 'king of the whole of Britain' in the epigraphic records [Figure 1.2].[143] The reign also included the first documentation of minting and moneyers in the law codes.[144] The Grateley Law Code of Æthelstan is the earliest known documentation of laws relating to the minting practices of late Anglo-Saxon England.[145] While it is possible that these laws were reiterations of previously held practices, the implication here is that Æthelstan, possibly capitalising on his recent success in consolidating control, solidified royal authority over the minting practices in England.

Figure 1.2. Circumscription type coin of Æthelstan.

Unfortunately, this was short-lived as later kings would not maintain this uniformity in minting and political events would disrupt the unified rule of England that Æthelstan enjoyed. This common practice was not revived until the recoinage of Edgar in the early 970s.[146] In the reign of Edgar, several important changes took place in the minting practices of late Anglo-Saxon England. Instead of local implementation of royal directives in regards to coin design, a central design was utilised throughout the kingdom.[147] Simon Keynes points to this shift as indication that the administrative functions of the Anglo-Saxon kingdom changed in order to accommodate the king's desire to utilise more control over the minting apparatus in England.[148] The scale and level of this shift, according to Keynes, points to the mints as part of a single network under central control.[149] Of the few surviving laws from Edgar that remain, one, *III Edgar 8*, does indicate that the kingdom would have one coinage valid 'throughout the king's dominion' (*ofer ealne þæs cyninges anweald*) but no law outlining the reform itself has been located.[150] Of course, this is a restating of *II Æthelstan 14*, but includes the additional caveat that no man is to reject the king's coinage (*þane nan man ne forsace*).[151] The level of organisation involved in transforming the coinage from a locally controlled to centrally designed framework and the imposition of a mandate of universal acceptance implies that further laws outlining the parameters of

[138] For a general summary of the potential monetary economy of the late Anglo-Saxon era see R. Naismith, 2015, 'Spending Power: Money and Power Relations in Early Medieval Europe', *Uppsala University Coin Cabinet Working Papers* 16, Uppsala.

[139] S. Foot, 2011, *Æthelstan: the First King of England*, New Haven, 25.

[140] *ASC* 937E; Foot, 2011, 23.

[141] Foot, 2011, 70–71.

[142] C. E. Blunt, 1960, 'The Anglo-Saxon Coinage and the Historian', *Medieval Archaeology* 4, 1–15 at 13; idem, 1974, 'The Coinage of Æthelstan, 924–939: A Survey', *BNJ* 42, 35–158.

[143] PAS, NCL-9C4317. The epigraphy on the obverse of this coin is EÐELSTAN REX TO BRIT. It was produced in York at some point during the reign of Æthelstan after 927.

[144] II Æthelstan 13.1–14.2, Liebermann, 156–9.

[145] M. A. S. Blackburn, 1996, 'Mints, burhs, and the Grately code, cap. 14.2', in D. Hill and A. R. Rumble, eds. *The Defence of Wessex: the Burghal Hidage and Anglo-Saxon Fortifications*, Manchester, 160–75 at 167. For discussion of the Grateley Code in general see S. Keynes, 'Royal Government and the Written Word in Late Anglo-Saxon England', in R. McKitterick, ed., 1990, *The Uses of Literacy in Medieval Europe*, Cambridge, 226–57 at 235–41; P. Wormald, 2001, *Making of English Law: King Alfred to the Twelfth Century, Legislation and its Limits*, Volume 1, Oxford, 291–308; D. Pratt, 2010, 'Written Law and the Communication of Authority in Tenth-Century England', in D. Rollason, C. Leyser, and H. Williams, eds., *England and the Continent in the Tenth Century: Studies in Honour of Wilhelm Levison (1876–1947)*, Turnhout, 331–50; Foot, 2011, 136–48; L. Roach, 2013b, 'Law Codes and Legal Norms in Later Anglo-Saxon England', *Historical Research* 86, 465–86 at 468–79.

[146] S. Keynes, 2008, 'Edgar, rex admirabilis', in D. Scragg, ed., *Edgar, King of the English, 959–975: New Interpretations*, Manchester, 3–59 at 24.

[147] Keynes, 2008, 23–4. Keynes outlines the shift from three different types of coinage being minted in different parts of the kingdom to the one centrally designed Reformed Coinage of *c.*973–975. See also H. Pagan, 2008, 'The Pre-Reform Coinage of Edgar', in D. Scragg, ed., *Edgar, King of the English, 959–975: New Interpretations*, Manchester, 192–208. See R. Naismith, 2013a, 'The English monetary economy, c. 973–1100: the contribution of single-finds', *EcHR* 66, 198–225 at 199.

[148] Keynes, 2008, 24. For further discussion on the implications of the coinage reform of Edgar see R. H. M. Dolley and D. M. Metcalf, 1961, 'The Reform of the English Coinage under Eadgar', in R. H. M. Dolley, ed., *Anglo-Saxon Coins: Studies Presented to F. M. Stenton on the Occasion of his 80th Birthday, 17 May 1960*, London, 136–68; J. J. North, 1980, *English Hammered Coinage*, Volume I: *Early Anglo-Saxon to Henry III c. 600–1272*, London, 109–13; K. Jonsson, 2006, 'The Pre-Reform Coinage of Edgar – the Legacy of the Anglo-Saxon Kingdoms', in B. Cook and G. Williams, eds., *Coinage and History in the North Sea World, c. AD 500–1250*, Leiden, 325–46; SCBI 34.

[149] Keynes, 2008, 24.

[150] III Edgar 8–8.3, Liebermann, 204. Translation from B. Thorpe, ed., 1840, *Ancient Laws and Institutes of England*, Ghent, 114.

[151] Naismith, 2014a, 56.

this reformation were written, but no such written documentation has been located.[152]

Following shortly after the reformation of the coinage under Edgar, the Scandinavians again attacked Anglo–Saxon England in the latter decades of the tenth century.[153] Within a decade of this resumption of violence, several disasters had occurred, most notably the Battle of Maldon on August 10, 991, which saw the disastrous defeat of an English war-band at the hands of the Danish king.[154] The Battle of Maldon witnessed the first wave of nobility killed, including influential and powerful people such as Byrhtnoth, the Ealdorman of Essex, along with most of his household. As a result of these disasters, King Æthelred II recognised the need to create a more efficient system of collection to pay off the Vikings in hopes of some sort of temporary reprieve from wholesale looting and slaughter.[155] Based upon an expansion of the land lease practices that were in existence at least three centuries before 1066, the geld collection consisted of a systematic taxation of the landholding populace based loosely upon a calculation of hidage for an individual landowner.[156] This allowed for a more stable estimation of yearly income. Hidage was defined as the 'land of one household' by Bede and was utilised to assess the value of a conquered or subjugated family to determine the level of taxation to be levied against them.[157] Though terminology would shift over time to include ploughs as a means of measurement, the system of taxation maintained hidages as its basis throughout the period in which geld was collected.[158] This system of measurement allowed the provincial kings to collect vast sums of silver and gold in order to pay off the invading Danish armies and fleets.[159] The mint system was the facility through which this tax collection process would be implemented. Also, during the earlier parts of Æthelred II's reign, the coinage, carrying forward under the reform of Edgar, underwent further changes. Æthelred's mints operated on a cycle of regular, or at least semi-regular, recoinages.[160] This process of recoinage was immediately apparent in the coinages of London and some of the larger mints and widespread within the first two coinages of Æthelred's reign.[161] This cycle of recoinages allowed for the regular assessment of the coins, providing a steady revenue stream and the ability to regulate the purity and regularity of the coins being produced.

The *Anglo–Saxon Chronicle* outlines in some detail the frequency and amounts of these tributes. Notable early payments include 24,000 pounds of silver in 1002, 30,000 pounds in 1007, 3,000 pounds in security payments in 1009, 21,000 pounds in 1014 and so on, all while those responsible for paying the taxes were taking part in battles and defenses against the invading bands.[162] This process of taxation to fund military expedition, or to forestall military defeat and subjugation, became the foundation of the geld system. These accounts outline a pattern of invasion and payouts that illustrate indirectly the evident complexity and efficiency of the geld collection system. In order to provide such large payments on regular intervals, especially in the midst of intermittent warfare, the method by which the assessments and collection took place needed to be significant in scope. According to Campbell, this complexity was established through the administrative local offices of the reeves and sheriffs, giving them responsibility for the geld collection.[163] The reeves were themselves responsible for overseeing the quality of the coinage and ensuring that the mints produced coins to the king's specifications, although it is unclear whether or not a reeve would have had the expertise to make this determination.[164] Grierson states that moneyers could also have been responsible for collecting geld payments as part of their normal duties in their local communities.[165] This might support the assertion by Tsurushima that some moneyers also acted as reeves.[166] The shire network, controlled locally, facilitated this collection of taxes and dues.[167] This localised administration was continuous from the time of Æthelred through Cnut and later carried on by William, sometimes with the benefit of the same office holders carrying out the taxation under multiple monarchs.[168] By the time Cnut had firmly secured himself on the throne, the geld payments were sufficiently high enough – 72,000 pounds from the nation and 10,500 pounds

[152] E. Screen, 2007, 'Anglo-Saxon Law and Numismatics: A Reassessment in Light of Patrick Wormald's *The Making of English Law*', *BNJ* 77, 150–172 at 154.
[153] H. R. Loyn, 1984, The Governance of Anglo-Saxon England, 500–1087, Stanford, 120.
[154] *ASC*, 991C.
[155] There are numerous references to the Battle of Maldon as a turning point, notably Loyn, 1984, 121; A. Williams, 1999, *Kingship and Government in Pre–Conquest England, c. 500–1066*, New York, 145; eadem, 2008, *The World Before Domesday: The English Aristocracy, 900–1066*, London, 70.
[156] Loyn, 1991, 183. Loyn outlines the land lease process as beginning in the early seventh-century and formulating into a process of land being leased to a family for 'three lives' during the tenth-century. 'Three lives' is calculated as the life of the original lessee plus two heirs.
[157] Williams, 1999, 33.
[158] *ASC* 999–1002C.
[159] L. Roach, 2016, *Æthelred the Unready*, New Haven, 178.
[160] P. Grierson, 1962, 'The President's Address: Numismatics and the historian', *NC* 2, i–xiv at x; R. Naismith, 2012a, *Money and Power in Anglo-Saxon England: the Southern English Kingdoms, 757–865*, Cambridge, 181–3.
[161] R. H. M. Dolley, 1978, 'An Introduction to the Coinage of Æthelred II', in D. Hill, ed., *Ethelred the Unready: Papers from the Millenary Conference*, Oxford, 115–33; J. D. Brand, 1984, *Periodic Change of Type in the Anglo-Saxon and Norman Periods*, Rochester; B. H. I. H. Stewart, 1990, 'Coinage and Recoinage after Edgar's Reform', in K. Jonsson, ed., *Studies in Late Anglo-Saxon Coinage in Memory of Bror Emil Hildebrand*, Stockholm, 455–85.
[162] *ASC* 1002C, 1008C, 1009C, 1014C.
[163] Campbell, 2000, 203–4.
[164] S. Harvey, 2014, *Domesday: Book of Judgement*, Oxford, 143–4.
[165] P. Grierson, 1987, 'The Monetary System under William I', in A. Williams, ed., *Domesday Book Studies*, London, 75–9.
[166] Tsurushima, 2012, 44.
[167] Loyn, 1984, 133–40; S. Keynes, 2014, 'Shire' in M. Lapidge, J. Blair, S. Keynes, and D. Scragg, eds., *The Wiley-Blackwell Encyclopedia of Anglo-Saxon England*, Chichester, 434–5.
[168] For illustration of the continuity of the local administrative units see Douglas, 1953, 463–4, regarding the writs of the local sheriffs documenting the maintenance of local officials. Specifically, in S 1116 and S 1427, Tofi is recorded as the sheriff of Somerset under Edward the Confessor and an individual with the same name kept that role post-Conquest under William I.

from London directly in 1018 alone – that the system not only had to be complex but widespread as well, covering at least the bulk of the southern portions of Britain in its entirety.[169] It was in this context that the Anglo–Saxons established not only the most efficient economic structure of the age in Western Europe but also laid the groundwork for their demise.

It is important to point out, however, that many scholars do not take the values presented by the *Chronicle* at face value and quite a bit of academic debate has circled around the geld collections as reported. The most direct challenge to the reported amounts comes from Gillingham and centres on his debate with Lawson concerning the possibility and likelihood of a widespread taxation method being in place to compensate for the totals outlined within the source material.[170] Both parties make strongly-supported claims about the calculations, with perhaps the advantage going towards Lawson's quantitative assessment based upon his explanation of the totals paid to ship crews, which protected the coasts against Viking incursions, from the source material and firm mathematical calculation.[171] However, neither scholar disputes the fact that gelds were collected and while the amounts of the varying collections might have differed between what was recorded and what was actually counted, the end result, that the taxation system was in place and at least somewhat effective, is generally accepted.

The debate on the size of the Anglo-Saxon coinage has done much to systematise the process by which the coins themselves are studied. Through the establishment of quantitative methodologies for calculating the estimated production of a coinage issue through the use of die records, in conjunction with the distribution of coins within various hoard finds, the purity of the metal composition and the weight of the coins in question, a more uniform approximation of the total volume of the Anglo-Saxon coinage can be determined.[172] Other methods of calculating the volume of the coinage around die usage have been developed, primarily around the work of Warren Etsy.[173] The legitimacy of the geld system is thus not in question and for the purposes of this text, the amounts, while potentially relevant, are not necessarily binding to its conclusions. The basic point was that the collection process itself sufficiently acclimatized the populace to a purposeful societal norm that was easily incorporated into the ruling apparatus of the Norman conquerors after William I claimed the throne.

The centuries–long cycle of raiding and payoff between the Scandinavians and the Anglo–Saxons waned as the midpoint of the eleventh century approached. This was due primarily to a Danish king also holding the throne of England, in the person of Cnut or his heirs.[174] Cnut, sought conquest in England in 1013 before finding his prospective inheritance lost upon the untimely death of his father, only to return to take an unsteady throne in 1016.[175] Yet, from the reign of Cnut, even in its infancy and possible uncertainty, to the reign of Edward the Confessor, the heregeld was a regular annual tax collection for the payment of soldiers and sailors.[176] What is also evident is that during Cnut's reign a number of royal advisors were brought into England from Denmark, similar to the method used by William half a century later.[177] There were several years between geld assessments for some of the larger collections from Cnut's reign. This may have contributed to the reason for such large sums as the 72,000-pound collection in 1018, which was preceeded by 4 years of no gelding.[178] The ability to manage the collection of such large sums illustrates the importance of the Danegeld

[169] Williams, 1999, 101. Æthelred died in 1016. His son Edmund took the throne. Cnut defeated and killed him and took up the crown of England directly, marrying Æthelred's widow and exiling all heirs. After solidifying power, he made the large geld demand presented here, which was considered severe and caused some economic hardship according to Williams. Cnut used this payment to pay off the Danish fleet.

[170] J. Gillingham and M. K. Lawson published a debate in the April 1989 volume of the *English Historical Review*. The debate was sparked by Gillingham's attempt to refute the assertions made by Lawson in an earlier article that the geld amounts within the Anglo-Saxon Chronicle were valid. Both parties presented evidence in support of their argument with no conclusive determination. This book favours Lawson's viewpoint. See M. K. Lawson, 1984, 'The collection of Danegeld and Heregeld in the reigns of Æthelred II and Cnut', *EHR* 99, 721–38; J. Gillingham, 1989, "The Most Precious Jewel in the English Crown': levels of Danegeld and heregeld in the early eleventh century', *EHR* 104, 373–84; M. K. Lawson, 1989, "Those stories look true': levels of taxation in the reigns of Æthelred II and Cnut', *EHR* 104, 385–406; M. K. Lawson, 1990, 'Danegeld and Heregeld Once More', *EHR* 105, 951–61.

[171] Lawson, 1984, 721–38.

[172] P. Grierson, 1979, 'The Volume of Anglo-Saxon Coinage', in *Dark Age Numismatics: Selected Studies*, London, 153–60. For further discussion on the topic see also: C. N. L. Brooke, B. H. I. H. Stewart, J. G. Pollard, and T. R. Volk, eds., 1983, *Studies in Numismatic Method presented to Philip Grierson*, Cambridge.

[173] W. W. Etsy, 1986, 'Estimation of the Size of a Coinage: a Survey and Comparison of Methods', *NC* 146, 185–215; idem, 2006, 'How to estimate the original number of dies and the coverage of a sample', *NC* 166, 359–64. Etsy outlines a method of utilising random samples of coins and determining how representative the collection is based upon the regularity of die links between various coins in the selection. Other viewpoints and discussions on the establishment of coin production numbers based on die numbers and die links can be found in G. F. Carter, 1981, 'Comparison of Methods for Calculating the Total Number of Dies from Die-Link Statistics', in C. Carcassone and T. Hackens, eds., *Statistics and Numismatics*, Strasbourg, 204–13; T. V. Buttrey, 1993, 'Calculating Ancient Coin Production: Facts and Fantasies', *NC* 153, 335–51; idem, 1994, 'Calculating Ancient Coin Production II: Why it cannot be done', *NC* 154, 341–52; F. De Catallaÿ, 1995, 'Calculating Ancient Coin Production: Seeking a Balance', *NC* 155, 289–311; M. Allen, 2004, 'Medieval English Die-Output', *BNJ* 74, 29–49; idem, 2006b, 'The Volume of the English Currency, c.973–1158', in Cook, 2006, 487–523. The arguments made by Buttrey and Catallaÿ are primarily geared towards ancient Roman coinage production with Buttrey arguing that the overuse of statistics in numismatic evaluation provides false evidence while Catallaÿ refutes Buttrey's suppositions.

[174] T. Bolton, 2009, The Empire of Cnut the Great: Conquest and Consolidation of Power in Northern Europe in the Early Eleventh Century, Leiden, 9.

[175] *ASC* 1013D; Bolton, 2009, 10, n. 6.

[176] Loyn, 1984, 121. Loyn notes the geld as an annual payment but there were instances of multi-year separations in collections.

[177] Bolton, 2009, 18–9. Bolton outlines how several prominent families that became powerful aristocrats *TRE* first gained power during the reign of Cnut through the gifts of large estates, primarily in Kent. This replacement of aristocratic positions was not as widespread as the Conqueror's however, but does illustrate that the moneyers, who were not similarly displaced, maintained control over their craft through at least two conquests.

[178] *ASC*, 991C, 994C, 1002C, 1007C, 1009C, 1014C, 1018C.

system and how it likely served as a temptation to the Vikings, the Danes, and the Normans. Its integration into Anglo-Saxon society assisted in the transition of authority during both the Danish and Norman Conquests. In 1049, Edward paid off his ships and transferred direct control of naval defense to the Cinque Ports, thereby abolishing the heregeld, but the overall taxation under the Danegeld was maintained at a lower level, calculated in Domesday Book at a rate of 2s. per hide.[179] It is of some importance to distinguish the various terminologies. The heregeld was specifically designated as a tax for the payment of the armed forces of the king. From the Old English term for army *(here)* one can separate, at least at this stage in Anglo–Saxon political development, the military from the civil in regard to general monetary practices. This differentiation becomes somewhat ambiguous within two decades, once the Normans take control, but the separation during the period from Cnut to Edward is clear. During this time, the general taxation consisted of all other forms of royal revenue in regard to collection from landed populace, trade impositions, and minting fees. The dissolution of heregeld, prompted by the diminishing frequency of Viking raids, by Edward the Confessor was not a complete halting of taxation but was a ceasing of the military funding aspect of his reign. This complicated exchange system helped established a wide–ranging minting system that outlined the measure of sophistication within the English economic structure. The complex organisation of coinage and minting developed within England stands as testament to the cohesion of the society that grew before the Norman Conquest. Æthelred, before his death in 1016, oversaw the greatest growth in minting since before the fall of the Roman Empire across southern Britain, primarily so that the Danegeld could be paid.[180] Between 1049 and 1067 the geld payments were kept low enough to offset any overall disposition and burden, but the arrangement of minting, commerce exchange, and taxation was firmly in place and stood ready for exploitation when William drove his ships ashore.

To facilitate the wide scale taxation of the population, a process by which enforcement for non–payment could be accomplished needed to be implemented outside of military action, which was impractical on a long–term basis. To that end, the king allowed any man that could pay to submit the geld for those that could not, and in return, the lands of the non–payer were confiscated and taken over by the payer.[181] This land seizure system of tax enforcement allowed individuals to increase their own landed influence while maintaining fiduciary support for the crown. Sources have shown that this was likely the most common means of practical tax enforcement, although not the only one.[182] While not inexpensive or practical for long–term engagement, military reprisal for nonpayment was also practiced, especially in the early days of the system under Cnut. Cnut utilised the geld to hire a mercenary army that could be used to enforce his taxation system after he sent his main invasion force back to Denmark. This expression of martial force was necessary in the early years of his reign while the English people grew accustomed to his rule.[183]

In regard to its relation on taxation and the geld system, the position of Cnut as king of England was somewhat different than that of William half a century later. Cnut had conquered England but was forced to maintain a standing army well into his reign because of the existing noble class within the Anglo–Saxon hierarchy. Cnut did not replace the aristocracy, as William would do later. Instead, he took over the existing geld system and empowered the local reeves to collect it on his behalf. Since he was an invader king, the standing army, which was largely compliant based upon the possibility of plunder and profit, was somewhat suspect in regard to their loyalty to the crown. This mandated a mercenary force that supported Cnut based on pay rather than direct fealty.[184] His enforcement by military threat was harsher and more direct than that which the Conqueror assumed when pressing his geld demands upon his own nobility. Therefore, it is likely, and supported by the quantitative assessments provided for within the *Anglo–Saxon Chronicle*, that Cnut was able to press for and receive higher geld payments than those of later monarchs because of the constant threat of force beyond the normative violence of the age.[185] Later rulers

[179] *ASC*, 1050–1D. The chronicler states that Edward abolished the heregeld in 1049. The *Chronicle* also states that the military tax took precedent over all other taxation and was the most severe. See also Loyn, 1984, 121: The ability to collect such a tax is a testament to the prosperity of the land and why it was a ready target. As Loyn puts it: 'They indicate not only the fluid wealth available in England, but also the capacity to tap it'. See also J. A. Green, 1981, 'The Last Century of Danegeld', *EHR* 96, 241–58.

[180] Loyn, 1984, 122–5. Loyn states that the development of a complex coinage system 'is one of our best indications of the strength…and of the general coherence of the English community'. Along with this 'tremendous increase to the output of the mints' moneyer regulations were installed to support the 'integrity of the coinage'.

[181] II Cnut 79, Leibermann, 366. And se ðe land gewerod hæbbe on scire gewitnesse & se noble oððe ne mihte, þe hit ær ahte, hæbbe unbesacen on dæge & æfter dæge to syllenne & to gyfenne þam þe him leofost sy. Hemming, Chartularium Ecclesiae Wigorniensis, 278, in T. Hearne, ed., 1723, Hemingi Chartularium Ecclesiae Wigorniensis, Volume 1. Constituerunt enim, ut, siquid vectigalis ad iliam, constituti diei deesset, quisquis prius peccuniam pro ea solveret, ejus possessioni subjaceret; Lawson, 1984, 724. Lawson argues that Cnut's law allowed another person to take possession of land whose owner failed to pay the Danegeld when it was due. This activity carried forward to at least the Normans with examples of the practice apparent in Domesday Book. See GDB 216v.

[182] William of Malmesbury, Gesta pontificum Anglorum, v.258, in M. Winterbottom, ed., 2007, William of Malmesbury: Gesta pontificum Anglorum (The History of the English Bishops). Volume IL Text and Translation, Oxford, 614. Brihtwoldus, ut ex ascriptis Anglicis animadvertimus, multa incommoda cenobio intulit, terras vel omnino distrahendo vel parvo pretio invadando. Sed enim excusatur, quod magno illo geldo, qui tunc Danis dabatur, oppressus unicum inveniebat malorum remedium; quod futurorum incautus, non videbas obesse posse inposterum.... Brihtwold, an abbot of Malmesbury, had to sell and mortgage church lands in order to pay the heavy geld that was imposed by Cnut early in his reign, most likely the large geld of 1018 based upon the chronology specified by William of Malmesbury in the passage.

[183] Lawson, 1984, 734.

[184] Lawson, 1984, 734.

[185] Campbell, 2000, 203–4. Campbell states that while the source material is limited in regard to expression of military enforcement of taxation there

would not have the same apparatus in place to enforce those threats. Notably, just two generations removed from Cnut, Edward the Confessor paid off his navy, which was manned by his army, and more or less contracted naval defense for the island to semi–autonomous cities, thereby removing the military threat somewhat but also in turn removing the means by which the threat was funded.[186]

Nevertheless, this process of taxing, collecting, and giving tribute created an apparatus, which was a means of security and prosperity for the English royalty for generations. This apparatus also stood as a temptation to the Normans when the formal invasion began and would be an essential part of the Normans' actions after the Battle of Hastings.[187] When the English lined up to fight at Hastings, Harold II had just fought off a Norwegian invasion force led by Harald Hardraada at the Battle of Stamford Bridge.[188] The weakening that resulted from this battle and other losses before William's landing led to the defeat of the native English in the main battle, but it was not the end of the invasion or a definitive close to the Conquest as a whole.[189] The Anglo–Saxon elite were decimated in the Battle of Hastings, leaving large gaps in the aristocracy. The absence of land owning elites, who were responsible for providing troops and taxes to the king, among the Anglo–Saxon ranks allowed the Normans to install their own nobility into the most prominent positions of governance within the kingdom.[190] Indeed, some four or five thousand landed Anglo–Saxon tenants-in-chief were displaced, their lands consolidated, and control passed to a mere 180 Normans.[191] This consolidation allowed Norman England to maintain a much tighter grip on the means of commerce, through direct control of the landed estates, than even the sophisticated pre-Conquest methods allowed.[192]

However, this wholesale replacement did not occur within the ranks of the moneyers, even though they maintained royal prerogative in their practice. This text will not only demonstrate that the moneyers maintained significant linear familial placement within the period prior to the Conquest, at least in regard to patterns associated with naming practices, but will also show that those placements survived afterwards until at least Domesday. Further, the book will outline, as mentioned above, that this continuity resulted in a cross-dynastic organisation that led to a complex system of mint management that spread to nearly all corners of late Anglo-Saxon England. This continuity along family lines and a possible system of mint administration, discussed in detail in chapter six, was addressed in a limited capacity in relation to mints in Kent by Hirokazu Tsurushima in 2012.[193] Tsurushima notes that the minting of the Benediction Hand type (*c*.991) by an unusually named Osferth at three geographically widely separated mint places could indicate that a master-moneyer had workers operating for him under his name.[194] While the conclusions reached herein do not exactly match his conclusion, his work has been inspirational in the development of the mint administrative system outlined in chapter five below. The work carried out in the construction of the database, and the study that follows is an attempt to take up the large-scale analysis

are notable examples in both the *Anglo-Saxon Chronicle* and 'Florence' for Harthacnut and others using their housecarls in this manner. Considering the oppressive nature of the gelds, Campbell concludes that the use of a standing army, whether mercenary or housecarl, to enforce the collection is a reasonable assumption. There is no reason or support to dispute this assumption within the current argument.

[186] Campbell, 2000, 205–6. Campbell acknowledges the work of Lawson on the Danegeld collection in relation to the naval forces of Edward and C. Warren Hollister's work on the pre–Norman Anglo-Saxon military institutions. His conclusion is that the paying off of the navy by Edward precipitated the end of the geld altogether. The leap to this being a causal event in turn is not so difficult.

[187] D. C. Douglas, 1964, *William the Conqueror: the Norman Impact upon England*, Berkeley, 279–80. Douglas states that William needed to utilise large contingents of mercenary forces to carry out his military campaigns and that in order to maintain these standing armies he had to utilise the geld system of Anglo–Saxon England and tax heavily. Douglas also points out that William was taking the tax on conquered continental lands and using those funds directly to pay for further campaigns in 1078 (according to his interpretation of Orderic Vitalis). It is reasonable to extrapolate, since taxation was a continual process in England and Domesday Book was just a few years distant, that this method of taxation for military utilisation was common throughout William's reign. See also: D. Bates, 2016, *William the Conqueror*, New Haven, 294. Bates states that the wealth of England was used to gain favour, reward, and secure the kingdom after the Conquest. He states '[e]xceptional wealth and power were given to newcomers from France from a very early date.'

[188] *ASC*, 1066C, 1066D, 1066E: The *Chronicle* outlines the Battle of Stamford Bridge in versions C, D, and E. Harold II, upon hearing of the loss by Earls Morcar and Edwin against the Scandinavian invaders at the Battle of Fulford on September 20, 1066, rode with a large force north to Stamford Bridge, where he defeated his brother, Tostig, and Hardraada in a large battle. The king and his army gathered, armed, and rode the 185-mile distance in just under 4 days in order to catch the Norwegians off-guard. This worked but resulted in a weary and fatigued force.

[189] Bates, 2016, 232–3. Bates states that the defeat of Earls Edwin and Morcar severely depleted Harold's army. He also points to contemporary sources for the number of ships the army arrived in for the Fulford and Stamford Bridge battles (300 in *ASC* 1066D and 520 in John of Worchester) and that they departed in only 24, signifying a huge reduction in strength. Bates also states that Harold's practice of not distributing loot likely led to a demoralization of his troops as well. See also: B. Golding, 1994, *Conquest and Colonisation: The Normans in Britain, 1066–1100*, New York, 30.

[190] Green, 2017, 36–7. Green notes that the Normans took advantage of the power vacuum left with the fall of the house of Godwin at Hastings. With the accumulation of power after the Danish conquest into the hands of just a few individuals, and the regular taxation of the English during this period and after, the Normans were able to quickly take control of powerful positions in the kingdom. Green states 'the destruction of the power of some great aristocratic families had eaten away at the fabric of Edgar's England'. See also: H. Thomas, 2008, *The Norman Conquest: England After William the Conqueror*, Plymouth, 55–6. Thomas states that William initially offered some of the aristocracy the right to keep their land but decided to crush 'all but the lowest fringes of the Anglo-Saxon aristocracy through systematic dispossession of their land'. Also: W. E. Kapelle, 1979, *The Norman Conquest of the North: The Region and Its Transformation, 1000–1135*, Chapel Hill, 121. Kapelle specifically highlights the appointments in the northern Yorkshire provinces following the Harrying of the North. But the general trend toward aristocratic replacement was foundational to the Norman Conquest even prior to the northern campaign. Nearly all levels of governance were affected by the military campaigns before Hastings, the battle itself, and succeeding endeavours. For discussion on York in the period see D. M. Palliser, 2014, *Medieval York: 600–1540*, Oxford.

[191] Williams, 1999, 331. This figure is compiled by Williams as the sum total of those named nobles of William the Conqueror that were granted titles and estates following the Conquest. Many areas that were spread amongst several nobles were consolidated.

[192] Williams, 1999, 331. The question of loyalty among those collecting the tax was not evidently in question since William knew all title-holders before his landing in England and they were landholders in Normandy.

[193] Tsurushima, 2012.

[194] Tsurushima, 2012, 41.

that Tsurushima's work makes necessary to push the study of the moneyers further.[195] The organisational structure that resulted in the administrative model outlined herein, particularly the rotational aspect of moneyer placement in chapter six, while potentially derivative of Tsurushima's suppositions on the Kentish moneyers, have not been espoused in scholarship to date. Within this context, the development of a database of the moneyers facilitates and permits a wide-scale review of the moneyers as a collective group.

Minting and Coinage in Anglo-Saxon England

Despite their importance to the monetary system, and thus their importance to the development of an Anglo-Saxon 'state' overall, relatively little is known about the moneyers, as discussed above. Most of the information we have about the individual minters comes from the coins that have survived the last thousand years in various hoards and single coin finds. But, in order to frame even that small amount of information an understanding of the coinage itself, how it was structured and how modern numismatists and historians have discovered the processes by which it was manufactured must be understood. Perhaps the most important aspect of this is the order in which the coinages were made because without that information the names and mint places from the coins would not have any structure. While we could state that a moneyer with a certain name was likely present at a certain mint place, without the factor of temporality that information is not very helpful overall. The late Anglo-Saxon coinage consists of one currency produced at anywhere from two dozen mint places at the time of Edgar's reform to over five times this number almost a century later. This varied and large number of mint places makes ordering the coinage a necessary component of identifying individual moneyers. The study of the order of coin types is an expansive work in and of itself, but selective discussion of the key findings and debates is included below.

The first documentation of the Anglo-Saxon coinages as distinct types is generally traced back to the work of Swedish Antiquarian Nicolaus Keder in 1708.[196] Keder however made no notice of Edgar's potential coinage reform and it was not until Bror Emil Hildebrand's still foundational work over a century later that the post-reform coinage was acknowledged as unique and ordered. Hildebrand, a Swedish archaeologist, numismatist, and founder of the Swedish History Museum, began his cataloguing of coins located in the Swedish Royal Coin Cabinet in the 1820s, first published his catalogue with ordered types of coins in 1846, and produced a much-revised edition in 1881.[197] His cataloguing of the coin types is still largely accepted, although modifications to the ordering have taken place over the last century and a half.[198] In 1867, Head praised the work of Hildebrand in the ordering of the coins of Edward the Confessor, but provided an alternative ordering for Hildebrand Types H and G, reversing the order in which they were produced based upon mule finds in England.[199] The problem of mules, or coins that were likely produced in small numbers between distinct types and having an obverse or reverse of the old coin type and the new, was consistent in Hildebrand's work and has led to the most direct revisions to his ordering of the coinages as he classified them as distinct types.[200] After Hildebrand, more complete listings that corrected his errors and incorporated coin information that was likely not available to Hildebrand in Sweden were prepared. Carlyon-Britton produced a complete ordering of the coins of Edward the Confessor in 1905 that later helped Seaby to better frame and define the king's reign.[201] In 1910 a debate on the ordering of the coinages during the reign of Æthelred II between Parsons and Brooke led to a more complete ordering and a better picture of the king's reign overall.[202] This was readdressed in 1921 by Carlyon-Britton and Nordman resulting in further modifications to the type ordering.[203] A major component and obstacle to ordering the coinages is the process of periodic type changes that began shortly after Edgar's reform in the early 970s. In 1905, Chadwick commented on the shift in coinage during Edgar's reign but did not elaborate on this as a substantial change.[204] The type changes themselves were mentioned by Brooke as early as 1929 when he noted that they must have existed *TRE* because of the manner in which they are mentioned in Domesday.[205] He would later comment on the type changes as an 'incomplete stage' in the development of the Anglo-Saxon monetary system.[206] Further work on the periodic changing of coinage types was spearheaded by Dolley in the last half of the twentieth century. Dolley pushed for a rigid system of recoinages based upon what would later be termed the 'sexennial

[195] Tsurushima, 2012.

[196] N. Keder, 1708, Nummorum in Hibernia antequam haec insula sub Henrico II. Angliae rege Anglici facta sit juris cusorum indagatio; Accessit catalogus nummorum Anglo-Saxonicor. & Anglo-Danicor. Musei Kederiani, Leipzig.

[197] K. Jonsson, ed., 1990, Studies in Late Anglo-Saxon Coinage in Memory of Bror Emil Hildebrand, Stockholm, 37; B. E. Hildebrand, 1846, Anglosachsiska mynt i Svenska kongl. myntkabinett funna i Sveriges jord, Stockholm; idem, 1881, Anglosachsiska mynt i Svenska kongl. myntkabinett funna i Sveriges jord, 2nd Edition, Stockholm.

[198] K. Jonsson, 1987b, Viking-Age Hoards and Late Anglo-Saxon Coins: A Study in Honour of Bror Emil Hildebrand's Anglosachsiska mynt, Stockholm, 79–80.

[199] B. V. Head, 1867, 'An account of the hoard of Anglo-Saxon coins found at Chancton Farm, Sussex', *NC* 7, 63–126 at 65 and 70–71.

[200] C. S. S. Lyon, 2003, 'Anglo-Saxon numismatics', *BNJ* 73, 58–75 at 58 and 67.

[201] P. W. P. Carlyon-Britton, 1905b, 'Eadward the Confessor and his coins', *NC* 5 (Fourth Series), 179–205; P. Seaby, 1955, 'The sequence of Anglo-Saxon coin types', *BNJ* 28, 112–46.

[202] H. A. Parsons, 1910a, 'The coin types of Aethelred II', *NC* 10 Fourth Series, 251–90; idem, 1910b, 'Mr G. C. Brooke on "the coin types of Aethelred II." A reply', *NC* 10 Fourth Series, 381–7; G. C. Brooke, 1910, 'Mr Parsons' arrangement of the coin types of Aethelred II. A criticism', *NC* 10 Fourth Series, 370–80.

[203] P. W. P. Carlyon-Britton, 1921, 'The chronological sequence of the types of Eadweard the Martyr and Æthelræd II', *BNJ* 16, 5–31; C. A. Nordman, 1921, *Anglo-Saxon Coins Found in Finland*, Helsingfors.

[204] H. M. Chadwick, 1905, *Studies on Anglo-Saxon Institutions*, Cambridge, 35–6.

[205] G. C. Brooke, 1929, '*Quando moneta vertebatur*: the change of coin types in the eleventh century; its bearing on mules and overstrikes', *BNJ* 20, 105–16.

[206] G. C. Brooke, 1950, *English Coins*, 3rd Edition, London, 67.

thesis'.[207] Dolley's thesis would develop over several years as periodic expansions within his writings beginning in 1956.[208] The development of the rigid 'sexennial thesis' which states that coins were universally reminted at six-year intervals was not without its detractors. Grierson challenged the thesis in 1962 as being too exact, pointing to periods where coin types last longer or shorter than the prescribed period as evidence of its shortcomings.[209] In 1969, Petersson suggested that the theory be modified to a seven-year cycle instead to accommodate what he saw as inconsistency in the period of change from one coin type to the next.[210] But Dolley was a steadfast defender of his idea and it was not until after his death in 1983 that serious reconsideration of the theory emerged, although the underlying concept of periodic and universal type change has remained largely accepted. The first revisions emerged in 1984, with Brand giving critical review of the thesis.[211] Stewart outlined the theory in detail in 1990 and pointed out some flaws that resulted from discoveries taking place since the 1970s.[212] An increase in the study of mint places and types instead of large hoard finds has led to modifications of the 'thesis'. Detailed study of large mints like Lincoln and Winchester, as well as work on smaller mints such as Aylesbury, Huntingdon, and Wallingford have led to the realisation that the 'sexennial theory' could not be an absolute realisation of minting in late Anglo-Saxon England.[213] This has been compounded by studies of specific coinages and single coin finds.[214] Recent scholarship points to single finds in particular as an important indicator of how minting may have been in the late Anglo-Saxon era, pointing to the frequency of specific types in the find record as indication of how long specific coinages may have been produced. This has led to steps away from the absolute dating of specific coin types, although the order has remained the same.[215] The most recent example of this is in two new works by Naismith in which he suggests moving towards bands of time instead of exact years for each individual coinage.[216] His suggestions, while compelling, do not alter the order of the coinage types overall and still maintain the timing for each coinage closely to what has been used in research for the past few decades. For the purposes of this study, which is concentrated more specifically on the order of the types than the specific years in which they were produced, the traditional dates for the coinage types is maintained. Another important aspect of study on the minting practice of late Anglo-Saxon England was the recognition of local die production and the implications it had on the political landscape of the period. Dolley first postulated in 1958 that dies were created in regional centers and then distributed to local mints.[217] Later, in 1977, with Tuukka Talvio, Dolley analysed the coins of Æthered II in the British Museum and established, based on patterns in the surviving coins, that the coins were minted regionally at Canterbury, Chester, Lincoln, London, Norwich, and York.[218] The analysis indicates that the distribution centres at Canterbury and Chester disappeared and were subsumed by London while Lincoln and York would occasionally alternate which mints they supplied dies to.[219] Dolley ends the article with an invitation to input from an historian, which would appear in the following year in an article by Pauline Stafford.

In Stafford's 1978 article on the die distribution of the reign of Æthelred II, she provides political context for the process and some speculative reasons for it.[220] Stafford states that the regional production of dies provided local rulers with steady revenue and gave impetus for greater loyalty to the king, while also allowing the king to maintain greater control by providing those rulers, often ealdormen or bishops, with that revenue stream.[221] The local production and regional distribution of coin dies also provided the king with a means of administrative control and direct taxation, which is illustrated by the differentiation in coinage weights between the north and south. Coin distributed in the north and east were of lighter weight than those in the south and west.[222] Stafford's analysis here relies on earlier work by Stewart Lyon, who reiterates his position that the lighter weight coinages were likely the result of taxation to fund the heregeld in his 2016 addition to the *Sylloge of Coins of the British Isles*.[223] Another important aspect of the regional distribution of dies beyond simply profit for the royal household and local authorities was the concept of royal prestige and propaganda.[224] Here Stafford points back to the coinages

[207] Dolley and Metcalf, 1961.
[208] R. H. M. Dolley, 1956, 'The Shaftesbury hoard of pence of Æthelræd II', *NC* 16 Sixth Series, 267–80 at 267.
[209] P. Grierson, 1962, 'The President's Address: Numismatics and the historian', *NC* 2, i–xiv.
[210] H. B. A. Petersson, 1969, *Anglo-Saxon Currency: King Edgar's Reform to the Norman Conquest*, Lund.
[211] J. D. Brand, 1984, *Periodic Change of Type in the Anglo-Saxon and Norman Periods*, Rochester.
[212] Stewart, 1990, 458–60.
[213] For examples of mint place studies see: H. R. Mossop, 1970, *The Lincoln Mint, c. 890–1279*, Newcastle; Biddle, 1976; R. J. Eaglen, 1999, 'The mint of Huntingdon', *BNJ* 69, 47–145; W. N. Clarke and D. Symons, 2007, 'The mint of Aylesbury', *BNJ* 77, 173–89; T. J. T. Williams, 2012, 'The mint at Wallingford: an introduction to the corpus', *Yorkshire Numismatist* 4, 141–57.
[214] For examples of single-type studies see: H. E. Pagan, 1990, 'The coinage of Harold II', in K. Jonsson, ed., *Studies in Late Anglo-Saxon Coinage in Memory of Bror Emil Hildebrand*, Stockholm, 177–205; idem, 2011, 'The Pacx type of Edward the Confessor', *BNJ* 81, 9–106; Keynes and Naismith, 2011.
[215] Allen, 2012, 35–6; G. Williams, 2013b, 'Coins and kingship', in G. R. Owen-Crocker and B. W. Schneider, eds., *Royal Authority in Anglo-Saxon England*, Oxford, 37–61 at 60.
[216] Naismith, 2017a, 233; idem, 2017b, 'The Historian and Anglo-Saxon Coinage: The Case of Late Anglo-Saxon England', in R. Naismith and D. A. Woodman, eds., *Writing, Kingship and Power in Anglo-Saxon England*, Cambridge, 162–80.
[217] R. H. M. Dolley, 1958, Some Reflections on Hildebrand Type A of Æthelræd II, Stockholm.
[218] R. H. M. Dolley and T. Talvio, 1977, 'The Regional Pattern of Die-Cutting Exhibited by the First Hand pennies of Aethelraed II Preserved in the British Museum', *BNJ* 47, 53–65 at 64.
[219] Dolley, 1977, 64.
[220] P. Stafford, 1978, 'Historical Implications of the Regional Production of Dies Under Æthelred II', *BNJ* 48, 35–51.
[221] Stafford, 1978, 35.
[222] Stafford, 1978, 36.
[223] S. Lyon, 2016, *The Lyon Collection of Anglo-Saxon Coins* (*Sylloge of Coins of the British Isles* 68), Oxford, 114.
[224] Stafford, 1978, 36–7.

of Æthelstan and Dolley's suggestion that Edgar's Reform was timed to coincide with the king's second consecration and travel down the Dee.[225] Stafford states that after 973 during most coinage issues some regional die cutting occurred.[226] This move to regional die cutting seems to have been supported locally as moneyers and their respective lords would have likely gained a sizeable profit from the selling of the dies to smaller mints.[227] Regional die cutting also made it easier to differentiate die-links between coins minted at different mints and can thus help in the identification of individual moneyers who operated at multiple locations; this is discussed in detail below in the die-links section.

Perhaps the most important aspect of Stafford's work outlining the political importance of regional die cutting is the implication that the king may have traded minting rights for political support from prominent local officials. Ealdorman Æthelwine of East Anglia and Archbishop Dunstan of Canterbury were granted minting rights in exchange for supporting Edward the Martyr's bid for the throne, while a similar situation existed in the early reign of Æthelred II.[228] But, Stafford postulates, pointing to the work of Dolley and Talvio, that Æthelred changed this pattern soon after taking the throne. Dunstan evidently lost his minting privileges and the die distribution centre at Canterbury ceased to exist while Æthelwine maintained his control of regional minting rights in Norwich, as noted above.[229] Stafford indicates that this is likely the result of a dispute between Dunstan and Æthelred's mother, Ælfthryth, during the reign of Edward.[230] Dolley also noted the closure of the Chester distribution centre, which Stafford attributes to the sacking of the town by Vikings in 979.[231] The Chester mint would have its dies supplied by Lincoln after it reopened, likely as a means of supporting the authority of ealdorman Ælfhere, who ruled the Midlands for the king.[232] Stafford goes through Dolley's analysis of the movement of die distribution centres and makes political connections and rationalizations for each. Mark Blackburn and Stewart Lyon followed this with similar analyses of regional die distribution during the reign of Cnut.[233] Having a central record of all the moneyer activity for the period from Edgar's Reform Coinage to Domesday Book may make further work on the impact of local distribution possible and will certainly lend itself to work on tracing the movements of individual moneyers within that framework.

With the order of the coinage types established, comparing the information found on the coins to this arrangement allows the identification of a specific person at a specific location in a specific period of time, at least in relation to other moneyers from the same locale. Having this information to hand allowed for the creation of a database that consolidated all of the known moneyers from each of the recognised mints in the late Anglo-Saxon period. This database, the creation of which is described in more detail below, facilitates the preparation of a prosopography of the moneyers. Through the information contained within it work can be undertaken to identify these individuals and form a more complete picture of how they operated, and how the mints were organised, in late Anglo-Saxon England.

[225] Stafford, 1978, 36–7. See also: R. H. M. Dolley, 1979, 'Roger of Wendover's Date for Eadgar's Coinage Reform', *BNJ* 49, 1–11 at 6.
[226] Stafford, 1978, 40.
[227] Stafford, 1978, 41.
[228] Stafford, 1978, 42–3.
[229] See M. K. Lawson, 1984, 'The collection of Danegeld and Heregeld in the reigns of Æthelred II and Cnut', *EHR* 99, 721–38; J. Gillingham, 1989, ''The Most Precious Jewel in the English Crown': levels of Danegeld and heregeld in the early eleventh century', *EHR* 104, 373–84; M. K. Lawson, 1989, ''Those stories look true': levels of taxation in the reigns of Æthelred II and Cnut', *EHR* 104, 385–406; M. K. Lawson, 1990, 'Danegeld and Heregeld Once More', *EHR* 105, 951–61.
[230] Stafford, 1978, 43.
[231] Stafford, 1978, 43.
[232] Stafford, 1978, 43–4.
[233] M. A. S. Blackburn and C. S. S. Lyon, 1986, 'Regional die-production in Cnut's Quatrefoil issue', in M. A. S. Blackburn, 1986, *Anglo-Saxon Monetary History: Essays in Memory of Michael Dolley*, Leicester, 223–72; C. S. S. Lyon, 1998, 'Die-cutting in the Last Small Cross issue of c. 1009–1017 and some problematic East Anglian dies and die-links', *BNJ* 68, 21–41.

2

Methodology

Problems with the Current Resources on the Moneyers

The currently available resources for studying the moneyers, both individually and as a collective group, are insufficient to the task at hand. The primary repository for individuals in late Anglo-Saxon England is the *Prosopography of Anglo-Saxon England* database (hereinafter PASE).[1] While PASE is a valuable resource of information if the researcher has a specific variable or dataset from which to begin work, it is somewhat cumbersome if searching for a complete selection of any one piece of data. In researching and studying an entire group of specific individuals such as the moneyers, PASE is not sufficient despite, and potentially because of, the vastness of the information contained within it. This abundance of information makes the selection of individual groups difficult because of cross-referencing and unclear indicators. For example, if one searches for 'moneyer' in the text search, there are 10 results.[2] If the selection is 'occupation' and then 'moneyer', two examples are provided, but selection of 'moneyer' as an office provides 4545 records.[3] Likewise, if the location of a known mint, Lincoln for example, is selected then 86 records emerge, 19 of which are designated as moneyers during the time period 973–1086.[4] However, a review of Lincolnshire, compromising the same regional area as the Lincoln mint, provides 241 records on moneyers, over 50 of which operated during the designated timespan.[5] Therefore, in order to utilise PASE effectively as a means of measurement in regards to the validity of the collected data, all 4500-plus references of moneyer have been cross-referenced with one another because of numerous points where the given information is provided in an unrelated field. For example, when the references to the moneyers of Cambridgeshire are analysed there are cross-listed moneyers associated with Canterbury, Lincoln, London and York within the same listing.[6]

A further limitation in PASE is that it does not include numismatic data for the large corpus of late Anglo-Saxon coinage found within the British Museum. This is problematic for multiple reasons. First, this absence results in a dataset that is substantially smaller, on the magnitude of one-third less epigraphic information for moneyers operating between 973 and 1086 overall. And second, in conjunction with the first issue, is that the vast majority of coinage data, and thus moneyer data, in PASE comes from collections that are found outside of the United Kingdom. Specifically, the highest percentages of coins information found in PASE comes from Scandinavian hoards, which were taken from England as payments during the period of Viking incursions. The problem with this is that these payments tapered off after 1036 and are non-existent after 1042. So, the large-scale export of Anglo-Saxon coinage to Scandinavia that was so prevalent in the previous century no longer took place. This means that the numismatic information in PASE potentially consists of a large gap in information for the period 1042 to 1086 because it relies on information gathered from sources that do not include sizeable numbers of coins from the last half of the eleventh century.

Therefore, PASE provides a baseline of information, but further work is needed, as detailed below, in order to create a database specific to the moneyers. The purpose of extracting the information from PASE and adding to it information from various other sources, is so that the analytic aspects of this study could be completed without the need to cross-reference every instance of moneyer in the database in order to draw a baseline for each scenario. With one central database of information specific to the moneyers this group of individuals can be studied, individually and corporately, to see if any patterns are evident in their activity.

A Preparatory to a Prosopography

In this section, the steps taken to create the database of the moneyers is discussed in detail. The database presents a unique collection of information that goes beyond simply a list of names but falls a step short of being a full prosopography because of the limitations of the surviving source material. This intermediary step between an onomastic list and full individualization provides a preparatory to a prosopography that can still be used in analysis, as in chapters five and six below.

Mathisen estimated in 2007 that for the preceding 30 years there had been less than 10 'grand-scale' prosopographical databases created related to the ancient and medieval worlds.[7] His definition of 'grand-scale' is a database with over 2,000 person entries. Mathisen goes on to state that these are primarily created through the work of well-funded, professionally long-term staffed projects, making

[1] *Prosopography of Anglo-Saxon England* <http://www.pase.ac.uk/about/index.html>.
[2] PASE Search: moneyer.
[3] PASE Search: occupation; office: moneyer.
[4] PASE Search: Specific Location: Lincoln.
[5] PASE Search: Region: Lincolnshire. Crosslist: moneyer.
[6] PASE Search: Region: Cambridgeshire. Crosslist: moneyer.

[7] Mathisen, 2007, 122.

the idea of creating a large database independently with nearly double that number of individuals daunting. But, the need for a distinct collection of the moneyers that can be studied and reviewed in order to potentially learn more about their lives required the construction of a database to contain such a large volume of information. Having established that the current sources available are insufficient to address the placement of moneyers in late Anglo-Saxon society, a new database needed to be created. Because of the dearth of written source material for these men, other evidence must be used. Since the coinage that they produced within the mints bares an imprinting of their name and the mint location, along with iconography and monarch-specific epigraphy, this numismatic material can serve as the groundwork for this approach. From a single coin, it is possible to determine that a particular person existed at a specific time and location. This information in conglomeration can be used as a tool for measuring mint-place activity.[8] The lexicon of moneyer names can also serve as a means of looking into the social identity of a specific location at a certain time.[9]

But, prosopography is about the individual.[10] The epigraphic material on coins is finite and while there are lots of ways in which the iconography can be addressed and studied, when used for identification purposes the information is somewhat limited. The lack of written material about the individuals named on the coins prevents more extensive exposition on their status and how they might have lived. A few moneyers are also attested in written sources, such as mentions in charters, or associated with connected dies and discussed below; but by and large, the sources for the moneyers remain the coins that they produced. This places limits on the level of individualization that is possible for a study of moneyers. Also, as Verboven *et al* state in their manual on prosopography, the use of a single type of source can lead to problems in creating a prosopography.[11] The primary issue in Verboven's critique is the risk of using a single source to create a prosopography which might impact the researcher's interpretation.[12] Verboven was writing specifically about the utilisation of a single literary source but the same implication might be made if extrapolated to a single type of source, like coins. However, Verboven does state that a single source can provide homogeneity in the data, which coins almost certainly do.[13]

The nature of the extant source material does not at present, therefore, enable a full prosopography of the moneyers of late Anglo-Saxon England to be created. According to K. S. B. Keats-Rohan, the creation of a prosopography is conducted in two stages, first the preparation of a biographical dictionary or lexicon, which outlines details of each individual in the study population and second, the analysis of the data within the lexicon.[14] The first stage is the most critical in that it lays the groundwork for what follows.[15] This initial stage is the composed of three parts, first the identification of the study group, second the creation of an Index of Names and an Index of Persons, and third, a biographical catalogue for the entire study population.[16] The database provided with this book can only provide a necessary first step in the creation of a full prosopography. The database represents almost all of the steps outlined by Keats-Rohan but falls just short of realizing a full Index of Persons because of the limits of the source material in identifying the individual beyond a single mint. It has identified the study group, the moneyers of late Anglo-Saxon England active from Edgar's reform of *c.*973 and the Domesday survey of 1086. And an Index of Names has been created, through the transcription of the names attested on the coins. At this point, however, the resultant list will contain a great many names which are attested more than once, either at the same mint or at multiple mints. In order to transform an Index of Names into a true Index of Persons, one would necessarily need to determine how many distinct individuals lie behind these multiple attestations. Here, however, the specific limitations of the inscriptions on the coinage present inescapable difficulties, since it is impossible to determine definitively whether or not coins minted under a particular moneyer's name were all in fact minted by a single individual. This is true even when they were produced at the same time at the same mint. Numismatists have generally been content to assume that coins inscribed with the same name are likely to have been produced by the same moneyer if they were produced at a specific mint during a specific period of time. But there are instances where the same moneyer name appears on coins produced

[8] D. Hill, 1981, *An Atlas of Anglo-Saxon England*, Oxford, 130.

[9] Naismith, 2017a, 241.

[10] R. W. Mathisen, 2007, 'Where are all the PDBs?: The Creation of Prosopographical Databases for the Ancient and Medieval Worlds', in K. S. B. Keats-Rohan, ed., *Prosopography Approaches and Applications, A Handbook*, Oxford, 95–126 at 101. See also: P. Magdalino, 2003, 'Prosopography and Byzantine Identity' in A. Cameron, ed., *Fifty Years of Prosopography: The Later Roman Empire, Byzantium and Beyond*, Oxford, 41–56 at 47. Magdalino states that the 'essence of prosopography is to establish identity; the identity of an individual within a group, and individual identity as a part of group identity.'

[11] K. Verboven, M. Carlier, and J. Dumolyn, 2007, 'A Short Manual to the Art of Prosopography', in K. S. B. Keats-Rohan, ed., *Prosopography Approaches and Applications. A Handbook*, Oxford, 35–70 at 53.

[12] Verboven, 2007, 53.

[13] Verboven, 2007, 53–4. Verboven also points to specific problems associated with limited source selection. Specifically, that a lack of sources limits representativeness in the historical record, or that an overabundance of sources requires the historian to make selections, which detract from that representativeness, and finally that accessibility of sources limits the historian's ability to interact with the sources. However, these problems are not necessarily present in the current study. There is no lack of specific sources in that for the database assembly the corpus of material is large enough to provide an idea of what is 'ordinary', at least in regard to the minting activity of the moneyers at a specific time and place. And because all available sources have been included and access has not been limited, no selection has been made to restrict what is presented.

[14] K. S. B. Keats-Rohan, 2007, 'Biography, Identity and Names: Understanding the Pursuit of the Individual in Prosopography' in K. S. B. Keats-Rohan, ed., *Prosopography Approaches and Applications, A Handbook*, Oxford, 139–82 at 146–51.

[15] Keats-Rohan, 2007, 146.

[16] Keats-Rohan, 2007, 146.

Table 2.1. Example from the Index of Names ('Cild')

NameID	Name	Desc(Mint)	DocRef(CoinageRecord)
8026	Cild	Bedwin	Radiate Crown/Small Cross BM 1955.7.8.104
8027	Cild	Bedwin	Trefoil-Quadrilateral EMC 1024.0671
8028	Cild	Bedwin	Small Flan BM 1915.5.7.2270
8029	Cild	Bedwin	Small Flan BM 1962.3.4.3
8030	Cild	Bedwin	Small Flan EMC 1018.0747
8031	Cild	Bedwin	Expanding Cross EMC 1042.1182
8032	Cild	Bedwin	Hammer Cross BMC ii p.342 no.28
8033	Cild	Bedwin	Hammer Cross BMC ii p.342 no.29
8034	Cild	Bedwin	Hammer Cross BMC ii p.342 no.30
8035	Cild	Bedwin	Hammer Cross EMC 1009.0937
8036	Cild	Bedwin	Hammer Cross EMC 1024.0711
8037	Cild	Bedwin	Hammer Cross EMC 1030.0623
8038	Cild	Bedwin	Pyramids BM 1955.7.8.120
8039	Cild	Bedwin	Profile/Cross Fleury BMC i PE.I.2
8040	Cild	Marlborough	Canopy BMC iii 204
8041	Cild	Marlborough	Two Sceptres BMC iv 264.PE.IX.14
8042	Cild	Marlborough	Two Stars BMC v 356.PE.XII.14
8043	Cild	Marlborough	Two Stars CM.831-2001
8044	Cild	Marlborough	Sword BMC vi 424.PE.XV.5
8045	Cild	Marlborough	Paxs Crown 2 BMC viii 1985.7.82.38
8046	Cild	Marlborough	Paxs Crown 2 BMC viii 828.PE.XXII.16
8047	Cild	Marlborough	Paxs Crown 3 BMC viii 827.PE.XXII.15

over a very extended period of time; and even more cases in which multiple mints produced coins inscribed with the same name. These occurrences present more significant challenges to individualization. Because of the limited connections that can be made between moneyers at different mints and because different moneyers with the same name may have been acting over extended periods of time within a single mint, full individualization is not achieved in this study. This study does not seek to rectify these issues because the current evidence does not allow it beyond a very small minority. Future discoveries and additions may allow more complete individualization but at present the database represents the highest level that can be achieved uniformly across all mints.

What the database presents, then, is not a full Index of Persons, but rather a list of fused names. An example of the resultant layout of this step can be seen below [Table 2.1]. All coin entries are treated individually, with the name of the moneyer on the coin documented, as well as the mint. The coin type is also listed along with the provenance. The data was then alphabetized first by name, then by mint, and finally by type. After this was complete, each record was given a unique Name ID. For moneyers named 'Cild' the Name IDs range from 8026 to 8047. These records represent 22 coins produced at two mints, Bedwin and Marlborough.

At this point fusion is used to combine those records that first, are of the same coinage type, and second, that are temporally adjacent in manufacture.[17] While the dates ascribed to the coins can allow the determination of the period during which moneyers worked, there are problems associated with defining this range of activity through fusion. There are concerns relating to the use of fusion in defining individuals. Keats-Rohan states that the fusion of homonyms where other information to support distinction is lacking is problematic, but she goes on to indicate that where date records are available that such actions may be acceptable, provided the context from which the information is taken is carefully considered.[18] Since the dating of individual coins, at least within specific bands of years, is readily accepted in numismatics, and in light of other scholarly works using the same process in

[17] Prosopography Research, Modern History Research Unit, University of Oxford, 'Prosopography for Beginners, A Tutorial', <http://prosopography.modhist.ox.ac.uk/tutorial/tutorial_10.htm> Accessed 11 January 2018.

[18] Keats-Rohan, 2007, 170–1.

regards to the coinage of late Anglo-Saxon England, the context of the date ranges are sufficiently established to allow for the fusion of records from those individual coins that were produced by moneyers of the same name at the same mint.[19] Fusion of this kind results inescapably in an assumption that each occurrence of a particular name at the same location refers to the same individual. But this is an assumption which has been shared by previous scholars working on the onomasticon of late Anglo-Saxon moneyers. David Pelteret, for example, addresses fusion of this type in regard to ealdormen in PASE.[20] Pelteret's specific example is in relation to Osric, an ealdorman who appears as a witness on charters in 845 and 860 and was originally entered as two separate individuals.[21] Pelteret indicates that after review of Robertson's *Anglo-Saxon Charters* that he agreed with that scholar's attribution of these two Osrics as the same individual because of the placement of the name in the witness list order.[22] He notes that this is an assumed match, but the records have been fused.[23] The process of fusion allows for the creation of a database that is manageable and follows the general methodology utilised in PASE, although that database seemingly fuses some moneyer records and not others, thereby making PASE somewhat inconsistent in this respect.[24]

Here, in contrast, fusion adheres consistently to the following principles in order to maintain uniformity. If a moneyer is known only from one coin type (for example the Quatrefoil type of Cnut), then the range of activity is recorded as the period in which that type was produced (in this instance 1017–1023). If a coin is documented from the same mint with the same moneyer name for a coin on either side of this, then the range of activity will be expanded accordingly. So, a moneyer named Ælfweard operating at Lincoln with a coinage record inclusive of Æthelred II's Last Small Cross (1009–1016) and Cnut's Quatrefoil (1017–1023) has an active range of 1009–1023 within the database. If an Ælfweard were to appear again in the coinage record during Cnut's last type, the Short Cross (1029–1036), but has no records for the intervening coinage, Pointed Helmet (1023–1029), then this is entered as a separate period of activity and is treated as distinct from the first Ælfweard's activity.

In a few cases, this practice produces a single entry for a moneyer's name which is attested continuously for a suspiciously long period of time. Such cases appear so infrequently, however, that they are within an acceptable margin of error when compared to the entire corpus of material. For example, there is only one moneyer name operating consecutively at a mint for greater than 80 years. A moneyer, or moneyers, named Godwine was continuously active in London from 979 to 1062. Outside of this, there are two moneyer names linked to periods of activity greater than 60 years, nine further names operating more than 50 years, and an additional 33 names linked to periods of activity greater than 35 years within the database. This equates to 45 instances out of 3,646 records, or 1.2 per cent. This means that 98.8 per cent of the records in the database consist of moneyer names that have a range of activity of 35 years or less. The vast majority of records (94.4 per cent or 3,440 of 3,646) have a range of activity of 20 years or less. The differentiation between 20 years of activity and 10 years is a bit larger but still not significant overall, amounting to 14.2 per cent (520 of 3,646), meaning that 80.2 per cent (2,920 of 3,646) of the database consists of records that have a range of activity of 10 years or less. Therefore, it is reasonable, and accepted within this study, that the vast majority of biographical entries represent individual moneyers active for the presented periods. In practical terms, that means this study considers the 3,646 biographical entries to each represent an individual. But, this study also acknowledges that the number of actual individuals represented is likely to be less than this number because of potential links between moneyers of the same name operating at the same or close mints without clear connection.

No moneyer records from multiple mints have been fused, even if the likelihood of a match is high. The reason for this is that often there is no evidence that the moneyer of the same name operating at multiple locations are one and the same individual. In the few instances where such evidence is available, such as in die-links, as discussed below, there is still a certain level of assumption because of other possibilities (redistribution of dies, etc.). Therefore, in order to maintain uniformity in how each of the moneyers at each of the mints are dealt with, and to keep fusion to a minimum, moneyer names appearing at separate mints are kept separate. However, because of the way that the database is arranged, future work on these potential connections is possible and future iterations of the database could include tentative links between such

[19] Outside of the examples noted above, recent use of fusion in moneyers based only on their coins can be found in Biddle, 2012, 9–10 and S. Lyon, 2016, *The Lyon Collection of Anglo-Saxon Coins: Sylloge of Coins of the British Isles 68*, Oxford, 101. See also: D. C. Smythe, 2007, '"A Whiter Shade of Pale": Issues and Possibilities in Prosopography', in K. S. B. Keats-Rohan, ed., *Prosopography Approaches and Applications, A Handbook*, Oxford, 127–37 at 135–6. Smythe refers to fusion as one of the two 'cardinal sins' in prosopography. The other sin, fission, is viewed as the lesser of the two evils in that Smythe considers the later merging of two incorrectly split individuals easier than the division of two individuals that have incorrectly been merged. However, in the current study, the subsequent fission of incorrectly fused moneyer names is easily remedied because of the uniformity of information and fusion has been determined to be the better course of action because of the volume of source material being dealt with.

[20] D. E. Pelteret, 2007, 'Should One Include Unnamed Persons in a Prosopographical Study?' in K. S. B. Keats-Rohan, ed., *Prosopography Approaches and Applications, A Handbook*, Oxford, 183–96 at 190. 183–96 at 190.

[21] Pelteret, 2007, 190; S 313; S 317.

[22] Pelteret, 2007, 190; A. J. Robertson, ed., 1956, *Anglo-Saxon Charters*, Cambridge, 274–6.

[23] Pelteret, 2007, 190; PASE: Osric 7.

[24] For examples of this see PASE: Æthelwine 122, Æthelwine 123, Æthelwine 124, Æthelwine 125. These four moneyers in PASE are represented on coins minted in York between the reigns of Cnut and Edward. Some of these records have had the coinages for different types merged into one moneyer while others remain separated. The documentation on data collection and organisation does not address this differentiation in process but it appears that some effort has gone into separating some moneyers based on monarch instead of coinage production.

Table 2.2. Example from the Index of Fused Names ('Ada')

NameID	Name	FusedID	Desc(Mint)	Desc(Dates)	DocRef(CoinageRecord)
1	Ada	1	Cambridge	1017-1029	Quatrefoil EMC 1001.0752
2	Ada	1	Cambridge	1017-1029	Quatrefoil EMC 1013.1064
3	Ada	1	Cambridge	1017-1029	Quatrefoil EMC 1013.1065
4	Ada	1	Cambridge	1017-1029	Quatrefoil EMC 1013.1066
5	Ada	1	Cambridge	1017-1029	Quatrefoil EMC 1013.1067
6	Ada	1	Cambridge	1017-1029	Quatrefoil EMC 1013.1070
7	Ada	1	Cambridge	1017-1029	Quatrefoil EMC 1013.1071
8	Ada	1	Cambridge	1017-1029	Quatrefoil EMC 1051.0527
9	Ada	1	Cambridge	1017-1029	Pointed Helmet BMC ii p.271 no.230
10	Ada	1	Cambridge	1017-1029	Pointed Helmet EMC 1013.1068
11	Ada	1	Cambridge	1017-1029	Pointed Helmet EMC 1013.1069
12	Ada	1	Cambridge	1017-1029	Pointed Helmet EMC 1025.0751
13	Ada	1	Cambridge	1017-1029	Pointed Helmet EMC 1036.0677
14	Ada	2	Huntingdon	1029-1036	Short Cross EMC 1013.1259
15	Ada	2	Huntingdon	1029-1036	Short Cross EMC 1013.1260
16	Ada	2	Huntingdon	1029-1036	Short Cross EMC 1013.1261

moneyers. An example of moneyers operating at different mints that were potentially the same individual, but have been kept separate in the database, can be seen in the listing for moneyers named 'Ada' at the beginning of the Index of Fused Names [Table 2.2].

The name Ada only appears at these two mints in these coinages. An Ada is continuously active from Cnut's Quatrefoil type (1017–1023) to Pointed Helmet (1023–1029) in Cambridge. After 1029 no Ada is recorded in Cambridge, but in Huntingdon, only 18 miles to the northwest, an Ada is active for Cnut's last type, Short Cross, for the period 1029–1036. It seems very likely that these two individuals are one and the same, but since no record linking them directly exists, they remain fissioned in the database.

Die-Links

For future work to improve upon the present database and to create a true prosopography of the moneyers of late Anglo-Saxon England, additional evidence would need to be brought to bear. One category of additional evidence which would help in the identification of individual persons within the database is the evidence of die-linking. A die-link is the connection between coins struck with the same die. This provides a unique opportunity to identify individual moneyers who operated at multiple mints. Unfortunately, the number of such links based on current discoveries is limited and the examples of die-links, which have been used to great effect in scholarship to highlight the itinerant nature of minting in late Anglo-Saxon England, is a very small percentage when compared to the overall number of moneyers active in the nearly 100 mints operating over the period 973 to 1086.[25] This is in contrast to later records which demonstrate more widespread die-sharing (and thus die-links). For example, in Winchester after 1180 the moneyers shared workspace and tools but were fined for doing so just a few years earlier in the 1160s.[26] It is also evident in earlier records for Northumbria that extensive die-linking between mints occurred, implying that there was cooperation and possible shared workspace between moneyers in the north.[27] However, die-links in late Anglo-Saxon England are so infrequent that the conclusion is that each individual moneyer operated their own separate workshop.[28] But, those examples that are available do provide excellent insight into the movements of moneyers in the period and have been used to support larger trends in Anglo-Saxon minting history.

This work was largely started by Michael Dolley in the late 1950s. Dolley found several examples of coins that used dies from multiple locations in their production. The most common examples of these are obverse die-links, where the front facing portrait-side of the die is passed from moneyer to moneyer and thus potentially mint to mint. This practice does not necessarily assist in the identification of an individual operating at multiple locations however, as it is possible that an obverse die was used for a limited amount of time, returned to a distribution centre, and then

[25] Naismith, 2017a, 241. According to Naismith, 'inter-moneyer die-links occur but only occasionally' in the late Anglo-Saxon period.
[26] Allen, 2012, 56–7.
[27] Naismith, 2017a, 11.
[28] Naismith, 2017a, 11.

reissued to another moneyer, making any connectivity simply on this basis somewhat problematical. For example, in Dolley's work on the coinage of Hertford and London, he found an obverse link between moneyers of the same name operating between the two mints.[29] Dolley takes this as evidence that the two are likely one and the same person and goes on to extrapolate that moneyers of similar name working between the two mints during close or intersecting coinage issues are also likely one and the same.[30] Dolley and others used this type of analysis to make similar links at other mints. In their 1958 *Numismatic Chronicle* article, Dolley and Gay van der Meer used obverse die-links between coins minted at Winchester and Southampton to differentiate between the moneyer Leofwine working between these two mints and a moneyer of the same name operating at the same time in Northampton.[31] This link was verified in 1970 by Elmore Jones in his study of an obverse die-link between the moneyers Burgweald and Ælfweard operating at Winchester, who used an obverse die of Leofwine from Southampton.[32] Ian Stewart also used the die-links identified by Dolley to make connections between moneyers operating between the mints of London, Hertford, and Southwark.[33] Similar links between mints using an obverse die-link exist between Wilton and Salisbury for the moneyer Ælfred, identified for coins of Cnut by Dolley in 1962, and between Exeter and Gothaburh for two moneyers at the former, God and Byrhstan, and a Wulfmær at the latter, identified by Stewart Lyon.[34] Dolley would link the workings of the mints at London and Northampton as well as Winchester and Southampton with obverse die-links.[35] Specifically, the moneyer Æthelnoth from Northampton shared an obverse die with Æthelweard from London and Godman in Winchester used an obverse die also used by Ælfsige in Southampton.[36]

These links are debatable in that there are alternatives to these conclusions, especially when the mints in question are not geographically close. For example, the obverse die-link between Northampton and Cambridge identified in 1960 by Veronica Butler and Dolley was determined to likely be a reissuing of the die from the end of Sibwine's career at Cambridge to Wulfric at Northampton, potentially through the return of the die to London to be redistributed.[37] A similar conclusion is made in the 2007 study of the mint at Aylesbury by William Clarke and David Symons.[38] Their conclusion was that an obverse die-link between Æthelwine at Aylesbury and Brunman at London was most likely the case of a die being returned to London and then redistributed.[39]

But, in general, the use of obverse die-links has been acknowledged as a means of accepting, at least provisionally, that moneyers of similar name operating at geographically close mints at the same, or close to the same, time are one and the same individual. This has been extrapolated to include similarly named moneyers from those linked mints even where direct die-links do not exist. For example, in 1965, Dolley, Elliot, and Elmore Jones state that the moneyer Leofwine in operation in Aylesbury, Buckingham, and Wallingford were all the same moneyer although no actual die-link exists to support this position, only ancillary links through other moneyers.[40] This conclusion was supported by Metcalf in 1998.[41] Similar extrapolations were carried out in Pauline Stafford's 1978 work on die-distribution, which was discussed in some detail above.[42] Stafford points to several instances of like-named moneyers operating between different geographically close mints and indicates that these are likely the same individuals moving from one mint to another.[43] Stafford uses the work of Dolley and others to argue that moneyers moved from one mint to another and provides several examples.[44] The article also outlines that such links can be made 'on the basis of name identity alone'.[45] Stafford points to the movement of moneyers from Chester to supply both Hereford and Stafford, from London to Winchcombe, from Winchester to Gloucester, and from Gloucester to Shrewsbury as examples of the flexibility of the minting system.[46] A more detailed example of the use of name similarity and die-linking can be found in the work of Mark Blackburn on the mint of Watchet.[47] In looking at the uncommon name Hunewine, along with specific die-links between some of the mints, Blackburn reconstructs the career of this moneyer and illustrates how Hunewine was likely active at six mints over a long period.

Because relatively few die-links exist, and in order to maintain uniformity in the data, die-links are not included in the database and they have not been used to identify individual moneyers that may have operated at multiple mint locations. As they are so limited in number, die-links are best used in specific and small studies like those discussed above. In order to avoid including data that only

[29] R. H. M. Dolley, 1958b, 'Three More Anglo-Saxon Notes', *BNJ* 29, 51–60 at 56–7.
[30] Dolley, 1958b, 57.
[31] R. H. M. Dolley and G. van der Meer, 1958, 'A Group of Anglo-Saxon Pence at Sudeley Castle', *NC* 18 (Sixth Series), 123–29 at 126.
[32] F. Elmore Jones, 1970, 'Southampton/Winchester Die-Links in Canute's Quatrefoil Type', *BNJ* 39, 6–11 at 6.
[33] B. H. I. H. Stewart, 1971, 'The Early Coins of Ethered II's Crux Issue with Right-facing Bust', *NC* 11 (Seventh Series), 237–42 at 241–2.
[34] R. H. M. Dolley, 1962, 'Two Anglo-Saxon Notes', *BNJ* 31, 53–6 at 52–4; C. S. S. Lyon, 1962, 'Two Notes on the "Last Small Cross" Type of Æthelræd II', *BNJ* 31, 49–52 at 51–2.
[35] R. H. M. Dolley, 1966, 'Further Southampton/Winchester Die-Links in the Reign of Æthelræd II', *BNJ* 35, 25–33.
[36] Dolley, 1966, 28 and 30.
[37] V. J. Butler and R. H. M. Dolley, 1960, 'Two Die-Links Relative to the Anglo-Saxon Mint at Northampton', *BNJ* 30, 54–6 at 55–6.
[38] W. M. Clarke and D. Symons, 2007, 'The Mint of Aylesbury', *BNJ* 77, 173–89.
[39] Clarke, 2007, 180.
[40] R. H. M. Dolley, D. J. Elliott, and F. Elmore Jones, 1965, 'The Buckingham Mint', *BNJ* 34, 46–52 at 47.
[41] Metcalf, 1998, 222.
[42] Stafford, 1978.
[43] Stafford, 1978, 39–42.
[44] Stafford, 1978, 39.
[45] Stafford, 1978, 41.
[46] Stafford, 1978, 41.
[47] M. A. S. Blackburn, 1974, 'The Mint of Watchet', *BNJ* 44, 13–38.

impacted a very small percentage of the overall number of moneyers in the study, die-links are not included in the database. However, future work on the database could see them incorporated as an additional field that can be added to as new discoveries are made. In this way the database could be used as a support for such studies. For the present study adding the die-link connections between moneyers at multiple mints was not practical, but the inclusion of this material in future iterations would make it more useful for inquiries into the potential movement of moneyers from one location to another. This could be accomplished by adding a secondary Mint field, [Desc(Mint2)], into which the additional mints where a moneyer is thought to have been active due to die-links could be added. This field could then be used to further identify moneyers who were active at multiple locations.

Charters

In addition to die-links, charters would also offer a means of identifying persons within the database. But, like die-links, they present interpretative problems. The most prominent research into moneyer documentation from charters is the work of Ian Stewart on charters from the ninth to eleventh centuries.[48] Stewart located three instances of individuals appearing in charters with corresponding placement in time and location with moneyers appearing on coins. His example which is most relevant temporally to this study is from Devon during the reigns of Cnut and Edward the Confessor.[49] Coincidentally, the moneyer in question for his study is the same moneyer found through die-links by Michael Dolley, Hunewine, as discussed above. In looking at two charters, Stewart found that Hunewine acted as witness during the reign of Æthelred II and was a *minister* and granted land by Cnut.[50] Stewart notes a third charter that has a Hunewine 'Heca sunu' as witness, and states that this was likely so that this new Hunewine could be distinguished from the more prominent, and potentially related, namesake, but there is no evidence to support this link directly and the connection must be inferred as this is the only reference to Hunewine within the charter.[51] However, Stewart does note that on this third charter there are four other names listed as *minister* who acted as witness and which are found on coins at the mint in Exeter – Ælfric, Dodda, Leofwine 'æt Exon', and Wicing.[52] Stewart's conclusion is clear: he states 'because of the rarity of the name, and the coincidence of both period and locality, we can be confident that Hunewine the moneyer and Hunewine the minister were one and the same man'.[53] Dodda, another uncommon name, also appears as a witness on the charter from 1033, in which Hunewine is granted land, while Wicing, also uncommon, only appears in the 1046 charter.[54] As Dodda is an uncommon name and he was present and denoted as a *minister* in at least two instances in the time and place of a moneyer by the same name minting coins, further investigation into his appearances in charters may further define the individual beyond the coinage record.

For example, when looking at Dodda and other witnesses on the charters of Hunewine there is an interesting correlation between the *ministri* and correspondingly named moneyers active around the same time in the same geographic area. If we take Stewart's conclusion, that the appearance of Hunewine as a *minister* in charters local to his position as a moneyer at the same time confirms a match in identity and expand it to include others in similar circumstances then we can also ascribe the same characteristics to Dodda and others in the witness list. So, based on the two charters in which Dodda and Hunewine are present together and named as *minister*, it would appear that the moneyer Dodda in Exeter, who was active a few years before the 1046 charter is the same individual. Dodda also appears in charters dated 1042, 1043, and 1044.[55] The charter he witnesses in 1043 is a grant of 10 hides of land by King Edward to Ælfstan, another *minister*, who also happens to share the name of a moneyer of both Totnes and Exeter around the same time.[56] Using the database, it can be found that other *ministri* that acted as witnesses on this charter had correspondingly named moneyers in Exeter around the same time, including Leofing and Wulfnoth.[57] Æthelwig was a moneyer at Ilchester in the same period and a *minister* by that name was also witness.[58] A *minister* named Beorhtric was witness and a Beorhtric was a moneyer at Exeter for Harold's Pax type (1066).[59] There are also several coins of moneyers with indeterminate mint that correspond to this period. A Godsunu minted coins for Edward's Trefoil-Quadrilateral type (1046–1048) but the mint is unknown because of damage to the surviving coin.[60] A Godsunu was witness to this same charter and may very well have been this previously unlocated moneyer. There are three coins of an Æthelmær similarly documented and a *minister* by that name was witness to this charter as well.[61]

Table 2.3 lists *ministri* witnesses to the charters of Hunewine and Dodda and whether or not they have correspondingly named moneyers operating in the region at the same time [Table 2.3]. The table is organised by charter with the witness list on the left and any corresponding moneyer from the database on the right. Moneyers with indeterminate mint locations have not been included.

Using the database allows for the cross-referencing of every witness name on the charters with the Index of

[48] Stewart, 1988.
[49] Stewart, 1988, 169–70.
[50] S. 1452; S. 971.
[51] S. 1474.
[52] Stewart, 1988, 170.
[53] Stewart, 1988, 167–8.
[54] S. 971.
[55] S. 998; S. 999; S. 1005.
[56] SM1.Exeter.ix ; SM1.Totnes.i.
[57] SM1.Exeter.lxxi; SM1.Exeter.cviii–cix.
[58] SM1.Ilchester.xvi.
[59] SM1.Exeter.xviii.
[60] SM1.Indeterminate.lxx.
[61] SM1.Indeterminate.xxii–xxiii.

Fused Names, permitting a more complete listing of those *ministri* that might also have been moneyers operating regionally at the same time. While Stewart was able to identify Hunewine specifically and noted that some of the others might also have been moneyers during Edward the Confessor's reign his technique can be used to much greater effect when paired with the database. In the above illustration, taking six charters that apparently link the moneyers Hunewine and Dodda and reviewing all of the witnesses noted as *minister* on the charters it can be seen that over half (43 of 81) can be matched to a moneyer of the same name operating at the same time in the same general location. This comparison cannot be made using PASE, or any other single resource known to the author. For example, the only Cetel listings in PASE are moneyers and the variant spelling of Cytel refers only to later

Table 2.3. *Ministri* Witnesses and Corresponding Moneyers on Charters of Hunewine and Dodda

S. 1452 (968x93)		S. 971 (1033)		S. 998 (1042)	
Witness	**Moneyer**	**Witness**	**Moneyer**	**Witness**	**Moneyer**
Cetel	Cetel	Ælfgar	Ælfgar	Ælfgar	Ælfgar
Denisc		Æthelmær	Æthelmær	Ælfweard	Ælfweard
Eadwig		Dodda	Dodda	Æthelric	Æthelric
Eadwig Boga		Eadmær	Eadmær	Dodda	Dodda
Godwine	Godwine	Eadsige	Eadsige	Godwine	Godwine
Hunewine	Hunewine	Eadwine	Eadwine	Odda	
Sweta		Hunewine	Hunewine	Ordgar	
Wulfsige	Wulfsige	Leofsige		Osmær	
		Odda		Toki	
		Toki		Toui	
		Toui			

S. 999 (1043)		S. 1005 (1044)		S. 1474 (1046)	
Witness	**Moneyer**	**Witness**	**Moneyer**	**Witness**	**Moneyer**
Ælfgæt		Ælfgar	Ælfgar	Ælfgar	Ælfgar
Ælfstan	Ælfstan	Ælfstan	Ælfstan	Ælfgar æt Mynheafdon	
Æthelmær	Æthelmær	Ælfweard	Ælfweard	Ælfric	Ælfric
Æthelric	Æthelric	Ælfwine	Ælfwine	Ælfweard Ælfweald sunu	Ælfweard
Æthelwig	Æthelwig	Æthelric	Æthelric	Ælfweald sunu	
Beorhtric	Beorhtric	Dodda	Dodda	Ælfwig æt Hægdune	
Dodda	Dodda	Ecglaf		Æthelmær	Æthelmær
Esbern		Ecgulf		Alon	
Godsunu		Godwine	Godwine	Dodda	Dodda
Leofing	Leofing	Leofnoth		Escbern	
Leofric	Leofric	Odda		Hunewine Heca sunu	Hunewine
Leofwine		Ordgar		Leofwine æt Exon	Leofwine
Odda		Osgod		Lutsige on Wiht	
Ordgar		Osmær	Osmær	Odda	
Tofi		Wulfnoth	Wulfnoth	Ordgar	
Toki				Osmær	Osmær
Totig				Wicing	Wicing
Ulfcetel				Wulfweard æt Winesham	
Urki					
Wulfnoth	Wulfnoth				

instances.[62] This makes direct cross referencing between Cetel on the charter of 968–993, which is not included in PASE's sources currently, and moneyers of the same name operating at the same time difficult without a single point of reference.

But, like die-links, the number of instances in which this might be the case are very few in number and are not to included in the database because it only pertains to a very small minority of the moneyers being addressed. Future work on the database can incorporate this information on a case-by-case basis to include charters as a source and make appropriate links. This could also be expanded to include Domesday, especially where uncommon names are concerned.

Uses of the Database in Historical Analysis

Future work might therefore be able to build on the foundations laid by the present text, nevertheless even in its current state the database constitutes a useful resource for historical analysis in its own right. Scholars interested in the impact of the Danish conquests of Cnut could, for instance, use the activity of the mints and the onomastic information in the database to support arguments for Scandinavian importation of English workers and methods. Cnut adopted Anglo-Saxon law in his rule of England instead of imposing Danish customs and treated the English and Danes as equal under the law.[63] The creation of a single currency for his empire required the introduction of large-scale minting in his Scandinavian empire and the existing mint system in England was an ideal model for this. The need for imported labour and specialists to make this a reality is not so much in question, but the level at which Cnut relied upon English moneyers to establish minting in Denmark is a matter of some debate. Bolton argues that the importation of Scandinavian moneyers into English mints might have been a means of Cnut instituting control over the existing institutions.[64] While this may have been true to some extent, the dominance of English moneyers throughout most of England, including former Danelaw regions, during Cnut's reign seems to imply that this was not the ultimate aim, or at the very least was not an effective strategy. Bolton acknowledges this somewhat in his acknowledgement that many of the moneyers active during the reign of Cnut were also active under Æthelred II.[65] It seems more likely, based on the relative rarity of Scandinavian names in the mints, that any newly imported workers in the mints after 1016 were there to learn the trade that other English moneyers would carry to Denmark soon thereafter. The few instances of Scandinavian names first appearing in Wessex during the reign of Cnut might imply an importation of workers to be installed in the English mints, perhaps to learn the trade for later work in Denmark.[66]

Bolton's idea on the exporting of English moneyers to Denmark could be expanded upon and supported with the information in the database. When discussing the administration of England and Denmark, Bolton points to English names on the coins from Lund and Slagelse as evidence of English influence on the introduction and spread of minting in his homeland.[67] Bolton hypothesizes that the moneyers on the coins from Denmark may have been from the Anglo-Scandinavian Danelaw and enticed to leave England to serve the king in Denmark.[68] This is supported by Blackburn, who noted that the dies used in Lund were very similar to those cut in Lincoln.[69] A review of those names and periods of activity within the database may provide a more clear picture of the activity of moneyers and might provide more detail of how the minting structure was exported from Anglo-Saxon England to Denmark in the early eleventh century. Bolton bases his conclusions on Cinthio's earlier research work on the moneyers in Lund.[70] Looking at the same information in comparison to the database to see if further support for those conclusions can be established is detailed below.

Cinthio asserts that several of the moneyers on Cnut's first coinages in Lund were from England based on the names being derivative of Old English.[71] She notes that Ascetel, Ælfwine, Asferth, Farthegn, and Leofwine all came from England.[72] Bolton also names Godwine and Beortræd as moneyers from England active in Lund.[73] Cinthio names Sven, Thorcel, Ulfcetel, Toca, Asferth, and Thorstan as native Danish moneyers active in Lund because they have Old Norse names.[74] This is problematical. In basing conclusions only on the name structures an important aspect of Anglo-Saxon history is not considered: Danelaw. A number of the names that have been attributed as native Danish moneyers appear in Lincoln and York during the same period and could have very well been the same individuals. For example, an Ulfcetel is active in both Lincoln and York for the period immediately preceding the activity in Lund.[75] This is also true for a Toca in York,

---

[62] PASE: Cetel 1–9; Cytel 1–4.

[63] P. Stafford, 1982, 'The laws of Cnut and the history of Anglo-Saxon royal promises', *ASE* 10, 173–90 at 173–4 also 180: 'A conquering king is being asked to subscribe to the laws of the conquered people. See also: T. Bolton, 2017, *Cnut the Great*, New Haven, 106–7.

[64] T. Bolton, 2008, *The Empire of Cnut the Great, Conquest and the Consolidation of Power in Northern Europe in the Early Eleventh Century*, Leiden, 58–9. Bolton acknowledges that the idea originally came from Kenneth Jonsson at 59 n. 59.

[65] Bolton, 2008, 59 and 59 n. 60.

[66] Bolton, 2008, 56–7. Bolton points to the moneyer named Viking/Wicing active in Exeter and later listed in Domesday as evidence of this.

[67] T. Bolton, 2017, 142–4.

[68] Bolton, 2017, 144.

[69] M. A. S. Blackburn, 1990, 'Do Cnut the Great's First Coins as King of Denmark Date from Before 1018?', in K. Jonsson and B. Malmer, eds., *Sigtuna Papers: Proceedings of the Viking-Age Coinage Symposium at Sigtuna, 1989, Commentationes de nummis saeculorum IX–XI in Suecia repertis*, Nova Series, 6, Stockholm, 52–65 at 60.

[70] M. Cinthio, 1990, 'Myntverk och Myntare i Lund', *Kulturen: En Årsbok till Medlemmarna av Kulturhistoriska Föreningen för Södra Sverige*, 48–53 at 48–50.

[71] Cinthio, 1990, 48.

[72] Cinthio, 1990, 48.

[73] Bolton, 2017, 143.

[74] Cinthio, 1990, 50.

[75] SM1.Lincoln.clxxv; SM1.York.ccxvi.

who was active during Cnut's reign.[76] It can be argued that this is an example of Cnut bringing a Dane to England but there are earlier examples of Toca in Winchester, London, and Southwark.[77] Plus, the level of skill needed for the position makes it unlikely that a moneyer was imported from Denmark by Cnut since it seems apparent that Cnut used English moneyers to establish his minting there, not the other way round. An Asferth was active in Lincoln for the period and moneyers named Thorstan were present in Lincoln, Stamford, and York.[78] Another problem with Asferth is that the name appears in both lists, as a moneyer from England and a moneyer from Denmark. Cinthio resolves this by providing Asfrid as the name derived from Old Norse, but the Old English frith/ferth deuterotheme and the Old Norse frid deuterotheme both mean 'peace' and this may have simply been an example of a name spelling changing on subsequent dies, as occasionally occurred. This means that there may have been only one Asferth/Asfrid operating in Lund for Cnut but with a replacement die that had a variant spelling of the name. Regardless, the provenance of the name based on the name origin is problematic.

So, in looking at the moneyer names in Cinthio, which are used by Bolton to support the argument that Cnut imported English moneyers to help with the establishment of minting in his Danish kingdom, it would appear that it may not be only the 'English' named moneyers that took part in this exercise. It is wholly possible that those moneyers that Cinthio has stated as native to Denmark may possibly be Anglo-Scandinavian named moneyers from the Danelaw. If this was the case then it seems that of the 13 moneyers named on the coinages of Cnut from Lund a substantial number, 11, have like-named moneyer records in the Danelaw region that correspond to activity just before or during the reign of Cnut. Of the other two, the first, Sven, does not have a liked-name reference in the database for the period around Cnut's reign and the second, Thorcel, does have similar named moneyers in the records for the Danelaw, but not an exact match. This does not mean that these two individuals were not also from England, just that there are not currently available sources to support it. This supports Bolton's assertion that Cnut imported English moneyers to Denmark. It also enhances Bolton's argument that the administrative structure of Cnut's Danish kingdom was influenced by English structures that were exported to Jutland.[79] If Cnut was willing to entrust his new minting structure to newly conquered men of some status in their own right, and had the influence and authority to have them relocate from England to Denmark, how much of the rest of his governing structure was similarly influenced? Using the database, the argument can be made that while both Bolton, and Cinthio before him, attribute nearly half of the moneyers in Lund to Danish origins, it was far less than this and the majority of minting in Lund under Cnut was carried out by exported English moneyers [Table 2.4]. In this way, the examination provides a means of extending research for future scholars.

Local historians seeking to track the development of their town or city could look at the material collected in the database for evidential support of activity. Through local history, societal changes on a small scale can be illustrated. These changes might be representative of larger trends that are more relatable than grand-scale histories that study whole civilisations or political events. Local history provides a microcosm of events that may be difficult to relate to as an abstract concept. The idea of late Anglo-Saxon governance forming into a cohesive system in the century prior to the Norman Conquest can be studied through the political events of the period but in order to understand how this practically came into being functional examples need to be discovered, or at least clearly identified. In looking at how minting operated during this period, a better picture of the shift towards an Anglo-Saxon 'state' might be realised. In reviewing the activity of specific mints, using the information in the database to support the analysis, the efficiency of the coinage system can be illustrated and can be used to understand these transitions. Local history can also help in the understanding of the political events and how social change as a result of those events impacted local communities.

For example, the database can be used to study the activity of the mint in Wilton for the early eleventh century and find tangible support for the abandonment of the mint, and likely decreased influence of the town, following the Viking incursion of 1003. Prior to 1003 there were typically three to six moneyers operating in Wilton during each of the eight coinages produced from Edgar's Reform.[80] Minting stopped, and the moneyers moved to Salisbury from 1003, only to have a single moneyer, Winesige, return for the Last Small Cross type (1009–1016) at least half a decade later.[81] But, unlike pre-1003 minting, after the return to Wilton in 1009 only a single moneyer was active for the mint at any one time for the next 30 years, indicating that the need for a mint in the town had decreased, likely in response to depopulation, loss of regional influence, threat of repeat attack, or a combination of these and other factors. Using the database to look at the activity of minting in Wilton can provide the historian with a context through which to view the decline of the town's status in late Anglo-Saxon England.

The database could also be used to update and expand on the local histories contained in the Victoria County History series. For example, the entry for Huntingdon includes a detailed summary of the mint activity for the late Anglo-Saxon era, inclusive of moneyer names.[82] In contrast to this,

[76] SM1.York.ccx.

[77] SM1.London.ccclxvi; SM1.Southwark.lxii; SM1.Winchester.cxxxvii.

[78] SM1.Lincoln.xxix; SM1.Lincoln.clxvii; SM1.Stamford.xcvii; SM1.York.ccviii.

[79] Bolton, 2017, 144–5.

[80] SM1.Wilton.

[81] SM1.Wilton.liv.

[82] W. Page, G. Proby, and S. Inskip Ladds, eds., 1932, 'The borough of Huntingdon: Introduction, castle and borough', in *A History of the*

Table 2.4. Comparison of Moneyer Origins for Lund

Cnut's Moneyers of Lund	Language Derivation	Origin (Bolton & Cinthio)	Origin (database)
Ælfwine	OE	England	England
Ascetel	OE	England	England
Asferth	OE	England	England
Asferth (Asfrid)	OE (ON)	Denmark	England
Beortræd	OE	England	England
Farthegn	OE	England	England
Godwine	OE	England	England
Leofwine	OE	England	England
Sven	ON	Denmark	Denmark(?)
Thorcel	ON	Denmark	Denmark(?)
Thorsten	ON	Denmark	England
Toca	ON	Denmark	England
Ulfcetel	ON	Denmark	England
Percentage of Moneyers of Cnut in Lund of English origin		**53.8%**	**84.6%**

the volume on Buckinghamshire, which includes Aylesbury, only has a short reference to the mint with incomplete details relating to the mint's activity and the moneyers that were active.[83] The information in the database can be used to update this information. Beyond just updating existing local histories, the database can be used to analyse and research local economic and social histories. Small mints that have had little scholarship produced on them could be addressed and written about. The activity of the moneyers in Axbridge points to a small town that was active at the time of Edgar's reform but ceased all operation until Cnut's reign and was only active until 1042. The last analysis of the mint was by Elmore Jones in 1960 and this was a numismatic analysis of the five coins then attributed to the mint.[84] Using the information in the database, an argument for the activity of the mint being related to the need for higher coinage output during the reign of Cnut and his successors can be made.

The Coverage of the Database

The coinage of late Anglo-Saxon England is held in a number of museums and collections. Principal in these collections are the Department of Coins and Medals at the British Museum, London, the Fitzwilliam Museum, Cambridge and the Royal Coin Cabinet, Copenhagen. There are also various museums in Scandinavia, particularly Stockholm, which hold many thousands of Anglo-Saxon pennies taken during Viking raids and the era of Danegeld.[85] Smaller, but not insubstantial collections can also be found at the Ashmolean Museum in Oxford, Grosvenor Museum in Chester, the Hunterian Museum in Glasgow, and various local museums across England.

Because of the peculiarities of the *Sylloge of Coins of the British Isles* publication schedule, the volume on the late Anglo-Saxon coins is not yet in production or included in most of the online sources. The online catalogue for the British Museum does provide a great deal of information on these coins directly but a significant percentage of the coins listed on the website have some error in their listing. Specifically, when one searches for 'William' with the co-agent 'coin' in the Coins and Medals catalogue the listing returns 20,718 objects.[86] Further delineation to 'William the Conqueror' provides 481 objects, though the number of coins in the collection is closer to 1000. This is compounded by the fact that few of the objects on the online listing include photographs so verification via the iconography is impossible. Nearly all other collections are fully displayed online with photographs so that direct inspection is unnecessary. Many of the items on the catalogue were cross-listed between William I of England and William I of Scotland, who ruled nearly 100 years after the period in question. (Some of these errors have now been corrected but others remain.[87])

County of Huntingdon: Volume 2, London, 121–39. <http://www.british-history.ac.uk/vch/hunts/vol2/pp121-139> Accessed 7 May 2018.

[83] W. Page, ed., 1925, 'The borough of Aylesbury: Introduction and borough', in *A History of the County of Buckingham: Volume 3*, London, 1–11, <http://www.british-history.ac.uk/vch/bucks/vol3/pp1-11> Accessed 7 May 2018.

[84] F. Elmore Jones, 1960, 'The Mint at Axbridge', *BNJ* 30, 61–9.

[85] R. H. M. Dolley, 1970, *Anglo-Saxon Pennies*, London, 10.

[86] British Museum Collection Database <http://www.britishmuseum.org/research/collection_online/search.aspx?searchText=William&object=23360&view=list> [accessed 9/3/2017].

[87] British Museum Collection Database <http://www.britishmuseum.org/research/collection_online/collection_object_details.aspx?objectId=1072038&partId=1&searchText=william+the+conqueror&view=list&page=1> [accessed 9/3/2017]. The British Museum was notifed of this issue via email. The museum responded that due to multiple levels of cataloguing this error could not be overcome without direct inspection

This means that a direct review and study of the complete corpus of coins which date from between Edgar's Reform Coinage and William I coins within the British Museum was undertaken. This is beyond the collection of information from multiple online catalogues and databases that include clear photographs or epigraphic information from various coin collections. Most of the coinage record for the late Anglo-Saxon period, absent the British Museum, is available via online resources. This made collection of this data, which comprises nearly two-thirds of the total numismatic evidence in the database, easier.

Data Entry

The database collates the following information: the name of the moneyers, the location of the mint at which he worked, and the range of dates during which he was active at that mint. The processes by which this data was gathered is outlined below. The database is structured in a 'relational' model format.[88] The model takes specific points of data and links them based on information taken from a source and categorises them in table form. Specifically, the database is structured as a 'single table' database wherein each row represents a named moneyer while each column represents an aspect of that moneyer that can be derived from the coinage.[89] As Mathisen states, '[f]or most projects, especially personal PDBs, a database structure based on a single tabular file with individual person entries remains the most practical' method of constructing and presenting the information.[90]

The database utilises a format that is similar to the factoid model but the resultant entries are linear in their structure and information because it is 'source oriented', meaning that the individual entries and attributes are essentially defined by the coins themselves.[91] Since the database is not simply an onomastic listing of moneyer names, but utilises tabular datafiles to provide specific attributes for each individual moneyer record, this is a simple relational database.[92] According to Mathisen's terminology, the database can also be referred to as a 'File, Datafile, Dataset, [or] Table'.[93] Each row of the database may also be known as a 'Record, Entry, Entity, [or] Tuple'.[94] The columns are also known as 'Field, Attribute, [or] Domain'.[95] The preferred terms within the text, and used interchangeably, are database/dataset, entry/record, and field/attribute herein.

Information taken from a single coin is placed into several columns. The statement 'Cild was a moneyer' is derived from taking the moneyer's name from a specific coin. Likewise, expanding on this to state that 'Cild was a moneyer in Bedwin' draws upon the moneyer's name and the mint location, also taken from the coinage. By taking the iconography of the coin and the monarch's name from the front of the penny might allow a further expansion of this factoid to something like 'Cild was a moneyer in Bedwin under Edward the Confessor from 1044 to 1053'. This information is collated from different points of data derived from the study of the coinage. The reason coins are utilised exclusively in this study is that the medium is universal, meaning that every mint has some sources, in the form of surviving coins, that provide this information. The other extant source materials, primarily written documents, are very sporadic and generally limited to only a few regions, making them less representative overall of the moneyer group. Since the current study is focused upon the moneyers specifically, only those items that relate to the minters and their placement in the mints are specific times are included. Through this process, information can be collected and assembled from the database. The total number of moneyers associated with a specific mint, or specific coinage, or any other combination of this information is also readily available. For instance, the user could take the mint location as the primary datapoint in conjunction with the range of dates and thereby provide a statement of 'there were X moneyers in Y mint from 973 to 1086' or 'Z monarch had X moneyers in Y mint' or 'Y mint was active from [date] to [date]'. As this biographical collection is primarily derived from one type of source, it is a 'Limited' database.[96] There is only one moneyer per coin, only one mint, the date is determined by the iconography, and the monarch can be determined by the date and iconography, as well as the king's epigraphic listing. The coin provides the basis of the datapoints, which are then used to form the biographical entries, either singularly or in conjunction with the other items of information. These primary datapoints are outlined in more detail below. Monarch is not a distinct category as this information can be determined in conjunction with the establishment of the coin's date of production. This model can be utilised in other studies that look to only one source or seek to isolate only one aspect of the data. If a charter study is conducted to only look at witnesses of a specific class, for example Sheriffs or Reeves, then a similar model could be used since the information for each entry would contain information on the same points of data.

Moneyer Name

The names of the moneyers who worked during the late tenth and eleventh centuries are recorded on the coins

of the coins. The email exchange occurred between 16 and 17 October 2013.

88 Mathisen, 2007, 102–6.

89 Mathisen, 2007, 123.

90 Mathisen, 2007, 123.

91 Mathisen, 2007, 111. The factoid-based model was developed at King's College London and used in the creation of the *Prosopography of the Byzantine World*, the *Prosopography of Anglo-Saxon England*, the *People of Medieval Scotland*, and, most recently, in *The Making of Charlemagne's Europe* databases. The definition of factoid, taken from PBW, is 'small packets of information, a word or a sentence, sometimes with a word or two in the original language, and a source-reference'. <http://blog.pbw.cch.kcl.ac.uk/faq/#what-is-a-factoid-and-what-kinds-are-used-here>.

92 Mathisen, 2007, 111.

93 Mathisen, 2007, 111.

94 Mathisen, 2007, 111.

95 Mathisen, 2007, 111.

96 Mathisen, 2007, 107.

that they produced. The vast majority of Anglo-Saxon coinage has undergone this process of documentation and transcription numerous times but errors do occur and it is therefore necessary in many instances to visually verify these identifications directly.[97] Specifically, the Anglo-Saxon and early Norman coins of the British Museum are not fully documented online. An epigraphic review of all the coins produced in this period within this collection will therefore be carried out. This will follow the procedures developed by Cecily Clark and Fran Colman through a series of onomastic and phonological studies.[98] Further orthographic standardization has since incorporated more recent hoard finds and phonological discoveries, resulting in a uniform consideration of the epigraphy from Anglo-Saxon coins.[99] Whenever there are clear examples from previous records, most notably those normalisations found within Smart's *Cumulative Index* for the SCBI, and her work on correcting attribution and phonetic mistakes from Searle and Hildebrand, those names will be utilised.[100]

As we see below [Figure 2.1], the coins do not automatically lend themselves to quick interpretation because of wear and aging.[101] Therefore, each individual inspection can be time intensive.

For this First Hand type coin, the inscription on the obverse (left-hand side image) is patterned in a clockwise format

Figure 2.1. First Hand type coin of Æthelred II.

around the central profile of the reigning monarch, in this instance Æthelred II (the Unready) who ruled from 978 to 1016. The actual inscription is, beginning with the cruciform at 220° (indicated by the arrow on the left), +ÆĐELRÆD REX ANGLOX. This, along with the profiled image of the monarch and the hand on the the reverse, places the coinage within the second minting of Æthelred sometime between 979 and 985. The reverse (the right-hand side image) inscription, beginning with the cruciform at 0° (indicated by the arrow), is +EADSIGE M-O PINTONI. This provides the mint location, Winchester, along with the moneyer in charge of the stamping of the coin itself, in this instance, Eadsige. The moneyer designation was often abbreviated as MO, M-O, or M--O on the coinage for the period before Cnut and then ON from Cnut's reign.[102]

The names within the database are standardized to provide uniformity, especially in instances where a specific moneyer utilised multiple spellings on subsequent coin productions.[103] Standardization allows for the consolidation of moneyer records were successive mintings may have included slightly different spellings of individuals' names and allows for comparison between names from different mints in order to view correlation in naming practices in various geographic locations. Veronica Smart is the authority on the normalisation of Old English proper names as derived from coin epigraphy. The process by which this was achieved was via the use of Lemma-form tables for specific moneyers named within the coins of the initial *Sylloge of Coins of the British Isles*. Each variation of the spelling of a particular moneyer's name was included in the table and the occurrence percentages were calculated so that the higher occurrence spellings became the dominant classification. Unfortunately, the Lemma-form tables originally created by Smart were

[97] For example, in a review of 428 coins of William I held within the British Museum on one afternoon in November 2013, three errors in the catalogue were documented. One coin of Leicester by the moneyer Lierie is catalogued as a William I *BMC* type ii, but upon inspection of the iconography of the coin it became apparent that it was in fact a type viii, crown 2 coin (*BMC.* pl.iv.11). A coin of Norwich was transcribed as Ælgric but inspection of the coin seemed to clearly indicate Ælfwold or Ælfweald as the moneyer. The margin of error (0.7 per cent) is not included in the overall quantitative analysis since finding three errors in 428 coins extrapolated over the complete dataset equates to 200 errors. (The error is calculated as three of 428, where there was one miscategorisation and two transcription errors in the review of these 428 individual coins. The number of individual coin references for the 3,646 records in the *MED* is 28,576. 28,576*.007=200. This margin of error is less than 0.7 per cent so falls within an acceptable standard deviation.)

[98] F. Colman, 1989, 'Neutralization: On Characterizing Distinctions between Old English Proper Names and Common Nouns', *Leeds Studies in English* 20, 249–70. See also: eadem, 1990, 'Numismatics, Names and Neutralisations', *Transactions of the Philological Society* 88, 59–96; eadem, 1992, *Money Talks: Reconstructing Old English: Trends in Linguistics - Studies and Monographs* 56, New York; C. Clark, 1995, 'Clark's First Three Laws of Applied Anthroponymics', in P. Jackson, ed., *Words, Names, and History: Selected Writings of Cecily Clark*, Suffolk, 77–83; F. Colman, 2014, *The Grammar of Names in Anglo-Saxon England: The Linguistics and Culture of the Old English Onomasticon*, Oxford.

[99] P. Shaw, 2008, 'Orthographic Standardization and Seventh- and Eighth-Century Coin Inscriptions', in T. Abramson, ed., *Two Decades of Discovery: Studies in Early Medieval Coinage*, 97–112.

[100] B. E. Hildebrand, 1881, *Anglosachsiska Mynt i Svenska Kongliga Myntkabinettet*, Stockholm; W. G. Searle, 1897, *Onomasticon Anglo-Saxonicum, A List of Anglo-Saxon Proper Names from Bede to that of King John*, Cambridge; V. Smart, 1975, 'Corrections to Hildebrand's Corpus of Anglo-Saxon Moneyers: from Cnut to Edward the Confessor', *ASE* 4, 155–70; eadem, 1981, *Cumulative index of Volumes 1–20, in Sylloge of Coins of the British Isles*, London; eadem, 1987a, 'Moneyers of the late Anglo-Saxon coinage: the Danish Dynasty', *ASE* 16, 233–308; eadem, 2012, 'The Names of the Moneyers of the Winchester Mint' in M. Biddle, ed., *Winchester Studies 8: The Winchester Mint and Coins and Related Finds from the Excavations of 1961–71*, Oxford, 66–78.

[101] PAS, IOW-34EEEC.

[102] Early examples of the use of MO, and infrequently just M, in epigraphy are found in Northumbria during the reign of King Eanred (*c.*810–*c.*850) for the moneyers Folcnoth and Odilo. See: A. Anscombe, 1918, 'Odilo, A Northumbrian Moneyer of the Tenth Century, and His Issues', *BNJ* 14, 1–12 at 2.

[103] V. Smart, 1981, *Cumulative index of Volumes 1–20*, in *Sylloge of Coins of the British Isles*, London. See also: eadem, 1987a, 'Moneyers of the late Anglo-Saxon coinage: the Danish Dynasty', *ASE* 16, 233–308; eadem, 1987b, 'Moneyers of the late Anglo-Saxon Coinage, 973–1016', in *Commentationes de Nummis Saeculorum IX-XI in Suecia Repertis*, Volume II, Stockholm, 193–276.

lost when her research transferred from St. Andrews to the British Academy, making it difficult to reconcile any differences that occur within this collection and the work she accomplished.[104] The study normalisation differs somewhat from that presented nearly four decades ago in that certain occurrences within the records illustrate a divergence from that originally presented by Smart. For example, the maintenance of the 'beorht' form over the 'briht' form and the incorporation of standard West Saxon spelling throughout. The reason for this is to conform with other contemporary resources, such as PASE, in providing late Anglo-Saxon names in a uniform fashion.[105] Thus a moneyer documented in Smart as Brihtmær will appear as Beorhtmær in the database.

Mint

Coins from this period also give the name of the mint at which they were struck. Knowledge of the mint at which a particular moneyer practised his craft assists in the geographic placement of the moneyer at a specific point in time. The mint location also allows for the collection of a wide range of moneyers in order to establish continuity over a set interval. This information additionally permits cross-referencing with extant charters, deeds and wills within the same geographic location in order to ascertain if any correlation between the moneyer and other practices might exist. There are some areas of difficulty in identifying specific mints from coin epigraphy. Because of the limited space on the reverse of the coins, often the name of the mint is abbreviated, making it difficult to determine mint location between coins produced at mints with closely related names. For example, coins have been incorrectly attributed to mints based on phonetic similarities only to have later research specify the error through die link connections or the presence of coins from the same moneyer on either side of the questionable production located clearly at another minting location.[106] In the instance of London in particular, the mint markers on the coinage issues from 973 to 1086 are varied to such a degree that identification of the mint itself is sometimes problematic. This variation is outlined in the table below [Table 2.5]. Throughout the study period there were 28 different spellings of London on coins from that mint, many of them appearing concurrently with others. The name could be truncated because of errors in the cutting of the die, or because of a moneyer having a particularly long name and requiring the space on the reverse of the coin. While most of the markers clearly point to London as the point of origin, some of the different characterisations of the name make quick identification difficult. Without cross-checking information from the iconography, moneyer name, and occasionally die-links with other mints, it would be difficult to differentiate a worn coin from LII (London) to one from LI (Lincoln).

Table 2.5. Epigraphy variations of London on late Anglo-Saxon coins

LENDON	LV	LVNDEN	LVNDNIE
LII	LVD	LVNDENE	LVNDO
LIINDNI	LVDO	LVNDI	LVNDON
LINI	LVI	LVNDII	LVNDONI
LUN	LVN	LVNDNE	LVNDONIA
LUND	LVND	LVNDNEN	LVNEI

Errors in transcription can also cause mistakes in identification. For instance, the mint epigraphy of a coin of the moneyer Beorhtric of Petherton was misread in the early twentieth century as REDI instead of PEDI and led to several decades of incorrect attribution to a late Anglo-Saxon mint at Reading, which did not, at least according to current extant coin records, exist.[107] In such instances, reliance upon the most recent and widespread consideration for a given mint name is the designation. Future revisions to the database may require shifts in some descriptions as further research is carried out, or if new hoard discoveries indicate a shift in a currently common attribution.

Range of Active Dates

Determining when a specific moneyer operated at a specific mint can only be achieved by dating the coinage which they produced. Understanding this sequential nature within the late Anglo-Saxon coinage is important, because determining the timeframe within which an individual moneyer was active is paramount. As discussed in detail above, work on the dating of specific coinages in the modern era derives most directly from, and revisions to, the work of Dolley, who developed what is commonly known as the sexennial theory of recoinage.[108] This theory outlines the idea of coinages after Edgar's reform of the late 970s to the end of Cnut's reign as lasting six years before a universal reissue. Numismatists and historians have refuted various aspects of this theory, most notably the uniformity associated with the recoinages because of aberrations in the cycle.[109] In leaving the strict six-year

[104] Confirmed via private correspondence with V. Smart.

[105] PASE, 'A guide to the PASE data-entry' <http://www.pase.ac.uk/redist/pdf/PaseDataCollectionGuide.pdf>; See also PASE, 'How have names been normalized?' <http //www.pase.ac.uk/help/faq.html>.

[106] The meaning of phonetic as sounds and their relation to symbols is the basis of this particular usage. Instances of this include notably Hildebrand's incorrect attribution of all Leicester coins to Chester and vice versa in his catalogue (Discussed in H. Montagu, 1891, 'The Anglo-Saxon Mints of Chester and Leicester', *NC* 11, 12–24.) and Brooke's attribution of a coin from Bruton to Bristol (Discussed in R. H. M. Dolley, 1959, 'The Earliest Penny of the Bruton Mint', *BNJ* 19, 183–5).

[107] R. H. M. Dolley, 1961b, 'A Note on the Anglo-Saxon mint of Reading', *BNJ* 30, 70–5 at 74. For other examples see Allen, 2012, 11–2; M. A. S. Blackburn, 2000, 'Metheltun not Medeshamstede: an Anglo-Saxon mint at Melton Mowbray rather than Peterborough Abbey', *BNJ* 70, 143–5 at 145.

[108] R. H. M. Dolley and D. M. Metcalf, 1961, 'The Reform of the English Coinage under Eadgar', in R. H. M. Dolley, ed., *Anglo-Saxon Coins: Studies Presented to F. M. Stenton on the Occasion of his 80th Birthday, 17 May 1960*, London, 152–8. For pre-sexennial theory sequence discussion see P. Seaby, 1955, 'The Sequence of Anglo-Saxon Coin Types, 1030–50', *BNJ* 28, 112–46.

[109] J. D. Brand, 1984, Periodic Change of Type in the Anglo-Saxon and Norman Periods, Rochester; B. H. I. H. Stewart, 1990, 'Coinage and Recoinage after Edgar's Reform', in K. Jonsson, ed., *Studies in Late*

cycle developed by Dolley, scholars such as Stewart and Brand propose a more fluid system in which recoinages were dictated as much by political circumstance as the calendar. Further work on this by Blackburn, Jonsson, Metcalf, and others has led to a generally accepted timeline of the late Anglo-Saxon coinages.[110] While these dates are not absolute, the sequence of the coinages is not in much dispute.[111] The dates currently ascribed to the various coinage types are presented in the table below [Table 2.6].

As can be seen, there are several issues, especially during the reign of Æthelred II, where some coinages overlap with others. This is possibly due to the process of recoinaging being under development at this point and not quite solidified as a stable process across all parts of the kingdom. The coinage types are named primarily in conjunction with specific aspects of their iconography. Going back to the example provided in Figure 2.1 above, the small, centred cross on the reverse provides the detail needed to categorise the coin properly within the context of the overall coinage issued during Æthelred II's reign. The 'small cross' form was utilised extensively before 1017, but when paired with the obverse portrait, it illustrates the last version, appropriately named the 'Last Small Cross' type, hammered some time between 1009 and 1016. Coins minted after 1017 maintained use of cross patterns, but often included more flourish in their designs. One further area of complication relates to the coinages of William I, which have recently been reexamined by Martin Allen.[112] Allen has renumbered the coinage issues of William I and credited the last coinages (William's Paxs Type) to his successor, William II.[113] Because of this, several mints that only have coins documented within this timeframe are recorded in the prosopography, but future consideration may require they be readdressed. The coins and related mints were maintained within the current structure because there is not consensus on the findings of Martin Allen at the time of this writing.[114]

The iconography itself is not without its own difficulties in classification and identification. While each series of coins is distinct in its markings, there are some similarities that can cause concern when attempting to place a specific coin within a particular monarch's reign. For example, when looking at three coins, one from Edgar's 'Reform Portrait' issue, one from Edward Martyr's 'Small Cross', and

Table 2.6. Coin Types by Date

Coin Type	Approximate Dates of Production	Monarch
Reform Portrait	973–975	Edgar
First Small Cross	975–978	Edward the Martyr
First Small Cross	978–979	Æthelred II
First Hand	979–985	Æthelred II
Second Hand	985–991	Æthelred II
Benediction Hand	991	Æthelred II
Crux	991–997	Æthelred II
Intermediate Small Cross	996	Æthelred II
Small Crux/ Transitional Crux	995–997	Æthelred II
Long Cross	997–1003	Æthelred II
Helmet	1003–1009	Æthelred II
Agnus Dei	1009	Æthelred II
Last Small Cross	1009–1016	Æthelred II
Quatrefoil	1017–1023	Cnut
Pointed Helmet	1023–1029	Cnut
Short Cross	1029–1036	Cnut
Jewel Cross	1036–1038	Harold I
Fleur-de-Lis	1038–1040	Harold I
Arm and Sceptre	1040–1042	Harthacnut
Pacx	1042–1044	Edward
Radiate Crown/ Small Cross	1044–1046	Edward
Trefoil-Quadrilateral	1046–1048	Edward
Short Cross	1048–1050	Edward
Expanding Cross	1050–1053	Edward
Pointed Helmet	1053–1056	Edward
Sovereign/Eagles	1056–1059	Edward
Hammer Cross	1059–1062	Edward
Facing Bust/Small Cross	1062–1065	Edward
Pyramids	1065–1066	Edward
Pax	1066	Harold II
Profile/Cross Fleury	1066–1068	William I
Bonnet	1068–1070	William I
Canopy	1070–1072	William I
Two Sceptres	1072–1074	William I
Two Stars	1074–1077	William I
Sword	1077–1080	William I
Profile/Cross and Trefoils	1080–1083	William I
Paxs	1083–1086	William I

Anglo-Saxon Coinage in Memory of Bror Emil Hildebrand, Stockholm, 455–85.

[110] D. M. Metcalf, 1980, 'Continuity and Change in English Monetary History', *BNJ* 50, 20–49; M. A. S. Blackburn, S. Keynes, and T. R. Volk, 1985, *Anglo-Saxon Coins*, Cambridge; K. Jonsson, 1987a, *The New Era*, London; R. Naismith, 2015, 'The Coinage of Æthelred II: A New Evaluation', *English Studies* 97, 124–39.

[111] C. S. S. Lyon, 1976, 'Some Problems in Interpreting Anglo-Saxon Coinage', *ASE* 5, 173–224; idem, 2003, 'Anglo-Saxon Numismatics', *BNJ* 73, 58–75.

[112] Allen, 2012.

[113] Allen, 2012, 300, 398.

[114] The major museum collections, including the Fitzwilliam Museum, where Martin Allen is Senior Assistant Keeper of the Department of Coins and Medals, maintain the Paxs type as a coin of William I in production between 1083 and 1086. No other numismatic study, to the author's knowledge, maintains the shift in provenance of the Paxs type to William II.

Figure 2.2. Coins of Edgar (1), Edward (2), and Æthelred II (3).

Æthelred II's 'First Small Cross' [Figure 2.2] side by side, it is difficult upon first inspection to see any significant difference.[115]

The reverse of each coin (1b, 2b, 3b) consists of a small cruciform in the centre of an open field surrounded by a raised ring and the inscription of the individual moneyer's name and the mint at which the coin was hammered. Even in reviewing the obverse of the coins (1a, 2a, 3a), it is not readily apparent that there is a difference between the left-facing profile images that are contained in the centre of the coins. However, the epigraphic inscriptions around each of these images are specific to the ruler issuing the coins. Unfortunately, the outer edges of the coins in many cases are not as easy to read as the examples presented herein, therefore the actual portrait itself must be analysed in order to ascertain its placement within the chronological history of the coinage. In the first coin, that of Edgar (1a), the profile includes two braids at 45° and a sloping bridge on the nose. In the obverse of the coin of Edward (2a), the braids have been lengthened and end at the 90–100° point. Also, the nose ends in more of a point, with a much less pronounced bridge. The obverse of the coin of Æthelred II (3a) includes the same stylistic qualities of the other two, but the head itself is much smaller and the neck is elongated.

Problems with quick identification such as this are common because of the wear associated with coins that have often been buried in less than ideal circumstances for the better part of a millennium. This makes the iconography incredibly important in determining when a coin was produced.[116] Familiarity with the various aspects of the iconography associated with the 38 different issues of coins for the period 973 to 1086 (inclusive of same coinages issued by multiple monarchs) is of paramount importance in this identification. But the coins themselves are small, measuring roughly 1.5cm in diameter. This small size makes direct examination of some coins difficult, especially if there is substantial wear on the coin. Fortunately, with good lighting and a magnifying glass, the iconography and epigraphy are typically discernable. The range is utilised as a general framework for the timescale involved with their activity in said mint. This range signifies a floruit band for the period of coinage in which a particular moneyer was responsible for the coins produced at a given mint.[117] Considering that there are records of die-links by moneyers over both short and long periods of activity at multiple mints there are implications that moneyers did take their equipment with them when they moved from location to location.[118] This implies that there was some level of direct residency associated with the name of the moneyer on the coins from a given mint at a specific point in time. This allows for the acknowledgement of a moneyer's activity range without necessarily indicating an exact date of residency. For example, a moneyer of Cnut's Pointed Helmet (1023–1029) from Lincoln would be noted as being active during this range of dates. It is not wholly clear whether this indicates if a moneyer was active for only part of this coinage cycle or for the duration, but it does outline that a moneyer with that specific name did operate at some point in Lincoln during that coinage. Further, if a moneyer of the same name was listed on the coinages of Cnut before or after this period then the range of activity can be expanded to include those coinage dates as well.

[115] PAS, NMS-6B70D1 (for 1a, 1b), IOW-657916 (for 2a, 2b), IOW-228A93 (for 3a, 3b).

[116] For discussion on the importance of coin iconography outside of type identification see I. Garipzanov, 1999, 'The Image of Authority in Carolingian Coinage: the image of a ruler and Roman imperial tradition', *Early Medieval Europe* 8, 197–218; M. A. S. Blackburn, 2007, 'Crosses and conversion: the iconography of the coinage of Viking York ca. 900' in K. L. Jolly, C. E. Karkov, and S. L. Keefer, eds., *Cross and Culture in Anglo-Saxon England: Studies in Honor of George Hardin Brown*, Morgantown, 172–200; A. Gannon, 2003, *The Iconography of Early Anglo-Saxon Coinage: Sixth to Eighth Centuries*, Oxford.

[117] A floruit band is the period of time in which a person is thought to have been active. See floruit, *Oxford English Dictionary*. <http://www.oed.com/view/Entry/71905?redirectedFrom=Floruit>.

[118] B. H. I. H. Stewart, 1992, 'The English and Norman Mints, *c.*600–1158', in C. E. Challis, ed., *A New History of the Royal Mint*, Cambridge, 1–82 at 74. Stewart states that '[s]everal of the mints where the same moneyers' names occur are connected by obverse die-links, which confirm the movement of their equipment.'

The Organisation of the Database

The table found in the supplementary material is a visualisation of each period of moneyer activity within the London mint for the period 973 to 1086. Every distinct iteration of a name is given a unique colour and categorised first alphabetically and then by longevity, from shortest period of activity to longest. The 68 by 38 grid has been given coordinates from A to AH on the X-axis and one to 38 on the Y-axis. This allows for a specific period of activity to be pinpointed on the chart for ease of use through an XY coordinate system. For example, a moneyer named Osmund was active from 1053 to 1062. He can be located on the chart under coordinates U21 and the footnote for this would be SM3.U21.

In order to facilitate the use of the *MED* beyond simply the study of the names of the moneyers, the mints themselves can be further organised into two primary categories, major and minor, which are then again divided into two subcategories each, high and low volume. The major mints are those that had over 30 distinct periods of moneyer activity between Edgar's reform in the early 970s and the Domesday survey in 1086. The minor mints are those that fall below 30 periods of moneyer activity. The high volume and low volume designations relate specifically to the available coinage records within each mint. Those with records of coin production for equal to, or greater than, half of the production years between 973 and 1086 are classified as high volume. Those that have records below half are low volume.

For example, Ipswich has representative activity over the entire spectrum of 973 to 1086, excepting the Profile/Cross Fleury type of William I (1066–1068), therefore making it a high-volume mint. Because there are 57 periods of activity within Ipswich, it is also a major mint. Conversely, Sudbury only contains coins for 37 years of the 113-year study period, making it a low volume mint. Likewise, with only nine distinct periods of activity, Sudbury is also a minor mint.

Moneyers with similar names are arranged alphabetically by name element and then chronologically in chapter six. This allows quick reference to the specific name groupings and illustrates how they flow in succession over time. The name element designation is separated by mint generational boundaries, meaning that successive series of moneyers with similar names are arranged together in the order of activity within a given mint. For concurrent moneyers with the same name element, further distinction can be made by using a secondary alpha-marker (e.g. 2a, 2b, 3a, 3b, etc.). Those moneyers noted with 'None' in the sequence do not have any corresponding moneyers within the mint that carry the same forename element.

Also included in the supplemental material is a list of the corresponding coin citations for each of the moneyers. They are organised chronologically by mint, then by moneyer. Full records for each named moneyer are documented and referenced throughout as the primary marker for every individual period of activity. Where a specific moneyer is referenced, a corresponding *MED* reference notation will be footnoted in the format [SupplementaryMaterial1.MintName.Moneyer#.Coin#].

For example, the fifth moneyer of the Lympne mint in the *MED* is Eatstan, who was active in the range 985–991. The footnote for this Eatstan would be SM1.Lympne.v. A coin number is not always included in the footnote.

The Moneyers of England Database, 973–1086

After identifying the study group, collecting the data, and organizing the Index of Names and Index of Fused Names the *Moneyers of England Database, 973–1086* took form. As noted above, many of the coin collections associated with the late Anglo-Saxon and first Norman coinages are digitized and available for review via online catalogues. Most of these collections are inclusive of high-resolution photographs of the coins, making verification of the epigraphic information readily available. The review of these online catalogues, briefly listed above and detailed in the bibliography, accounts for approximately two-thirds of the information collected in the *Moneyers of England, 973–1086* database. The process by which this information was collected is fairly straightforward. A coin record was reviewed, the provenance noted, and the epigraphy confirmed in order to gain the moneyer's name, the mint location, and determination of the coinage date reign. The bulk of this information pertains to coins produced before the reign of Edward the Confessor, as the exports of silver pennies to Scandinavia greatly decreased during his reign.[119] The reason for this is that the largest collections of the late Anglo-Saxon coinage, outside of that within the British Museum, are found in Scandinavian collections, gathered from hoards of Viking era Danegeld payments. Therefore, the information in the *MED* that derives solely from online sources is weighted towards the pre-1042 era. In order to balance this pre-1042 weighting, the collection within the British Museum was manually reviewed and added to the database. As discussed below, this information was not as easily collected as with other museum catalogues or online databases, therefore the process was somewhat more cumbersome and time consuming. Gathering and organising the information for this remaining one-third of the database information accounted for approximately two-thirds of the total research collection time for this project, which is why it is detailed more thoroughly.

One of the main obstacles in the collection of the British Museum data are problems with the online catalogue system it currently maintains. A review of the online searchable database reveals that there are 2,550 pennies in the British Museum collection produced between 973 and 1086. Upon arrival at the Study Room and the beginning inspection of the coins, it became apparent (based on

[119] B. H. I. H. Stewart, 1975, 'Reflections on some Wessex mints and their moneyers', *NC* 15, 219–29 at 222.

the number of cabinets that were slated for review) that the information collected from the online database was incorrect. The number of 2,550 was not aligning with the material available. In fact, it seemed that there were at least twice that number of coins that would need to be inspected. With this concern in mind, the method of data collection was quickly altered. In order to work through so many additional coins any in-process analysis or organisation was not possible. Generally, information specific to the parameters within the database would be expanded upon and included during the examination process. But, in this instance, the decision was made to collect the basic information in a cascading format without filling in each parameter for each coin until later. For example, lists of all coins for a certain type within a certain mint were set up and then only the catalogue number and moneyer name were recorded in the input fields. A list of London would include several sub-lists for each coinage type, thereby allowing this step to be skipped with each coin. Recording the coins only needed a switch from one type to another with an input of the basic information before moving on to the next coin. This allowed collection of the data at a much faster rate but increased the amount of work necessary to incorporate this information into the database and project.

By taking this shortcut in the collection process, rapid movement through the trays was possible, at a rate two to three times faster than previous attempts. After the first three days, information on over 2700 coins had been collected, more than the original total provided by the British Museum online database. The difference, evidently, has to do with the shifts in software that the museum is using for the online searches. All seven million plus objects held by the Coins and Medals Department are catalogued but because they were initially marked with different markers, newer software versions have not been able to correctly correlate these markers with new outputs. So basically, any research that involves information from the British Museum is reliant on first-hand review of the objects because there is no conceivable way to get all the relevant information on the website currently.

The cataloguing system internal to the Coins and Medals Department is somewhat confusing as well. While there is an overriding system in place it is not applied universally and coins that have been acquired since the last numbering are inserted into the corresponding type and mint section between concurrently organised items.[120] From the records, there are at least six completely different cataloguing schemes being utilised for the collection, often within types of coins for the same moneyer at the same mint. The original *British Museum Catalogue* published in the late nineteenth-century provides documentation for many of the coins that were in the collection at this time, along with a page number and series number. However, even this does not include some of the coins that are labelled with just a letter and a number and marked as being within the collection pre-1771 (assuming they were part of the museum collection added from its inception in 1753 to 1771) but with no other identifier or explanation as to why they were excluded from the original catalogue and with no provenance beyond their physical appearance in the museum.

Likewise, anything that was added to the collection after the catalogue is generally documented with the date of acquisition and a series number specific to the collection, irrespective of production period. Therefore, a coin of Æthelred II from 1012 can be number '300', while a coin of Edward the Confessor 50 years later might be numbered '20' if they came from the same collection. Including the coinages of William I and all of the Anglo-Saxon coins from Edgar's Reform Coinage, a direct inspection of nearly 8,000 coins took place during this phase of the database formation. This was accomplished through six multi-day trips to the British Museum. Careful review of the iconography and epigraphy is time consuming and difficult but ensures that accurate information is conveyed into the *MED*. In addition to this direct inspection, many hours were spent collating the information collected from the various online catalogues and database so that a cohesive useable version of the database might be realised.

The version utilised for this study is the fifteenth iteration of the database. As detailed in below, it contains information on over 3600 individual periods of moneyer activity. These periods are derived from over 28000 coins from 99 geographic locations. This constitutes the first comprehensive amalgamation of moneyer activity from all minting locations in England for the later tenth- and early eleventh-centuries. The database itself has been created utilising FileMaker Pro 12 Advanced, a comprehensive database construction and publishing program.[121]

The process of developing the *MED* from inception to this latest version constituted many visits to museums and coin collections, as well as comprehensive review of online repositories, requiring consecutive revisions in order to eliminate any duplicate records that may have been recorded in more than one location. The first version of the *MED* contained information from eight mints: Canterbury, Lincoln, London, Norwich, Stamford, Thetford, Winchester, and York. This first version consisted of 8,201 coins derived solely from the records contained within PASE and associated with each mint and the office of moneyer. The total number of individual periods of activity within this version was 526. After the removal of duplicate records through three subsequent versions which constituted verifying the information line by line, the fourth version, utilising this same information from eight mints, resulted in 457 moneyer periods of activity.

After the initial versions of the *MED* were completed, it became apparent that in order to gain a full picture

[120] The British Museum recently underwent a process of hiring a Curator with a specific remit of reorganising the Anglo-Saxon collection, so this may not be an impediment for future researchers.

[121] FileMaker Pro 12 Advanced <http://www.filemaker.com/products/filemaker-pro-advanced>.

of the moneyers, all of the minting locations that were active from 973 to 1086 would need to be included. This prompted Version 5, which consisted of reviewing all individual records within PASE and the *The Corpus of Early Medieval Coin Finds* and *Sylloge of Coins of the British Isles* at the Fitzwilliam Museum in order to capture information on each of the moneyers. Most important in this is PASE, but it contains its own difficulties in usage, as discussed above.

Comprehensive review of all moneyer records in PASE resulted in systematic analysis of the information, categorising each region by relevant dates and then recording the name of the moneyer, the monarch with whom they were associated, the mint to which they were linked, and the dates connected to the coins that they issued, as well as the specific examples of coins for each moneyer in the extant numismatic record. These were then cross-listed against those results with the data that was already collected. The source material, primarily coins, for this information was also analysed and recorded. The typical reference for an individual moneyer contained between 15 and 20 sources, several with many more. Ultimately, this resulted in the direct review, cross-checking, and recording of between 65000 and 90000 pieces of data from PASE. Subsequent versions built upon this by taking records from other sources such as auction catalogues and other online databases, as well as the British Museum, resulting in this latest version (16) with 3646 periods of moneyer activity, identified in the Index of Fused Names as individuals, at 99 geographic locations from the period 973 to 1086 based on 28,576 coin records.

3

Onomastic Patterns in the Late Anglo-Saxon Moneyers

Introduction

There are any number of analyses that can be done with the information collected in the *MED*. These can range from specific numismatic studies on the distribution of the coinage, to the production rates and activity of specific mints, to more general historical studies of the active dates of mints or individuals. Indeed, many mints have already been treated to these sorts of analysis, although the number of locations subjected to specific in-depth treatment is still outnumbered by those that have yet to get this level of attention. And while each of those studies would doubtless be fruitful, this analysis is more concerned with the general trends found within the moneyer group from amongst all the mints of late Anglo-Saxon England. Chapter five looks specifically at the data collected in the *MED* with the aim of determining if the idea of the minters working as familial groups holds true.

Inheritance in Late Anglo-Saxon England

Was the office of moneyer by the late Anglo-Saxon period an inherited office and was it similar to other royal offices or systems of inheritance known to scholars? Much of what we know about late Anglo-Saxon inheritance is centred around the movement of land, which was the most important indicator of wealth, between kinship groups.[1] Mumby addresses the inheritance of bookland (*bocland*) and how assumptive arguments about 'customary' practices do not necessarily translate into practical application when looking at the evidence.[2] This work goes on to outline the progress in inheritance studies over the last few decades, detailing how early work on Anglo-Saxon wills considered them illustrative of typical practice but how later work pointing to a lack of actual family inheritance in the wills seems to implicate the wills as an exceptional practice rather than the norm insofar as kinship inheritance is concerned.[3] Mumby notes that Wormald noticed the lack of sons specifically named within the wills and how this points to a differentiation between what earlier historians assumed as a standard practice and what was likely occurring within late Anglo-Saxon society.[4] The laws also provide limited support for the inheritance practices of late Anglo-Saxon England. II Cnut pointed back to the now lost VIII Æthelred in outlining successional inheritance in light of conflicting claims but do not provide much detail on the practice itself.[5] The constitution of bookland and the developing inheritance practices of it might be found in the Kentish Customary, but Mumby acknowledges this too is problematical in that it the records stem from thirteenth century sources, making provenance somewhat difficult.[6] The gavelkind practices within it do outline the preference to the eldest son in selecting his chosen land for inheritance, although the youngest son inherits the family home. Better and contemporary examples are found in Domesday, where partible inheritance *TRE* is found in four entries.[7] Some charters also outline the inheritance of land from fathers to sons, as well as the granting of this inheritance perpetually by the king. For example, a charter of Æthelred II outlines how a certain Ælfstan purchased land from King Edmund and how his son Ælfheah, upon inheritance, petitioned King Eadred to have it booked as a perpetual inheritance, part of which Ælfheah then granted to his brother Ælfric.[8] Hudson argues that the charters indicate that a primary purpose of bookland was to differentiate inheritors and solidify practices that were likely customary before the late Anglo-Saxon period.[9] Hudson also states that the inheritance of land was dependent upon the payment of heriot, or relief payment, to the lord, although he notes that evidence of land reverting to the lord prior to relief payment is unknown.[10] This is similar to R. S. Kinsey's analysis of the 'relief' payments made by successor moneyers at several mints wherein 'relief' payments were legally defined as the money thegns paid to a lord in order to succeed to an inheritance and H. R. Loyn's assertion that many of the moneyers held names that were commonly associated with the 'thegnly' class.[11] There is no documentation, to the author's knowledge, that outlines the inheritance of offices in a manner similar to the inheritance of land, but if the process of bequeathing the office of moneyer did follow similar lines then the practice of minting might

[1] J. Mumby, 2011, 'The decent of family land in later Anglo-Saxon England', *Historical Research* 84, 399–415 at 400.

[2] Mumby, 2011, 401.

[3] Mumby, 2011, 400–2. Mumby points to the work of Charles-Edwards, Loyn, Holt, and Garnett as important to the development of her argument, arguing a progression of a general idea of familial inheritance from fathers to sons to something more complex that is not explicitly clear from the wills.

[4] Mumby, 2011, 402 n.18. See also P. Wormald, 2001, 'On *þa Wæpnedhealfe*: Kingship and Royal Property from Æthelwulf to Edward the Elder', in N. J. Nighman and D. H. Hill, eds., *Edward the Elder, 899–924*, London, 264–79; idem, 2014, 'The Foundations of Title', in S. Baxter and J. Hudson, eds., *Patrick Wormald, Papers Preparatory to The Making of English Law: King Alfred to the Twelfth Century, Volume II: From God's Law to Common Law*, London, 212–28 at 223.

[5] Mumby, 2011, 403–4.

[6] Mumby, 2011, 403.

[7] Mumby, 2011, 405–6; J. Hudson, 2012, *The Oxford History of the Laws of England: 871–1216*, Oxford, 125.

[8] S 1458.

[9] Hudson, 2012, 128–9.

[10] Hudson, 2012, 123–4.

[11] Kinsey, 1960, 28; H. R. Loyn, 1991, *Anglo-Saxon England and the Norman Conquest*, 2nd Ed, London, 125.

have moved in a father-son progression similar to land ownership. Certainly, it seems that the process of securing the minting rights at least followed financial obligations similar to land inheritance.

Another avenue of support for the idea of minting being a hereditary office is in looking at how other royal offices during the late Anglo-Saxon period developed into hereditary placements. The position of ealdorman, for example, developed from a strictly royal appointment to a successive position often passed from father to son. The position of ealdorman was initially the appointed ruler over the *scirs*, or shires.[12] These men were generally relatives of the king or were powerful landholders that occasionally married the king's daughters.[13] Yorke states that early kings sought to name relatives to ealdorman positions in order to prevent rivalries.[14] John points out that eventually, this position of power and authority led to sons succeeding fathers into the role outside of direct royal appointment.[15] Fisher argues that this father to son movement was initially sporadic but became more commonplace in the later Anglo-Saxon period.[16] Fleming, drawing on Loyn, outlines that by the Danish Conquest and the move from ealdorman to earl during the time of Cnut the position was sufficiently solidified in the hereditary system that it was more a lateral move in title more than an institutional change in authority or power.[17] Fleming goes on to argue that the interconnectedness of the ealdorman group was widespread and that movement into the group from outside of those with direct kinship to previous ealdormen was unlikely.[18]

An example of this group of closely related men holding consecutive placement as ealdorman was detailed by Ann Williams in her work on the family of Ælfhere from the reigns of Eadwig and Eadgar in the last half of the tenth century.[19] Williams details the family connections of Ælfhere, ealdorman of Mercia.[20] Ælfhere was the son of an ealdorman and his brother, Ælfheah, was also an ealdorman (in central Wessex). His son, Ælfric, became ealdorman of Mercia upon his death. Ælfric's son, Ælfwine, was killed at the Battle of Maldon and is documented as a kinsman of another ealdorman, Beorhtnoth of Essex. What this illustrates is at least three generations of one family carrying forward in the office of ealdorman. This work was carried a step further in Mary Blanchard's recent work on the same topic, where she identifies five kin groups from the tenth century that gained and maintained control over the ealdorman positions.[21] Blanchard's argument is that these families utilised a strategy of secular office at the expense of religious appointments in order to solidify their authority.[22] The process by which they did this is not dissimilar to that conveyed herein regarding the office of moneyer.[23] Also evident is the continuation of the naming practices that were similar for the royal lineages and seem evident (as discussed in detail below) in the moneyers as well. While the office of moneyer was not as powerful or important in the administration of Anglo-Saxon England as the office of ealdorman, and later earl, proved to be, the processes by which families maintained control of the office may have been similar. If moneyer groups were related and the office was hereditary then further elucidation of how the mints were structured might be realised.

Moneyer Groups as Families

The idea that the moneyers working within a specific mint were related is not new. In 1953, Robert Lopez put forth his outline of how moneyers had established their own aristocracy of money by the late Middle Ages on the Continent, implying that the structures were in existence long before.[24] Lopez outlines that in the Frankish mints there were laws in place that specified no one could become a moneyer unless he was a descendant of a moneyer.[25] He goes on to state that the organisation of minting in Italy was likely a holdover from the late Roman era and that the general operation of mints throughout the Continent supported the idea of a predominance of kinship between the moneyers.[26] He specifies this shift to moneyer-

[12] E. John, 1996, *Reassessing Anglo-Saxon England*, Manchester, 11.
[13] John, 1996, 11.
[14] B. Yorke, 1990, Kings and Kingdoms of Early Anglo-Saxon England, London, 171.
[15] John, 1996, 11; T. S. M. Mommaerts-Browne, 2005, 'Anglo-Saxon Aristocracy: Tracing Lineages', *Foundations* 1, 404–13 at 405.
[16] D. J. V. Fisher, 1976, *The Anglo-Saxon Age, c.400–1042*, London, 259.
[17] R. Fleming, 1991, *Kings and Lords in Conquest England*, Cambridge, 22.
[18] Fleming, 1991, 23.
[19] A. Williams, 1981, '*Princeps Merciorum gentis*: the family, career and connections of Ælfhere, ealdorman of Mercia, 956–83', *ASE* 10, 143–72.
[20] Williams, 1991, 144.
[21] M. E. Blanchard, 2019, "A new perspective on family strategy in tenth- and eleventh-century England: ealdorman status and the Church," *Historical Research* 92, 1–23.
[22] Blanchard, "A new perspective on family strategy," 2.
[23] Blanchard, "A new perspective on family strategy," 3–16. Blanchard argues that those appointed to the role of ealdorman by the king eventually transitioned the office into an hereditary one, in which the ealdorman was replaced by their progeny. Blanchard also highlights how many of these most prominent families were able to have their second or third sons also appointed to royal offices outside of the ealdorman role. Examples of this being Leofric and Eadwine, noted by Stephen Baxter as shire-reeves in Worcestershire and Shropshire, who were later sons of ealdorman Leofwine. (14) See also: S. Baxter, 2007, *The Earls of Mercia: Lordship and Power in Late Anglo-Saxon England*, Oxford, 32–3.
[24] R. S. Lopez, 1953, 'An Aristocracy of Money in the Early Middle Ages', *Speculum* 28, 1–43. See also Andrew, 1901a, 279. Andrew outlines that the moneyer role was 'practically hereditary' because the same names were evident in the mints named in Domesday and in the Pipe Rolls, stating that in the latter 'usually, son succeeded father, or nephew uncle'.
[25] Lopez, 1953, 2. See P. Spufford, 1983, 'Mint organisation in the Burgundian Netherlands in the fifteenth century', in C. N. L. Brooke, B. H. I. H. Stewart, J. G. Pollard, and T. R. Volk, eds., *Studies in Numismatic Method presented to Philip Grierson*, Cambridge, 239–62 at 241; idem, 1989, *Money and Its Use in Medieval Europe*, Cambridge, 187–208; G. Romaneix, 2008, 'Les privilèges des monnayers du Serment de France aux XIIIe et XIVe siècles', in Y. Benhima, ed., *Actes des congrès nationaux des sociétés historiques et scientifiques*, 88–99.
[26] *CIL VI* 42-4. ...*familia monetaria*.... Lopez, 1953, 3–4. Lopez argues that the initial groups of minting slaves (*familia monetaria*) transitioned into freedmen and then over the centuries transitioned from the Roman Empire to the mid to late Middle Ages to form guilds in Continental Europe that witnessed hereditary membership. See R. Latouche, 1961,

descendent only as deriving from the early seventh-century Lombard mints.[27] Some of these laws governing mints are very similar to those adopted in Anglo-Saxon England, especially in regards to the punishments, the rights of the king, and the location for minting.[28] In 643, Rothari, a Lombard king, issued an edict outlining that moneyers operating outside of the king's approval would have their hands cut off.[29] This is remarkably similar to Æthelstan's Grately Code, which also stipulates that those caught illegally minting coins will have their hand removed or face the ordeal.[30] Edgar's Andover Code includes language restating the Grately Code's regulation that there would be a single coinage in the kingdom and includes that the coinage cannot be refused.[31] Æthelred II's Wantage Code repeats that there will be only one coinage and the option to face the ordeal for illegal minting with the alternative being execution.[32] IV Æthelred established that there would be three moneyers in the large towns and one moneyer in all the other towns under the king's domain.[33] This changed previous laws in limiting the number of moneyers, establishing that they would be allocated to the king only, and that they must mint their coins within the towns proper and not in the countryside outside of inspection. The law also reiterated the punishments for minting outside of the king's oversight and punishment for incorrect weight and purity within the coins' quality. Specifically, the moneyer's hand would be removed and hung from the front of the mint and he would be charged the *ouerhyrnessam* (a fine equating to the sum of 120 shillings). These laws and regulations mirrored the laws on the Continent. As Anglo-Saxon minting was in many ways reflective of minting from the Byzantine Empire, and later the Lombard Kingdoms and Holy Roman Empire, in the penalties, laws, and regulations, it is reasonable to conclude that internal structures relating to the hereditary right of practice might also be similar.[34]

Further work outlining the interconnectivity of the moneyers took place in 1982. Pamela Nightingale, expanding on a connection first noted by Walter Andrew in 1902, outlined a detailed study of one group in the London mint associated with the [Deor-] name element.[35] The name element is the prototheme from the Anglo-Saxon dithematic name structure and is used predominantly herein, although prototheme is also occasionally utilised. Nightingale's argument is that a group of moneyers with similar names in London demonstrated a multi-generational sequence of minters from within one family operating over a significant period of time. Primary in this analysis was the series of Deormans that was active, in her study, from Domesday Book to the middle of the twelfth century.[36] The impetus of that analysis was to provide genealogical support for ideas that were evident, but not wholly clear, in earlier research. Nightingale addresses Martin Biddle's earlier work on Winchester, in which he notes that moneyers were the most prominent members of society outside of the royal officials and that sons likely succeeded fathers at the mints.[37] But, Nightingale notes that both Biddle and Veronica Smart outline that there are difficulties in comparing the names of the moneyers from the coins to the written records for the late Anglo-Saxon period, making the analysis, absent some form of genealogy, complicated.[38] Thus, in noting these assumptions from earlier research, she states that having 'even one fairly reliable genealogy of a family of moneyers may yield more information about their social standing and suggest some clues to the organization of the mints'.[39] Nightingale's analysis compares coinage records with land holding evidence from the eleventh and twelfth centuries. By looking at the land ownership and documents witnessed by the Deormans and Theoderics, two names

The Birth of the Western Economy: Economic Aspects of the Dark Ages, London, 13.

[27] Lopez, 1953, 4. See also P. Grierson and M. A. S. Blackburn, 1986, *Medieval European Coinage, Volume 1: The Early Middle Ages (5th–10th centuries)*, Cambridge, 50–73.

[28] II Æthelstan 13.1–14.2; III Edgar 8–8.3; III Æthelred 8–8.2; IV Æthelred 5–9.3, in Liebermann.

[29] *Edictum Rothari* 242, translation from 'Rothair's Edict', in K. F. Drew, ed., 1973, *The Lombard Laws*, Philadelphia, 39–130; Lopez, 1953, 6; Foot, 2011, 151. Lopez states that Æthelstan's law likely derives from the Edict of Rothair, which he posits derives from earlier Byzantine law. Foot does not indicate any Byzantine influence. See also F. S. Lear, 1950, 'Treason and Related Offenses in the Anglo-Saxon Dooms', *Rice Institute Pamphlet - Rice University Studies* 37, Houston, 1–20 at 8. Lear argues that the introduction of specific penalties for moneyers relating to illegal minting points to increased Roman influence in the law code, but does not specify the origin of this assumption.

[30] II Æthelstan 14.1, Liebermann, 159. R. S. Kinsey, 1960, 'Anglo-Saxon Law and Practice Relating to Mints and Moneyers', *BNJ* 29, 12–50 at 14–6.

[31] III Edgar 8–8.3, Liebermann, 204.

[32] III Æthelred 8–8.2, Liebermann, 230.

[33] IV Æthelred 5–9.3, Liebermann, 234–6. *Et ut monetarii pauciores sint quam antea fuerint: in omni summo portu sint tres monetarii, et in omni alio portu sit unus monetarius* 'And in order that there might be fewer moneyers than in the past, in all major ports/towns there are three moneyers, and in all other ports/towns one moneyer.' This shift is perhaps the most important as it is a new regulation, but in practice it appears there was not a regular enforcement of this regulation as there were many more than three moneyers operating at some mints at a given time. A possible reason for this is discussed in detail in chapter six below.

[34] Lopez's 'An Aristocracy of Money' is a truncated English version of his detailed and more fully referenced 1949 work 'Continuità e adattamento nel medio evo: Un millenio di storia delle associazioni di monetieri nell'Europa meridionale'. Text available in R. S. Lopez, 1986, *The Shape of Medieval Monetary History*, London, 74–117. Lopez outlines the progression of minting laws from the late Byzantine Empire, through the Italian peninsula, into the Lombard kingdoms, and on to the Frankish and Germanic regions over a period of roughly one-thousand years. The discussion on the structure of the mints can be found primarily at 89–92.

[35] Because of the nature of this study and the inherent need for some level of clarification in dealing with the repetition of a multitude of similar names, the name element nomenclature will always be in brackets.; P. Nightingale, 1982, 'Some London Moneyers and Reflections on the Organization of English Mints in the Eleventh and Twelfth Centuries', *NC* 142, 34–50; Andrew, 1901b, 280.

[36] Nightingale, 1982, 35.

[37] Nightingale, 1982, 34; M. Biddle, ed., 1976, *Winchester in the Early Middle Ages*, Oxford, 397–400, 445–7, and 463. Biddle points to records from the Winton Domesday survey of *c.*1110 that outlines seven forges belonging to the son of a moneyer near the palace precinct. The forges are documented as active and the conclusion was that the father passed these down, along with the working knowledge of coin production to the son.

[38] Nightingale, 1982, 34; Biddle, 1976, 404, 408, 413; V. Smart, 1968, 'Moneyers of the late Anglo-Saxon Coinage, 973–1016', in *Commentationes de Nummis Saeculorum IX-XI in Suecia Repertis*, Volume II, Stockholm, 193–276 at 211.

[39] Nightingale, 1982, 34.

that are not common amongst late Anglo-Saxon moneyers, or the general population overall, Nightingale concludes that these men were directly related, specifying three or four Deormans and two Theoderics from one family.[40] She suggests that this family operated within the mints of London and passed the trade down from father to son, or nephew.[41] It is important to point out that Nightingale also notes the prevalence of the Deorman name in the London moneyers from the time of Æthelred II, Harold I, and Edward the Confessor, but she restricts her study to the post-Domesday era because of the greater volume of written source material like landholding records.[42] Another important point here is that the sequence of moneyers does include two different names (Deorman and Theoderic), thereby making it difficult to match pre-Domesday moneyers that may have maintained certain naming patterns overall but included differentiation because of something like multiple sons within the family. But, the inference is clear: groups of moneyers with similar names operating in the same locale in the same, or successive, periods of time are potentially related. If the first recorded Deorman after Domesday was indeed, as posited by Nightingale, the grandson of the last Deorman of Edward the Confessor, then predominantly, the [Deor-] name element is preferred, meaning that first sons are likely to carry this prototheme, and at least some relation between those named individuals might be surmised.[43]

Beyond just the Deormans of London, there are other incidences of potential families taking up the role of moneyer as a generational practice. In his analysis of the moneyers of Kent, Hirokazu Tsurushima outlines that the moneyers were skilled craftsmen that typically passed their skill from father to son.[44] Tsurushima also outlines the potential kinship between moneyers with the first name element at various minting locations, citing the existence of unusual names repeating after long absences in the coinage record as possible indications of this multi-generational apparatus.[45] Also suggested here is a different interpretation of multiple locations for a single moneyer of an unusual name. Instead of there being three Osferths, to take Tsurushima's example, operating at three different mint locations simultaneously, might it be a group of moneyers operating collectively under the name of a 'master-moneyer' with that name?[46] Tsurushima calls this a 'brand-name' process in which the moneyers work under the auspices of their group leader, similar to practices utilised by swordsmiths in Scandinavia and northern Europe from the ninth to twelfth centuries.[47]

Tsurushima undertook some comparative analysis of names from PASE and determined that there are several names that occur most frequently associated with the moneyer group, thereby concluding that these men were either directly related or undertaking work on a 'brand' model.[48] This would result in a scenario that would look like both hereditary moneyer practice and the incorporation of moneyers under a specific name or set of names to maintain a certain level of overarching control of the production cycle. Since we know that the former definitively took place in later periods, concurrently on the continent, and that certain laws imply hereditary status, then it is very likely that it was also happening within the mints of late Anglo-Saxon England as well.[49] The mint structure may have mirrored other metalworking trades during the same period. The moneyers at a given mint could therefore consist not only those connected by direct familial relation but also through the incorporation of their practice under the name of the master-moneyer responsible for the coinage that they produce. This means that moneyers operating over multiple coinages under the same name may be connected - whether through blood or commerce - and that this connection signifies continuity in the internal operation and organisation of the mint over an extended period of time. This is born out by the high regularity of repeating names occurring consecutively at various mints across late Anglo-Saxon England.

If this was the case, then the classification of moneyer groups as 'families' may be true in more than a direct blood-relation sense and would certainly speak directly to the prevalence of certain names as more common among moneyers than within the general population. This can also explain why some moneyers appear to operate for extremely long periods of time at a single mint. With the average period of activity for a single moneyer within the *MED* being 10.5 years before 1036 and 4 years after 1036, those moneyer names that have continuous activity for periods of 40 to 60 years in one location could be either men working under a single 'brand-name' or direct descendants carrying forward with the same name. However, it is important to point out that the moneyers operating for extended periods of time make up a very small minority of the overall records within the database, therefore relegating the 'brand-name' theory to only a small portion of the moneyer population. The prevailing thought, at least as discussed herein, is that the vast majority of the moneyers taking part in the activity of the mints and sharing the same prototheme were part of a single family.

[40] Nightingale, 1982, 36.
[41] Nightingale, 1982, 38.
[42] Nightingale, 1982, 38.
[43] Nightingale, 1982, 40.
[44] H. Tsurushima, 2012, 'The Moneyers of Kent in the Long Eleventh Century', in D. Roffe, ed., *The English and Their Legacy, 900–1200: Essays in Honour of Ann Williams*, Woodbridge, 33–59 at 41.
[45] Tsurushima, 2012, 41.
[46] Tsurushima, 2012, 41.
[47] Tsurushima, 2012, 41, n. 57; cf. I. G. Peirce, 2002, *Swords of the Viking Age*, Woodbridge.

[48] Tsurushima, 2012, 42–4. The names Boia, Man, and Brunman were reviewed. For Boia in the *Prosopography of Anglo-Saxon England* there are 37 instances and 32 are moneyers. For Man there are 51 occurrences with all being moneyers. He also notes that there are also nine records of Mann, with one being a goldsmith, who could also have been a moneyer, and three instances of Manna. Brunman appears 19 times with 10 being moneyers. Analysis herein of certain names being highly prevalent with the moneyer group concurs with this finding.
[49] Lopez, 1953, 2–3.

Interpretation of this is that there were traditional families associated with the mints as noted on the Continent from at least the seventh century and in the written sources for the post-Conquest period in England that passed operation from father to son/nephew and so on. In conjunction with this, there appears to have been the possibility, as outlined by Tsurushima, as can be seen in other metalworking crafts, of moneyers taking up the trade and operating under the name of one of these family members, thereby expanding the 'family' at least in the sense defined above. This can likely explain why there are some names that seem to be in operation continuously for extended periods of time while other names from within the same name-group arrive and disappear in the coinage record. For those moneyers that are not associated with either one of the prominent name elements or were operating in conjunction with them at the same location it could very well have been extended family members, second sons, or cousins operating at infrequent intervals to assist in times of higher demand.[50] As the majority of the moneyers at the largest mints were in fact associated with only a few name elements, it would appear that more often than not, the master-moneyer and his extended family did manage the production of the coinage without these added men.

Therefore, a possible hierarchy of the mints based upon the idea of name appropriation could be described as a master-moneyer establishing his name as the mint mark for a given coinage, probably with royal support, followed by a series of moneyers operating on his behalf who also utilised the same mint mark, potentially at multiple locations, over several periods of coin production. Once this master-moneyer retires or otherwise passes on his monopoly over a given mint to his son, grandson, or other direct descendent, the name shifts to a similar name with the same prototheme, or first element, and the process begins again. This could have happened within several minting families simultaneously at some of the larger mints, like London, where there were seven dominant name elements among the moneyers. The coordination of such practices amongst thousands of individuals at nearly 100 locations on such a consistent and uniform basis is astounding. There are complications to this scenario, which are discussed in some detail in chapter six below, but the overall concept appears to hold true for nearly all the largest mints and many of the smaller ones. This could explain why some names appear for extended periods of time at multiple locations and why the names on the coinage of the late Anglo-Saxon era are generally connected to a small minority of the names that appear in the extant sources, as discussed below.

The sequential patterns associated with the moneyers' names within a mint over various generational shifts indicate that some level of continuity exists. According to R. S. Kinsey, the personal names of the Anglo-Saxons, were traditionally derived from a combination of the father's name with that of the mother or another common ending.[51] For example, Winterlida could be a combination of Winterfugol (male) and Leoflida (female), with the prominent position falling to the father's name. This was, however, not universal and often the female name did not automatically lend itself to such combinations. In this manner, even common names, such as Æthelstan can be utilised to demonstrate patterns within the named sequences of the moneyers. This is further supported in the work of Fran Colman, who has produced multiple works on the onomastic structures of Anglo-Saxon personal names based on coin epigraphy.[52] Colman built upon the work of H. B. Woolf, who developed the concept of alliteration and variation as key components of Anglo-Saxon naming patterns.[53] Alliteration in Anglo-Saxon dithematic personal names primarily occurs in the prototheme, while variation is mostly limited to the deuterotheme, or second element, for example the name element [Wulf-] would appear in successive generations while the second element shifted from one generation to the next.[54] This would occasionally skip generations so that the grandfather and grandson would have the same first element. Woolf argues that the diversification of names within families became more widespread in the tenth and eleventh centuries as English families intermixed with families from alternative naming conventions, notably Scandinavian and Norman traditions.[55] This diversification of names within the moneyer group did not take place at this time and, as can be seen in chapter four below, alliteration and variation in naming practices maintained consistency through both the Danish and Norman Conquests.

Further instances of this are pointed out as recently as 2012 in Rory Naismith's work on eighth- and ninth-century England.[56] Naismith outlines that the moneyers were likely connected through families, pointing out not only the alliteration of the name structures as outlined above, but also the necessity of the moneyers to come from a small group of specialists because of the requirements associated

[50] Nightingale, 1982, 42.

[51] Kinsey, 1960, 12–50. See also Searle, 1897, ix–xxxi; T. Forssner, 1916, *Continental Germanic Personal Names in England in Old and Middle English Times*, Uppsala; M. A. Redin, 1919, *Studies of Uncompounded Personal Names in Old English*, Uppsala; H. Kokeritz, 1939, *Notes on the Pre-Conquest Personal Names of Domesday Book*, Uppsala; G. Fellows Jensen, 1968, *Scandinavian Personal Names in Lincolnshire and Yorkshire*, Copenhagen; R. A. G. Carson, 1949, 'The Mint of Thetford', *NC* 6, 189–236 at 194; D. E. Beeaff, 1978, 'Aelfraed and Haranfot: Anglo-Saxon Personal Names', *History Today* 28, 688–90.

[52] F. Colman, 1989, 'Neutralization: On Characterizing Distinctions between Old English Proper Names and Common Nouns', *Leeds Studies in English* 20, 249–70. See also: eadem, 1990, 'Numismatics, Names and Neutralisations', *Transactions of the Philological Society* 88, 59–96; eadem, 1992, *Money Talks: Reconstructing Old English: Trends in Linguistics - Studies and Monographs* 56, New York.

[53] H. B. Woolf, 1939, *The Old Germanic Principles of Name-Giving*, Baltimore, 118–9.

[54] F. Colman, 2014, *The Grammar of Names in Anglo-Saxon England: The Linguistics and Culture of the Old English Onomasticon*, Oxford, 106–8.

[55] Woolf, 1939, 119.

[56] Naismith, 2012a.

with the craft regarding metallurgy.[57] Considering Colman's assessment of Anglo-Saxon naming structures, the overall pattern is that there is some level of kinship associated between like-named individuals within the mints. Therefore, the likelihood increases that those with similar names within a given location at a specific point in time are related. While it is certainly possible, if not probable, that not all the similarly named moneyers within a given mint are directly related, the pattern of repeating protothemes indicates that it is still likely that this is the case at least a significant portion of the time, compensating for the lack of explicit statements of kinship in the existing documentation.

Onomastic Trends in the MED

When looking specifically at the *Moneyers of England Database, 973–1086* it seems that certain names, or at least name elements, appear quite frequently at multiple locations. On first glance, it is easy enough to determine that the obvious reason for this is that moneyers were part of the general population and therefore utilised common name structures. The most common name elements in the database certainly seem to support this supposition. The [God-], [Leof-], and [Wulf-] name elements are common at almost all the largest mints and were so for large sections of the study period. These names are attested to in many sources outside of the coinage record, for example in charters, wills, and deeds, and therefore, potentially speak against a uniformity based upon families in the organisation of the mints.

But, that is only a surface level comparison. When looking a bit deeper, it can be seen, as noted by Tsurushima's research above, that the name structures in use at the mints are not random and do not simply conform to the common naming practices of the day. First, in looking at the prevalence of the common name elements in general, there are comparisons to be made between the coinage record and the rest of the corpus of late Anglo-Saxon source material. Because of the number of coins available, any amalgamation of sources should indicate a prevalence of the moneyers' names by sheer numbers. The mathematical dominance of these records would indicate that, of course, the names of the moneyers are common in comparison with the rest of the records because they make up such a significant portion of the dataset.

But is this what happens when the analysis is carried out? If looking at the *Prosopography of Anglo-Saxon England*, a repository of names taken from coins, charters, wills, and other documents from the late Anglo-Saxon era, there are 4,925 unique names.[58] The unique names belonging to moneyers, meaning distinct spellings of names, in PASE make up less than 20 per cent of this total (885 of 4,925 or 17.9 per cent) even though the extant coinage record makes up a significantly higher percentage of the overall number of sources utilised in the creation of the database. This seems to run counter to the supposition above. If the coins make up a substantial percentage of the data then the representation of the moneyer names should be similarly represented if they were truly only an extension of the most common naming patterns of the era.

And indeed this does occur in some instances. Some names, like those beginning with [God-], [Leof-], or [Wulf-] as mentioned above, appear frequently at multiple mints and in multiple texts so these names have quite a bit of overlap between PASE and the *MED*. However, a further review of these most prominent name elements within PASE reveals that of those individuals so named, a notable number, in the range of 60 per cent to 70 per cent overall, from among those with known occupations, are in fact moneyers.[59] In this and further instances, 'known occupation' refers to those identified with a particular occupation, office, or title, such as moneyer, bishop, monk, slave, etc. In general, between 80 per cent–90 per cent of all named individuals addressed within PASE exist within a dataset that includes a known occupation. Those that are excluded are listed individuals marked only as witness, landowner, or with no further specific occupation or status noted. This disparity, that a large number of the records are moneyers, is understandable considering that the majority of sources for these names are coins. However, this does not account for the lack of moneyer names being prevalent throughout the entire database. If a large percentage of the records in PASE are derived directly from coin epigraphy, then an equally large percentage of the unique names of individuals in the database should correspondingly come from coins. But this does not hold true outside of these most prevalent name elements, which could be argued as being prevalent partially because of their association with the number of moneyer records. If the protothemes with the highest number of occurrences are discounted, there is a significant disparity between the 'common' names within PASE and those belonging to moneyers in the *MED*.

---

[57] Naismith, 2012a, 146. Outside of the restrictive candidate pool specialism in metallurgy would have required, Naismith outlines several potential families of moneyers from the London, Ipswich, and Canterbury mints based on prototheme repetition. While this text does not deal with the scientific aspects of metallurgy and the skills involved, it is important to point out that the ability of the moneyers to maintain specific percentages of silver content within the coinage alloys was an integral part of the minting practice. For discussion on the alloy specification in medieval coinage, including periodic debasement in the silver content percentages, see D. M. Metcalf and J. P. Northover, 1986, 'Interpreting the alloy of the later Anglo-Saxon coinage', *BNJ* 56, 35–63; idem, 2002, 'Sporadic debasement in the English coinage, c.1009–1052', *NC* 162, 217–36. Metcalf and Northover (1986) analyse the metal content in sample coins from several mints utilising electron-probe micro-analysis to identify 11 elements in the alloy of Anglo-Saxon pennies. This analysis led to speculation that the silver utilised in the post-reform coinage likely came from mines in Germany. A primary conclusion of the study is that moneyers maintained quality and consistency in the coinage they produced, even at mints widely separated geographically. Further, there were common practices of adding brass without tin to the alloy, which required specialised skill since bronze scrap was a common raw material in coin production.

[58] Prosopography of Anglo-Saxon England,<http:/www.pase.ac.uk>.

[59] PASE Search; person: God, Leof, Wulf.

Beyond this comparison with PASE, a similar situation occurs with regards to the records of the *MED* as compared with the Domesday survey of 1086, which marks the end of the study period. For example, the Domesday records on Colchester contain 276 names from 91 different name elements.[60] 87 per cent of these names are derived from Old English. In comparison, there are 57 recorded moneyers from the same time period in Colchester within the *MED*. All but nine of these are from eight name element groups and all but Toca are derived from Old English (98.3 per cent). The differentiation in names for the general population of the town, as recorded in 1086, is significantly more diverse (three names per name element) than those of the moneyers (seven names per name element).[61] The most common elements like [Leof-] and [Wulf-] are present in the general population of Colchester as well but not to the same level of repetition or iteration.[62] While name derivation cannot be utilised absolutely as a means of determining lineage, the overriding pattern seems to indicate that the majority of the moneyers were more English than Continental.[63]

This is born out in reviewing the work of Smart on the moneyers of Chester under the Danish monarchs.[64] Smart's work, first in her 1981 PhD thesis, and subsequently in a 1987 article on the same topic, notes that Chester has a significant percentage of moneyers with names derivative of Old Irish.[65] Smart identified three moneyers during this period as having names of Old Irish origin and originally hypothesized that this was due to the town's placement along the Scandinavian-Irish trade route and its relative isolation from other Anglo-Saxon mints, being north of the Alfred Guthrum treaty line.[66] She also notes that a possible cause for this differentiation in names was due to Norse settlement in the Wirral, drawing on Wainwright's mapping of *TRE* manors from Domesday.[67] Regardless, the implication is the same, that a higher percentage of the moneyers in Chester were likely of Irish origin than elsewhere. Admittedly, and as Smart states, this number is still small - only three moneyers out of 32 have names derivative of Old Irish.[68] Smart, however, adds the Old Irish and Scandinavian/Old Norse names together in her calculations and reasons that nearly 40 per cent of the moneyers in Chester had names not derivative of Old English (11 of 28) according to her 1981 calculations.[69] The updated information in her 1987 article only has 10 moneyers with Old Irish or Scandinavian names and 19 moneyers with Old English names, making the percentage closer to 34 per cent (10 of 29).[70] The calculations in the database are close to those produced by Smart. Based on current coin finds, there are 11 Old Irish/Scandinavian named moneyers recorded for Chester out of 32 for the same period 1016–1042 or 34 per cent. This is significantly higher than the number of non-Old English names found elsewhere, as exampled by Colchester above, but considering the isolation of the mint and the fact that Domesday identifies nearly half of all landholders in Chester as having names not derivative of Old English, it still seems to indicate that the moneyer's themselves were more likely to be of Old English lineage than not, even above Watling Street.[71] This is evident in York as well, the

[60] P. Crummy, 1981, 'Aspects of Anglo-Saxon and Norman Colchester', in *Colchester Archaeological Reports*, London, 1–91 at 75–7. Colchester is utilised as an example because it falls outside of the largest mints but is also of significant size to provide an example without any major gaps in the coinage record from 973 to 1086. Also, as the aim is to look at a comparison for a mint outside of London before approaching the largest mint directly, a mint of similar potential structural make-up should be considered. As Colchester maintained a subordinate mint at Maldon, like London and Southwark, this seemed to be a logical selection. See Andrew, 1901b, 279.

[61] Crummy, 1981, 75–7, Appendix 1, 'Origins of personal names of burgesses in Colchester Domesday and of moneyers operating in Colchester during the period 979–1087'. Crummy provides a full list of all 276 names in Colchester Domesday, along with the origin and reference for the derivation. The listing of moneyers contains only 33 records, with all but Toca being derivative of Old English. The additional records in the *MED* support this conclusion, with Toca as the only name that is not one of the known Old English names. The breakdown of the general population of the Colchester Domesday from Crummy's report is 241 persons with Old English names (87.5 per cent), 13 persons with Scandinavian names (4.5 per cent), 12 persons with Old German names (4.5 per cent), and 10 names noted as 'other' (3.5 per cent). The moneyers have less diversity in that the Colchester Domesday numbers are 32 Old English named moneyers versus one Scandinavian named moneyer (97 per cent had names derived from Old English). For Colchester within the *MED*, this number is 56 moneyers with Old English names and one with a Scandinavian name (Toca), or 98.2 per cent. There are three unique names associated with each prototheme in the general population but seven associated with each prototheme within the moneyer population, meaning that there was more diversification within the naming patterns of the general population versus the moneyer population.

[62] Crummy, 1981, 75–7, Appendix 1. There are 41 attestations of [Wulf-] names and 14 attestations of [Leof-] names in the Colchester records from Domesday. These equate to 14.9 per cent and 5.1 per cent respectively of the total number of names in the record (51 of 276 and 14 of 276). For the *MED* records of the moneyers in Colchester there are 13 [Wulf-] names and six [Leof-] names, making their representative levels 22.8 per cent and 10.5 per cent respectively (13 of 57 and 6 of 57). The level of repetition of these common name elements are 34.6 per cent greater amongst the moneyers than the general population for minters with the [Wulf-] prototheme and 51.4 per cent greater for moneyers with the [Leof-] prototheme.

[63] For discussion on naming practices in late Anglo-Saxon England and how the derivation of the name may indicate lineage in a broad sense see E. Björkman, 1910, *Nordische Personennamen In England In Alt- Und Frühmittel-Englischer Zeit*, Halle; O. von Feilitzen, 1937, *The Pre-Conquest Personal Names of Domesday Book*, Uppsala, 31–2; idem, 1976, 'The Personal Names and Bynames of the Winton Domesday', in M. Biddle, ed., *Winchester in the Early Middle Ages*, Oxford, 143–229.

[64] V. Smart, 1981, 'Moneyers of the Late Anglo-Saxon Coinage, 1016–1042', Unpublished PhD thesis, Nottingham; eadem, 1987a, 'Moneyers of the late Anglo-Saxon coinage: the Danish Dynasty', *ASE* 16, 233–308.

[65] Smart, 1981, 198; eadem, 1987a, 248.

[66] Smart, 1981, 198.

[67] Smart, 1987a, 248; F. T. Wainwright, 1942, 'North-west Mercia A.D. 871–924', *Transactions of the Historical Society of Lancashire and Cheshire* 94, 3–53 at 35.

[68] Smart, 1987a, 243 and 248–9.

[69] Smart, 1981, 193–4 and 196.

[70] Smart, 1987a, 241–3. Smart also identifies the moneyer Gillacrist of Chester as 'the only instance of this name in the Anglo-Saxon period' (243). The current study includes a Gillacrist active at Taunton immediately after the end of the moneyer's activity in Chester from 1042–1044. As this is the only other instance of this very rare name, it would appear that this moneyer moved 180 miles south.

[71] Wainwright, 1942, 35. Wainwright identified 96 *TRE* landholders in the Domesday survey for Cheshire and found that 41 of them had Scandinavian names, or 43 per cent. This means that while almost half of the *TRE* landholders in Domesday likely had some Scandinavian lineage, only a third of the moneyers held this same distinction. This is a significantly closer percentage than the 87.5 per cent of Domesday people in Colchester verses the 98.2 per cent of moneyers that had Old English names, but is still a significant difference that supports the idea of the moneyers being predominantly from certain groups.

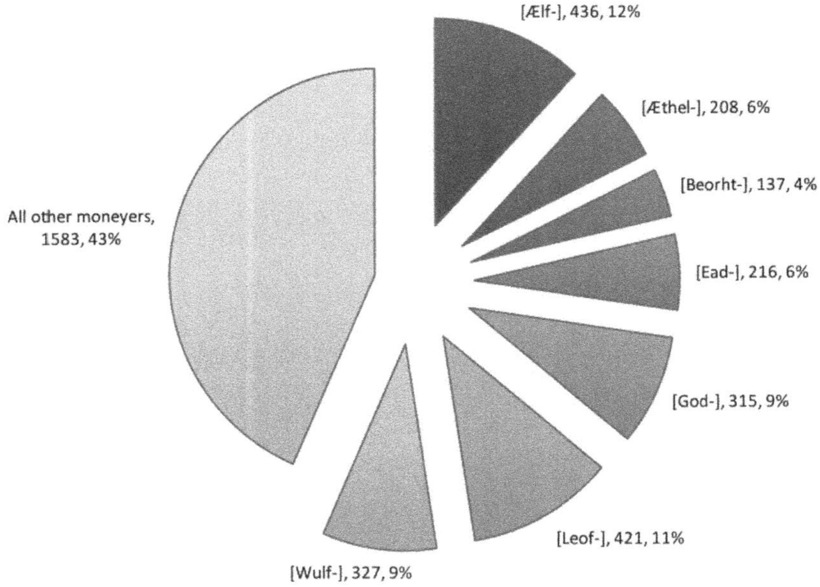

Figure 3.1. Instances and percentages of moneyers with the top seven protothemes as compared with all other moneyers' in the *MED*.

only other northern mint with significant activity during the study period.

If there are certain names that are connected more to the moneyer group than others and these names illustrate the pattern of successive generations of moneyers from the same name element over extended periods of time in multiple locations, could that lead to a more expansive view of the activities of moneyers from those most common protothemes? From the 3,646 records in the *MED*, there are 323 distinct name elements. The majority of these (2,060 of 3,646 or 56.5 per cent) belong to the top seven name element groups [Figure 3.1]. For the purposes of this study, these 'name element groups' or groups of moneyers with the same prototheme are called name sequences. By reviewing the frequency of the name sequences and outlining how those sequences might have operated within the mint, a picture of overriding administrative structure within the money-making enterprise becomes clear, perhaps pointing to the creation of a construct with internal rules and regulations regarding the assumption of responsibility for the coinage. The name sequence, which draws upon basic Anglo-Saxon naming patterns in order to link successive generations of moneyers with their predecessors, is the primary tool in linking the moneyers to one another over time.[72] While not universal, and problematic with regards to specific individuals, the general naming practices of the late Anglo-Saxons indicate that the likelihood of a sequential naming pattern across multiple time periods could define direct kinship.[73] Thus, the name of a moneyer group from the earliest periods of the database can be linked to the names of later groups.

The numbers of moneyers whose names begin with the seven most common protothemes is: [Ælf-] with 436, [Leof-] with 421, [Wulf-] with 327, [God-] with 315, [Ead-] with 216, [Æthel-] with 208, and [Beorht-] with 137. This means that over half of all the names in the *MED* belong to one of these few groups that comprise only 2 per cent of the total number of protothemes used by the moneyers from 973 to 1086 [Figure 3.2]. If we expand this to include all name sequences that have at least 10 iterations over the study period, which is over three times the number of iterations found in the general population in the example from Colchester described above, then the total number of individuals included in these few name sequences increases to 2,984, or 81.9 per cent of the total [Figure 3.3]. So, four-fifths of the database is dominated by only 13.6 per cent, or 44 of 323, of the name sequences [Figure 3.4].

Conversely, there are only 337 instances of moneyers belonging to name sequences with three or less iterations, which is the number of iterations found within the general population of the Colchester Domesday. This is only 9.2 per cent of the overall number of periods of moneyer activity but consists of 68.7 per cent of the total number of name sequences. The overall average per name sequence within the database is 11.3 names per element, but this average is obviously offset by the incredibly high numbers at the top and the wide range of very low numbers at the bottom. Considering that such a high percentage of the overall total is concentrated in the name sequences with 10 or more iterations, this examination will therefore be concentrating at first on those elements that are outside of the largest seven sequences but higher than 10 instances of activity. The average names per element for the group of sequences with 10 or more iterations but less than the top seven is 25 (924 periods of activity over 37 name elements). Therefore, it is apparent that not only did the moneyers

[72] Nightingale, 1982; Colman, 2014.

[73] For discussion on various genealogical and onomastic methods of calculating or establishing generations within subsets of data see: D. E. Thornton, 2003, *Kings, Chronologies, and Genealogies: Studies in the Political History of Early Medieval Ireland and Wales*, Oxford, 57–8; D. Herlihy, 1985, *Medieval Households*, Cambridge, 46.

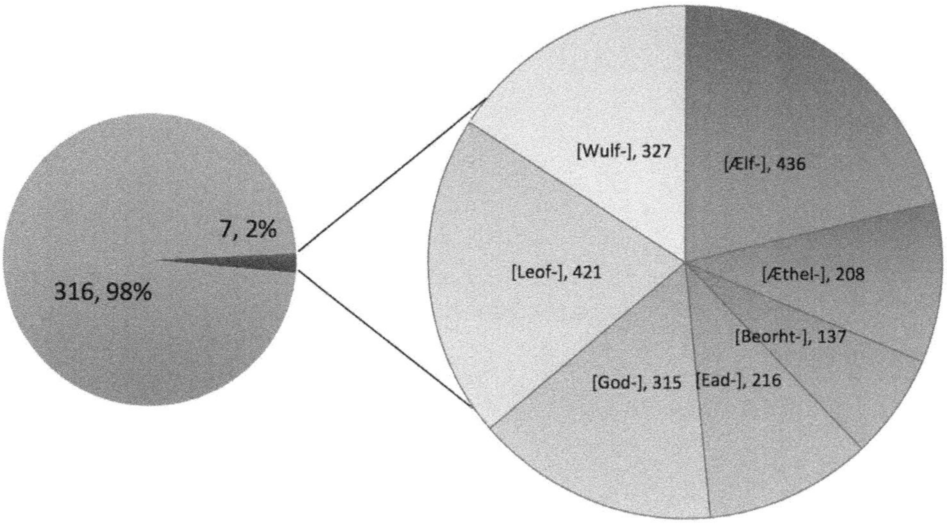

Figure 3.2. The seven most frequently occurring name elements as a percentage of all protothemes and the number of moneyers with those top name elements.

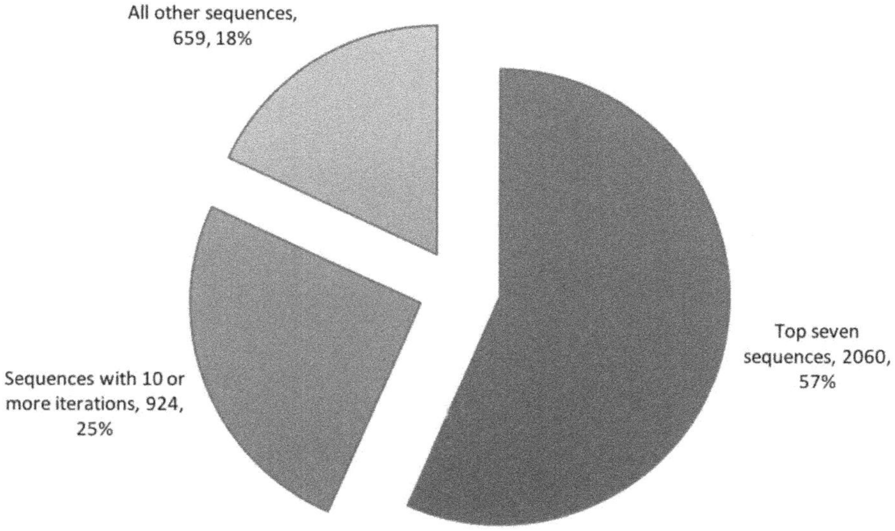

Figure 3.3. Number and percentage of moneyers from the top seven name sequences, the next largest sequences with ten or more iterations, and all other sequences.

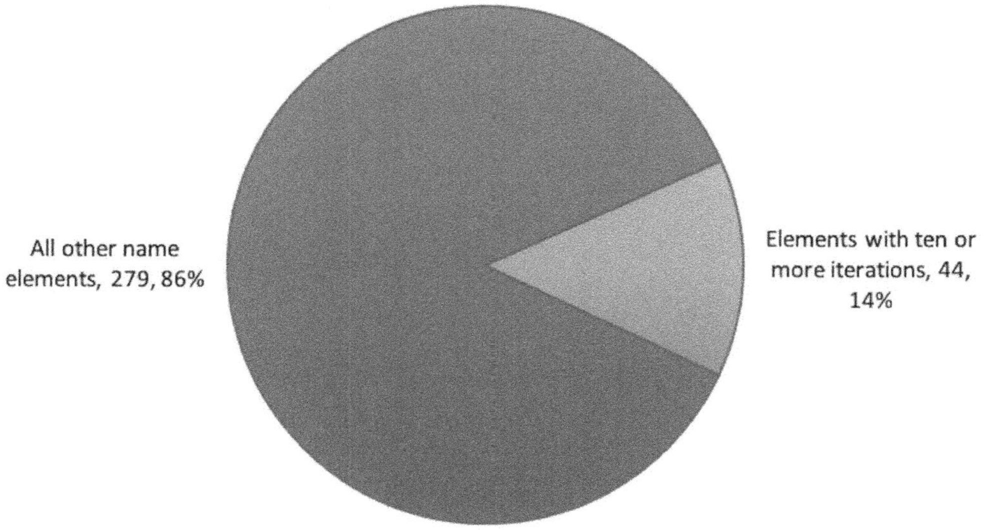

Figure 3.4. Total number and percentage of protothemes with ten or more iterations and all other name elements.

maintain a high percentage of insular naming, and thus potentially a high percentage of geographic nativity but the inclusion of so few name elements in that insularity points towards a very high percentage of genealogical continuity as well. This results in a group of craftsmen that were highly skilled, relatively few in number, and in most instances directly related controlling a substantial and important aspect of the royal finances.

In order to ascertain if the model outlined above exists outside of the most prevalent name groups, a review of some of the less common name sequences within London is below. This will help determine if there are parallels to the arrangement of moneyers within specific name sequences that are not part of the prevailing groups but within much of the overall activity. Beginning with sequences that are uncommon in London with more than 10 iterations, then expanding the selection to some sequences with fewer representative examples to see if a similar pattern is evident. If a pattern of name element repetition outside of the dominant groups exists, then the study will expand to those larger groups and outline in detail the placement processes of those moneyers. In showing that a regular organisation of the moneyers from smaller to larger groups within the mints existed in London, it may then be possible to extend beyond London to incorporate similar reviews of mints in other geographic locations. The tabular representations found below and in the next chapter detail the specific name sequences within a specified mint. The sequences themselves are arranged alphabetically by moneyer name and then chronologically. This allows quick reference to a specific name within the group and illustrates how they flow in succession over time. The name sequence designation is separated by mint generational boundaries, meaning that successive series of moneyers with similar names are arranged together in the order of activity within a given mint. Breaks between a moneyer of group of moneyers of a name sequence and another succeeding moneyer or group from the same group are defined as 'generations' within the mint. For example, if three moneyers from the [Wulf-] name sequence were in operation within a mint consecutively from the period 973 to 975 and then two different [Wulf-] moneyers were in operation for the period 975 to 978 this would constitute two different generations of moneyers. This could be stated as 'five moneyers from the [Wulf-] name sequence were active for two generations in mint X'. For concurrent moneyers of the same sequence, further delineation is characterized by a secondary alpha-marker (e.g. 2a, 2b, 3a, 3b, etc.).

Case Study 1: The [Brun-] Name Sequence

As noted earlier within the discussion on the work of Tsurushima, the name Brunman specifically is predominantly associated with the office of moneyer across nearly all records for the late Anglo-Saxon period.[74]

[74] Tsurushima, 2012, 42–4.

Table 3.1. Moneyers of the [Brun-] sequence in London

Moneyer Name	Sequence Position	Activity Range
Brunsige	Brun - 1	979–985
Brunstan	Brun - 2	997–1009
Brunman	Brun - 3	1009–1038
Brun	Brun - 4	1017–1023
Brungar	Brun - 5a	1023–1046
Brunic	Brun - 5b	1023–1029
Brunmar	Brun - 6	1029–1036
Brun	Brun - 7	1036–1038
Brun	Brun - 8a	1040–1042
Brunman	Brun - 8b	1040–1042
Brunman	Brun - 9	1046–1048
Brungar	Brun - 10	1053–1056
Brunic	Brun - 11	1083–1086

Similarly, the name element [Brun-] is not common at most locations and is all but absent from the records of London excepting the extant coinage material. There are 13 iterations of [Brun-] moneyers within the records of London from 973 to 1086, covering nearly the entire period of this study [Table 3.1]. It is possible that the name Brun could be an abbreviation for one of the other [Brun-] names, but as it appears in three separate instances and overlaps with a Brunman for both the first and last instances, and immediately precedes a Brungar in the first instance and immediately succeeds a Brunmar in the second instance, it is not clear for which moneyer this would be an abbreviation. What can also be observed in this sequence of moneyers is a repetition of names beginning with the first Brunman in 1009 and carrying forward with both Brunic and Brungar, both of which first appear concurrently in 1023.[75] This could illustrate sons preparing to take over for their father. The reiterations of the names in later issues could be a continuation of this process to grandsons or other relations.

Case Study 2: The [Os-] Name Sequence

Similar to the [Brun-] sequence above, the [Os-] name element is not widely found in London during the study period outside of the coinage record, even though it is common in some other regions.[76] There are 11 instances of [Os-] named moneyers operating in London from 979 to 1066 [Table 3.2]. Unlike [Brun-] there are no instances of possible abbreviation so the differentiation between the different moneyers over successive periods of minting is clearer. There are a few names that repeat but the sequence is dominated primarily by the name Osmund, which was

[75] SM1.London.cxxxiv–cxli.

[76] Excluding the coinage record from PASE, there are only four individuals during the study period with the [Os-] prototheme in London.

Table 3.2. Moneyers of the [Os-] sequence in London

Moneyer Name	Sequence Position	Activity Range
Oscetel	Os - 1a	979–1003
Osulf	Os - 1b	979–1023
Osfrith	Os - 2	985–0991
Osmund	Os - 3	991–0997
Osmund	Os - 4a	1009–1023
Oswald	Os - 4b	1009–1016
Oswig	Os - 4c	1009–1016
Osfrith	Os - 5a	1029–1036
Osulf	Os - 5b	1029–1036
Osmund	Os - 6	1053–1062
Osmund	Os - 7	1066–1066

active over four distinct periods, the first two and last two being widely separated temporally.[77] This likely indicates a familial continuation, potentially from grandfather to grandson, or even great-grandson.

Case Study 3: The [Deor-] Name Sequence

As discussed above, Nightingale identified the [Deor-] name sequence as an established moneyer dynasty from at least Domesday with very probable links to the Deormans that operated in London before 1066.[78] Deorman is the most common name in the sequence but there are also two iterations of Deorsige, which may indicate a shift in the name sequence from the latter to the former [Table 3.3].[79] This could signify a hereditary passing of the office from father/uncle/grandfather to son/nephew/grandson during the reign of Æthelred II. The establishment of the Deorman name could then represent the creation of the 'Deorman Brand' which would carry forward to at least Edward the Confessor and potentially beyond with multiple people operating under the name regardless of direct familial descent. Although the possibility of this being a father-son transition at some point between the first appearance in 1009 and the last in 1059 is certainly valid, it seems unlikely that this would be the same individual for the entire five-decade span because of the large break in activity between 1016 and 1036, during which a Deorsige is again active. Alternative explanations for this sort of break in activity is explored further in chapter six.

Case Study 4: The [Eald-] Name Sequence

The [Eald-] sequence consists of eight periods of activity from 1003 to 1072. Primary in this sequence are the names Ealdgar, which appears at four different intervals, and

Table 3.3. Moneyers of the [Deor-] sequence in London

Moneyer Name	Sequence Position	Activity Range
Deorsige	Deor - 1	991–997
Deorwulf	Deor - 2	997–1003
Deorman	Deor - 3	1009–1016
Deorsige	Deor - 4	1017–1023
Deorman	Deor - 5	1036–1038
Deorman	Deor - 6	1044–1046
Deorman	Deor - 7	1048–1050
Deorman	Deor - 8	1056–1059

Table 3.4. Moneyers of the [Eald-] sequence in London

Moneyer Name	Sequence Position	Activity Range
Ealdgar	Eald - 1	1003–1009
Ealdred	Eald - 2	1009–1023
Ealdgar	Eald - 3	1042–1046
Ealdwine	Eald - 4	1044–1046
Ealdgar	Eald - 5	1048–1059
Ealdred	Eald - 6	1050–1053
Ealdulf	Eald - 7	1053–1056
Ealdgar	Eald - 8	1062–1072

Ealdred, which appears twice [Table 3.4].[80] It seems likely that the Ealdgar name has been passed from father to son or potentially grandson with an intermittent Ealdred, who could have been a second son or a cousin helping in a period of greater need, from 1009 to 1023 and then a break in the sequence from 1023 to 1042. The large geld collection recorded in the *Anglo-Saxon Chronicle* for 1018 may account for this additional moneyer.[81]

Case Study 5: The [Gold-] Name Sequence

Consisting of only five periods of activity from two distinct names, the [Gold-] sequence provides an example of an uncommon name element maintaining representation in the coinage record for an extended period of time [Table 3.5]. The moneyers named Goldwine and Goldsige appear to alternate activity within the mint. It seems plausible that the first Goldwine may have operated over two different periods from 991 to 997 and then from 1009 to 1016 before passing the mint onto his descendant Goldsige.[82] Of course, both of these Goldwines could have been different individuals operating in close proximity temporally, with

[77] SM1.London.cccxxiv; SM1.London.cccxxvii; SM1.London.cccxxx–cccxxxi.
[78] Nightingale, 1982, 36–8.
[79] SM1.London.clvii; SM1.London.clx.
[80] SM1.London.ccxix–ccxxi; SM1.London.ccxxiii–ccxxiv; SM1.London.ccxxvi.
[81] *ASC* 1018C, 1018D, 1018E. Cnut took a geld collection of £72,000 for the entire county and £10,500 for London is recorded for 1018.
[82] SM1.London.cclxxvi–cclxxviii.

Table 3.5. Moneyers of the [Gold-] sequence in London

Moneyer Name	Sequence Position	Activity Range
Goldwine	Gold - 1	991–997
Goldwine	Gold - 2	1009–1016
Goldsige	Gold - 3	1036–1044
Goldsige	Gold - 4	1046–1056
Goldwine	Gold - 5	1059–1062

Table 3.6. Moneyers of the [Theod-] sequence in London

Moneyer Name	Sequence Position	Activity Range
Theodred	Theod - 1	985–991
Theodred	Theod - 2	1003–1009
Theodred	Theod - 3	1023–1029
Theodred	Theod - 4	1042–1046

one being a father or grandfather to the other. Similarly, Goldsige has two periods of activity from 1036 to 1044 and then 1046 to 1056.[83] After this, another Goldwine, possibly the grandson of the first, appears in the coinage record as active in the period 1059 to 1062.[84]

Case Study 6: The [Theod-] Name Sequence

The last case study of the smaller uncommon name sequences of London consists of the other name element that was part of Nightingale's study of the Deormans: [Theod-]. With the lack of attestations overall in the *MED*, the [Theod-] sequence provides a clear example of a specific name operating within the mints over an extended period of time, either through the transition of hereditary rights or via the creation of a brand-name. All the [Theod-] named moneyers in London operated under the name Theodred [Table 3.6].[85]

The Primary Name Sequences of London

With 425 periods of moneyer activity between 973 and 1086 derived from extant numismatic records within the mints at London, all but 31 belong within a name sequence that consists of two or more generations of minting practice. These 31, as discussed earlier, may have been distant relations that were added to the mint at times of need.[86] Therefore, there were 394 moneyers within the records operating in London during the study period that were a part of a name sequence, which could indicate kinship.

Specifically, there were 41 distinct name sequences within the London mints, by far the most of any mint in Anglo-Saxon England during this period. This equates to 85.4 per cent of the moneyers being part of a name sequence that consisted of three or more individuals from the same name group. Further delimitation to the most common name sequences, or those with substantially more generations of moneyers than the average, reveals that the top seven sequences, make up 60.2 per cent of the total number of moneyers, or 256 individual periods of activity, operating at the mints over the entire spectrum of this study.[87] Therefore, nearly two-thirds of the moneyers working in the mints within London from 973 to 1086 were a part of one of the seven largest name sequences, or 17.1 per cent of the total number of sequences overall (seven of 41). An analysis of the seven largest name sequences also reveals certain patterns in the number of moneyers present in certain periods and how those patterns can illustrate that the native population maintained systemic control over the process of coinage even when the monarchy was fluid or subverted via war or invasion.

First, in reviewing the seven primary name sequences, the continuity of these particular names at the London mint can be observed to have proceeded fairly unhindered for the entirety of the period 973 to 1086. In studying the occurrence of those most common name sequences over the whole timespan [Figure 3.5] it would appear on the surface that nearly all the main sequences operated in an almost perfect linear flow from Edgar's monetary reform in *c.*973 to the Domesday survey in 1086. The most prolific of the name sequences ([Ælf-], [Æthel-], [Beorht-], [Ead-], [God-], [Leof-], and [Wulf-]) have moneyer representation on nearly every one of the 36 coinage issues minted during this period. Even the relatively smaller name sequences, such as [Brun-], have moneyers active within most of the coinages. This implies that the mint operations under these specific groups in London were effectively continuous without pause for the entirety of the late Anglo-Saxon period. This is not surprising considering the prominence of London in the overall structure of the Anglo-Saxon state.[88]

Name Sequence Variation in the London and Southwark Mints

Having outlined how the pattern of name repetition is evident within the more uncommon name sequences, an expansion of this idea to the larger more prominent protothemes seems possible. If the activity of familial continuation was widespread amongst the smaller minting families, thus providing them with a certain level of security and protection in regard to their monopoly

[83] SM1.London.cclxxviii–cclxxix.
[84] SM1.London.cclxxx.
[85] SM1.London.ccclix–ccclxii.
[86] Lopez, 1953, 2–3.

[87] The average number of moneyer records per sequence for London is 10.4 (41 name sequences / 395 moneyer records within a name sequence). Consideration for the largest sequences were those that contained moneyer records at least double this average.
[88] Naismith, 2013, 44–74; Campbell, 2000, 203–4.

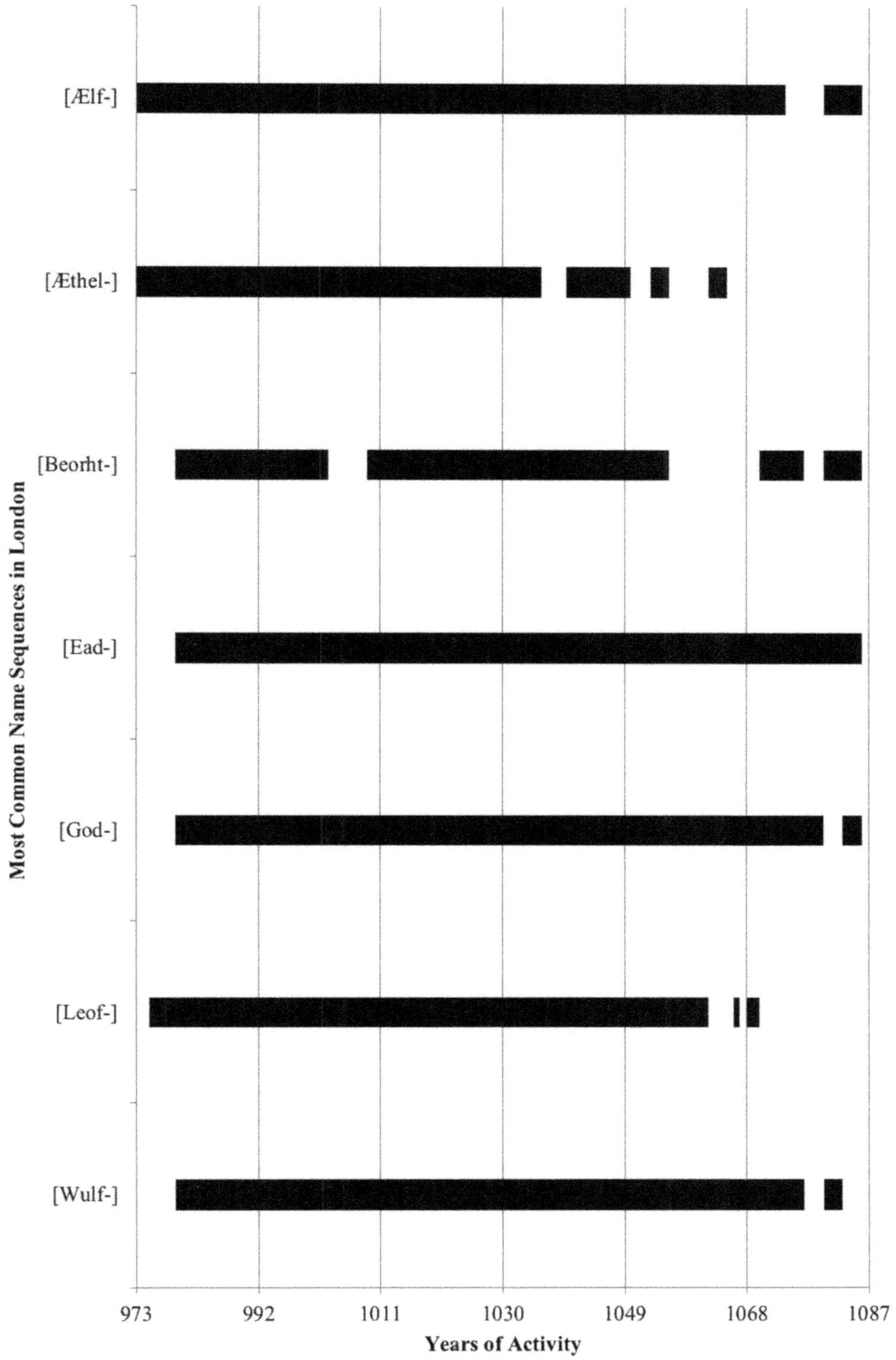

Figure 3.5. Occurrences of the most common Name Sequences over time in London.

on the practice, it stands to reason that larger families would utilise the same principles. To outline how this pattern recognition may illustrate such consistencies over the entire period of minting between 973 and 1086, the largest sequences in London are detailed below. This is followed by a short discussion on the mint at Southwark, since it was closely linked to the London mints. When this exercise is repeated across all such name sequences at all 99 minting locations that operated at some point between Edgar's reform and the Domesday survey, the regular repetition, especially when compared to the whole corpus of Anglo-Saxon names in general, compels the idea that an underlying paradigm in the associated naming process was in place. If the moneyers operating at a given mint did so under the name of a master-moneyer who was ultimately responsible for the coinage before passing this onto his heir and descendent then this would explain this widespread repetition. Likewise, if these moneyers were all, or predominantly, related through extended families then the repetition would also manifest itself. In either scenario, the repetition would be in place, as is evident in the coinage record.

Table 3.7. Moneyers of the [Ælf-] sequence in London

Moneyer Name	Sequence Position	Activity Range
Ælfnoth	Ælf - 1	973–975
Ælfweard	Ælf - 2	975–978
Ælfgar	Ælf - 3a	979–997
Ælfstan	Ælf - 3b	979–985
Ælfweald	Ælf - 3c	979–985
Ælfwine	Ælf - 3d	979–985
Ælfgæt	Ælf - 4a	985–997
Ælfnoth	Ælf - 4b	985–997
Ælfweard	Ælf - 4c	985–1003
Ælfric	Ælf - 5a	991–1003
Ælfstan	Ælf - 5b	991–997
Ælfwig	Ælf - 5c	991–997
Ælfwine	Ælf - 5d	991–1038
Ælfred	Ælf - 6	997–1003
Ælfwig	Ælf - 7	1003–1036
Ælfgæt	Ælf - 8a	1009–1016
Ælfnoth	Ælf - 8b	1009–1016
Ælfric	Ælf - 8c	1009–1016
Ælfsige	Ælf - 8d	1009–1016
Ælfweard	Ælf - 8e	1009–1016
Ælf	Ælf - 9a	1017–1023
Ælfstan	Ælf - 9b	1017–1036
Ælfgæt	Ælf - 10a	1023–1029
Ælfgar	Ælf - 10b	1023–1029
Ælfred	Ælf - 10c	1023–1038
Ælfric	Ælf - 10d	1023–1042
Ælfweard	Ælf - 10e	1023–1036
Ælfwig Swencel	Ælf - 11	1029–1036
Ælfnoth	Ælf - 12a	1036–1038
Ælfweald	Ælf - 12b	1036–1038
Ælfred	Ælf - 13a	1040–1042
Ælfweard	Ælf - 13b	1040–1046
Ælfwine	Ælf - 13c	1040–1056
Ælfwig	Ælf - 14	1042–1050
Ælfgar	Ælf - 15a	1044–1048
Ælfred	Ælf - 15b	1044–1062
Ælfsige	Ælf - 16	1046–1048
Ælf	Ælf - 17a	1048–1050
Ælfgæt	Ælf - 17b	1048–1050
Ælfstan	Ælf - 17c	1048–1050
Ælfweald	Ælf - 17d	1048–1050
Ælfgar	Ælf - 18a	1050–1053
Ælfsige	Ælf - 18b	1050–1053
Ælfweard	Ælf - 19a	1053–1066
Ælfwig	Ælf - 19b	1053–1056
Ælfsige	Ælf - 20	1056–1066
Ælfwine	Ælf - 21	1059–1062
Ælfsige	Ælf - 22a	1066–1072
Ælfwine	Ælf - 22b	1066–1070
Ælfwine	Ælf - 23	1072–1074
Ælfwine	Ælf - 24	1080–1083
Ælfred	Ælf - 25	1083–1086

Considering the records in existence for the London mint, the organisation of named sequences can be problematic. With 425 named individuals included for the period 973 to 1086, London has the highest volume of successively named generations of moneyers. To illustrate how these sequences operated over the minting period, the top seven sequences ([Ælf-], [Æthel-], [Beorht-], [Ead-], [God-], [Leof-], and [Wulf-]) are detailed below, along with a coalesced analysis of them and how they relate to the entirety of the mint's records as a whole.

The [Ælf-] Name Sequence in London

With 52 specific moneyer records, the [Ælf-] name sequence was the most prominent in London [Table 3.7]. A review of the sequence over the full term of 973 to 1086 outlines the nearly continuous presence of at least one moneyer with the forename element [Ælf-]. These records represent 25 generations of moneyer activity in the London mint. The name element is present in all but two coinage issues for the entire period, those being the Two Stars (1074–1077) and Sword (1077–1080) types of William I. Considering the consistency of the name element throughout the rest of the 113-year period, it is likely that this absence is related more to the lack of surviving source material than the lack of a moneyer of the name sequence working within London during this period. Also apparent is the large number of moneyers from the sequence in operation during some periods that have distinct demarcation into separate groups that end activity while another group begins.

The first moneyer of the [Ælf-] sequence was Ælfnoth, who was active for Edgar's Reform Coinage (973–975).[89] He was immediately followed by Ælfweard from 975 to 978.[90] Four moneyers began operation within the mint during the First Hand type (979–985) of Æthelred II: Ælfgar, Ælfstan, Ælfweald, and Ælfwine.[91] Only one

[89] SM1.London.xvii.
[90] SM1.London.xviii.
[91] SM1.London.xix–xxii.

of these, Ælfgar, produced coins of the Second Hand type (985–991) and Crux type (991–997) immediately afterwards. Three new moneyers from the [Ælf-] sequence began in 985: Ælfgæt, a repeat of Ælfnoth, and another Ælfweard.[92] Ælfgæt and Ælfnoth stopped activity in 997, with Ælfweard continuing to 1003.

Concurrent with the activity of these four moneyers, four more minters began operation during the Crux type: Ælfstan (991–997), Ælfwig (991–997), Ælfric (991–1003), and Ælfwine (991–1038).[93] In 997, the Long Cross type (997–1003) saw the addition of one new moneyer, Ælfred.[94] Ælfwig reappears after this and is recorded in every issue from 1003 to 1036.[95] In 1009, for the Last Small Cross type (1009–1016), the last coinage of Æthelred II, five new moneyers are included: Ælfgæt, Ælfnoth, Ælfric, Ælfsige, and Ælfweard.[96] Three of these, Ælfgæt, Ælfnoth, and Ælfweard, are repeating names from earlier in the mint record.

There are only two additions to the moneyer list for Cnut's first coinage, the Quatrefoil type (1017–1023), Ælf and Ælfstan.[97] Ælf could be an abbreviation for any of the moneyers that were already operating within the mint at this time but since it is hammered into the epigraphy separately it has been treated as distinct herein. Ælfstan continued until 1036. Other moneyers were appointed during the reign of Cnut, including five for the Pointed Helmet type (1023–1029): Ælfgæt (1023–1029), Ælfgar (1023–1029), Ælfweard (1023–1036), Ælfred (1023–1038), and Ælfric (1023–1042).[98] A uniquely named moneyer, Ælfwig Swencel, is documented on coins for 1029 to 1036.[99] Ælfnoth and Ælfweald both repeat in the record for 1036 to 1038.[100] In 1040 another Ælfred (1040–1042) and Ælfweard (1040–1046) return to activity in the mint.[101] Ælfwine first appears in the coinage record for London in 1040 as well and is initially active until 1056.[102] An Ælfwig is again active from 1042 to 1050.[103]

Ælfgar reappears for 1044–1048, along with Ælfred, who was active from 1044 to 1062.[104] An Ælfsige was then active from 1046 to 1048, followed by four moneyers beginning activity in 1048 before ending in 1050: Ælf, Ælfgæt, Ælfstan, and Ælfweald.[105] These four were followed by a repeat Ælfgar and Ælfsige from 1050 to 1053.[106] In 1053, two more repeated names appear in the coinage record: Ælfwig (1053–1056) and Ælfweard (1053–1066).[107] Ælfsige repeats again in 1056 and operates to the end of Edward's reign (1066) and into the first part of William I's rule until 1072.[108] No coins of Harold II's Pax type (1066) for Ælfsige are recorded. The post-1066 coinage of the [Ælf-] sequence is predominantly under one moneyer name, Ælfwine, who was active from 1066 to 1070, 1072 to 1074, and 1080 to 1083.[109] For the Paxs type (1083–1086) there is also an Ælfred recorded.[110]

These 52 instances of moneyer activity for the period 973 to 1086 outline the repetitious nature of the most prominent name sequences and support the idea of there being familial continuity within the moneyer group over important watershed events, like both the Danish and Norman Conquests.

The [Æthel-] Name Sequence in London

The [Æthel-] name sequence was active consistently in London until the end of Edward the Confessor's reign, when it disappeared from the coinage record. There were 31 periods of activity for the [Æthel-] sequence over 13 generations [Table 3.8].

The first [Æthel-] sequence moneyers in London were Æthelsige (973–975), Æthelstan (973–978), Æthelweald (973–979), and Æthelred (973–997).[111] In 979 two additional moneyers are recorded, Æthelweard and Æthelstan, both of whom were active from 979 to 985.[112] An Æthelulf was active for Æthelred II's Second Hand type (985–991).[113]

Beginning in 991, there is a sequence of three pairs of moneyers beginning operation together with one stopping after one coinage issue and the other continuing for an extended period of activity. The first of these are Æthelwine and Æthelweard, the first being active from 991 to 997 and the second continuing until 1029.[114] Following these two are Æthelfrith and Æthelric. Æthelfrith was active from 997 to 1003 and Æthelric was active from 997 to 1029.[115] The final pair included Æthelmær (1003–1009) and a repeat of Æthelwine (1003–1036).[116]

Operating concurrently with this Æthelwine, four moneyers began operation in 1009: Æthelnoth, Æthelred, and Æthelwig, who were all active from 1009 to 1016, and Æthelman, who was active from 1009 to 1023.[117] This was the first grouping of four moneyers beginning

[92] SM1.London.xxiii–xxv.
[93] SM1.London.xxvi–xxix.
[94] SM1.London.xxx.
[95] SM1.London.xxxi.
[96] SM1.London.xxxii–xxxvi.
[97] SM1.London.xxxvii–xxxviii.
[98] SM1.London.xxxix–xliii.
[99] SM1.London.xliv.
[100] SM1.London.xlv–xlvi.
[101] SM1.London.xlvii–xlviii.
[102] SM1.London.xlix.
[103] SM1.London.l.
[104] SM1.London.li–lii.
[105] SM1.London.liii–lvii.
[106] SM1.London.lviii–lix.
[107] SM1.London.lx–lxi.
[108] SM1.London.lxii; SM1.London.lxv.
[109] SM1.London.lxiii–lxiv; SM1.London.lxvi–lxvii.
[110] SM1.London.lxviii.
[111] SM1.London.lxx–lxxiii.
[112] SM1.London.lxxiv–lxxv.
[113] SM1.London.lxxvi.
[114] SM1.London.lxxvii–lxxviii.
[115] SM1.London.lxxix–lxxx.
[116] SM1.London.lxxxi–lxxxii.
[117] SM1.London.lxxxiii–lxxxvi.

Table 3.8. Moneyers of the [Æthel-] sequence in London

Moneyer Name	Sequence Position	Activity Range
Æthelred	Æthel - 1a	973–997
Æthelsige	Æthel - 1b	973–975
Æthelstan	Æthel - 1c	973–978
Æthelweald	Æthel - 1d	973–979
Æthelweard	Æthel - 2a	979–985
Æthelstan	Æthel - 2b	979–985
Æthelulf	Æthel - 3	985–991
Æthelweard	Æthel - 4a	991–1029
Æthelwine	Æthel - 4b	991–997
Æthelfrith	Æthel - 5a	997–1003
Æthelric	Æthel - 5b	997–1029
Æthelmær	Æthel - 6a	1003–1009
Æthelwine	Æthel - 6b	1003–1036
Æthelman	Æthel - 7a	1009–1023
Æthelnoth	Æthel - 7b	1009–1016
Æthelred	Æthel - 7c	1009–1016
Æthelwig	Æthel - 7d	1009–1016
Æthelbeorht	Æthel - 8a	1023–1029
Æthelgæt	Æthel - 8b	1023–1029
Æthelnoth	Æthel - 8c	1023–1029
Æthelwig	Æthel - 8d	1023–1036
Æthelweard	Æthel - 9a	1040–1044
Æthelwine	Æthel - 9b	1040–1042
Æthelgar	Æthel - 10a	1044–1046
Æthelman	Æthel - 10b	1044–1046
Æthelric	Æthel - 10c	1044–1046
Æthelwig	Æthel - 10d	1044–1050
Æthelric	Æthel - 11	1048–1050
Æthelric	Æthel - 12	1053–1056
Æthelwig	Æthel - 13a	1062–1065
Æthelwine	Æthel - 13b	1062–1065

together with three stopping after one issue and the fourth continuing to one additional coinage production.

The second set of four began in 1023, with three operating only for Cnut's Pointed Helmet type (1023–1029) and the fourth remaining active until the end of the following Short Cross type (1029–1036). The first three were: Æthelbeorht, Æthelgæt, and Æthelnoth.[118] The fourth moneyer in this group was another, or possibly the same, Æthelwig.[119]

[118] SM1.London.lxxxvii–lxxxix.
[119] SM1.London.xc.

Following this set of four, two moneyers began activity in 1040: Æthelwine (1040–1042) and Æthelweard (1040–1044).[120]

In 1044 another set of four moneyers began activity together. Three of these moneyers operated until 1046: Æthelgar, Æthelman, and Æthelric.[121] The fourth, Æthelwig, was active for two coinages until 1050.[122] Æthelwig and Æthelman are both repeating names from early groupings in this sequence. This group is followed by a short gap in the coinage record, and then a return of Æthelric for the period 1048–1050.[123] Æthelric is again active from 1053 to 1056.[124]

Two moneyers, both repeating names from earlier in the record, are active from 1062 to 1065: Æthelwig and Æthelwine.[125] The operational years of the moneyers illustrate a pattern of grouping that can be observed throughout London and most of the other major mints of the late Anglo-Saxon and early Anglo-Norman eras. This is discussed in detail in chapter five below.

The [Beorht-] Name Sequence in London

The [Beorht-] name sequence is the smallest of the seven largest sequences in the London mint, with only 21 iterations [Table 3.9]. The sequence itself is potentially negatively impacted, in regard to its status as a major name sequence for the mint overall, by the fact that almost a third of its periods of activity are under one name, Beorhtmær, which could conceivably be only one or two moneyers. If this is the case, then argument against [Beorht-] as a primary sequence for the mint is feasible. Regardless of this, these 21 periods of activity do place it over the threshold for consideration as a primary name sequence, and it is addressed as such herein.

Beorhtsige was the first [Beorht-] sequence moneyer in London for the period 973 to 1086. He was active from 979 to 985.[126] In 985, Beorhtlaf began activity and was operating in London until 1003.[127] From 991 to 997, Beorhtmær was first active.[128] In 1009, four moneyers began operation together: Beorhtfrith (1009–1023), Beorhtweald (1009–1023), Beorhtnoth (1009–1036), and Beorhtmær (1009–1042).[129] Beorhtræd was active from 1023 to 1036.[130] Also stopping in 1036 was Beorhtwine, who first appeared in the coinage record in 1029.[131] Beorhtræd reappeared for the period 1038–1040.[132] Beorthtwine returned from 1040

[120] SM1.London.xci–xcii.
[121] SM1.London.xciii–xcv.
[122] SM1.London.xcvi.
[123] SM1.London.xcvii.
[124] SM1.London.xcviii.
[125] SM1.London.xcix–c.
[126] SM1.London.cv.
[127] SM1.London.cvi.
[128] SM1.London.cvii.
[129] SM1.London.cviii–cxi.
[130] SM1.London.cxii.
[131] SM1.London.cxiii.
[132] SM1.London.cxiv.

Table 3.9. Moneyers of the [Beorht-] sequence in London

Moneyer Name	Sequence Position	Activity Range
Beorhtsige	Beorht - 1	979-985
Beorhtlaf	Beorht - 2	985-1003
Beorhtmær	Beorht - 3	991-997
Beorhtfrith	Beorht - 4a	1009-1023
Beorhtmær	Beorht - 4b	1009-1016
Beorhtnoth	Beorht - 4c	1009-1036
Beorhtweald	Beorht - 4d	1009-1023
Beorhtmær	Beorht - 5	1017-1042
Beorhtræd	Beorht - 6	1023-1036
Beorhtwine	Beorht - 7	1029-1036
Beorhtræd	Beorht - 8	1038-1040
Beorhtwine	Beorht - 9	1040-1044
Beorhtmær	Beorht - 10a	1044-1046
Beorhtræd	Beorht - 10b	1044-1056
Beorhtsige	Beorht - 11a	1050-1053
Beorhtwine	Beorht - 11b	1050-1056
Beorhtmær	Beorht - 12	1053-1056
Beorhtric	Beorht - 13	1070-1072
Beorhtmær	Beorht - 14a	1074-1077
Beorhtric	Beorht - 14b	1074-1077
Beorhtwine	Beorht - 15	1080-1086

to 1044 before being replaced by repeats of Beorhtmær (1044–1046) and Beorhtræd (1044–1056).[133]

A reappearance of the first name associated with this sequence, Beorhtsige, is recorded for the period 1050 to 1053.[134] It seems unlikely that this would be the same individual considering the six-decade gap in activity. Also starting in 1050 was another Beorhtwine, who was active until 1056.[135] A Beorhtmær was also active in this period, from 1053 to 1056.[136] After 1056, there was a large gap in production by this name sequence within London.

After the Norman Conquest, in 1070, the [Beorht-] sequence resurfaces in the London mint with a new name: Beorhtric (1070–1072).[137] Beorhtric was also active from 1074 to 1077 with a repeat Beorhtmær.[138] The last [Beorht-] sequence moneyer in London for the study period was Beorhtwine, who was active from 1080 to 1086.[139] These 21 records for the [Beorht-] sequence illustrate 14 generations of activity within the mint.

The [Ead-] Name Sequence in London

The [Ead-] name sequence of London consisted of moneyers active in 47 distinct intervals covering all but the very first segments of the 113-year study period [Table 3.10]. The [Ead-] sequence, like the [Ælf-] sequence above, was active for 25 generations in London and is the second largest sequence group. As with the other large sequences, there are multiple instances of groups of moneyers with the [Ead-] name element beginning together in the London mint. This may indicate some level of coordination in regard to the operational years of the moneyers beyond simply one moneyer passing his office onto his descendent. An alternative interpretation of this is discussed in detail in chapter six below.

The first generation of [Ead-] moneyers are Eadweald, who is documented from 979 to 985 as a minter of the First Hand type of Æthelred II, and Eadhelm, who minted both the First Hand and Second Hand types to 991.[140] In 985 six additional [Ead-] moneyers were added to the London mint: Eadnoth (985–991), Eadsige (985–991), Eadwi (985–991), Eadwig (985–997), Eadmund (985–1036), and Eadwine (985–1040).[141] These last two, along with Eadweald, who began in 991, had long careers. A moneyer with the name Eadweald is documented on every type from 991 to 1046.[142] Obviously, these three may not be individuals operating on long timescales and could be multiple minters with the same name overlapping, but for the purposes of this study, moneyers with the same name that have overlying mint productions have been conflated.

Outside of these three long-term moneyers, and one Eadric who is noted as minting only the Long Cross type from 997–1003, the latter period of Æthelred II's reign and the first part of Cnut's typically consists of groupings of two or three moneyers beginning at the same time with typically one or two of them ending concurrently before being replaced by another group of three.[143] Three moneyers, Eadweard, another Eadwi, and another Eadsige begin minting together in 995 on the Small Crux type.[144] This Eadwi and Eadsige could very well be those documented earlier. Eadwi and Eadweard stop at the end of the Small Crux/Transition Crux type in 997. Eadsige continues until the end of Cnut's Pointed Helmet type in 1029.

In 1003, in the Helmet type, three more moneyers begin: Eadgar (1003–1009), another Eadwig (1003–1029), and another Eadweard (1003–1036).[145] Again, these

133 SM1.London.cxv–cxvii.
134 SM1.London.cxviii.
135 SM1.London.cxix.
136 SM1.London.cxx.
137 SM1.London.cxxi.
138 SM1.London.cxxii–cxxiii.
139 SM1.London.cxxiv.
140 SM1.London.clxxii–clxxiii.
141 SM1.London.clxxiv–clxxix.
142 SM1.London.clxxx.
143 SM1.London.clxxxiv.
144 SM1.London.clxxxi–clxxxiii.
145 SM1.London.clxxxv–clxxxvii.

Table 3.10. Moneyers of the [Ead-] sequence in London

Moneyer Name	Sequence Position	Activity Range
Eadhelm	Ead - 1a	979–991
Eadweald	Ead - 1b	979–985
Eadnoth	Ead - 2a	985–991
Eadmund	Ead - 2b	985–1036
Eadsige	Ead - 2c	985–991
Eadwi	Ead - 2d	985–991
Eadwig	Ead - 2e	985–997
Eadwine	Ead - 2f	985–1040
Eadweald	Ead - 3	991–1046
Eadsige	Ead - 4a	995–1029
Eadweard	Ead - 4b	995–997
Eadwi	Ead - 4c	995–997
Eadric	Ead - 5	997–1003
Eadgar	Ead - 6a	1003–1009
Eadweard	Ead - 6b	1003–1036
Eadwig	Ead - 6c	1003–1029
Eadric	Ead - 7a	1009–1048
Eadsme	Ead - 7b	1009–1016
Eadwi	Ead - 7c	1009–1016
Eadgar	Ead - 8a	1017–1029
Eadnoth	Ead - 8b	1017–1023
Eadhelm	Ead - 9a	1023–1029
Eadred	Ead - 9b	1023–1038
Eadwulf	Ead - 9c	1023–1036
Eadnoth	Ead - 10	1029–1036
Eadwig	Ead - 11	1036–1038
Eadweard	Ead - 12	1038–1042
Eadwig	Ead - 13	1040–1042
Eadmund	Ead - 14	1042–1048
Eadwi	Ead - 15a	1044–1046
Eadwine	Ead - 15b	1044–1056
Eadred	Ead - 16	1046–1048
Eadweald	Ead - 17a	1048–1050
Eadwig	Ead - 17b	1048–1059
Eadmund	Ead - 18a	1050–1053
Eadred	Ead - 18b	1050–1056
Eadsige	Ead - 18c	1050–1053
Eadric	Ead - 19a	1053–1056
Eadweald	Ead - 19b	1053–1056
Eadgar	Ead - 20a	1059–1062
Eadwine	Ead - 20b	1059–1077
Eadgar	Ead - 21a	1065–1066
Eadric	Ead - 21b	1065–1066
Eadric	Ead - 22	1070–1072
Eadwi	Ead - 23	1077–1086
Eadwig	Ead - 24	1080–1083
Eadric	Ead - 25	1083–1086

repeated names could point to the same individual with gaps in the extant coinage record, or gaps because of other mechanisms, such as placement rotation, which is addressed in more detail below. The Last Small Cross type, Æthelred II's final coinage, again had three new moneyers begin: Eadsme (1009–1016), Eadwi (1009–1016), and Eadric (1009–1048).[146] As before, two of the three moneyers stop at the end of the type while the third continues to be named. As noted above, there are arguments for and against including the 'wi' ending names with both 'wig' and 'wine', but since both exist in the record simultaneously, they are kept separate.[147]

This pattern of grouping moneyers beginning together continues into Cnut's reign, although the longevity of the individual's activity is reversed, meaning that in the groupings of three, two continue minting past the first type and the third stops. In 1017 the moneyers beginning are Eadnoth (1017–1023) and Eadgar (1017–1029).[148] In 1023, overlapping one of the previous two, there are three more moneyers: Eadhelm (1023–1029), Eadwulf (1023–1036), and Eadred (1023–1038).[149] Eadhelm is a repeat of a name associated with the first generation of moneyers in this sequence, who operated from 979 to 991. These two attestations are the only recordings of this name within the *Moneyers of England Database*. Considering the length of time between the two moneyers being active, it seems highly unlikely that these are the same individual and considering the rarity of the name, seems conversely highly likely that these two specific individuals are related, or at least closely associated.

After Cnut's reign, and until the second coinage of Edward the Confessor, the Radiate Crown/Small Cross type, there is a sequence of five short-span moneyers that carry the [Ead-] name element but do not otherwise fit the pattern that existed prior to 1036, although some of the names are familiar: Eadnoth (1029–1036), Eadwig (1036–1038), Eadweard (1038–1042), another (or likely the same) Eadwig (1040–1042), and Eadmund (1042–1048).[150] With the Radiate Crown/Small Cross type, it seems that the pattern of grouping moneyer placements together returns, although the groups are most commonly of only

[146] SM1.London.clxxxviii–cxc.
[147] B. H. I. H. Stewart and C. E. Blunt, 1978, 'The Droitwich Mint and *BMC* Type XIV of Edward the Confessor', *BNJ* 48, 52–8 at 54.
[148] SM1.London.cxci–cxcii.
[149] SM1.London.cxciii–cxcv.
[150] SM1.London.cxcvi–cc.

two, instead of three, moneyers. In 1044 there is Eadwi and Eadwine, which admittedly, as noted earlier, may be the same individual, although if the placement is likely to be with Eadwig over Eadwine it would remain the same.[151]

The Trefoil-Quadrilateral type of 1046–1048 had one new moneyer: Eadred.[152] Eadweald and Eadwig began in 1048, with the former minting in just the Short Cross type, and the latter carrying forward to the Sovereign/Eagles type (1056–1059).[153] 1050 had three new moneyers: Eadmund (1050–1053), Eadsige (1050–1053), and possibly the same Eadred (1050–1056).[154] It is noteworthy here that two stopped minting and the third continued to the next type, along the pattern associated with Æthelred II's placements more so than Cnut's.

In 1053 two moneyers were added for Edward's Pointed Helmet type (1053–1056): Eadric and Eadweald.[155] In 1059 Eadgar, who minted only the Hammer Cross type (1059–1062), and Eadwine, who carried forward to the Two Stars type (1074–1077) of William I, began minting.[156] Possibly the same Eadgar returned in 1065 to mint Edward's last coin, the Pyramids type (1065–1066).[157] An Eadric also began in 1065 and minted both the Pyramids type and Harold II's Pax type in 1066.[158] After the Norman Conquest, four moneyers were added (or were carried forward but with broken coinage records): Eadric (1070–1072), Eadwi (1077–1086), Eadwig (1080–1083), and Eadric (1083–1086).[159]

The [God-] Name Sequence in London

There were 31 periods of activity for moneyers within the [God-] name sequence [Table 3.11]. A distinction of the [God-] sequence is that there were several moneyers with seemingly long periods of activity, far above the overall average of 10.5 years for the pre-1036 period. Most prominent is the first recorded Godwine. A moneyer by this name is recorded on every coinage issue from 979 to 1062.[160] The likelihood of this being the same individual over this 83-year period is very remote. What seems more likely is that this was a series of related moneyers succeeding one another over time, perhaps uncle to nephew or grandfather to grandson.

In reviewing the operational years of the moneyers, with this extended period of activity from a single moneyer included, the groupings for the mint are somewhat problematical but not completely absent. There are still groupings at several points between the first recorded [God-] sequence moneyers in 979 and the end of the study period in 1086. The first such grouping consisted of four moneyers beginning together in 979: God (979–985), Godric (979–985), Goda (979–997), and the previously mentioned Godwine.[161] Two moneyers began together in 991, Godhere, who was active until 997, and Godric, who, like Godwine above, is recorded on coins covering an extensive period of time (to 1040) and was likely more than one individual operating with the same name.[162] This occurs again after another God and a uniquely named

Table 3.11. Moneyers of the [God-] sequence in London

Moneyer Name	Sequence Position	Activity Range
God	God - 1a	979–985
Goda	God - 1b	979–997
Godric	God - 1c	979–985
Godwine	God - 1d	979–1062
Godhere	God - 2a	991–997
Godric	God - 2b	991–1040
God	God - 3a	995–997
Godra	God - 3b	995–997
Godman	God - 4	997–1042
Goda	God - 5a	1003–1038
Godhere	God - 5b	1003–1036
Godwig	God - 6	1017–1023
God	God - 7a	1029–1036
Goding	God - 7b	1029–1036
Godsige	God - 8a	1036–1040
Godwine Stew	God - 8b	1036–1038
God	God - 9	1038–1040
Goda	God - 10a	1040–1042
Godric Calic	God - 10b	1040–1042
Godwig	God - 11	1042–1044
Godman	God - 12a	1044–1046
Godsunu	God - 12b	1044–1053
Godric	God - 13a	1046–1077
Godwig	God - 13b	1046–1050
Godhere	God - 14a	1053–1056
Godman	God - 14b	1053–1056
Godwig	God - 14c	1053–1056
Godwine	God - 15	1068–1072
Godwine	God - 16	1074–1080
Godric	God - 17a	1083–1086
Godwine	God - 17b	1083–1086

[151] SM1.London.cci–ccii.
[152] SM1.London.cciii.
[153] SM1.London.cciv–ccv.
[154] SM1.London.ccvi–ccviii.
[155] SM1.London.ccix–ccx.
[156] SM1.London.ccxi–ccxii.
[157] SM1.London.ccxiii.
[158] SM1.London.ccxiv.
[159] SM1.London.ccxv–ccxviii.
[160] SM1.London.ccxlviii.
[161] SM1.London.ccxlv–ccxlvii.
[162] SM1.London.ccxlix–ccl.

Godra are active for Æthelred II's Transitional Crux type (995–997).[163] After these two, a Godman is recorded on coins from 997 to 1042.[164]

If these three likely multi-generation moneyer names were separated out into distinct individuals, it is likely that the [God-] sequence would prove to be even more prominent in the mint overall. Although not as extensive, two more long-active moneyer names are added to the record from 1003: Godhere (1003–1036) and Goda (1003–1038).[165] While above the average, it is not unreasonable to believe that these could have been single individuals operating over three decades, as such instances appear periodically among the other mints.

A Godwig is recorded as active from 1017 to 1023.[166] Two moneyers began activity together in 1029 and operated until 1036: God and Goding.[167] Following their disappearance from the coinage record are two more moneyers beginning together in 1036, Godwine Stew, who was active until 1038, and Godsige, who operated until 1040.[168] Overlapping with the latter, God returned for the period 1038 to 1040.[169]

From 1040 to 1042, Goda and an unusually named Godric Calic are active.[170] Another Godwig is active from 1042 to 1044.[171] Two moneyers begin operation in 1044, a repeat of Godman, who was active until 1046, and Godsunu, whose activity carried forward to 1053. [172] In 1046, Godwig repeats and is active until 1050.[173] From Harthacnut and into Edward the Confessor's rule, the average span of activity for the moneyers in the [God-] sequence generally conformed to the average observed in the mint as a whole and elsewhere, with one exception. A Godric is recorded from 1046 continuously until 1077, and again from 1083 to 1086.[174] The Godric name was active for three distinct periods from 973 to 1086, covering eighty-nine of the 113 years addressed in this study.

Three moneyers operated together for the Expanding Cross type (1050–1053): Godhere, Godman, and Godwig.[175] After this, and outside of the above noted Godric and Godwine, there is no other [God-] sequence moneyer record from 1053 to 1068, when a Godwine reappears from a short break in the record to be active again for 1068–1072, 1074–1080, and 1083–1086.[176] Including the post-1062 period, the Godwine name has four iterations covering 96 total years. Similarly, the Godric name was active for three distinct periods from 973 to 1086, covering 89 of the 113 years addressed in this study. These 31 records represent 17 generations of [God-] sequence moneyer activity in the London mint.

The [Leof-] Name Sequence in London

The first [Leof-] recorded at London for the period spanning 973 to 1086 is Leofheah, who was active from 975 to 978.[177] After this Leofheah, two new moneyers began operation in London: Leofric (979–985) and Leofstan (979–1003).[178] A Leofwine began in 985 and was active for a long period until 1040.[179] Like the [God-] sequence above, the [Leof-] sequence has several moneyer names that are continuously represented on the epigraphy of the surviving coinage record for extended periods of time. A Leofwine began in 985 and was active until 1040.[180] Three other examples of [Leof-] names existing in the record for an extended period began operation together in 991: Leofing (991–1042), Leofric (991–1046), and Leofred (991–1056).[181] These were followed by the first Leofnoth, who was active from 997 to 1003.[182]

A Leofweald was active from 1003 to 1036.[183] He was followed by a group of four moneyers beginning in 1009, which included repeats of Leofheah (1009–1016), Leofnoth (1009–1016), and Leofstan (1009–1046), as well as a Leofwig (1009–1036).[184] Two moneyers began in 1017, Leofsige, who was active until 1029, and Leofweard, who was on the coinage epigraphy until 1036.[185] For Cnut's Pointed Helmet type (1023–1029) three new moneyers are recorded: Leofgar, Leofmær, and Leofman.[186] These three were followed by Leofa for the 1029–1036 coinage of Cnut's last type, Short Cross.[187]

There were no new moneyers of the [Leof-] sequence added between 1036 and 1046. The only recorded [Leof-] moneyers of this period were the earlier noted group that began operation in 991: Leofing, Leofric, and Leofred. As discussed in the [God-] sequence section above, it is conceivable these were different individuals with the same name operating separately. There are obvious concerns with this determination, most notable being the lack of separation in the coinage record. Also, this would indicate that these three moneyer names began together in 991 and then moneyers of the same exact names also began together in the same grouping of three over four decades later, which seems improbable, at least without some interim grouping or alteration with others. Possibly

[163] SM1.London.ccli–cclii.
[164] SM1.London.ccliii.
[165] SM1.London.ccliv–cclv.
[166] SM1.London.cclvi.
[167] SM1.London.cclvii–cclviii.
[168] SM1.London.cclix–cclx.
[169] SM1.London.cclxi.
[170] SM1.London.cclxii–cclxiii.
[171] SM1.London.cclxiv.
[172] SM1.London.cclxv–cclxvi.
[173] SM1.London.cclxvii.
[174] SM1.London.cclxviii; SM1.London.cclxxiv.
[175] SM1.London.cclxix–cclxxi.
[176] SM1.London.cclxxii–cclxxiii; SM1.London.cclxxvi.
[177] SM1.London.cclxxxvi.
[178] SM1.London.cclxxxvii–cclxxxviii.
[179] SM1.London.cclxxxix.
[180] SM1.London.cclxxxix.
[181] SM1.London.ccxc–ccxcii.
[182] SM1.London.ccxciii.
[183] SM1.London.ccxciv.
[184] SM1.London.ccxcv–ccxcviii.
[185] SM1.London.ccxcix–ccc.
[186] SM1.London.ccci–ccciii.
[187] SM1.London.ccciv.

this was accomplished via connection with the other name sequences.

In 1046, two moneyers from the [Leof-] sequence appear in the coinage record: a Leofing who was active until 1053 and a repeat of Leofwine, a name that was active for an extended period until 1040 and in this iteration was active until 1059.[188] From 1048 to 1050 a repeat of two names that began together in 1009 appear, Leofnoth and Leofwig.[189] Another Leofsige was then active from 1050 to 1053.[190] A new name appears in 1056, Leofæg (1056–1059), along with a repeat of Leofing (1056–1062).[191] Leofric joins Leofing in 1059 and is active until 1062.[192] The last recorded [Leof-] of the London mint is Leofsige, who minted the single Pax type (1066) of Harold II and the Bonnet type (1068–1070) of William I.[193]

There were 29 iterations of the [Leof-] name sequence at London [Table 3.12].

Table 3.12. Moneyers of the [Leof-] sequence in London

Moneyer Name	Sequence Position	Activity Range
Leofheah	Leof - 1	975–978
Leofric	Leof - 2a	979–985
Leofstan	Leof - 2b	979–1003
Leofwine	Leof - 3	985–1040
Leofing	Leof - 4a	991–1042
Leofred	Leof - 4b	991–1056
Leofric	Leof - 4c	991–1046
Leofnoth	Leof - 5	997–1003
Leofweald	Leof - 6	1003–1036
Leofheah	Leof - 7a	1009–1016
Leofnoth	Leof - 7b	1009–1016
Leofstan	Leof - 7c	1009–1046
Leofwig	Leof - 7d	1009–1036
Leofsige	Leof - 8a	1017–1029
Leofweard	Leof - 8b	1017–1036
Leofgar	Leof - 9a	1023–1029
Leofmær	Leof - 9b	1023–1029
Leofman	Leof - 9c	1023–1029
Leofa	Leof - 10	1029–1036
Leofing	Leof - 11a	1046–1053
Leofwine	Leof - 11b	1046–1059
Leofnoth	Leof - 12a	1048–1050
Leofwig	Leof - 12b	1048–1050
Leofsige	Leof - 13	1050–1053
Leofæg	Leof - 14a	1056–1059
Leofing	Leof - 14b	1056–1062
Leofric	Leof - 15	1059–1062
Leofsige	Leof - 16	1066–1066
Leofsige	Leof - 17	1068–1070

The [Wulf-] Name Sequence in London

Covering nearly the entire span of this study, the common name element [Wulf-] includes 45 distinct periods of activity over 23 successive generations at the London mint, from 979 to 1083, crossing both the Danish and Norman conquests [Table 3.13].

The first moneyers in the sequence were Wulfmær and Wulfric, both active during Æthelred II's First Hand (979–985) and Second Hand (985–991) types, and Wulfstan, who was active until 1029.[194] Then there was Wulfgar, who minted from 991 to 997, and Wulfwine, active from 991 to 1040.[195] Concurrent to these was Wulfnoth, active from 995 to 997.[196] In 997, two moneyers began activity together: Wulfsige (997–1003) and another Wulfric (997–1036).[197] Wulfgar reappears in 1003 and is in the coinage record until 1009.[198] He is joined by Wulfred who was active from 1003 to 1036.[199] During this tenure, Wulfbeald operated from 1009 to 1016, followed by several other moneyers beginning in 1017: another Wulfsige (1017–1023), Wulfweard (1017–1023), Wulfnoth (1017–1029), and Wulfgar (1017–1038).[200] After the large group of moneyers beginning in 1017, there is another Wulfmær operating from 1023 to 1029.[201] From 1036 to 1038, for the short Jewel Cross type of Harold I, there is only Wulfnoth distinctly.[202]

A Wulf without a secondary name element is documented in the coin epigraphy from 1038 to 1040, although this could very easily have been a die replacement, or possibly a die simplification, for any of the other moneyers active at this time.[203] Another Wulfsige and Wulfstan also began operation in 1038 and minted coins until 1040 and 1044, respectively.[204] A second Wulfred and a fourth iteration of Wulfgar are recorded as beginning activity in 1040, with the first stopping in 1042 and the second operating until 1044.[205]

[188] SM1.London.cccv–cccvi.
[189] SM1.London.cccvii–cccviii.
[190] SM1.London.cccix.
[191] SM1.London.cccx–cccxi.
[192] SM1.London.cccxii.
[193] SM1.London.ccc.
[194] SM1.London.ccclxxxi–ccclxxxiii.
[195] SM1.London.ccclxxxiv–ccclxxxv.
[196] SM1.London.ccclxxxvi.
[197] SM1.London.ccclxxxvii–ccclxxxviii.
[198] SM1.London.ccclxxxix.
[199] SM1.London.cccxc.
[200] SM1.London.cccxci–cccxcv.
[201] SM1.London.cccxcvi.
[202] SM1.London.cccxcvii.
[203] SM1.London.cccxcviii.
[204] SM1.London.cccxcix–cd.
[205] SM1.London.cdi–cdii.

Table 3.13. Moneyers of the [Wulf-] sequence in London

Moneyer Name	Sequence Position	Activity Range
Wulfmær	Wulf - 1a	979–991
Wulfric	Wulf - 1b	979–991
Wulfstan	Wulf - 1c	979–1029
Wulfgar	Wulf - 2a	991–997
Wulfwine	Wulf - 2b	991–1040
Wulfnoth	Wulf - 3	995–997
Wulfric	Wulf - 4a	997–1036
Wulfsige	Wulf - 4b	997–1003
Wulfgar	Wulf - 5a	1003–1009
Wulfred	Wulf - 5b	1003–1036
Wulfbeald	Wulf - 6	1009–1016
Wulfgar	Wulf - 7a	1017–1038
Wulfnoth	Wulf - 7b	1017–1029
Wulfsige	Wulf - 7c	1017–1023
Wulfweard	Wulf - 7d	1017–1023
Wulfmær	Wulf - 8	1023–1029
Wulfnoth	Wulf - 9	1036–1038
Wulf	Wulf - 10a	1038–1040
Wulfsige	Wulf - 10b	1038–1042
Wulfstan	Wulf - 10c	1038–1044
Wulfgar	Wulf - 11a	1040–1042
Wulfred	Wulf - 11b	1040–1042
Wulfgar	Wulf - 12a	1042–1044
Wulfric	Wulf - 12b	1042–1044
Wulfwine	Wulf - 12c	1042–1059
Wulfred	Wulf - 14a	1044–1053
Wulfsige	Wulf - 14b	1044–1046
Wulfric	Wulf - 15a	1046–1050
Wulfsic	Wulf - 15b	1046–1048
Wulfsige	Wulf - 16a	1048–1050
Wulfwig	Wulf - 16b	1048–1050
Wulfcrdd	Wulf - 17a	1050–1053
Wulfweard	Wulf - 17b	1050–1053
Wulfgar	Wulf - 18a	1053–1066
Wulfric	Wulf - 18b	1053–1059
Wulfnoth	Wulf - 19a	1056–1059
Wulfred	Wulf - 19b	1056–1059
Wulfsi	Wulf - 20a	1062–1065
Wulfsige	Wulf - 20b	1062–1066

Wulfric (1042–1044) and Wulfwine (1042–1056) were next in the sequence.[206] Another pair of repeating names follows these two: Wulfsige (1044–1046) and Wulfred (1044–1053).[207] A uniquely named Wulfsic and another Wulfric begin together in 1046, with the first active until 1048 and the second operating until 1050.[208] Wulfsige repeats again, along with a Wulfwig, from 1048 to 1050.[209] Another pair is active for the Expanding Cross type (1050–1053): Wulfcrdd and Wulfweard.[210] Wulfcrdd is only attested to on a single coin and this name does not appear anywhere else in the coinage record. It is possible that this was a mistake on a die that saw very limited use. If the 'c' and 'r' were reversed, the epigraphy would look very close to Wulfred, who was active just before and shortly after this potential moneyer. In 1053, another pair started together, with the first, Wulfric, operating until 1059 and the second, yet another Wulfgar, active until 1066.[211]

Two moneyers minted the Sovereign Eagles type (1056–1059), Wulfnoth and Wulfred.[212] In 1062, three moneyers started together: Wulfsi (1062–1065), Wulfsige (1062–1066), and Wulfweard (1062–1066).[213] After the Norman Conquest, a Wulfwine was active for two periods, 1066 to 1072 and 1080 to 1083.[214] Between these two periods of activity, three moneyers operated from the [Wulf-] sequence in London. A Wulfie and a Wulfric both operated from 1072 to 1074 and Wulfweard repeats for the period 1074 to 1077.[215]

The [Wulf-] sequence at London illustrates the repetitious pattern often associated with the more common name sequences. Some names are utilised multiple times, making differentiation between generational shifts difficult. There are 45 distinct periods of activity of [Wulf-] named moneyers within the London mint in this sequence from 973 to 1086, and of those, 73 per cent utilise one of seven specific names. There are six instances of Wulfric and Wulfsige in the record, with the first having activity as early as 979 and as late as 1074, making it nearly impossible for this to have been one individual operating sporadically. The name Wulfsige, similarly, has periods of activity from 997 to 1066. Wulfgar had five iterations covering a broad timespan. There are four instances of Wulfnoth, Wulfred, Wulfweard, and Wulfwine as well. If Wulfcrdd could be considered a variant of Wulfred this would increase the overall percentage. These, along with the 27 per cent of [Wulf-] moneyers not included as one of the primary names, were active for 23 generations in London. While [Wulf-] was a common name element used in late Anglo-Saxon England, it is apparent that some level

[206] SM1.London.cdiii–cdiv.
[207] SM1.London.cdv–cdvi.
[208] SM1.London.cdvii–cdviii.
[209] SM1.London.cdix–cdx.
[210] SM1.London.cdxi–cdxii.
[211] SM1.London.cdxiii–cdxiv.
[212] SM1.London.cdxv–cdxvi.
[213] SM1.London.cdxvii–cdxix.
[214] SM1.London.cdxx; SM1.London.cdxxiv.
[215] SM1.London.cdxxi–cdxxiii.

of connection existed in the London mints where these individuals took up their craft.

The Southwark Mint

The mint at Southwark, across the Thames from the Tower in London, had 68 distinct periods of moneyer activity from 973 to 1086. These were predominantly in two distinct eras of operation, 991 to 997 and 1017 to 1029. Of the 48 individually named moneyers that were active in Southwark, only four were not also active in London. So, 91.7 per cent of all the names of moneyers active in Southwark for the period 991 to 1086 are repeats of moneyers active, typically concurrently or within a single coinage issue, across the Thames as well. This lends credence to the argument of Southwark being more of a supplement to the monetary enterprise of London than a cohesive independent mint.[216]

Southwark was predominantly manned by an Osmund in Edward the Confessor's later reign, alternating placement with a Godric and a Leofwine, both also active in London. Osmund was active from 1053 to 1066 and again from 1083 to 1086.[217] A Godric was active in Southwark as early as 991, operating until 1003.[218] A moneyer named Godric was active again later, from 1062 to 1065 and from 1080 to 1086.[219] A moneyer, or some moneyers, named Leofwine, similarly, was active in Southwark early in the study period, 991–1003 and 1009–1016, and then over three periods late in Edward's reign and into William I's rule for the periods 1046–1050, 1068–1070, and 1074–1080.[220] There are also two other moneyers unique to Southwark operating in the post-Norman Conquest period from 1083 to 1086: Ælfdoulf and Lifweard.[221] The second is likely a variant of the very common [Leof-] sequence that saw widespread transition to this spelling after 1066.

Conclusion

Representing 19.9 per cent of the total coinage record, and 13.5 per cent of the total number of moneyers recorded from 973 to 1086 within the database, London and Southwark provide the best single-site example, when taken together, of the entire minting endeavour in Anglo-Saxon England and illustrate patterns that are evident in many of the other 97 minting locations from this period. By outlining how the name sequences in place illustrated continuity over nearly the entire range of this study, London and Southwark encapsulates the idea of the native population working within a skilled craft with seemingly minimum outside interference in its internal hierarchy and is illustrative of the patterns evident in other minting locations.

In reviewing the uncommon name sequences found within London, there consistently seems to be a pattern of like-named individuals operating within the mints over consecutive periods of activity. This practice can also be seen in the largest of the name sequences, which dominate the coinage record for London and the mints of Anglo-Saxon England overall. Certain name elements appear again and again within the coinage record irrespective of their overall prevalence within the general population, as discussed above. This repetition, based upon the ideas of Anglo-Saxon naming patterns as outlined in the beginning of this chapter, supports the idea that these were groups of men that were somehow connected to one another operating collectively. This process may have been managed solely by the hereditary passing of the mint and office from father to son, or some other direct descendent, as was mandated by laws on the Continent and found to be evident within some of the later structures within England.[222] Or it could have been a series of 'master-moneyers' overseeing the operation of the mint with the lesser moneyers minting coins under their name or in conjunction with the name of their family, as took place in the Northern European sword making industry. Perhaps it was a combination of the two, thereby allowing for the dynastic control of the mints over a prolonged period of time while providing the fluidity to incorporate workers outside of the family into the practice provided they became subservient to the overarching 'family' associated with the specific name element. In most instances, however, it appears that it is the family which takes precedence and is directly in control of the minting apparatus. While branding is a possibility, the overriding evidence seems to point to the familial over the commercial connections.

What is definite is that the moneyers of London belonged to a non-noble, but wealthy, class of men who were responsible for the production of the king's coins for the use in trade, taxation, and whatever else the economic structures of late Anglo-Saxon England allowed. By illustrating that there was a continuous progression of moneyers with likely links, either through direct familial connection or through the incorporation of certain naming patterns, over important watershed events like the Danish and Norman Conquests, it is apparent that there were possibly structures in place within England that are traditionally considered to have arrived after 1066.[223] The preponderance of the evidence supporting linkages between individuals acting within specific minting locations heavily implies that some mechanism was in place to maintain family control

216 Naismith, 2013, 59. See also J. Evelyn, ed., 1783, *The Charters of the City of London which have been granted by the Kings and Queens of England since the Conquest*, London, 36; Andrew, 1901b, 279. Naismith points to the repetition of names between the London and Southwark mints as a link between the two. Andrew notes that the *Charters* characterises Southwark as subject to London in the payment of taxes and that the moneyers in London paid the taxes for the mints in Southwark, indicating a subordinate position for the latter, similar to the arrangement held by Colchester and Maldon as discussed above.

217 SM1.Southwark.lvi–lvii.

218 SM1.Southwark.xxxviii.

219 SM1.Southwark.xxxix–xl.

220 SM1.Southwark.l–liv.

221 SM1.Southwark.ii; SM1.Southwark.lv.

222 Andrew, 1901a, 29; Lopez, 1953, 2–3; Nightingale, 1982.

223 S. Ogilvie, 2014, 'The Economics of Guilds', *The Journal of Economic Perspectives* 28, 169–92 at 170. Ogilvie outlines that guilds in Europe were sporadic after the fall of the Roman Empire and that there

of the craft through successive generations. A guild-like structure of master and apprentice moneyers may not be too strong of an explanation. At the very least, it seems likely that there was some sort of pre-guild framework in place before the idea of organised artisans arrived on the British Isles. Of course, there is no extant documentation that supports the idea of these moneyers forming any sort of collective management or trade protection society. But, there were laws in place that sought to protect the currency itself, in weight, purity, and minting, and outlined who could take part in the hammering of coins.[224]

was not a large-scale resurgence until after 1000, and that craft guilds specifically were not evident in Europe until after 1100. See T. De Moor, 2009, 'The Silent Revolution: A New Perspective on the Emergence of Commons, Guilds and Other Forms of Corporate Collective Action in Western Europe', in J. Lucassen, T. De Moor, and J. L. van Zanden, eds., *The Return of the Guilds, International Review of Social History*, Supplement 16, 179–212 at 188. The incorporation of craft guilds is markedly different from the ecclesiastical guilds which predated them. For discussion on religious guild practices see G. Rosser, 1988, 'The Anglo-Saxon Gilds', in J. Blair, ed., *Minsters and Parish Churches: The Local Church in Transition, 950–1200*, Oxford, 31–43.

[224] IV Æthelred 5–9.3, Liebermann, 234–6. There is some debate on the exact dating of IV Æthelred but it is generally credited to around 1009.

4

The Moneyers and Mints of Late Anglo-Saxon England

Mint Classification and Name Sequence Organisation

The mints of late Anglo-Saxon England within the *MED* can be classified most directly by the volume of the extant coinage record and the number of active moneyers operational within the mint from 973 to 1086. As detailed in chapter three above, these factors provide for two levels of classification: major/minor and high/low volume mints. What follows is a listing of the name sequences within the three largest mints arranged by volume, beginning with the complete listing for London. The major mints are listed first with some examples of the minor mints following. The name sequences are arranged alphabetically and then chronologically. [Tables 4.1–4.77]

What is evident is that each of the major mints contained multiple instances of the patterns of name continuity as outlined in London above. This pattern of just a few name structures controlling much of the coinage production was widespread in Anglo-Saxon England. Each of the major mints exhibit this behaviour, with many of the minor mints containing it as well. This listing of the mints illustrates the widespread nature of this continuity among the moneyer group as each of the major mints and many of the minor mints demonstrate patterns like those outlined above.

The moneyers that do not belong to any specific name sequence are included in the mint listings and labelled as 'None' in the corresponding column. This number is generally a small minority of the overall number of moneyers active within the mints. Those mints with only one or two instances of moneyer activity that do not illustrate any clear name element continuity are not included in this section. Each of these mints, excepting those only active during the later period of William I, is located geographically close to a major mint. Those major mints generally fall in line with the shire system, established by the West Saxon kingdom in the eight century and spread when Wessex consolidated its authority through a series of campaigns to the early tenth century.[1]

The minor mints that are not graphically represented are: Caistor, Cardiff, Cuer, Droitwich, Durham, Frome, Horncastle, Horndon, Hythe, Launceston, Milbourne Port, Newark, Niwan, Pershore, Peterborough, Petherton, Pevensey, Rhuddlan, St Davids, Stes, Twynham, and Wilton (East Anglia).[2] These 22 mint locations account for only 29 periods of activity and 55 coins within the *MED*, or 0.8 per cent of the former and 0.2 per cent of the latter. Only two of these mints, Launceston and Milbourne Port, have three instances of activity. A further three have two periods of moneyer activity and the rest are only attested to by a single moneyer operating for a single period of time, often with only a single coin as evidence that they ever minted at the given location. Unfortunately, it is unlikely that any clear reason for this sporadic activity at these mint locations will ever be determined, but it is possible that these locations were test markets for silver exchanges that proved unprofitable and were summarily abandoned.

The geographic proximity of some of these smallest mints to much larger minting locations was likely a cause of their sporadic and limited activity, and thus the limitations of their name sequence representation. The exact location of the Caistor mint is not known, but a likely analysis places it in or near the town of the same name in Lindsey, which would have been close to Lincoln.[3] Similar connections to Lincoln were evident in the low production mints of Frome, Horncastle, and Newark, all of which utilised dies that were in the 'Lincoln' style, likely pointing to a direct connection with the larger mint.[4] Stamford and Torksey, while not very low production mints like these others, were similarly linked to Lincoln through the type of die that they utilised.[5]

---

1 B. Yorke, 1990, *Kings and Kingdoms of Early Anglo-Saxon England*, London, 130.

2 Several of these mints are discussed below in relation to their activity as it relates to larger geographically close mints, further information on the others can be found in these sources. For Droitwich see C. E. Blunt and B. H. I. H. Stewart, 1978, 'The Droitwich Mint and *BMC* Type XIV of Edward the Confessor', *BNJ* 48, 52–8; For Durham see M. Allen, 2003, *The Durham Mint*, London; For Milbourne Port see R. H. M. Dolley, 1958a, Three West Country Notes', *BNJ* 29, 61–8; For Pershore and Petherton see P. W. P. Carlyon-Britton, 1909, '"Uncertain" Anglo-Saxon Mints and some new Attributions', *BNJ* 6, 13–47 at 34–5. There are some speculative attestations of Droitwich on late coinages of Edward the Confessor, but these are not conclusive and are currently not attributed to this mint within the *MED*. Milbourne Port was a mint in Somerset. Pershore was located in Worcestershire. There is some ambiguity as to whether Petherton refers to North Petherton or South Petherton, but the former is the more common attribution.

3 R. H. M. Dolley, 1955a, 'Three Late Anglo-Saxon Notes', *BNJ* 28, 88–105 at 90–1.

4 For Frome see R. H. M. Dolley, 1955b, 'Two Anglo-Saxon Notes', BNJ 28, 499–508 at 508; For Horncastle see idem, 1958b, 'Three More Late Saxon Notes', *BNJ* 29, 51–60 at 54; For Newark see idem, 1955b, 501. The attestation of Frome is still a matter of some debate but the die type linking appears to place it in the vicinity of Lincoln according to Dolley. For more general discussion on the mint at Lincoln see F. Hill, 1948, *Medieval Lincoln*, Cambridge, 15; F. M. Stenton, 1970, 'Lindsey and Its Kings', in D. M. Stenton, ed., *Preparatory to Anglo-Saxon England: The Collected Papers of Frank Merry Stenton*, Oxford, 127–35. For discussion on Lincoln in general and how it may have been connected to these other locations see F. Hill, 1948, *Medieval Lincoln*, Cambridge.

5 Dolley, 1955b, 502–3; C. Mahany and D. Roffe, 1983, 'Stamford: The Development of an Anglo-Scandinavian Borough', *ANS* 5, 197–219.

Similar geographic connections existed between Horndon and London, Gothaburh and Exeter, Wilton (EA) and Thetford, Berkeley and Gloucester, Peterborough and Stamford, and Aylesbury and Buckingham.[6] Most of these maintained enough activity to illustrate the name sequences as outlined below, but one mint often dominated production, leaving the other as only periodically active. This is evident in the relationship between the mints at Salisbury and Wilton, as well as Ilchester and Cadbury. In the former pairing, Wilton was abandoned in favour of Salisbury after it was attacked in 1003, resulting in both mints being active in very close proximity after the Wilton mint reopened.[7] While several of the Wilton moneyers relocated to Salisbury and did not return, there are several die-links between the two mints indicating that some moneyers maintained activity at both.[8] At Ilchester, threat of invasion prompted a move to Cadbury around 1009–1010 and then a return to activity once the danger had subsided.[9] Ilchester is also linked to the small mints at Langport and Crewkerne, with some moneyers appearing to operate between the primary mint and the smaller ones intermittently.[10] The Dorset mints of Bridport, Dorchester, and Wareham share moneyers named Hwætman and Blacman, with the former appearing at Dorchester and Bridport and the latter at Dorchester and Wareham.[11] The moneyer Cild moved, apparently by order of the king, to Marlborough in the reign of William I.[12] It also appears that some of the smaller mints were replacements for, or replaced by, other more active mints. For example, it appears that Bath, although maintaining an active mint from at least the reign of Eadward the Elder (899–924/5), saw its activity dwindle with the development of Bristol as a commercial port.[13] Likewise, there is speculation that Hythe was a replacement for Lympne, perhaps even being the same mint altogether, but undergoing a name shift in the eleventh century.[14]

The nearness that many of the smallest mints shared with larger mints, resulted in their production output being smaller, and thus their name sequence contribution correspondingly small as well. However, several of the mints that are not included below have so few records attached to their production that pinpointing their location and their possible connection to a large mint difficult. The locations of the mints of Cuer, Dernt, Niwan, and Stes are not known, making comparative analysis with a major mint difficult.[15] A handfull of the mints were ecclesiastical in nature, meaning that the operators might have been subject directly to the local bishopric or abbey and potentially part of the monastic order, making the likelihood of progeny significantly lower. Bury St Edmunds may have been operated by such a moneyer as Edward the Confessor named a moneyer to the abbots in 1065.[16] Almost certainly, in the reign of William I, Launceston was operated by such a moneyer. The uniquely marked Sasoti Stefani moneyer for William I's Two Stars type (1074–1077) is the first indication of a move back to monastic minting under the Conqueror.[17] The epigraphy, +SASOTI STEFANII, is in the Latin genitive case and implies that the coinage is by a moneyer associated with the Canons of St. Stephen.[18] Other mints were part of a defensive fortification and may have been utilised only during times of conflict. Mints such as Cissbury, Cricklade, and Pevensey likely fall into this category.[19] Similarly, Bedford, a moderately active major mint, was on the border between Wessex and the Danelaw, marking it as a potentially strategic point for trade, thereby requiring a higher mint output.[20] A complete listing of the

[6] For Horndon and London see Dolley, 1958b, 53; For Gothaburh and Exeter see R. H. M. Dolley and F. Elmore Jones, 1955, 'The Mints "ÆT GOTHABYRIG" and "ÆT SITH(M)ESTEBYRIG"', *BNJ* 28, 270–82; C. S. S. Lyon, 1962, 'Two Notes on the "Last Small Cross" Type of Æthelræd II', *BNJ* 31, 49–52 at 51; For discussion on the location of Gothaburh as likely being at the location of Gotha Castle in Cornwall see S. Keynes, 2013c, 'Wulfstan I', in M. Lapidge, ed., *The Wiley-Blackwell Encyclopedia of Anglo-Saxon England*, 513; For Wilton (EA) and Thetford see R. A. G. Carson, 1949, 'The Mint at Thetford', *NC* 9, 189–236 at 189–90; Metcalf, 1998, *An Atlas of Anglo-Saxon and Norman Coin Finds, C.973–1086*, London, 217; For Berkeley and Gloucester see R. H. M. Dolley, 1961, 'A Note on the Anglo-Saxon Mint at Berkeley', *Transactions* of the Bristol and Gloucestershire Archaeological Society 80, 80–9; For Peterborough and Stamford see W. C. Wells, 1934, 'The Stamford and Peterborough Mints', *BNJ* 6, 35–77; For Aylesbury and Buckingham see W. N. Clarke and D. Symons, 2007, 'The Mint of Aylesbury', *BNJ* 77, 173–90; R. H. M. Dolley, D. J. Elliott, and F. Elmore Jones, 1965, 'The Buckingham Mint', *BNJ* 34, 46–52.

[7] Metcalf, 1998, 238.

[8] R. H. M. Dolley, 1962, 'Two Anglo-Saxon Notes', *BNJ* 31, 53–6; Metcalf, 1998, 238.

[9] Blunt, 1960, 14.

[10] Dolley, 1955a, 101; Dolley, 1962, 56.

[11] L. Keen, 1984, 'The Towns of Dorset', in J. Haslam, ed., *Anglo-Saxon Towns in Southern England*, Chichester, 203–47 at 241; Bridport has been postulated as located close to the town of Stockbridge, in the vicinity of Winchester, although this is contested. See W. J. Andrew, 1929, 'Stockbridge, an Anglo-Saxon Mint', *BNJ* 20, 49–61; H. Symonds, 1922, 'Bridport as an Anglo-Saxon Mint', *NC* 5, 144–5; Dolley, 1955a, 88–105.

[12] P. W. P. Carlyon-Britton, 1902, 'Bedwin and Marlborough and the Moneyer Cilda', *NC* 2, 20–5.

[13] L. V. Grinsell, 1973, *The Bath Mint, an Historical Outline*, Oxford, 36–7.

[14] J. Carroll and D. Parsons, 2007, *Anglo-Saxon Mint Names*, Nottingham, 176–7.

[15] Cuer is thought to be Cuerdale in the Cumbria region. Personal communication with Dr. Stewart Lyon; The location of Dernt has been the subject of some debate with the consensus pointing to Suffolk as a likely location without specificity. See F. Elmore Jones, 1962, 'The Mysterious Mint of 'Dernt'', *BNJ* 31, 66–8; R. H. M. Dolley, 1960, 'A New Late Saxon Mint in Suffolk', *NCirc* 68, 236; Niwan has been attributed to both Newark and Newport Pagnell but without definitive conclusion. See Dolley, 1955a, 98; An early attribution placed Niwan in Gloucester with a possible correlation to Newent. See R. S., 1837–8, 'An Attempt to Locate Some Coins of Unappropriated Mints, in Ruding from Domesday, and the New Topographical Dictionary', *TNJ* 2, 45–51 at 45; The location of Stes remains uncertain. See Allen, 2012, 21.

[16] S 1085.

[17] SM1.Launceston.iii.

[18] P. W. P. Carlyon-Britton, 1906, 'Cornish Numismatics', *BNJ* 8, 107–16 at 111.

[19] For Cissbury see M. Daunt, 1955, 'A Philological and Topographical note on Cissbury', *BNJ* 28, 281–2; For Cricklade see H. D. S. Shortt, 1948, 'The Mints of Wiltshire: From Eadgar to Henry III', *Archaeological Journal* 104, 112–32 at 116; For Pevensey see Metcalf, 1998, 237. The Cissbury mint was most likely located in Sussex, on a fortified hill described as 'west of Lewes and east of Chichester', both of which were major mints. Cricklade was a royal burgh in Wiltshire that was possibly fortified as a defense on the Thames against the Danes. Pevensey mint was attached to the castle of the same name.

[20] S. Keynes, 2013b, 'Cynethryth', in M. Lapidge, ed., *The Wiley-Blackwell Encyclopedia of Anglo-Saxon England*, 133. Bedford is also

name sequences for every mint in operation from 973 to 1086 can be found in the fourth set of downloadable supplemental materials accompanying this book.

Table 4.1. Name Sequences of the London Mint

Moneyer Name	Name Sequence	Activity Range
Ægnulf	Æg - 1	995–997
Ægfrie	Æg - 2	1023–1029
Ægelweard	Ægel - 1a	1023–1029
Ægelwine	Ægel - 1b	1023–1036
Ægelweard	Ægel - 2	1040–1044
Ægelwig	Ægel - 3	1046–1050
Ægelric	Ægel - 4	1048–1050
Ægelred	Ægel - 5	1050–1053
Ægelric	Ægel - 6a	1053–1056
Ægelwig	Ægel - 6b	1053–1056
Ægelwine	Ægel - 6c	1053–1056
Ægelweard	Ægel - 6d	1053–1059
Ægelwine	Ægel - 7	1062–1065
Ægelwine	Ægel - 8	1068–1070
Ægelric	Ægel - 9	1070–1072
Ægelwine	Ægel - 10	1072–1074
Ælfnoth	Ælf - 1	973–975
Ælfweard	Ælf - 2	975–978
Ælfstan	Ælf - 3a	979–985
Ælfweald	Ælf - 3b	979–985
Ælfwine	Ælf - 3c	979–985
Ælfgar	Ælf - 3d	979–997
Ælfgæt	Ælf - 4a	985–997
Ælfnoth	Ælf - 4b	985–997
Ælfweard	Ælf - 4c	985–1003
Ælfstan	Ælf - 5a	991–997
Ælfwig	Ælf - 5b	991–997
Ælfric	Ælf - 5c	991–1003
Ælfwine	Ælf - 5d	991–1038
Ælfred	Ælf - 6	997–1003
Ælfwig	Ælf - 7	1003–1036
Ælfgæt	Ælf - 8a	1009–1016
Ælfnoth	Ælf - 8b	1009–1016
Ælfric	Ælf - 8c	1009–1016
Ælfsige	Ælf - 8d	1009–1016
Ælfweard	Ælf - 8e	1009–1016
Ælf	Ælf - 9a	1017–1023
Ælfstan	Ælf - 9b	1017–1036
Ælfgæt	Ælf - 10a	1023–1029
Ælfgar	Ælf - 10b	1023–1029
Ælfweard	Ælf - 10c	1023–1036
Ælfred	Ælf - 10d	1023–1038
Ælfric	Ælf - 10e	1023–1042
Ælfwig Swencel	Ælf - 11	1029–1036
Ælfnoth	Ælf - 12a	1036–1038
Ælfweald	Ælf - 12b	1036–1038
Ælfred	Ælf - 13a	1040–1042
Ælfweard	Ælf - 13b	1040–1046
Ælfwine	Ælf - 13c	1040–1056
Ælfwig	Ælf - 14	1042–1050
Ælfgar	Ælf - 15a	1044–1048
Ælfred	Ælf - 15b	1044–1062
Ælfsige	Ælf - 16	1046–1048
Ælf	Ælf - 17a	1048–1050
Ælfgæt	Ælf - 17b	1048–1050
Ælfstan	Ælf - 17c	1048–1050
Ælfweald	Ælf - 17d	1048–1050
Ælfgar	Ælf - 18a	1050–1053
Ælfsige	Ælf - 18b	1050–1053
Ælfwig	Ælf - 19a	1053–1056
Ælfweard	Ælf - 19b	1053–1066
Ælfsige	Ælf - 20	1056–1066
Ælfwine	Ælf - 21	1059–1062
Ælfwine	Ælf - 22a	1066–1070
Ælfsige	Ælf - 22b	1066–1072
Ælfwine	Ælf - 23	1072–1074
Ælfwine	Ælf - 24	1080–1083
Ælfred	Ælf - 25	1083–1086
Æthelsige	Æthel - 1a	973–975
Æthelstan	Æthel - 1b	973–978
Æthelweald	Æthel - 1c	973–979
Æthelred	Æthel - 1d	973–997
Æthelweard	Æthel - 2a	979–985
Æthelstan	Æthel - 2b	979–985
Æthelulf	Æthel - 3	985–991
Æthelwine	Æthel - 4a	991–997
Æthelweard	Æthel - 4b	991–1029

thought to be the burial place of Offa.

Table 4.1 ***continued***

Moneyer Name	Name Sequence	Activity Range
Æthelfrith	Æthel - 5a	997–1003
Æthelric	Æthel - 5b	997–1029
Æthelmær	Æthel - 6a	1003–1009
Æthelwine	Æthel - 6b	1003–1036
Æthelnoth	Æthel - 7a	1009–1016
Æthelred	Æthel - 7b	1009–1016
Æthelwig	Æthel - 7c	1009–1016
Æthelman	Æthel - 7d	1009–1023
Æthelbeorht	Æthel - 8a	1023–1029
Æthelgæt	Æthel - 8b	1023–1029
Æthelnoth	Æthel - 8c	1023–1029
Æthelwig	Æthel - 8d	1023–1036
Æthelwine	Æthel - 9a	1040–1042
Æthelweard	Æthel - 9b	1040–1044
Æthelgar	Æthel - 10a	1044–1046
Æthelman	Æthel - 10b	1044–1046
Æthelric	Æthel - 10c	1044–1046
Æthelwig	Æthel - 10d	1044–1050
Æthelric	Æthel - 11	1048–1050
Æthelric	Æthel - 12	1053–1056
Æthelwig	Æthel - 13a	1062–1065
Æthelwine	Æthel - 13b	1062–1065
Æwi	Æw - 1	1050–1053
Æwi	Æw - 2	1083–1086
Beorhtsige	Beorht - 1	979–985
Beorhtlaf	Beorht - 2	985–1003
Beorhtmær	Beorht - 3	991–997
Beorhtfrith	Beorht - 4a	1009–1023
Beorhtweald	Beorht - 4b	1009–1023
Beorhtnoth	Beorht - 4c	1009–1036
Beorhtmær	Beorht - 4d	1009–1042
Beorhtræd	Beorht - 5	1023–1036
Beorhtwine	Beorht - 6	1029–1036
Beorhtræd	Beorht - 7	1038–1040
Beorhtwine	Beorht - 8	1040–1044
Beorhtmær	Beorht - 9a	1044–1046
Beorhtræd	Beorht - 9b	1044–1056
Beorhtsige	Beorht - 10a	1050–1053
Beorhtwine	Beorht - 10b	1050–1056
Beorhtmær	Beorht - 11	1053–1056
Beorhtric	Beorht - 12	1070–1072
Beorhtmær	Beorht - 13a	1074–1077
Beorhtric	Beorht - 13b	1074–1077
Beorhtwine	Beorht - 14	1080–1086
Beornwulf	Beorn - 1	979–991
Beornfrith	Beorn - 2	1009–1016
Brunsige	Brun - 1	979–985
Brunstan	Brun - 2	997–1009
Brunman	Brun - 3	1009–1038
Brun	Brun - 4	1017–1023
Brunic	Brun - 5a	1023–1029
Brungar	Brun - 5b	1023–1046
Brunmar	Brun - 6	1029–1036
Brun	Brun - 7	1036–1038
Brun	Brun - 8a	1040–1042
Brunman	Brun - 8b	1040–1042
Brunman	Brun - 9	1046–1048
Brungar	Brun - 10	1053–1056
Brunic	Brun - 11	1083–1086
Burred	Bur - 1	1044–1046
Burred	Bur - 2	1048–1053
Burnsige	Burn - 1	979–991
Burnmær	Burn - 2	995–997
Coleman	Col - 1	1017–1023
Colspegen	Col - 2	1072–1074
Cynesige	Cyne - 1	979–991
Cyneweald	Cyne - 2a	1036–1038
Cynewig	Cyne - 2b	1036–1038
Cynemær	Cyne - 3	1048–1050
Deorsige	Deor - 1	991–997
Deorwulf	Deor - 2	997–1003
Deorman	Deor - 3	1009–1016
Deorsige	Deor - 4	1017–1023
Deorman	Deor - 5	1036–1038
Deorman	Deor - 6	1044–1046
Deorman	Deor - 7	1048–1050
Deorman	Deor - 8	1056–1059
Duding	Dud - 1	1036–1038
Duding	Dud - 2	1042–1046
Duding	Dud - 3	1048–1053
Durred	Dur - 1	1048–1050
Duric	Dur - 2	1059–1062
Eawig	Ea - 1	1046–1048
Eawig	Ea - 2	1050–1053

Table 4.1 ***continued***

Moneyer Name	Name Sequence	Activity Range
Eadweald	Ead - 1a	979–985
Eadhelm	Ead - 1b	979–991
Eadnoth	Ead - 2a	985–991
Eadsige	Ead - 2b	985–991
Eadwi	Ead - 2c	985–991
Eadwig	Ead - 2d	985–997
Eadmund	Ead - 2e	985–1036
Eadwine	Ead - 2f	985–1040
Eadweald	Ead - 3	991–1046
Eadweard	Ead - 4a	995–997
Eadwi	Ead - 4b	995–997
Eadsige	Ead - 4c	995–1029
Eadric	Ead - 5	997–1003
Eadgar	Ead - 6a	1003–1009
Eadwig	Ead - 6b	1003–1029
Eadweard	Ead - 6c	1003–1036
Eadsme	Ead - 7a	1009–1016
Eadwi	Ead - 7b	1009–1016
Eadric	Ead - 7c	1009–1048
Eadnoth	Ead - 8a	1017–1023
Eadgar	Ead - 8b	1017–1029
Eadhelm	Ead - 9a	1023–1029
Eadwulf	Ead - 9b	1023–1036
Eadred	Ead - 9c	1023–1038
Eadnoth	Ead - 10	1029–1036
Eadwig	Ead - 11	1036–1038
Eadweard	Ead - 12	1038–1042
Eadwig	Ead - 13	1040–1042
Eadmund	Ead - 14	1042–1048
Eadwi	Ead - 15a	1044–1046
Eadwine	Ead - 15b	1044–1056
Eadred	Ead - 16	1046–1048
Eadweald	Ead - 17a	1048–1050
Eadwig	Ead - 17b	1048–1059
Eadmund	Ead - 18a	1050–1053
Eadsige	Ead - 18b	1050–1053
Eadred	Ead - 18c	1050–1056
Eadric	Ead - 19a	1053–1056
Eadweald	Ead - 19b	1053–1056
Eadgar	Ead - 20a	1059–1062
Eadwine	Ead - 20b	1059–1077
Eadgar	Ead - 21a	1065–1066
Eadric	Ead - 21b	1065–1066
Eadric	Ead - 22	1070–1072
Eadwi	Ead - 23	1077–1086
Eadwig	Ead - 24	1080–1083
Eadric	Ead - 25	1083–1086
Ealdgar	Eald - 1	1003–1009
Ealdred	Eald - 2	1009–1023
Ealdgar	Eald - 3	1042–1046
Ealdwine	Eald - 4	1044–1046
Ealdgar	Eald - 5	1048–1059
Ealdred	Eald - 6	1050–1053
Ealdulf	Eald - 7	1053–1056
Ealdgar	Eald - 8	1062–1072
Ealhstan	Ealh - 1	979–997
Ealhsige	Ealh - 2	1044–1046
Eastmær	East - 1	1044–1046
Eastmund	East - 2	1053–1056
Eastmund	East - 3	1062–1065
Etsige	Et - 1	1023–1029
Etsige	Et - 2	1050–1053
Frith	Frith - 1a	1017–1023
Frithwine	Frith - 1b	1017–1023
Frithwine	Frith - 2	1029–1036
God	God - 1a	979–985
Godric	God - 1b	979–985
Goda	God - 1c	979–997
Godwine	God - 1d	979–1062
Godhere	God - 2a	991–997
Godric	God - 2b	991–1040
God	God - 3a	995–997
Godra	God - 3b	995–997
Godman	God - 4	997–1042
Godhere	God - 5a	1003–1036
Goda	God - 5b	1003–1038
Godwig	God - 6	1017–1023
God	God - 7a	1029–1036
Goding	God - 7b	1029–1036
Godwine Stew	God - 8a	1036–1038
Godsige	God - 8b	1036–1040
God	God - 9	1038–1040
Goda	God - 10a	1040–1042
Godric Calic	God - 10b	1040–1042

Table 4.1 ***continued***

Moneyer Name	Name Sequence	Activity Range
Godwig	God - 11	1042–1044
Godman	God - 12a	1044–1046
Godsunu	God - 12b	1044–1053
Godwig	God - 13a	1046–1050
Godric	God - 13b	1046–1077
Godhere	God - 14a	1053–1056
Godman	God - 14b	1053–1056
Godwig	God - 14c	1053–1056
Godwine	God - 15	1068–1072
Godwine	God - 16	1074–1080
Godric	God - 17a	1083–1086
Godwine	God - 17b	1083–1086
Goldwine	Gold - 1	991–997
Goldwine	Gold - 2	1009–1016
Goldsige	Gold - 3	1036–1044
Goldsige	Gold - 4	1046–1056
Goldwine	Gold - 5	1059–1062
Grim	Grim - 1	1009–1023
Grim	Grim - 2	1029–1036
Leofheah	Leof - 1	975–978
Leofric	Leof - 2a	979–985
Leofstan	Leof - 2b	979–1003
Leofwine	Leof - 3	985–1040
Leofing	Leof - 4a	991–1042
Leofric	Leof - 4b	991–1046
Leofred	Leof - 4c	991–1056
Leofnoth	Leof - 5	997–1003
Leofweald	Leof - 6	1003–1036
Leofheah	Leof - 7a	1009–1016
Leofnoth	Leof - 7b	1009–1016
Leofwig	Leof - 7c	1009–1036
Leofstan	Leof - 7d	1009–1046
Leofsige	Leof - 8a	1017–1029
Leofweard	Leof - 8b	1017–1036
Leofgar	Leof - 9a	1023–1029
Leofmær	Leof - 9b	1023–1029
Leofman	Leof - 9c	1023–1029
Leofa	Leof - 10	1029–1036
Leofing	Leof - 11a	1046–1053
Leofwine	Leof - 11b	1046–1059
Leofnoth	Leof - 12a	1048–1050
Leofwig	Leof - 12b	1048–1050
Leofsige	Leof - 13	1050–1053
Leofæg	Leof - 14a	1056–1059
Leofing	Leof - 14b	1056–1062
Leofric	Leof - 15	1059–1062
Leofsige	Leof - 16	1066–1066
Leofsige	Leof - 17	1068–1070
Man	Man - 1	1036–1038
Manic	Man - 2	1077–1080
Ecferth	None	985–991
Sidewine	None	985–997
Heahwulf	None	991–1003
Drihtweald	None	995–997
Blundered	None	1003–1009
Ælman	None	1009–1016
Sunegod	None	1009–1016
Eardnoth	None	1009–1023
Borstig	None	1017–1023
Holeman	None	1017–1023
Aslac	None	1023–1029
Dunstan	None	1023–1029
Gauti	None	1023–1029
Sæwine	None	1023–1029
Enfdici	None	1029–1036
Swan	None	1029–1036
Wadweald	None	1029–1036
Farmann	None	1036–1038
Ulfcetel	None	1036–1038
Widia	None	1036–1038
Corf	None	1036–1042
Orlaf	None	1042–1044
Alric	None	1046–1048
Sneiman	None	1046–1048
Wihtred	None	1046–1048
Burgræd	None	1050–1053
Bricsige	None	1050–1053
Spracling	None	1050–1053
Glifwine	None	1053–1056
Idcefis	None	1068–1070
Blacsunu	None	1072–1074
Beriteri	None	1080–1083
Oda	Od - 1	991–997
Oda	Od - 2	1009–1016

Table 4.1 ***continued***

Moneyer Name	Name Sequence	Activity Range
Oda	Od - 3	1036–1037
Oscetel	Os - 1a	979–1003
Osulf	Os - 1b	979–1023
Osfrith	Os - 2	985–991
Osmund	Os - 3	991–997
Osmund	Os - 4a	1009–1023
Oswald	Os - 4b	1009–1016
Oswig	Os - 4c	1009–1016
Osfrith	Os - 5a	1029–1036
Osulf	Os - 5b	1029–1036
Osmund	Os - 6	1053–1062
Osmund	Os - 7	1066–1066
Sibwine	Sib - 1	979–985
Sibwine	Sib - 2	991–1016
Sibode	Sib - 3	1070–1072
Sigeweard	Sige - 1a	1017–1023
Sigenoth	Sige - 1b	1017–1029
Sigered	Sige - 2	1023–1029
Sigered	Sige - 3	1053–1056
Sired	Sir - 1	1023–1029
Sired	Sir - 2	1053–1056
Stithulf	Stith - 1	1003–1009
Stithulf	Stith - 2	1023–1029
Swarting	Swart - 1	995–1003
Swartgar	Swart - 2	1003–1009
Swetman	Swe - 5	1062–1068
Swegen	Sweg - 1	1009–1016
Swegen	Sweg - 2	1029–1036
Sweting	Swet - 1	985–1023
Sweting	Swet - 2a	1029–1036
Swetman	Swet - 2b	1029–1036
Swetman	Swet - 3	1044–1050
Swetman	Swet - 4	1053–1056
Theodred	Theod - 1	985–991
Theodred	Theod - 2	1003–1009
Theodred	Theod - 3	1023–1029
Theodred	Theod - 4	1042–1046
Thorcetel	Thor - 1	1023–1029
Thor	Thor - 2a	1048–1050
Thorfrith	Thor - 2b	1048–1050
Toca	Toc - 1	997–1009
Toca	Toc - 2	1023–1029
Uhtred	Uht - 1	1046–1048
Uhtred	Uht - 2	1070–1072
Wigfrith	Wig - 1	973–978
Wigfend	Wig - 2	975–978
Winesige	Wine - 1	979–985
Winesige	Wine - 2	1009–1042
Winestan	Wine - 3	1017–1029
Wine	Wine - 4	1062–1065
Winediec	Wine - 5	1072–1074
Wulfmær	Wulf - 1a	979–991
Wulfric	Wulf - 1b	979–991
Wulfstan	Wulf - 1c	979–1029
Wulfgar	Wulf - 2a	991–997
Wulfwine	Wulf - 2b	991–1040
Wulfnoth	Wulf - 3	995–997
Wulfsige	Wulf - 4a	997–1003
Wulfric	Wulf - 4b	997–1036
Wulfgar	Wulf - 5a	1003–1009
Wulfred	Wulf - 5b	1003–1036
Wulfbeald	Wulf - 6	1009–1016
Wulfsige	Wulf - 7a	1017–1023
Wulfweard	Wulf - 7b	1017–1023
Wulfnoth	Wulf - 7c	1017–1029
Wulfgar	Wulf - 7d	1017–1038
Wulfmær	Wulf - 8	1023–1029
Wulfnoth	Wulf - 9	1036–1038
Wulf	Wulf - 10a	1038–1040
Wulfsige	Wulf - 10b	1038–1042
Wulfstan	Wulf - 10c	1038–1044
Wulfgar	Wulf - 11a	1040–1044
Wulfred	Wulf - 11b	1040–1042
Wulfric	Wulf - 12a	1042–1044
Wulfwine	Wulf - 12b	1042–1059
Wulfsige	Wulf - 13a	1044–1046
Wulfred	Wulf - 13b	1044–1053
Wulfsic	Wulf - 14a	1046–1048
Wulfric	Wulf - 14b	1046–1050
Wulfsige	Wulf - 15a	1048–1050
Wulfwig	Wulf - 15b	1048–1050
Wulfcrdd	Wulf - 16a	1050–1053
Wulfweard	Wulf - 16b	1050–1053
Wulfric	Wulf - 17a	1053–1059

Table 4.1 ***continued***

Moneyer Name	Name Sequence	Activity Range
Wulfgar	Wulf - 17b	1053–1066
Wulfnoth	Wulf - 18a	1056–1059
Wulfred	Wulf - 18b	1056–1059
Wulfsi	Wulf - 19a	1062–1065
Wulfsige	Wulf - 19b	1062–1066
Wulfweard	Wulf - 19c	1062–1066
Wulfwine	Wulf - 20	1066–1072
Wulfie	Wulf - 21a	1072–1074
Wulfric	Wulf - 21b	1072–1074
Wulfweard	Wulf - 22	1074–1077
Wulfwine	Wulf - 23	1080–1083

Table 4.2. Name Sequences of York Mint

Moneyer Name	Name Sequence	Activity Range
Ægelwine	Ægel - 1	1029–1036
Ægelmær	Ægel - 2	1038–1040
Ælfstan	Ælf - 1	975–978
Ælfstan	Ælf - 2	979–985
Ælfhere	Ælf - 3	991–997
Ælfstan	Ælf - 4	1009–1029
Ælfwine	Ælf - 5a	1038–1040
Ælfhere	Ælf - 5b	1038–1050
Ælfwine	Ælf - 6	1044–1053
Ælfstan	Ælf - 7	1046–1048
Æthelweald	Æthel - 1	975–978
Æthelwine	Æthel - 2	1023–1036
Æthelmær	Æthel - 3a	1038–1040
Æthelwine	Æthel - 3b	1038–1046
Aleof	Aleof - 1	1065–1066
Aleof	Aleof - 2	1072–1077
Aleof	Aleof - 3	1083–1086
Althwulf	Alth - 1	1068–1070
Althwulf	Alth - 2	1074–1077
Arncetel	Arn - 1	978–979
Arnthor	Arn - 2	991–1016
Arncetel	Arn - 3	995–997
Arncetel	Arn - 4	1017–1042
Arnolf	Arn - 5	1023–1029
Arngrim	Arn - 6	1029–1036
Arncill	Arn - 7a	1038–1040
Arngrim	Arn - 7b	1038–1065
Arncetel	Arn - 8	1044–1056
Arncetel	Arn - 9	1059–1066
Arncetel	Arn - 10	1068–1070
Asbeorn	As - 1	979–985
Asgout	As - 2	1023–1029
Beorhtwine	Beorht - 1	1003–1009
Beorhtnoth	Beorht - 2	997–1029
Beorhtwine	Beorht - 3	991–997
Beornnoth	Beorn - 1	1017–1023
Beorn	Beorn - 2	1029–1046
Cetel	Cetel - 1	991–1029
Cetelbeorn	Cetel - 2	1003–1009
Cetel	Cetel - 3	1040–1046
Colgrim	Col - 1	979–985
Colgrim	Col - 2	1003–1023
Colgrim	Col - 3	1029–1036
Coll	Col - 4	1046–1053
Ellaf	El - 1	979–985
Elfere	El - 2	1044–1046
Eltan	El - 3	1046–1050
Farmann	Far - 1	978–985
Fargrim	Far - 2	1017–1036
Farthegn	Far - 3	1023–1036
Fastolf	Fast - 1	973–975
Fastolf	Fast - 2	978–985
Fastolf	Fast - 3	1017–1023
Frostulf	Frost - 1	979–985
Frostulf	Frost - 2	991–1003
Godman	God - 1	1017–1036
Goding	God - 2a	1038–1040
Godman	God - 2b	1038–1040
Golla	Golla - 1	979–985
Golla	Golla - 2	991–997
Gunner	Gun - 1a	975–978
Gunnulf	Gun - 1b	975–978
Gunhwæt	Gun - 2	991–997
Gunhwæt	Gun - 3	1017–1023
Gunnulf	Gun - 4	1044–1046
Harthulf	Harth - 1	1068–1070
Harthulf	Harth - 2	1072–1080
Hrafn	Hrafn - 1	1029–1036
Hrafn	Hrafn - 2	1044–1050

Table 4.2 ***continued***

Moneyer Name	Name Sequence	Activity Range
Hrafn	Hrafn - 3	1053–1056
Hundulf	Hun - 1	979–985
Hundulf	Hun - 2	991–1009
Iohan	Io - 1	973–975
Iole	Io - 2	991–997
Iole	Io - 3	1042–1062
Iocil	Io - 4a	1044–1046
Iolana	Io - 4b	1044–1046
Io	Io - 5a	1046–1048
Iocetel	Io - 5b	1046–1050
Iola	Io - 6	1048–1059
Iocetel	Io - 7	1053–1066
Ire	Ir - 1	997–1009
Ire	Ir - 2	1023–1029
Isulf	Is - 1	973–985
Isulf	Is - 2	1009–1016
Iustan	Iu - 1	975–978
Iurerel	Iu - 2	1046–1048
Leofman	Leof - 1a	991–997
Leofwine	Leof - 1b	991–997
Leofstan	Leof - 1c	991–1003
Leofwine	Leof - 2	1009–1016
Leofwine	Leof - 3	1017–1023
Leofnoth	Leof - 4	1046–1059
Leofing	Leof - 5	1066–1066
Leofsige	Leof - 6	1068–1070
Leifinc	Leof - 7	1080–1086
Man	Man - 1a	973–975
Manna	Man - 1b	973–975
Man	Man - 2	978–979
Man	Man - 3	1044–1046
Brentinc	None	973–975
Dunn	None	973–978
Beaniene	None	975–978
Boiga	None	975–978
Ealhstan	None	975–978
Surclos	None	975–978
Winbeald	None	975–978
Beolan	None	975–985
Cieolog	None	978–979
Uri	None	978–979
Fællan	None	979–985
Herewulf	None	979–985
Hwætman	None	979–985
Scadwine	None	979–985
Scanig	None	979–985
Wineman	None	979–985
Oge	None	991–997
Eadric	None	991–1003
Wengos	None	991–1003
Hildulf	None	991–1036
Theodred	None	997–1003
Deorwulf	None	1009–1016
Bretecol	None	1009–1023
Dagfin	None	1009–1023
Selecol	None	1017–1023
Toca	None	1017–1029
Frithcol	None	1017–1036
Crinan	None	1023–1029
Grurn	None	1023–1029
Oustman	None	1023–1029
Surtinc	None	1023–1029
Crucan	None	1023–1038
Grimulf	None	1023–1046
Earngrim	None	1029–1036
Landfrith	None	1029–1036
Ucede	None	1029–1042
Duracan	None	1036–1038
Swegen	None	1036–1044
Scule	None	1036–1066
Thærdine	None	1040–1042
Sæfugel	None	1042–1050
Egann	None	1044–1046
Æitel	None	1050–1053
Etyrcol	None	1050–1053
Sutere	None	1066–1066
Roscetel	None	1066–1070
Inleif	None	1068–1070
Arthulf	None	1072–1074
Oban	Ob - 1	979–985
Oban	Ob - 2	991–1009
Oda	Oda - 1	973–985
Oda	Oda - 2	991–1003
Osmund	Os - 1	973–975

Table 4.2 ***continued***

Moneyer Name	Name Sequence	Activity Range
Osulf	Os - 2a	973–978
Oscetel	Os - 2b	973–979
Osulf	Os - 3	979–985
Osulf	Os - 4	991–997
Oscetel	Os - 5	995–1003
Osgot	Os - 6	1003–1036
Osfrith	Os - 7	1017–1023
Othgrim	Oth - 1	979–985
Othcetel	Oth - 2a	991–997
Othulf	Oth - 2b	991–997
Othgrim	Oth - 2c	991–1023
Othan	Oth - 3a	1029–1036
Othin	Oth - 3b	1029–1042
Othen	Oth - 4a	1044–1046
Othin	Oth - 4b	1044–1048
Othgrim	Oth - 5	1056–1070
Othbeorn	Oth - 6	1059–1070
Othulf	Oth - 7	1062–1066
Othgrim	Oth - 8	1072–1074
Othbeorn	Oth - 9	1083–1086
Pitherwine	Pither - 1	1023–1029
Pitherwine	Pither - 2	1036–1040
Rægenbeald	Ræ - 1	975–979
Ræfen	Ræ - 2	1029–1036
Ræfen	Ræ - 3	1044–1048
Ræfen	Ræ - 4	1053–1056
Snecol	Sne - 1	979–985
Snecol	Sne - 2	1009–1023
Snebeorn	Sne - 3	1056–1066
Stirgar	Stir - 1a	975–978
Stir	Stir - 1b	975–985
Stirgar	Stir - 2	979–985
Stirgar	Stir - 3	991–1003
Stircol	Stir - 4	1009–1029
Stirgar	Stir - 5	1017–1023
Stircol	Stir - 6	1036–1042
Stircol	Stir - 7	1044–1048
Stircol	Stir - 8	1050–1056
Sumerlida	Sumer - 1	991–1003
Sumerlida	Sumer - 2	1009–1016
Sunulf	Sun - 1	979–985
Sunulf	Sun - 2	991–1003
Sunulf	Sun - 3	1009–1038
Swerting	Swert - 1	978–979
Swertcol	Swert - 2a	991–997
Swerting	Swert - 2b	991–997
Swert	Swert - 2c	991–1003
Swerting	Swert - 3	1017–1029
Swert	Swert - 4	1038–1040
Swertcol	Swert - 5	1050–1066
Swertcol	Swert - 6	1068–1070
Thorstan	Thor - 1	978–985
Thorcetel	Thor - 2	979–985
Thorcetel	Thor - 3a	991–997
Thorstan	Thor - 3b	991–1016
Thorulf	Thor - 4	997–1016
Thorgrim	Thor - 5	1029–1042
Thorgrim	Thor - 6	1044–1048
Thor	Thor - 7	1046–1066
Thor	Thor - 8	1068–1070
Thor	Thor - 9	1077–1080
Thor	Thor - 10	1083–1086
Tuma	Tum - 1	973–975
Tuma	Tum - 2	978–985
Tumne	Tum - 3	979–985
Ulf	Ulf - 1	979–985
Ulfcetel	Ulf - 2	991–1023
Ulfcetel	Ulf - 3	1040–1066
Ulfcetel	Ulf - 4	1068–1070
Unspac	Un - 1	973–975
Unolf	Un - 2	1042–1046
Winterlida	Winter - 1	991–997
Winterfugol	Winter - 2	1050–1056
Withrin	With - 1	1023–1029
Withrin	With - 2	1036–1042
Wulfric	Wulf - 1	973–975
Wulfstan	Wulf - 2	979–985
Wulfsige	Wulf - 3	991–1016
Wulfstan	Wulf - 4	1009–1029
Wulfgrim	Wulf - 5	1017–1023
Wulfnoth	Wulf - 6	1023–1036
Wulfric	Wulf - 7	1040–1042
Wulfwine	Wulf - 8	1046–1048
Wulf	Wulf - 9	1066–1068

Table 4.3. Name Sequences of Lincoln Mint

Moneyer Name	Name Sequence	Activity Range
Ælfgeat	Ælf - 1a	997–1003
Ælfsige	Ælf - 1b	997–1003
Ælfric	Ælf - 2	1009–1023
Ælfnoth	Ælf - 3	1017–1042
Ælfwici	Ælf - 4	1038–1040
Ælfnoth	Ælf - 5	1044–1046
Ælfnoth	Ælf - 6	1048–1062
Ælfwine	Ælf - 7	1059–1062
Ælfgeat	Ælf - 8a	1065–1066
Ælfmær	Ælf - 8b	1065–1066
Ælfmær	Ælf - 9	1068–1070
Æscman	Æsc - 1	973–975
Æscman	Æsc - 2	979–985
Æscman	Æsc - 3	991–1003
Æscman	Æsc - 4	1009–1016
Æthelnoth	Æthel - 1	991–1016
Æthelred	Æthel - 2a	1009–1016
Æthelnoth	Æthel - 2b	1009–1023
Æthelmær	Æthel - 2c	1009–1036
Æthelnoth	Æthel - 3	1038–1040
Æthelnoth	Æthel - 4	1046–1048
Æthelmær	Æthel - 5	1065–1066
Agmund	Ag - 1	1062–1065
Agmund	Ag - 2	1062–1065
Agmund	Ag - 3	1068–1070
Aslac	As - 1	1017–1029
Asferth	As - 2	1023–1029
Aslac	As - 3	1059–1062
Beorhtric	Beorht - 1	1029–1038
Beorhtric	Beorht - 2	1040–1053
Cetelbeorn	Cetel - 1	991–997
Cetelbeorn	Cetel - 2	1003–1016
Colgrim	Col - 1	979–985
Colgrim	Col - 2	991–1003
Colswegen	Col - 3	1009–1016
Colgrim	Col - 4	1023–1042
Colgrim	Col - 5	1044–1056
Eadsige	Ead - 1	991–1003
Eadweald	Ead - 2	1003–1009
Eadsige	Ead - 3	1009–1016
Eadmund	Ead - 4a	1017–1023
Eadweald	Ead - 4b	1017–1023
Eadric	Ead - 5a	1036–1038
Eadwine	Ead - 5b	1036–1038
Eadmund	Ead - 6a	1040–1044
Eadric	Ead - 6b	1040–1050
Eadric	Ead - 7	1062–1066
Eanwulf	Ean - 1	973–978
Eanmund	Ean - 2	1062–1065
Farthegn	Far - 1	975–978
Farthegn	Far - 2	979–985
Garfin	Gar - 1	991–997
Garfin	Gar - 2	1062–1066
Garwig	Gar - 3	1066–1068
Gife	Gif - 1	991–997
Gife	Gif - 2	1059–1065
Gifel	Gif - 3	1068–1072
Goding	God - 1	975–985
Godwine	God - 2	1003–1036
Godric	God - 3	1017–1062
Goda	God - 4	1023–1029
Godric Spot	God - 5	1029–1036
Godwine	God - 6	1038–1040
Grim	Grim - 1	978–979
Grim	Grim - 2	991–1003
Grimcetel	Grim - 3	997–1003
Grimcetel	Grim - 4	1017–1029
Grind	Grind - 1	973–985
Grind	Grind - 2	991–997
Leofing	Leof - 1	973–985
Leofwig	Leof - 2	975–978
Leofman	Leof - 3	991–997
Leofric	Leof - 4	997–1003
Leofing	Leof - 5	1003–1038
Leofric	Leof - 6a	1009–1023
Leofwine	Leof - 6b	1009–1050
Leofman	Leof - 7a	1023–1029
Leofthegn	Leof - 7b	1023–1029
Leofa	Leof - 8	1029–1036
Leofric	Leof - 9a	1036–1038
Leofthegn	Leof - 9b	1036–1038
Leofnoth	Leof - 9c	1036–1040
Leofwig	Leof - 9d	1036–1044
Leofing	Leof - 10	1040–1042

Table 4.3 ***continued***

Moneyer Name	Name Sequence	Activity Range
Leofnoth	Leof - 11	1044–1046
Leofwine	Leof - 12	1062–1065
Leofnoth	Leof - 13	1070–1072
Man	Man - 1	1009–1029
Man	Man - 2	1048–1059
Manna	Man - 3	1050–1053
Manna	Man - 4	1056–1059
Matathan	Mat - 1	1017–1040
Matan	Mat - 2a	1023–1029
Matathan Balluc	Mat - 2b	1023–1038
Adelaver	None	975–978
Hafgrim	None	975–979
Levig	None	975–979
Rodbert	None	975–985
Rægenweald	None	997–1016
Dreng	None	997–1023
Boiga	None	1003–1016
Bruntat	None	1003–1029
Sunegod	None	1003–1029
Eamær	None	1009–1016
Snelling	None	1009–1023
Iustan	None	1009–1029
Crinan	None	1017–1036
Ægelmær	None	1023–1029
Eustan	None	1023–1029
Cnut	None	1029–1036
Harthacnut	None	1029–1038
Swafa	None	1029–1044
Wælræfn	None	1029–1044
Conrin	None	1036–1038
Hildulf	None	1036–1038
Pælræfen	None	1036–1038
Pororie	None	1038–1040
Wororic	None	1038–1040
Guthfrith	None	1042–1044
Udd	None	1044–1046
Wineman	None	1046–1048
Wilgrip	None	1048–1050
Auti	None	1050–1066
Outti	None	1065–1066
Ginch	None	1066–1068
Iegner	None	1068–1070
Sinferth	None	1072–1074
Wihtric	None	1074–1077
Ansthuc	None	1074–1080
Osfrith	Os - 1	978–979
Oscut	Os - 2a	997–1003
Osmund	Os - 2b	997–1009
Osgeat	Os - 2c	997–1029
Osfrith	Os - 2d	997–1059
Osfram	Os - 3	1009–1016
Oslac	Os - 4	1017–1038
Osfram	Os - 5a	1023–1029
Osmund	Os - 5b	1023–1029
Osmund	Os - 6	1036–1042
Oslac	Os - 7	1050–1053
Oslac	Os - 8	1059–1066
Othgrim	Oth - 1	997–1023
Othbeorn	Oth - 2	1009–1023
Othbeorn	Oth - 3	1036–1038
Othgrim	Oth - 4	1036–1042
Othbeorn	Oth - 5	1040–1042
Othgrim	Oth - 6	1048–1066
Othbeorn	Oth - 7	1050–1056
Othgrim	Oth - 8	1068–1070
Siferth	Si - 1	1068–1070
Siferth	Si - 2	1083–1086
Sifweard	Sif - 1	1068–1070
Sifweard	Sif - 2	1074–1077
Sigeweard	Sige - 1	1070–1072
Sigeferth	Sige - 2	1074–1077
Sigeferth	Sige - 3	1083–1086
Stegenbit	Stegen - 1	991–1003
Stegencetel	Stegen - 2	1003–1009
Sumerlida	Sumer - 1	997–1029
Sumerlida	Sumer - 2	1036–1044
Swarting	Swart - 1	978–1009
Swartebrand	Swart - 2	1017–1038
Swarting	Swart - 3	1023–1046
Swart	Swart - 4	1029–1036
Swart	Swart - 5	1065–1066
Theodgeld	Theod - 1	979–985
Theodred	Theod - 2a	991–997
Theodgeld	Theod - 2b	991–1003
Theodulf	Theod - 3	1003–1009
Thorcetel	Thor - 1	1009–1016

Table 4.3 *continued*

Moneyer Name	Name Sequence	Activity Range
Thorstan	Thor - 2	1036–1038
Thorgrim	Thor - 3	1040–1048
Thorcetel	Thor - 4	1056–1062
Thorstan	Thor - 5	1074–1077
Ulf	Ulf - 1	991–997
Ulfcetel	Ulf - 2	997–1029
Ulf	Ulf - 3	1042–1053
Ulf	Ulf - 4	1056–1066
Ulf	Ulf - 5	1072–1074
Ulf	Ulf - 6	1083–1086
Unbegn	Un - 1	979–985
Unbegn	Un - 2	991–1003
Unspac	Un - 3	1072–1074
Wedlos	Wed - 1	1029–1038
Wedlos	Wed - 2	1040–1042
Wulfmær	Wulf - 1a	997–1003
Wulfred	Wulf - 1b	997–1003
Wulfric	Wulf - 1c	997–1003
Wulfgeat	Wulf - 2a	1003–1009
Wulfwine	Wulf - 2b	1003–1009
Wulfric	Wulf - 3a	1009–1023
Wulfgrim	Wulf - 3b	1009–1023
Wulfheah	Wulf - 3c	1009–1023
Wulfbeorn	Wulf - 3d	1009–1036
Wulfgeat	Wulf - 4a	1017–1023
Wulfnoth	Wulf - 4b	1017–1023
Wulfwine	Wulf - 5	1023–1036
Wulfric	Wulf - 6	1029–1036
Wulfgeat	Wulf - 7	1036–1040
Wulfbeorn	Wulf - 8a	1038–1042
Wulfnoth	Wulf - 8b	1038–1042
Wulfric	Wulf - 9	1040–1044
Wulf	Wulf - 10	1044–1048
Wulfgar	Wulf - 11	1046–1048
Wulfric	Wulf - 12a	1056–1062
Wulfbeorn	Wulf - 12b	1056–1065
Wulfgar	Wulf - 13	1059–1062
Wulfgar	Wulf - 14	1065–1066
Wulfmær	Wulf - 15	1066–1066
Wulfsige	Wulf - 16	1068–1070
Wulfstan	Wulf - 17	1072–1074

Table 4.4. Name Sequences of the Winchester Mint

Moneyer Name	Name Sequence	Activity Range
Æstan	Æ - 1	1046–1048
Æstan	Æ - 2	1056–1059
Æstan	Æ - 3	1077–1080
Æstan	Æ - 4	1083–1086
Ægelric	Ægel - 1	1029–1038
Ægelwine	Ægel - 2	1038–1040
Ægelwine	Ægel - 3	1042–1044
Ægelwine	Ægel - 4	1050–1053
Ælfsige	Ælf - 1	973–975
Ælfsige	Ælf - 2	979–1003
Ælfweald	Ælf - 3	997–1016
Ælfheah	Ælf - 4a	1009–1016
Ælfmær	Ælf - 4b	1009–1016
Ælfhelm	Ælf - 4c	1009–1023
Ælfstan	Ælf - 4d	1009–1029
Ælfsige	Ælf - 4e	1009–1036
Ælfric	Ælf - 5	1017–1023
Ælfweald	Ælf - 6a	1023–1029
Ælfwine	Ælf - 6b	1023–1029
Ælfheah	Ælf - 6c	1023–1036
Ælfred	Ælf - 7a	1036–1038
Ælfweard	Ælf - 7b	1036–1038
Ælfwine	Ælf - 7c	1036–1042
Ælfwine	Ælf - 8	1044–1072
Ælfstan	Ælf - 9	1048–1050
Æthelstan	Æthel - 1	979–985
Æthelweard	Æthel - 2	985–991
Æthelstan	Æthel - 3a	991–997
Æthelgar	Æthel - 3b	991–1009
Æthelmær	Æthel - 4a	1009–1016
Æthelwine	Æthel - 4b	1009–1023
Æthelric	Æthel - 5	1017–1038
Æthelstan	Æthel - 6	1023–1059
Æthelwig	Æthel - 7	1038–1042
Æthelric	Æthel - 8	1040–1042
Anderboda	Ander - 1	1056–1068
Anderboda	Ander - 2	1070–1080
Beorhtræd	Beorht - 1a	979–997
Beorhtnoth	Beorht - 1b	979–1003
Beorhtsige	Beorht - 1c	979–1009
Beorhtmær	Beorht - 2	985–1003

Table 4.4 ***continued***

Moneyer Name	Name Sequence	Activity Range
Beorhtweald	Beorht - 3	996–1003
Beorhtric	Beorht - 4a	1009–1016
Beorhtstan	Beorht - 4b	1009–1016
Beorhtnoth	Beorht - 4c	1009–1023
Beorhtweald	Beorht - 5	1023–1029
Beorhtweald	Beorht - 6	1050–1053
Beorhtmær	Beorht - 7	1053–1062
Brunstan	Brun - 1	1003–1029
Brunstan	Brun - 2	1036–1038
Brunic	Brun - 3	1080–1086
Eadsige	Ead - 1	979–997
Eadwine	Ead - 2	985–991
Eadnoth	Ead - 3	991–997
Eadwine	Ead - 4	1009–1023
Eadweard	Ead - 5	1017–1029
Eadwine	Ead - 6	1038–1040
Eadwine	Ead - 7	1046–1050
Eadwig	Ead - 8	1048–1050
Eadric	Ead - 9	1050–1053
Frithmund	Frith - 1	973–978
Frithmund	Frith - 2	979–985
Godwine	God - 1	991–1003
Godman	God - 2	997–1016
Goda	God - 3a	1023–1029
Godioluwa	God - 3b	1023–1029
Godwine	God - 3c	1023–1062
Godman	God - 4a	1036–1038
Godwine Ceoc	God - 4b	1036–1038
Godwine Ceoc	God - 5a	1040–1042
Godman	God - 5b	1040–1044
Godric	God - 6	1044–1050
Godman	God - 7a	1053–1056
Godwine Ceoc	God - 7b	1053–1056
Godwine Widia	God - 7c	1053–1056
Godric	God - 8	1062–1065
Godwine	God - 9	1065–1066
Godric	God - 10	1066–1066
Godnoth	God - 11	1068–1072
Godwine	God - 12	1070–1072
Godwine	God - 13	1074–1086
Heahwulf	Heah - 1	991–997
Heahwulf	Heah - 2	1065–1066
Ifing	If - 1	1042–1046
Ifing	If - 2	1048–1050
Leofweald	Leof - 1	979–1029
Leofwine	Leof - 2	1003–1029
Leofsunu	Leof - 3	1009–1023
Leofstan	Leof - 4	1017–1023
Leofstan	Leof - 5	1029–1036
Leofstan	Leof - 6a	1038–1040
Leofwine	Leof - 6b	1038–1040
Leofing	Leof - 7	1040–1059
Leofwine	Leof - 8	1044–1053
Leofweald	Leof - 9	1059–1083
Leofing	Leof - 10	1062–1066
Leofwine	Leof - 11	1066–1070
Leofing	Leof - 12	1070–1080
Lifinc	Leof - 13	1080–1086
Lifweald	Leof - 14	1083–1086
Marscalc	None	973–975
Thihtsige	None	973–975
Eatstan	None	975–978
Mægenfrith	None	975–978
Ingalric	None	979–985
Toca	None	979–997
Herewulf	None	991–997
Cynna	None	997–1023
Seolca	None	1003–1023
Ordbeorht	None	1009–1023
Oda	None	1009–1029
Siboda	None	1009–1029
Sigegar	None	1017–1023
Sparafuc	None	1017–1023
Burgweald	None	1017–1029
Ladmær	None	1023–1056
Elawine	None	1038–1040
Coll	None	1048–1050
Loc	None	1048–1053
Brand	None	1050–1053
Ertan	None	1053–1056
Swerting	None	1066–1066
Garulf	None	1074–1077
Ægstan	None	1080–1083
Dimund	None	1083–1086

Table 4.4 ***continued***

Moneyer Name	Name Sequence	Activity Range
Rægenweald	Rægen - 1a	973–975
Rægenulf	Rægen - 1b	973–978
Rægenulf	Rægen - 2	979–985
Siwine	Si - 1	1017–1023
Siweard	Si - 2	1038–1044
Siwine	Si - 3	1040–1044
Siweard	Si - 4	1072–1086
Spileman	Spile - 1	997–1023
Spileman	Spile - 2	1029–1044
Spracling	Sprac - 1	1038–1040
Spracling	Sprac - 2	1056–1066
Spracling	Sprac - 3	1083–1086
Widia	Wid - 1	1036–1042
Widia	Wid - 2	1044–1046
Widia	Wid - 3	1050–1056
Wihtsige	Wiht - 1	975–978
Wihtsige	Wiht - 2	1017–1029
Wine	Wine - 1	1017–1029
Wine	Wine - 2	1040–1042
Wulfstan	Wulf - 1	979–985
Wulfgar	Wulf - 2	991–997
Wulfnoth	Wulf - 3	997–1016
Wulfric	Wulf - 4a	1017–1023
Wulfnoth	Wulf - 4b	1017–1040
Wynstan	Wyn - 1	991–997
Wynstan	Wyn - 2	1029–1036
Wynstan	Wyn - 3	1050–1053

Table 4.5. Name Sequences of the Exeter Mint

Moneyer Name	Name Sequence	Activity Range
Ælfstan	Ælf - 1	973–975
Ælfstan	Ælf - 2a	979–997
Ælfnoth	Ælf - 2b	979–1016
Ælfric	Ælf - 3	991–1009
Ælfmær	Ælf - 4	1003–1009
Ælfstan	Ælf - 5a	1023–1029
Ælfwine	Ælf - 5b	1023–1036
Ælfric	Ælf - 6	1029–1036
Ælfstan	Ælf - 7	1040–1042
Ælfwine	Ælf - 8	1044–1048
Ælfric	Ælf - 9	1048–1062
Ælfwine	Ælf - 10	1068–1072
Ælfwine	Ælf - 11	1074–1077
Beorhtfrith	Beorht - 1a	979–985
Beorhtsige	Beorht - 1b	979–997
Beorhtstan	Beorht - 2	985–997
Beorhtfrith	Beorht - 3	996–1003
Beorhtric	Beorht - 4	997–1003
Beorhtstan	Beorht - 5	1009–1016
Beorhtric	Beorht - 6	1066–1066
Byrhfrith	Byrh - 1	979–985
Byrhsige	Byrh - 2	985–991
Byrhstan	Byrh - 3	991–997
Byrhred	Byrh - 4	995–997
Byrhtric	Byrh - 5	997–1003
Byrhstan	Byrh - 6	1009–1016
Carla	Carl - 1	997–1023
Carla	Carl - 2	1036–1038
Carla	Carl - 3	1040–1042
Dodda	Dodda - 1	1023–1029
Dodda	Dodda - 2	1040–1042
Eadwine	Ead - 1a	991–997
Eadric	Ead - 1b	991–1003
Eadwine	Ead - 2	1003–1009
Eadstan	Ead - 3a	1009–1016
Eadmær	Ead - 3b	1009–1029
Eadsige	Ead - 4	1017–1038
Eadsige Ware	Ead - 5a	1029–1036
Eadwine	Ead - 5b	1029–1036
Eadmær	Ead - 6	1036–1042
Eadwine	Ead - 7	1040–1042
Eadmær	Ead - 8	1044–1046
Eadsige	Ead - 9a	1050–1053
Eadwig	Ead - 9b	1050–1053
Godwine	God - 1	979–985
Goda	God - 2	985–1029
God	God - 3	997–1003
God	God - 4	1009–1016
Godwine	God - 5	1017–1023
Godberht	God - 6	1023–1029
Godwine	God - 7	1040–1042
Hærra	Hær - 1	1036–1038
Hærra	Hær - 2	1040–1042

Table 4.5 *continued*

Moneyer Name	Name Sequence	Activity Range
Hunwine	Hun - 1	991–997
Hunwine	Hun - 2	1017–1023
Huna	Hun - 3a	1029–1036
Hunman	Hun - 3b	1029–1038
Hunwine	Hun - 4	1050–1053
Leofsunu	Leof - 1a	985–991
Leofric	Leof - 1b	985–997
Leofwine	Leof - 2	1023–1029
Leofwine	Leof - 3	1038–1046
Leofing	Leof - 4	1046–1048
Leofing	Leof - 5	1053–1065
Leofwine	Leof - 6	1059–1062
Leofing	Leof - 7a	1066–1066
Leofwig	Leof - 7b	1066–1066
Leofwine	Leof - 7c	1066–1068
Lifwine	Leof - 8	1083–1086
Mangod	Man - 1a	997–1003
Manna	Man - 1b	997–1003
Man	Man - 2	997–1009
Man	Man - 3	1017–1029
Mana	Man - 4	1023–1029
Manleof	Man - 5	1036–1042
Iohan	None	973–978
Brun	None	979–985
Luda	None	979–997
Cetel	None	991–997
Dunstan	None	997–1003
Dudel	None	1003–1009
Æthelstan	None	1009–1016
Eatstan	None	1009–1016
Isegod	None	1009–1023
Thurgod	None	1009–1023
Wine	None	1017–1023
Ealdbeard	None	1023–1029
Scule	None	1023–1036
Etsige	None	1040–1042
Ifing	None	1042–1044
Wicing	None	1059–1062
Spotinc	None	1070–1074
Sigewine	None	1072–1074
Esmær	None	1077–1080
Simær	None	1080–1086
Sæwine	Sæ - 1	1009–1016
Sæwine	Sæ - 2	1023–1029
Sæwulf	Sæ - 3a	1050–1053
Sæwine	Sæ - 3b	1050–1059
Sæwine	Sæ - 4	1062–1066
Sæweard	Sæ - 5a	1074–1077
Sæwine	Sæ - 5b	1074–1086
Thegnwine	Thegn - 1	1029–1038
Thegnwine	Thegn - 2	1040–1042
Tuna	Tun - 2	991–997
Tuna	Tun -1	979–985
Wulfsige	Wulf - 1	997–1023
Wulfric	Wulf - 2a	1017–1023
Wulfsie	Wulf - 2b	1017–1023
Wulfstan	Wulf - 2c	1017–1036
Wulfweard	Wulf - 3	1023–1029
Wulfnoth	Wulf - 4	1036–1042
Wulfnoth	Wulf - 5	1042–1044
Wulfmær	Wulf - 6	1046–1062
Wulfnoth	Wulf - 7a	1065–1066
Wulfwine	Wulf - 7b	1065–1066
Wulfwine	Wulf - 8	1072–1080
Wynstan	Wyn - 1	995–997
Wynsige	Wyn - 2	997–1003

Table 4.6. Name Sequences of the Thetford Mint

Moneyer Name	Name Sequence	Activity Range
Ægelsige	Ægel - 1	1044–1048
Ægelsige	Ægel - 2	1050–1056
Ælfgar	Ælf - 1	973–975
Ælfgar	Ælf - 2	991–1003
Ælfwine	Ælf - 3	997–1003
Ælfcetel	Ælf - 4a	1009–1016
Ælfgar	Ælf - 4b	1009–1016
Ælfweald	Ælf - 4c	1009–1016
Ælfwine	Ælf - 4d	1009–1042
Ælfwig	Ælf - 5	1017–1023
Ælfwig	Ælf - 6a	1029–1036
Ælfweald	Ælf - 6b	1029–1038
Ælfwig	Ælf - 7	1038–1040
Ælfsige	Ælf - 8a	1048–1050
Ælfric	Ælf - 8b	1048–1053

Table 4.6 *continued*

Moneyer Name	Name Sequence	Activity Range
Ælfwine	Ælf - 9	1059–1066
Ælfwine	Ælf - 10	1083–1086
Æthelweald	Æthel - 1	1003–1016
Æthelmær	Æthel - 2	1036–1038
Æthelsige	Æthel - 3	1044–1046
Æthelsige	Æthel - 4	1048–1053
Beorhtric	Beorht - 1	991–997
Beorhtnoth	Beorht - 2	1017–1023
Beorhtwine	Beorht - 3	1068–1070
Blachere	Blac - 1	1053–1065
Blacsunu	Blac - 2	1068–1070
Brunstan	Brun - 1	1017–1044
Brunstan	Brun - 2	1046–1048
Cyneric	Cyne - 1a	1066–1077
Cynewig	Cyne - 1b	1066–1068
Cyneric	Cyne - 2	1083–1086
Deorwine	Deor - 1	1003–1009
Deorwine	Deor - 2	1017–1023
Eadgar	Ead - 1	979–997
Eadweard	Ead - 2a	991–997
Eadwig	Ead - 2b	991–997
Eadric	Ead - 3a	1003–1029
Eadwine	Ead - 3b	1003–1029
Eadwig	Ead - 4	1009–1023
Eadric	Ead - 5	1038–1046
Eadric	Ead - 6	1050–1053
Eadwig	Ead - 7	1053–1056
Eastmær	East - 1a	1044–1056
Eastmund	East - 1b	1044–1056
Eastbeorn	East - 2	1072–1077
Folcard	Folc - 1	991–997
Folcard	Folc - 2	1059–1062
Folcard	Folc - 3	1074–1080
Folcard	Folc - 4	1083–1086
Godman	God - 1	991–997
Godman	God - 2	1017–1023
Godwine	God - 3	1040–1044
Godleof	God - 4	1053–1065
Godeln	God - 5a	1059–1062
Godric	God - 5b	1059–1066
Godwine	God - 6	1062–1065
Godwig	God - 7	1065–1066
Godleof	God - 8a	1066–1066
Godwine	God - 8b	1066–1068
God	God - 8c	1066–1072
Goda	God - 9a	1068–1070
Godric	God - 9b	1068–1070
Godwine	God - 10	1070–1072
Godric	God - 11	1072–1080
Godred	God - 12	1074–1080
Goding	God - 13a	1083–1086
Godleof	God - 13b	1083–1086
Godred	God - 13c	1083–1086
Godric	God - 13d	1083–1086
Grim	Grim - 1a	997–1003
Grimcetel	Grim - 1b	997–1003
Leofthegn	Leof - 1	978–979
Leofwine	Leof - 2	991–997
Leofæg	Leof - 3a	1009–1016
Leofthegn	Leof - 3b	1009–1016
Leofric	Leof - 3c	1009–1029
Leofwine	Leof - 4	1017–1023
Leofing	Leof - 5	1023–1029
Leofwine	Leof - 6	1036–1050
Leofric	Leof - 7	1048–1053
Leofwine	Leof - 8	1053–1056
Manna	Man - 1a	997–1016
Man	Man - 1b	997–1023
Manna	Man - 2	1044–1046
Boiga	None	991–997
Fugolta	None	991–997
Fastolf	None	1009–1016
Palgist	None	1009–1016
Wælgist	None	1009–1023
Ealdred	None	1017–1023
Sprunt	None	1017–1023
Stanmær	None	1017–1023
Wineman	None	1023–1036
Runstan	None	1029–1036
Rincolf	None	1038–1040
Sægrim	None	1040–1044
Atsere	None	1056–1065
Goelic	None	1059–1062
Otbeorn	None	1068–1070

Table 4.6 ***continued***

Moneyer Name	Name Sequence	Activity Range
Osfrith	Os - 1	979–985
Osfrith	Os - 2a	991–997
Osbeorn	Os - 2b	991–1009
Osulf	Os - 3	997–1009
Osulf	Os - 4	1017–1023
Osbeorn	Os - 5	1070–1072
Sperling	Sperl - 1	975–978
Sperling	Sperl - 2	979–997
Sumerlida	Sumer - 1	1009–1023
Sumerlida	Sumer - 2	1056–1065
Thorfrith	Thor - 1	1023–1029
Thorfrith	Thor - 2	1056–1062
Thorgod	Thor - 3	1066–1066
Tidred	Tid - 1	1023–1029
Tidred	Tid - 2	1040–1046
Wulfnoth	Wulf - 1	1009–1016
Wulfmær	Wulf - 2	1017–1023

Table 4.7. Name Sequences of the Stamford Mint

Moneyer Name	Name Sequence	Activity Range
Ælfweald	Ælf - 1	973–978
Ælfweald	Ælf - 2	979–991
Ælfgar	Ælf - 3a	991–997
Ælfgeat	Ælf - 3b	991–997
Ælfweald	Ælf - 4	995–997
Ælfweard	Ælf - 5a	997–1003
Ælfwine	Ælf - 5b	997–1003
Ælfwig	Ælf - 6	1017–1023
Ælfheah	Ælf - 7	1023–1029
Ælfwine	Ælf - 8	1036–1038
Ælfheah	Ælf - 9	1038–1046
Ælfnpne	Ælf - 10	1070–1072
Æscman	Æsc - 1	973–979
Æscwig	Æsc - 2	997–1016
Æscea	Æsc - 3	1003–1009
Æscman	Æsc - 4	1009–1029
Æthelfrith	Æthel - 1	985–991
Æthelberht	Æthel - 2	1003–1009
Æthelwine	Æthel - 3	1009–1016
Æthelstan	Æthel - 4	1023–1029
Arncetel	Arn - 1	1038–1040
Arngrim	Arn - 2	1042–1044
Arnfrith	Arn - 3	1046–1056
Brun	Brun - 1	991–997
Brunstan	Brun - 2	1009–1023
Brunwine	Brun - 3	1029–1042
Brunwine	Brun - 4	1046–1050
Brunwine	Brun - 5	1053–1068
Brunwine	Brun - 6	1070–1072
Brunstan	Brun - 7	1083–1086
Eadwig	Ead - 1	997–1003
Eadwine	Ead - 2	1009–1029
Eadwine	Ead - 3	1046–1048
Fargrim	Far - 1	1017–1023
Fargrim	Far - 2	1029–1042
Fargrim	Far - 3	1048–1053
Godwine	God - 1	979–985
Godwine	God - 2a	991–997
Godleof	God - 2b	991–1023
Godæg	God - 3	997–1016
Godelc	God - 4a	1009–1016
Godhere	God - 4b	1009–1016
Godric	God - 4c	1009–1023
Godwine	God - 4d	1009–1042
Godric	God - 5	1029–1046
Godwine	God - 6	1044–1046
Godwine	God - 7	1053–1059
Godwine	God - 8	1066–1066
Godelef	God - 9	1083–1086
Harcin	Har - 1	1038–1040
Harcin	Har - 2	1046–1048
Harcin	Har - 3	1050–1053
Harcin	Har - 4	1059–1062
Leofing	Leof - 1	975–985
Leofæg	Leof - 2	979–985
Leofwine	Leof - 3	1009–1042
Leofsige	Leof - 4	1017–1029
Leofing	Leof - 5a	1023–1029
Leofric	Leof - 5b	1023–1029
Leofweald	Leof - 5c	1023–1029
Leofthegn	Leof - 6a	1029–1036
Leofæg	Leof - 6b	1029–1038
Leofing	Leof - 7a	1036–1038

Table 4.7 ***continued***

Moneyer Name	Name Sequence	Activity Range
Leofric	Leof - 7b	1036–1066
Leofwine	Leof - 8	1046–1053
Leofwine	Leof - 9	1056–1065
Leofwine	Leof - 10	1066–1070
Leofwine	Leof - 11	1072–1077
Cnapa	None	973–978
Man	None	973–978
Oge	None	973–979
Wacer	None	975–978
Wine	None	975–978
Hild	None	975–979
Iole	None	975–979
Grim	None	975–985
Boiga	None	975–991
Goldwine	None	991–997
Cristin	None	991–1003
Ælebeorht	None	997–1003
Brand	None	1017–1023
Capelin	None	1017–1029
Ceawlin	None	1017–1029
Eadweard	None	1017–1036
Morulf	None	1017–1036
Agisman	None	1023–1029
Baldwin	None	1044–1046
Ærfra	None	1048–1053
Osmund	Os - 1	1009–1016
Osweald	Os - 2	1017–1029
Osweard	Os - 3	1023–1038
Osweard	Os - 4	1059–1066
Swartgar	Swart - 1	991–1016
Swart	Swart - 2a	1009–1023
Swartebrand	Swart - 2b	1009–1023
Swart	Swart - 3	1029–1042
Swartcol	Swart - 4	1062–1066
Thorstan	Thor - 1	1009–1038
Thorulf	Thor - 2	1023–1044
Thor	Thor - 3	1029–1036
Thorstan	Thor - 4	1040–1042
Thorstan	Thor - 5	1044–1046
Wilgrip	Wil - 1	1038–1042
Wilgrip	Wil - 2	1044–1048
Wilgrip	Wil - 3	1056–1062
Wulfgar	Wulf - 1	973–991
Wulfstan	Wulf - 2	975–991
Wulfstan	Wulf - 3	995–997
Wulfnoth	Wulf - 4	1042–1044
Wulfric	Wulf - 5	1046–1048
Wulfwine	Wulf - 6	1050–1053
Wulfweard	Wulf - 7	1066–1066
Wulfweard	Wulf - 8	1083–1086

Table 4.8. Name Sequences of the Chester Mint

Moneyer	Name Sequence	Active Range
Ælfstan	Ælf - 1	975–985
Ælfstan	Ælf - 2	991–1009
Ælfsige	Ælf - 3a	997–1003
Ælfwine	Ælf - 3b	997–1003
Ælfnoth	Ælf - 3c	997–1036
Ælfsige	Ælf - 4	1009–1042
Ælfsi	Ælf - 5a	1017–1023
Ælfweard	Ælf - 5b	1017–1023
Ælfsige	Ælf - 6	1044–1062
Ælfsic	Ælf - 7	1046–1048
Ælfwine	Ælf - 8	1048–1050
Ælfsie	Ælf - 9	1050–1053
Ælfgar	Ælf - 10	1053–1056
Ælfsi	Ælf - 11	1059–1066
Ælfsige	Ælf - 12	1065–1066
Ælfsi	Ælf - 13a	1068–1070
Ælfweard	Ælf - 13b	1068–1070
Ælfsi	Ælf - 14	1083–1086
Æthelmod	Æthel - 1	979–985
Æthelmod	Æthel - 2	991–997
Æthelnoth	Æthel - 3a	997–1003
Æthelwine	Æthel - 3b	997–1038
Æthelnoth	Æthel - 4	1009–1023
Æthelric	Æthel - 5	1017–1023
Æthelnoth	Æthel - 6	1029–1036
Æthelwine	Æthel - 7	1059–1062
Boiga	Boiga - 1	975–978
Boiga	Boiga - 2	991–997
Bruning	Brun - 1	1040–1066
Brun	Brun - 2	1048–1050
Colbeinn	Col - 1	1040–1042

Table 4.8 *continued*

Moneyer Name	Name Sequence	Activity Range
Colthegn	Col - 2	1042–1044
Colbrand	Col - 3	1044–1059
Croc	Croc - 1	1017–1042
Croc	Croc - 2	1044–1046
Deorlaf	Deor - 1	978–979
Deorlaf	Deor - 2	985–991
Dunstan	Dun - 1	1053–1056
Duninc	Dun - 2	1056–1062
Eadric	Ead - 1	979–985
Eadric	Ead - 2	991–1003
Ealhsige	Ealh - 1	1009–1023
Ealhsige	Ealh - 2	1050–1062
Ealhsige	Ealh - 3	1065–1066
Elemod	Ele - 1	995–997
Elewine	Ele - 2	1017–1023
Elewine	Ele - 3	1036–1038
Fargrim	Far - 1	1040–1042
Fargrim	Far - 2	1044–1046
Fargrim	Far - 3	1050–1053
Godric	God - 1a	1017–1023
Godwine	God - 1b	1017–1029
Leofman	Leof - 1	979–985
Leofwine	Leof - 2	997–1044
Leofnoth	Leof - 3	1003–1029
Leofa	Leof - 4a	1017–1023
Leofman	Leof - 4b	1017–1023
Leofing	Leof - 4c	1017–1029
Leofwig	Leof - 4d	1017–1029
Leofsige	Leof - 4e	1017–1036
Leofwig	Leof - 5a	1036–1040
Leofnoth	Leof - 5b	1036–1044
Leofing	Leof - 6	1040–1042
Leofwi	Leof - 7a	1042–1044
Leofwig	Leof - 7b	1042–1044
Leofnoth	Leof - 8	1046–1048
Leofwine	Leof - 9	1048–1053
Leofnoth	Leof - 10	1050–1066
Lifinc	Leof - 11a	1083–1086
Lifwine	Leof - 11b	1083–1086
Mælsuthain	None	973–978
Hringwulf	None	991–997
Sigewine	None	991–997
Oscetel	None	997–1003
Othulf	None	997–1003
Gunleof	None	1003–1036
Lific	None	1017–1023
Macsuthan	None	1017–1023
Trotan	None	1017–1029
Ceolnoth	None	1017–1036
Snell	None	1017–1042
Gillacrist	None	1036–1042
Arngrim	None	1042–1044
Huscarl	None	1048–1066
Sprot	None	1056–1059
Wigal	None	1056–1059
Ordric	None	1059–1062
Thrond	None	1065–1066
Frithegist	None	1068–1070
Sunolf	None	1083–1086
Unnulf	None	1083–1086
Swarting	Swart - 1	1009–1029
Swarting	Swart - 2	1036–1040
Swartcol	Swart - 3	1053–1062
Swegen	Sweg - 1	997–1023
Swegen	Sweg - 2	1036–1038
Thorald	Thor - 1	1009–1016
Thormod	Thor - 2	1017–1023
Wulflaf	Wulf - 1	991–991
Wulfnoth	Wulf - 2	1023–1029
Wulfnoth	Wulf - 3	1038–1040

Table 4.9. Name Sequences of the Canterbury Mint

Moneyer Name	Name Sequence	Activity Range
Ælfstan	Ælf - 1	975–978
Ælfred	Ælf - 2	997–1003
Ælfred	Ælf - 3	1009–1036
Ælfric	Ælf - 4	1029–1038
Ælfred	Ælf - 5	1036–1062
Ælfric	Ælf - 6	1059–1062
Ælfwine	Ælf - 7a	1062–1065
Ælfweard	Ælf - 7b	1062–1066
Ælfwine	Ælf - 8	1066–1066
Ælfred	Ælf - 9	1074–1080
Ælfred	Ælf - 10	1083–1086

Table 4.9 ***continued***

Moneyer Name	Name Sequence	Activity Range
Æthelstan	Æthel - 1	975–978
Æthelræd	Æthel - 2	1050–1053
Æthelwine	Æthel - 3	1059–1062
Beorhtræd	Beorht - 1	1029–1038
Beorhtweald	Beorht - 2	1083–1086
Boiga	Boiga - 1	973–975
Boiga	Boiga - 2	978–991
Eadweald	Ead - 1	979–1023
Eadwine	Ead - 2	1023–1029
Eadweard	Ead - 3	1046–1068
Eadmær	Ead - 4	1053–1056
Eadwine	Ead - 5	1066–1066
Godwine	God - 1	991–1016
Godman	God - 2a	1003–1016
Godric	God - 2b	1003–1029
Godman	God - 3	1023–1029
Godwine	God - 4	1029–1036
Godwine	God - 5	1053–1056
Godric	God - 6	1080–1086
Goldwine	Gold - 1	991–997
Goldwine	Gold - 2	1048–1050
Goldwine	Gold - 3	1070–1072
Heahwulf	Heah - 1	979–985
Heahwulf	Heah - 2	1003–1009
Leofing	Leof - 1a	979–997
Leofric	Leof - 1b	979–1009
Leofstan	Leof - 1c	979–1023
Leofnoth	Leof - 2	1009–1040
Leofwine	Leof - 3	1017–1038
Leofwig	Leof - 4	1029–1038
Leofing	Leof - 5	1036–1038
Leofstan	Leof - 6	1038–1040
Leofwine	Leof - 7	1040–1042
Leofstan	Leof - 8	1044–1062
Leofwine	Leof - 9	1046–1065
Manna	Man - 1	1042–1044
Man	Man - 2	1046–1056
Manna	Man - 3	1048–1066
Man	Man - 4	1059–1065
Man	Man - 5	1066–1066
Manna	Man - 6	1066–1068
Man	Man - 7	1068–1077
Manna	Man - 8	1074–1077
Garwig	None	973–975
Dudda	None	991–997
Ulf	None	1009–1016
Wynhere	None	1017–1038
Cetel	None	1036–1044
Gildewine	None	1036–1065
Caldwine	None	1040–1042
Rudcarl	None	1046–1048
Brunman	None	1046–1050
Thurstan	None	1050–1053
Stanherd	None	1059–1059
Æcereard	None	1059–1062
Ædric	None	1062–1065
Sigered	None	1062–1066
Burnoth	None	1083–1086
Pinedi	None	1083–1086
Sired	Si - 1	1062–1066
Simær	Si - 2	1083–1086
Wine	Wine - 1	973–985
Winedæg	Wine - 2a	1017–1038
Winred	Wine - 2b	1017–1023
Winred	Wine - 3	1029–1036
Windei	Wine - 4	1040–1042
Wulfwine	Wulf - 1	985–991
Wulfwig	Wulf - 2	991–1003
Wulfwi	Wulf - 3	995–997
Wulfstan	Wulf - 4	1009–1029
Wulfwig	Wulf - 5	1023–1040
Wulfwine	Wulf - 6	1029–1036
Wulfric	Wulf - 7	1036–1038
Wulfwine	Wulf - 8	1038–1040
Wulfwig Ubi	Wulf - 9	1040–1042
Wulfgeat	Wulf - 10	1044–1046
Wulfred	Wulf - 11a	1050–1053
Wulfstan	Wulf - 11b	1050–1056
Wulfnoth	Wulf - 12a	1053–1056
Wulfgeat	Wulf - 12b	1053–1059
Wulfwine	Wulf - 13	1059–1062
Wulfweard	Wulf - 14	1062–1065
Wulfred	Wulf - 15	1066–1068
Wulfric	Wulf - 16	1072–1077
Wulfbold	Wulf - 17a	1083–1086
Wulfric	Wulf - 17b	1083–1086

Table 4.10. Name Sequences of the Norwich Mint

Moneyer Name	Name Sequence	Activity Range
Ælfwine	Ælf - 1a	997–1003
Ælfric	Ælf - 1b	997–1029
Ælfrith	Ælf - 2	1029–1036
Ælfric	Ælf - 3a	1036–1038
Ælfwine	Ælf - 3b	1036–1038
Ælfweald	Ælf - 3c	1036–1040
Ælfwine	Ælf - 4	1059–1062
Ælfweald	Ælf - 5	1074–1077
Æthelwine	Æthel - 1	991–997
Æthelfrith	Æthel - 2	1029–1036
Branting	Brant - 1	973–975
Branting	Brant - 2	979–991
Cyneric	Cyne - 1	1009–1016
Cynehelm	Cyne - 2	1050–1053
Cyneric	Cyne - 3	1066–1066
Eadmund	Ead - 1	991–997
Eadwacer	Ead - 2	1003–1023
Eadwine	Ead - 3	1009–1016
Eadmund	Ead - 4	1017–1023
Eadwine	Ead - 5	1062–1065
Eadwine	Ead - 6	1066–1070
Eadweald	Ead - 8	1074–1077
Eadweald	Ead - 9	1083–1086
Folcard	Folc - 1	979–985
Folcard	Folc - 2	991–997
Godwine	God - 1	1017–1023
Godwine	God - 2	1044–1046
Godman	God - 3	1053–1056
Godfrith	God - 4	1062–1065
Godwine	God - 5	1062–1066
Godric	God - 6	1072–1074
Godrun	God - 7	1074–1077
Godric	God - 8	1080–1086
Godric brd	God - 9a	1083–1086
Godwid	God - 9b	1083–1086
Godwig	God - 9c	1083–1086
Godwine	God - 9d	1083–1086
Hringwulf	Hring - 1	1017–1029
Hringwulf	Hring - 2	1038–1042
Hringwulf	Hring - 3	1044–1046
Hringwulf	Hring - 4	1053–1056
Leofing	Leof - 1	973–975
Leofing	Leof - 2	979–985
Leofing	Leof - 3	991–997
Leofwine	Leof - 4	997–1003
Leofstan	Leof - 5	1003–1009
Leofwine	Leof - 6a	1009–1023
Leofric	Leof - 6b	1009–1029
Leofwine	Leof - 7	1029–1048
Leofwig	Leof - 8	1040–1044
Leofwig	Leof - 9	1048–1050
Leofwine	Leof - 10	1050–1056
Leofric	Leof - 11	1056–1062
Leofwine	Leof - 12	1059–1065
Leofold	Leof - 13	1068–1070
Manning	Man - 1	975–997
Man	Man - 2	1009–1040
Manna	Man - 3	1017–1042
Man	Man - 4	1040–1046
Man	Man - 5	1066–1068
Hwætman	None	997–1029
Edelwine	None	1003–1009
Weimund	None	1017–1023
Ægelferth	None	1029–1036
Grim	None	1040–1042
Wrice	None	1062–1065
Howorth	None	1083–1086
Inhuhe	None	1083–1086
Ulfcetel	None	1083–1086
Oslac	Os - 1	973–975
Osfrith	Os - 2	978–979
Osweald	Os - 3	1009–1023
Oslac	Os - 4	1023–1029
Osmund	Os - 5	1040–1046
Rægenulf	Rægen - 1	1017–1036
Rægenulf	Rægen - 2	1038–1042
Sigeric	Sige - 1	1017–1023
Sigeric	Sige - 2	1029–1036
Swerting	Swert - 1	985–991
Swerting	Swert - 2	995–1003
Swerting	Swert - 3	1017–1023
Thorstan	Thor - 1	1009–1023
Thorfrith	Thor - 2	1017–1029
Thorfrith	Thor - 3	1048–1062

Table 4.10 ***continued***

Moneyer Name	Name Sequence	Activity Range
Thorstan	Thor - 4	1050–1066
Thorman	Thor - 5	1053–1056
Thorgrim	Thor - 6	1065–1066
Wulfmær	Wulf - 1	1009–1016
Wulfsige	Wulf - 2	1056–1062
Wulfstan	Wulf - 3	1059–1062

Table 4.11. Name Sequences of the Oxford Mint

Moneyer Name	Name Sequence	Activity Range
Ægelric	Ægel - 1	1023–1029
Ægelwig	Ægel - 2	1036–1038
Ægelwig	Ægel - 3	1046–1048
Ægelwig	Ægel - 4	1053–1056
Ægelwine	Ægel - 5	1040–1042
Ægelwine	Ægel - 6	1050–1062
Ægelwine	Ægel - 7	1070–1074
Ælfwine	Ælf - 1	991–1009
Ælfmær	Ælf - 2	997–1003
Ælfweald	Ælf - 3	1009–1036
Ælfwine	Ælf - 4	1017–1029
Ælfwine Tosti	Ælf - 5	1029–1038
Ælfwine	Ælf - 6	1036–1042
Ælfwig	Ælf - 7	1038–1044
Ælfwine	Ælf - 8	1044–1046
Ælfwine	Ælf - 9a	1048–1050
Ælfwig	Ælf - 9b	1048–1066
Ælfwi	Ælf - 10	1050–1053
Ælfwine	Ælf - 11	1053–1056
Ælfwi	Ælf - 12	1065–1066
Ælfwig	Ælf - 13a	1068–1070
Ælfwine	Ælf - 13b	1068–1070
Ælfwine	Ælf - 14	1074–1077
Æthelwine	Æthel - 1	973–975
Æthelmær	Æthel - 2a	991–1003
Æthelwine	Æthel - 2b	991–1003
Æthelric	Æthel - 3	1003–1046
Æthelwine	Æthel - 4a	1036–1038
Æthelwig	Æthel - 4b	1036–1066
Æthelmær	Æthel - 5	1038–1040
Æthelwine	Æthel - 6	1040–1042
Æthelwine	Æthel - 7	1050–1053
Æthelwine	Æthel - 8	1056–1062
Æthelric	Æthel - 9	1059–1062
Beorhtwine	Beorht - 1	1003–1023
Beorhtnoth	Beorht - 2	1009–1016
Beorhtweald	Beorht - 3	1042–1053
Beorhtweald	Beorht - 4	1056–1059
Beorhtræd	Beorht - 5	1059–1062
Beorhtweald	Beorht - 6	1062–1066
Beorhtræd	Beorht - 7	1080–1086
Eadwig	Ead - 1	991–997
Eadwine	Ead - 2	997–1003
Eadwig	Ead - 3	1017–1036
Eadwine	Ead - 4	1029–1036
Eadwig	Ead - 5	1038–1042
Eadwine	Ead - 6	1053–1059
Goding	God - 1	979–1003
Godman	God - 2a	1017–1023
Godwine	God - 2b	1017–1042
Godwine	God - 3	1044–1050
Godwine	God - 4	1059–1065
Godwine	God - 5	1066–1066
Godwine	God - 6	1068–1074
Heregod	Here - 1	1044–1050
Heregod	Here - 2	1059–1066
Heregod	Here - 3	1072–1074
Heregod	Here - 4	1080–1083
Leofman	Leof - 1	997–1016
Leofwine	Leof - 2	1003–1009
Leofing	Leof - 3	1017–1042
Leofwine	Leof - 4	1036–1040
Seleweald	None	973–975
Coleman	None	1003–1040
Sæwine	None	1017–1023
Sibwine	None	1017–1023
Lafdensic	None	1036–1038
Agulf	None	1074–1077
Swetman	Swet - 1	1050–1062
Swetman	Swet - 2	1083–1086
Wulfred	Wulf - 1	973–978
Wulfwine	Wulf - 2	991–1003
Wulfmær	Wulf - 3a	1017–1023
Wulfwig	Wulf - 3b	1017–1023

Table 4.11 *continued*

Moneyer Name	Name Sequence	Activity Range
Wulfwine	Wulf - 3c	1017–1036
Wulfwig	Wulf - 4	1062–1066
Wulfwi	Wulf - 5	1062–1065
Wulfwine	Wulf - 6	1068–1074
Wulfwine	Wulf - 7	1077–1080
Wulfwi	Wulf - 8	1083–1086

Table 4.12. Name Sequences of the Southwark Mint

Moneyer Name	Name Sequence	Activity Range
Ælfnoth	Ælf - 1a	991–997
Ælfric	Ælf - 1b	991–997
Ælfwig	Ælf - 1c	991–997
Ælfwine	Ælf - 2	1009–1036
Ælfsige	Ælf - 3a	1017–1023
Ælfweard	Ælf - 3b	1017–1023
Ælfgar	Ælf - 3c	1017–1029
Ælfric	Ælf - 4	1023–1029
Ælfwine	Ælf - 5	1038–1040
Ælfric	Ælf - 6	1040–1046
Ælfwine	Ælf - 7	1048–1050
Ælfdoulf	Ælf - 8	1083–1086
Æthelweard	Æthel - 1	991–997
Æthelsige	Æthel - 2a	1017–1023
Æthelwig	Æthel - 2b	1017–1023
Æthelwine	Æthel - 2c	1017–1023
Æthelric	Æthel - 3	1023–1029
Æthelwig	Æthel - 4	1029–1036
Æthelwine	Æthel - 5	1040–1042
Beorhthelm	Beorht - 1a	991–997
Beorhtlaf	Beorht - 1b	991–997
Beorhtric	Beorht - 1c	991–997
Beorhtmær	Beorht - 2	1017–1023
Brunman	Brun - 1	1017–1023
Brunræd	Brun - 2	1040–1042
Eadwig	Ead - 1a	991–997
Eadwine	Ead - 1b	991–1003
Eadwi	Ead - 2	995–997
Eadwine	Ead - 3	1009–1023
Eadweard	Ead - 4	1017–1023
Eadnoth	Ead - 5	1023–1029
Goda	God - 1a	991–997
Godric	God - 1b	991–1003
Godwine	God - 1c	991–997
Godwine	God - 2	1023–1029
Godman	God - 3	1056–1059
Godric	God - 4	1062–1065
Godric	God - 5	1080–1086
Leofstan	Leof - 1a	991–997
Leofwine	Leof - 1b	991–1003
Leofwine	Leof - 2	1009–1016
Leofric	Leof - 3	1017–1023
Leofing	Leof - 4	1023–1038
Leofric	Leof - 5	1036–1038
Leofric	Leof - 6	1040–1042
Leofwine	Leof - 7	1046–1050
Leofred	Leof - 8	1050–1056
Leofwine	Leof - 9	1068–1070
Leofwine	Leof - 10	1074–1080
Lifweard	Leof - 11	1083–1086
Boiga	None	991–997
Heahwulf	None	991–997
Swegen	None	1017–1023
Swarting	None	1017–1023
Toca	None	1023–1029
Ægelwig	None	1040–1042
Burred	None	1042–1042
Burgræd	None	1042–1046
Osmund	Os - 1	1053–1066
Osmund	Os - 2	1083–1086
Swetman	Swet - 1	1053–1056
Swetman	Swet - 2	1059–1062
Tuneman	Tun - 1	991–997
Tuneman	Tun - 2	1009–1016
Wulfric	Wulf - 1a	1017–1023
Wulfstan	Wulf - 1b	1017–1023
Wulfwine	Wulf - 2	1042–1046
Wulfwine	Wulf - 3	1048–1053

Table 4.13. Name Sequences of the Cambridge Mint

Moneyer Name	Name Sequence	Activity Range
Ælfwine	Ælf - 1	978–997
Ælfric	Ælf - 2	991–1003
Ælfric	Ælf - 3a	1009–1016

Table 4.13 ***continued***

Moneyer Name	Name Sequence	Activity Range
Ælfwi	Ælf - 3b	1009–1023
Ælfwig	Ælf - 3c	1009–1023
Ælfwine	Ælf - 4	1023–1029
Ælfwig	Ælf - 5	1029–1042
Ælfwi	Ælf - 6	1038–1040
Ælfwig	Ælf - 7a	1050–1059
Ælfwine	Ælf - 7b	1050–1053
Ælfwi	Ælf - 8	1053–1059
Alfcil	Ælf - 9	1083–1086
Eadmund	Ead - 1a	991–997
Eadric	Ead - 1b	991–997
Eadwine	Ead - 1c	991–1003
Eadric	Ead - 2	1017–1023
Eadwine	Ead - 3	1023–1036
Eadwacer	Ead - 4	1036–1038
Eadwine	Ead - 5	1040–1042
Eadstan	Ead - 6a	1044–1046
Eadweard	Ead - 6b	1044–1046
Eadstan	Ead - 7a	1048–1050
Eadweard	Ead - 7b	1048–1065
Godwine	God - 1	991–997
Godric	God - 2	997–1003
Godwine	God - 3	1017–1023
Godwine	God - 4a	1040–1042
Godsunu	God - 4b	1040–1046
Godsunu	God - 5	1050–1053
Godwine	God - 6	1053–1059
Godwine	God - 7a	1062–1065
Godlamb	God - 7b	1062–1066
Godwine	God - 8	1066–1066
Godric	God - 9	1066–1068
Hunstan	Hun - 1	975–978
Hunstan	Hun - 2	979–985
Hunstan	Hun - 3	991–997
Leofnoth	Leof - 1	991–997
Leofsige	Leof - 2	1003–1029
Wilmund	None	979–985
Sidewine	None	991–997
Cniht	None	1003–1023
Clern	None	1009–1016
Stængrim	None	1017–1023
Ada	None	1017–1029
Ornost	None	1017–1029
Grim	None	1023–1029
Stircere	None	1038–1040
Wibearn	None	1062–1065
Beorhtric	None	1066–1066
Othbeorn	None	1072–1074
Ægelmie	None	1074–1077
Ulfcetel	None	1083–1086
Oscetel	Os - 1	991–997
Osgeat	Os - 2	1036–1038
Sæcoll	Sæ - 1	1056–1065
Sægolf	Sæ - 2	1059–1062
Wulfgar	Wulf - 1	991–997
Wulfsige	Wulf - 2	997–1029
Wulfwine	Wulf - 3	1036–1040
Wulfmær	Wulf - 4	1040–1042
Wulfwine	Wulf - 5	1050–1053
Wulfwig	Wulf - 6a	1059–1062
Wulfwine	Wulf - 6b	1059–1062
Wulfwi	Wulf - 7	1066–1066

Table 4.14. Name Sequences of the Shrewsbury Mint

Moneyer Name	Name Sequence	Activity Range
Ægelric	Ægel - 1	1062–1065
Ægelric	Ægel - 2	1068–1070
Ælfric	Ælf - 1	979–985
Ælfheah	Ælf - 2	997–1003
Ælfstan	Ælf - 3	1009–1016
Ælfhelm	Ælf - 4	1017–1023
Ælfheah	Ælf - 5	1040–1042
Ælfheah	Ælf - 6	1050–1056
Ælfgæt	Ælf - 7a	1059–1062
Ælfheah	Ælf - 7b	1059–1062
Ærnwig	Ærn - 1	1056–1066
Ærnwi	Ærn - 2	1068–1070
Ærnwi	Ærn - 3	1072–1074
Ærnwine	Ærn - 4	1074–1077
Ærnwi	Ærn - 5	1083–1086
Æthelsige	Æthel - 1	973–975
Æthelnoth	Æthel - 2	1009–1016
Brungar	Brun - 1	995–1003
Brungar	Brun - 2	1017–1036

Table 4.14 *continued*

Moneyer Name	Name Sequence	Activity Range
Eadsige	Ead - 1	1003–1009
Eadsige	Ead - 2	1017–1036
Eadstan	Ead - 3	1023–1029
Godwine	God - 1	1017–1036
Godhere	God - 2	1036–1038
Godsbrand	God - 3	1050–1066
Godwine	God - 4	1059–1066
Godsbrand	God - 5	1068–1070
Godsbrand	God - 6	1083–1086
Leofhelm	Leof - 1	979–985
Leofnoth	Leof - 2a	997–1003
Leofsige	Leof - 2b	997–1003
Leofstan	Leof - 3	1023–1042
Leofwine	Leof - 4	1036–1042
Leofwine	Leof - 5	1046–1048
Leofwine	Leof - 6a	1050–1056
Leofstan	Leof - 6b	1050–1059
Hildic	None	973–975
Ævic	None	979–985
Martin	None	991–997
Ordgar	None	997–1003
Oswald	None	997–1003
Unspac	None	997–1009
Crinan	None	1017–1023
Grim	None	1017–1023
Wada	None	1017–1023
Wudeman	None	1059–1066
Goldwine	None	1062–1065
Lernwi	None	1077–1080
Sægrim	None	1083–1086
Sigeweald	Sige - 1	973–975
Sigered	Sige - 2	1009–1016
Sigewine	Sige - 3	1074–1077
Winesige	Wine - 1	991–1003
Winesige	Wine - 2	1009–1016
Wulfred	Wulf - 1	1017–1040
Wulfweard	Wulf - 2a	1023–1036
Wulfgeat	Wulf - 2b	1023–1046
Wulfmær	Wulf - 3	1040–1042
Wulfmær	Wulf - 4	1044–1046
Wulfgeat	Wulf - 5a	1048–1053
Wulfmær	Wulf - 5b	1048–1056
Wulfmær	Wulf - 6	1059–1062
Wulfmær	Wulf - 7	1065–1066
Wulfmær	Wulf - 8	1072–1074

Table 4.15. Name Sequences of the Gloucester Mint

Moneyer Name	Name Sequence	Activity Range
Ægelric	Ægel - 1	1029–1036
Ægelric	Ægel - 2	1050–1053
Æleric	Æl - 1	1038–1042
Æleric	Æl - 2	1053–1056
Ælfsige	Ælf - 1	1036–1040
Ælfsige	Ælf - 2	1042–1044
Ælfsige	Ælf - 3	1046–1048
Ælfric	Ælf - 4a	1050–1053
Ælfsige	Ælf - 4b	1050–1062
Ælfsi	Ælf - 5	1059–1062
Ælfsige	Ælf - 6	1065–1066
Æthelstan	Æthel - 1	973–975
Æthelric	Æthel - 2	1029–1042
Æthelmær	Æthel - 3	1038–1040
Æthelwulf	Æthel - 4	1040–1042
Æthelric	Æthel - 5	1046–1053
Æthelric	Æthel - 6	1056–1062
Beorhtstan	Beorht - 1	975–978
Beorhtnoth	Beorht - 2	1059–1065
Beorhtnoth	Beorht - 3	1083–1086
Godwine	God - 1	991–1029
Godric	God - 2	1017–1042
Godric	God - 3	1044–1046
Godric	God - 4	1048–1056
Godwine	God - 5	1056–1059
Leofsige	Leof - 1	979–991
Leofsige	Leof - 2	997–1029
Leofnoth	Leof - 3	1023–1042
Leofnoth	Leof - 4	1048–1059
Leofwine	Leof - 5	1056–1065
Leofwine	Leof - 6	1070–1072
Leofwine	Leof - 7	1074–1077
Wynsige	None	973–975
Wihtsige	None	985–1003
Bolla	None	1017–1029
Sired	None	1017–1036

Table 4.15 ***continued***

Moneyer Name	Name Sequence	Activity Range
Æwulf	None	1048–1053
Eadwig	None	1056–1059
Guolcwine	None	1059–1062
Ordric	Ord - 1	1056–1059
Ordric	Ord - 2	1066–1070
Seolcwine	Seolc - 1	1056–1065
Seolcwine	Seolc - 2	1066–1066
Sigered	Sige - 1	1009–1036
Sigelac	Sige - 2	1056–1059
Sigelac	Sige - 3	1062–1066
Silac	Sil - 1	1056–1059
Silac	Sil - 2	1062–1066
Silac	Sil - 3a	1083–1086
Silacwine	Sil - 3b	1083–1086
Wulfnoth	Wulf - 1	1029–1038
Wulfred	Wulf - 2	1036–1038
Wulfweard	Wulf - 3	1038–1042
Wulfheard	Wulf - 4	1040–1042
Wulfwig	Wulf - 5	1042–1046
Wulfweard	Wulf - 6	1044–1046
Wulfwig	Wulf - 7	1048–1050
Wulfweard	Wulf - 8	1050–1062
Wulfred	Wulf - 9a	1053–1056
Wulfgæt	Wulf - 9b	1053–1062
Wulfgæt	Wulf - 10	1066–1066
Wulfgæt	Wulf - 11	1070–1072
Wulfgæt	Wulf - 12	1083–1086

Table 4.16. Name Sequences of the Wallingford Mint

Moneyer Name	Name Sequence	Activity Range
Ægelwig	Ægel - 1	1042–1044
Ægelwig	Ægel - 2	1050–1053
Ægelwine	Ægel - 3	1083–1086
Ælfred	Ælf - 1a	991–997
Ælfweard	Ælf - 1b	991–997
Ælfwine	Ælf - 1c	991–997
Ælfric	Ælf - 1d	991–1003
Ælfweald	Ælf - 1e	991–1003
Ælfwig	Ælf - 1f	991–1003
Ælfmær	Ælf - 2	997–1003
Ælfweard	Ælf - 3	1003–1009
Ælfric	Ælf - 4	1009–1016
Ælfwine	Ælf - 5	1023–1042
Ælfwig	Ælf - 6	1036–1042
Ælfric	Ælf - 7	1040–1042
Ælfwi	Ælf - 8a	1050–1053
Ælfwine	Ælf - 8b	1050–1053
Æthelwine	Æthel - 1	1029–1036
Æthelric	Æthel - 2	1038–1040
Æthelwig	Æthel - 3	1040–1046
Beorhtric	Beorht - 1	979–985
Beorhtric	Beorht - 2a	1040–1042
Beorhtwine	Beorht - 2b	1040–1042
Beorhtric	Beorht - 3a	1046–1048
Beorhtwine	Beorht - 3b	1046–1050
Beorhtric	Beorht - 4	1050–1059
Beorhtwine	Beorht - 5	1053–1059
Beorhtmær	Beorht - 6	1059–1072
Brand	Brand - 1	1053–1065
Brand	Brand - 2	1066–1077
Brunwine	Brun - 1	1040–1042
Brunwine	Brun - 2	1050–1062
Brunwine	Brun - 3	1065–1066
Burewine	Bur - 1	1036–1042
Burewine	Bur - 2	1053–1056
Burewine	Bur - 3	1059–1066
Eadric	Ead - 1	997–1003
Eadwig	Ead - 2	1003–1009
Eadwine	Ead - 3	1017–1023
Eadweard	Ead - 4	1023–1036
Eadweard	Ead - 5	1038–1042
Eadweard	Ead - 6	1044–1046
Leofwine	Leof - 1	991–997
Leofric	Leof - 2	995–997
Leofstan	Leof - 3	1009–1016
Leofwine	Leof - 4	1029–1036
Leofwine	Leof - 5	1038–1044
Man	Man - 1	997–1003
Man	Man - 2	1017–1029
Siolf	None	991–991
Eoda	None	991–997
Sigewulf	None	991–997
Oda	None	991–1003

Table 4.16 ***continued***

Moneyer Name	Name Sequence	Activity Range
Wine	None	1009–1016
Colman	None	1017–1029
Godwine	None	1029–1036
Withman	None	1083–1086
Swarting	Swart - 1a	1066–1086
Swartlind	Swart - 1b	1066–1068
Swartwine	Swart - 2	1070–1072
Wulfstan	Wulf - 1	973–975
Wulfwine	Wulf - 2	997–1009
Wulfwine	Wulf - 3	1038–1042

Table 4.17. Name Sequences of the Worcester Mint

Moneyer Name	Name Sequence	Activity Range
Ægelwine	Ægel - 1	1038–1040
Ægelwine	Ægel - 2	1056–1062
Ælfsige	Ælf - 1	997–1003
Ælfweald	Ælf - 2	1017–1036
Ælf	Ælf - 3a	1023–1029
Ælfwine	Ælf - 3b	1023–1036
Ælfwine	Ælf - 4	1042–1044
Ælfwine	Ælf - 5	1046–1048
Ælfwine	Ælf - 6	1050–1053
Ælfwine	Ælf - 7	1062–1065
Ælfweard	Ælf - 8	1072–1074
Ælfgeat	Ælf - 9	1077–1080
Ælfgærd	Ælf - 10	1080–1086
Æthelmær	Æthel - 1	991–1003
Æthelstan	Æthel - 2	1009–1016
Æthelwine	Æthel - 3	1023–1040
Æthelwig	Æthel - 4	1038–1040
Æthelric	Æthel - 5	1053–1056
Æthelwine	Æthel - 6	1059–1062
Æthelwine	Æthel - 7	1065–1066
Baldric	Bald - 1	1062–1065
Baldric	Bald - 2	1072–1074
Baldric	Bald - 3	1083–1086
Eastmær	East - 1	1062–1065
Eastmær	East - 2	1066–1066
Eastmær	East - 3	1068–1072
Eastmær	East - 4	1083–1086
Garwulf	Gar - 1	1009–1023
Garwulf	Gar - 2	1053–1056
Garwulf	Gar - 3	1059–1062
Garwulf	Gar - 4	1066–1066
Garwulf	Gar - 5	1068–1072
Goda	God - 1	991–1009
Goda	God - 2	1017–1029
God	God - 3	1023–1029
Godwine	God - 4	1029–1036
Godwine	God - 5	1048–1050
Heathwulf	Heath - 1	1062–1065
Heathwi	Heath - 2	1066–1066
Leofric	Leof - 1	1023–1029
Leofstan	Leof - 2	1029–1046
Leofric	Leof - 3	1036–1042
Leofric	Leof - 4a	1048–1050
Leofstan	Leof - 4b	1048–1050
Leofing	Leof - 5	1050–1053
Leofstan	Leof - 6	1056–1062
Leofric	Leof - 7	1059–1062
Leofric	Leof - 8	1066–1070
Man	Man - 1	975–978
Man	Man - 2	979–985
Martin	None	979–985
Durant	None	991–1009
Ealdwine	None	1050–1053
Wicing	None	1053–1066
Refwine	None	1068–1072
Sæwine	None	1083–1086
Sigefrith	Sige - 1a	991–997
Sigewine	Sige - 1b	991–997
Wulfric	Wulf - 1	997–1003
Wulfmær	Wulf - 2	1017–1023
Wulfwine	Wulf - 3	1048–1050
Wulfwine	Wulf - 4	1066–1066

Table 4.18. Name Sequences of the Lewes Mint

Moneyer Name	Name Sequence	Activity Range
Ælfnoth	Ælf - 1a	991–997
Ælfgar	Ælf - 1b	991–1003
Ælfweard	Ælf - 2	1009–1016
Ælfwine	Ælf - 3	1017–1023
Ælfweard	Ælf - 4	1023–1036

Table 4.18 ***continued***

Moneyer Name	Name Sequence	Activity Range
Ælfsige	Ælf - 5	1050–1053
Ælfric	Ælf - 6	1072–1074
Ælfric	Ælf - 7	1083–1086
Deoring	Deor - 1	1048–1050
Deoring	Deor - 2	1059–1062
Eadweard	Ead - 1	991–997
Eadweard	Ead - 2	1009–1016
Eadwine	Ead - 3	1023–1042
Eadweard	Ead - 4	1036–1042
Eadwine	Ead - 5	1042–1044
Eadweard	Ead - 6	1046–1048
Eadwig	Ead - 7a	1048–1050
Eadwine	Ead - 7b	1048–1050
Eadweard	Ead - 8	1050–1059
Eadwine	Ead - 9	1053–1059
Godfrith	God - 1	997–1003
Godfrith	God - 2	1009–1036
Godman	God - 3a	1017–1023
Godwig	God - 3b	1017–1023
Godwine	God - 4	1038–1040
Godric	God - 5	1046–1048
Godwine	God - 6	1050–1066
Goldstan	Gold - 1	973–975
Goldstan	Gold - 2	979–985
Herebreht	Here - 1	985–991
Hereberht	Here - 2	997–1003
Leofstan	Leof - 1	979–991
Leofwine	Leof - 2	991–1029
Leofnoth	Leof - 3	995–1003
Leofa	Leof - 4	1003–1029
Leofstan	Leof - 5a	1009–1016
Leofnoth	Leof - 5b	1009–1023
Leofnoth	Leof - 6	1046–1048
Leofman	Leof - 7a	1048–1050
Leofwig	Leof - 7b	1048–1050
Leofwine	Leof - 7c	1048–1053
Leofweard	Leof - 8	1059–1066
Leofweald	Leof - 9	1062–1065
Theodgar	None	973–985
Seaxberht	None	975–978
Merewine	None	997–1009
Olaf	None	1009–1016
Ealdred	None	1017–1023
Coling	None	1023–1029
Northman	None	1036–1046
Winered	None	1072–1086
Osweald	Os - 1	991–997
Osweald	Os - 2a	1046–1048
Osmund	Os - 2b	1046–1050
Osweald	Os - 3	1050–1066
Osweald	Os - 4	1072–1077
Osweald	Os - 5	1083–1086
Wulfstan	Wulf - 1	991–997
Wulfric	Wulf - 2	1040–1042
Wulfwine	Wulf - 3	1059–1062

Table 4.19. Name Sequences of the Bedford Mint

Moneyer Name	Name Sequence	Activity Range
Ægelman	Ægel - 1	1029–1036
Ægelman	Ægel - 2	1038–1040
Ælfstan	Ælf - 1	975–985
Ælfstan	Ælf - 2	991–1003
Ælfwig	Ælf - 3	997–1003
Ælfman	Ælf - 3	1050–1056
Æthelgeat	Æthel - 1	1017–1023
Æthelman	Æthel - 2	1023–1040
Æthelman	Æthel - 3	1042–1048
Æthelman	Æthel - 4	1050–1053
Baldric	Bald - 1	975–979
Bealdwulf	Bald - 2	978–979
Beorhtwine	Beorht - 1	979–985
Beorhtric	Beorht - 2	1066–1066
Beorht	Beorht - 3	1074–1077
Godric	God - 1	1009–1023
Godwine	God - 2	1017–1023
Godcild	God - 3	1044–1046
Godwine	God - 4	1050–1053
Godric	God - 5a	1056–1059
Godwine	God - 5b	1056–1062
Leofnoth	Leof - 1	991–1003
Leofing	Leof - 2a	1009–1016
Leofwine	Leof - 2b	1009–1036
Leofsige	Leof - 3	1017–1023
Leofthegn	Leof - 4	1036–1040

Table 4.19 ***continued***

Moneyer Name	Name Sequence	Activity Range
Leofwine	Leof - 5	1038–1040
Leofthegn	Leof - 6	1059–1065
Grim	None	973–978
Byrnwine	None	978–979
Gunni	None	997–1003
Deorwine	None	997–1009
Ælmon	None	1050–1053
Sigebrand	None	1083–1086
Oswi	Os - 1	979–985
Oswig	Os - 2	991–997
Sigod	Si - 1	1053–1056
Sigod	Si - 2	1059–1066
Sibrand	Si - 3	1066–1070
Sigod	Si - 4	1068–1077
Sibrand	Si - 5	1074–1077
Sibrand	Si - 6	1083–1086
Swet	Swet - 1	1029–1036
Swet	Swet - 2	1038–1042
Swet	Swet - 3	1048–1053
Swet	Swet - 4	1056–1059
Ulfcetel	Ulf - 1	1042–1044
Ulfcetel	Ulf - 2	1048–1050
Ulfcetel	Ulf - 3	1053–1056
Wulfmær	Wulf - 1a	1050–1053
Wulfwig	Wulf - 1b	1050–1053
Wulfwi	Wulf - 2	1053–1056
Wulfwig	Wulf - 3	1056–1062
Wulfwi	Wulf - 4	1059–1059
Wulfwine	Wulf - 5	1062–1065
Wulfwi	Wulf - 6a	1066–1066
Wulfwig	Wulf - 6b	1066–1066

Table 4.20. Name Sequences of the Colchester Mint

Moneyer Name	Name Sequence	Activity Range
Ælfwine	Ælf - 1	991–997
Ælfwine	Ælf - 2	1017–1029
Ælfwine	Ælf - 3	1046–1048
Ælfsi	Ælf - 4	1083–1086
Beorhthelm	Beorht - 1	991–997
Beorhtric	Beorht - 2	1046–1059
Beorhtric	Beorht - 3	1062–1065
Beorhtric	Beorht - 4	1066–1066
Beorhtric	Beorht - 5	1068–1070
Brunman	Brun - 1	1017–1023
Brunhuse	Brun - 2	1044–1048
Brunnus	Brun - 3a	1050–1053
Brunhuse	Brun - 3b	1050–1056
Brunhuse	Brun - 4	1059–1065
Deorman	Deor - 1	1053–1056
Deorman	Deor - 2	1059–1062
Dorman	Deor - 3	1077–1080
Dirman	Deor - 4	1083–1086
Eadwig	Ead - 1a	991–997
Eadsige	Ead - 1b	991–1009
Eadmund	Ead - 2	997–1003
Eadsige	Ead - 3	1003–1009
Eadwine	Ead - 4	1009–1023
Godwine	God - 1	991–997
Godric	God - 2	997–1003
Godric	God - 3	1009–1040
Godwine	God - 4	1059–1062
Goldman	Gold - 1	1059–1062
Goldman	Gold - 2	1066–1066
Goldstan	Gold - 3	1066–1070
Leofred	Leof - 1	991–997
Leofweald	Leof - 2a	997–1003
Leofwig	Leof - 2b	997–1003
Leofwine	Leof - 3	1029–1036
Leofweard	Leof - 4	1044–1048
Leofweard	Leof - 5	1050–1056
Manwine	None	991–997
Sweting	None	991–997
Toca	None	991–997
Sidwine	None	995–997
Elewine	None	1009–1016
Druman	None	1074–1077
Standre	Stan - 1a	1044–1046
Stanmær	Stan - 1b	1044–1056
Wulfnoth	Wulf - 1a	991–997
Wulfric	Wulf - 1b	991–997
Wulfwine	Wulf - 1c	991–1003
Wulfred	Wulf - 2	1009–1016
Wulfwine	Wulf - 3	1017–1042

Table 4.20 ***continued***

Moneyer Name	Name Sequence	Activity Range
Wulfwine	Wulf - 4	1046–1048
Wulfwine	Wulf - 5	1053–1066
Wulfwi	Wulf - 6a	1066–1066
Wulfwig	Wulf - 6b	1066–1066
Wulfwine	Wulf - 7	1074–1077
Wulfric	Wulf - 8a	1083–1086
Wulfwine	Wulf - 8b	1083–1086
Wulfweard	Wulf - 8c	1083–1086

Table 4.21. Name Sequences of the Ipswich Mint

Moneyer Name	Name Sequence	Activity Range
Ægelbeorht	Ægel - 1	1068–1070
Ægelbeorht	Ægel - 2	1072–1074
Ægelwine	Ægel - 3	1083–1086
Ælfbeorht	Ælf - 1	1038–1040
Ælfwine	Ælf - 2	1062–1066
Ælfwine	Ælf - 3	1080–1086
Ælfric	Ælf - 4	1083–1086
Æthelbeorht	Æthel - 1	1003–1009
Æthelbeorht	Æthel - 2	1017–1036
Æthelbeorht	Æthel - 3	1038–1040
Æthelbeorht	Æthel - 4	1068–1074
Æthelwine	Æthel - 5	1083–1086
Branting	Brant - 1	979–985
Branting	Brant - 2	1017–1023
Bruning	Brun - 1	1044–1046
Bruning	Brun - 2	1048–1056
Brunman	Brun - 3	1056–1066
Bruning	Brun - 4	1059–1065
Eadric	Ead - 1	1017–1029
Eadwig	Ead - 2	1048–1050
Godric	God - 1a	991–997
Godwine	God - 1b	991–997
Godric	God - 2	1003–1009
Leofric	Leof - 1	973–975
Leofman	Leof - 2a	979–985
Leofric	Leof - 2b	979–985
Leofstan	Leof - 3	991–997
Leofsige	Leof - 4	991–1023
Leofing	Leof - 5	1009–1048
Leofman	Leof - 6a	1017–1023
Leofric	Leof - 6b	1017–1023
Leofric	Leof - 7a	1040–1042
Leofstan	Leof - 7b	1040–1046
Leofing	Leof - 8	1050–1053
Leofweald	Leof - 9	1053–1056
Leofweald	Leof - 10	1059–1065
Leofstan	Leof - 11	1066–1066
Leofstan	Leof - 12	1068–1070
Leofstan	Leof - 13	1074–1080
Lifwine	Leof - 14	1083–1086
Osulf	None	979–985
Rodbert	None	979–985
Waldfrith	None	979–985
Lytelman	None	979–1003
Erlewin	None	1003–1009
Sigeweald	None	1009–1016
Oda	None	1009–1023
Folcard	None	1017–1023
Widfara	None	1036–1040
Beorhtric	None	1059–1065
Spegen	None	1083–1086
Wilebeart	Wile - 1	975–978
Wilebeart	Wile - 2	979–985
Wulfsige	Wulf - 1	1048–1056
Wulfwine	Wulf - 2	1068–1070
Wulfweard	Wulf - 3	1074–1077
Wulfwine	Wulf - 4	1083–1086

Table 4.22. Name Sequences of the Dover Mint

Moneyer Name	Name Sequence	Activity Range
Ælfstan	Ælf - 1	1029–1036
Ælfwine	Ælf - 2	1029–1036
Boiga	Boiga - 1	1029–1042
Boiga	Boiga - 2	1044–1046
Brunman	Brun - 1	1070–1072
Brunman	Brun - 2	1074–1077
Cyneric	Cyne - 1	991–997
Cynesige	Cyne - 2	997–1016
Cynesige	Cyne - 3	1023–1036
Cynestan	Cyne - 4	1036–1044
Cynestan	Cyne - 5	1046–1059
Cynestan	Cyne - 6	1062–1065

Table 4.22 ***continued***

Moneyer Name	Name Sequence	Activity Range
Cynestan	Cyne - 7	1066–1066
Cynestan	Cyne - 8	1080–1083
Eadsige	Ead - 1	997–1003
Eadsige	Ead - 2	1017–1038
Eadwig	Ead - 3a	1029–1036
Eadwine	Ead - 3b	1029–1042
Eadsige	Ead - 4	1040–1042
Eadwine	Ead - 5	1044–1046
Eadweard	Ead - 6	1083–1086
Etsige	Et - 1	1023–1036
Etsige	Et - 2	1046–1048
Godwine	God - 1	995–1003
Godman	God - 2	1009–1023
Godwine	God - 3	1053–1062
Godwine	God - 4	1083–1086
Leofgar	Leof - 1	973–975
Leofwine	Leof - 2	991–997
Leofhyse	Leof - 3	997–1009
Leofstan	Leof - 4a	1017–1023
Leofwine	Leof - 4b	1017–1038
Leofric	Leof - 5	1029–1036
Leofwine	Leof - 6	1040–1042
Leofric	Leof - 7	1080–1086
Lifric	Leof - 8a	1083–1086
Lifwine	Leof - 8b	1083–1086
Manning	Man - 1	1003–1023
Manwine	Man - 2	1059–1066
Manwine	Man - 3	1066–1068
Manwine	Man - 4	1072–1077
Osfrith	None	979–991
Beorhtmær	None	1009–1023
Swertafe	None	1023–1029
Wynstan	None	1048–1050
Ceolwig	None	1053–1066
Lulfric	None	1083–1086
Goldwine	None	1083–1086
Wulfstan	Wulf - 1	997–1003
Wulfsi	Wulf - 2	1017–1023
Wulfweard	Wulf - 3	1062–1066

Table 4.23. Name Sequences of the Hereford Mint

Moneyer Name	Name Sequence	Activity Range
Ægelric	Ægel - 1	1056–1059
Ægelwine	Ægel - 2	1083–1086
Ælfstan	Ælf - 1	979–985
Ælfgeat	Ælf - 2	991–1003
Ælfwig	Ælf - 3	1056–1062
Ælfric	Ælf - 4a	1059–1062
Ælfwi	Ælf - 4b	1059–1065
Ælfwi	Ælf - 5	1066–1066
Ælfwi	Ælf - 6	1083–1086
Æthelwi	Æthel - 1a	997–1003
Æthelwig	Æthel - 1b	997–1003
Æthelwig	Æthel - 2	1009–1038
Æthelstan	Æthel - 3	1053–1056
Æthelric	Æthel - 4	1066–1068
Æthelwine	Æthel - 5	1083–1086
Beorhtstan	Beorht - 1	991–1003
Beorhtric	Beorht - 2	1068–1070
Beorhtric	Beorht - 3	1072–1074
Eadric	Ead - 1	1009–1016
Eadstan	Ead - 2	1017–1036
Eadwig	Ead - 3	1048–1056
Eadric	Ead - 4	1056–1059
Eadwi	Ead - 5	1059–1062
Eadric	Ead - 6	1065–1066
Earnwig	Earn - 1	1038–1042
Earnwig	Earn - 2	1059–1062
Earnwig	Earn - 3	1065–1066
Leofgar	Leof - 1	991–1009
Leofmær	Leof - 2	1009–1016
Leofgar	Leof - 3	1017–1029
Leofnoth	Leof - 4	1029–1044
Leofnoth	Leof - 5	1050–1062
Leofstan	Leof - 6	1072–1074
Lifstan	Leof - 7	1083–1086
Godman	None	979–985
Byrhstan	None	995–1003
Dilion	None	997–1003
Etstan	None	1023–1029
Elewig	None	1023–1038
Eielric	None	1046–1048
Rædulf	None	1046–1048

Table 4.23 ***continued***

Moneyer Name	Name Sequence	Activity Range
Æcepi	None	1070–1072
Hethwi	None	1074–1077
Ordric	Ord - 1	1017–1046
Ordwi	Ord - 2	1083–1086
Wulfsige	Wulf - 1	1017–1042
Wulfsige	Wulf - 2a	1044–1046
Wulfstan	Wulf - 2b	1044–1048
Wulfwi	Wulf - 3	1046–1048
Wulfwine	Wulf - 4	1053–1056
Wulfwine	Wulf - 5	1070–1072

Table 4.24. Name Sequences of the Wilton Mint

Moneyer Name	Name Sequence	Activity Range
Ælfsige	Ælf - 1	973–975
Ælfstan	Ælf - 2	1017–1040
Ælfred	Ælf - 3	1029–1036
Ælfwine	Ælf - 4	1040–1046
Ælfstan	Ælf - 5	1044–1048
Ælfwine	Ælf - 6a	1050–1059
Ælfweald	Ælf - 6b	1050–1066
Ælfweard	Ælf - 7	1059–1062
Ælfwine	Ælf - 8	1062–1065
Ælfwine	Ælf - 9	1074–1077
Ælfwine	Ælf - 10	1080–1086
Æthelstan	Æthel - 1	1023–1029
Æthelweald	Æthel - 2	1066–1066
Boiga	Boiga - 1	975–979
Boiga	Boiga - 2	995–997
Eadwine	Ead - 1	973–975
Eadwine	Ead - 2	978–979
Godwine	God - 1	991–1003
Godric	God - 2	1068–1074
Goldus	Gold - 1	997–1003
Goldstan	Gold - 2	1036–1040
Leofweald	Leof - 1	973–975
Leofweald	Leof - 2	991–997
Leofwine	Leof - 3	996–1003
Leofing	Leof - 4	1038–1040
Leofing	Leof - 5	1042–1048
Leofwine	Leof - 6	1062–1065
Wadwine	None	979–985
Wulfgar	None	991–997
Boca	None	995–997
Thorcetel	None	1050–1062
Swartric	None	1056–1062
Hærred	None	1056–1065
Brixi	None	1059–1062
Winus	None	1062–1066
Centwine	None	1065–1066
Opi	None	1066–1068
Osbeorn	Os - 1	973–975
Osbeorn	Os - 2	979–985
Sæwine	Sæ - 1	979–985
Sæwine	Sæ - 2	991–1003
Sæwine	Sæ - 3	1056–1062
Sæware	Sæ - 4	1070–1072
Sæwine	Sæ - 5	1072–1077
Sæwine	Sæ - 6	1083–1086
Sefar	Sef - 1	1068–1070
Sefmrol	Sef - 2	1083–1086
Winesige	Wine - 1	1009–1016
Wineman	Wine - 2	1044–1048

Table 4.25. Name Sequences of the Northampton Mint

Moneyer Name	Name Sequence	Activity Range
Ælfwine	Ælf - 1	1017–1023
Ælfwine	Ælf - 2	1036–1048
Ælfwine	Ælf - 3	1050–1062
Æthelnoth	Æthel - 1	997–1003
Æthelwine	Æthel - 2	1038–1040
Æthelwine	Æthel - 3	1044–1046
Godric	God - 1	1023–1029
Godric	God - 2	1038–1042
Godwine	God - 3	1065–1066
Leofsige	Leof - 1	973–978
Leofsige	Leof - 2	979–985
Leofing	Leof - 3	979–985
Leofsige	Leof - 4a	991–997
Leofstan	Leof - 4b	991–997
Leofwine	Leof - 4c	991–1003
Leofweald	Leof - 5a	997–1003
Leofgod	Leof - 5b	997–1009
Leofweald	Leof - 6a	1009–1023

Table 4.25 ***continued***

Moneyer Name	Name Sequence	Activity Range
Leofwine	Leof - 6b	1009–1040
Leofnoth	Leof - 7	1017–1029
Leofwine	Leof - 8	1042–1046
Leofwine	Leof - 9	1050–1053
Leofric	Leof - 10	1053–1059
Leofstan	Leof - 11	1065–1066
Mantat	Man - 1	973–975
Mancrent	Man - 2	975–979
Man	Man - 3	997–1003
Baldric	None	973–975
Eadnoth	None	973–975
Osweald	None	973–975
Cylm	None	973–978
Cetel	None	975–978
Bruning	None	991–1003
Thorcetel	None	995–997
Sæwine	Sæ - 1	1056–1062
Sæwine	Sæ - 2	1065–1066
Sæwine	Sæ - 3	1070–1080
Sæwig	Sæ - 4	1074–1077
Sæwine	Sæ - 5	1083–1086
Swetman	Swet - 1	1065–1066
Swetman	Swet - 2	1068–1070
Wulfric	Wulf - 1	997–1016
Wulfnoth	Wulf - 2	1009–1016
Wulfnoth	Wulf - 3	1053–1065
Wulfsi	Wulf - 4	1065–1066
Wulfwine	Wulf - 5	1070–1072

Table 4.26. Name Sequences of the Leicester Mint

Moneyer Name	Name Sequence	Activity Range
Ægelwine	Ægel - 1	1023–1029
Ægelwig	Ægel - 2	1029–1036
Ægelric	Ægel - 3	1056–1059
Ægelwine	Ægel - 4	1066–1066
Ægelwine	Ægel - 5	1070–1077
Ægelwine	Ægel - 6	1080–1083
Ælfric	Ælf - 1	991–997
Ælfric	Ælf - 2	1003–1016
Ælfwig	Ælf - 3	1017–1023
Ælfwine	Ælf - 4	1056–1062
Ælfric	Ælf - 5	1059–1065
Æthelwig	Æthel - 1	1009–1036
Æthelwig	Æthel - 2	1048–1050
Æthelric	Æthel - 3	1053–1062
Æthelwine	Æthel - 4	1059–1066
Æthelric	Æthel - 5	1065–1066
Godric	God - 1	1029–1036
Godric	God - 2	1046–1066
Godric	God - 3	1083–1086
Leofric	Leof - 1	1053–1056
Leofric	Leof - 2	1059–1062
Leofric	Leof - 3	1068–1070
Lierie	Lie - 1	1068–1070
Lierie	Lie - 2	1083–1086
Man	None	973–975
Styrcar	None	979–985
Dunn	None	979–991
Thorulf	None	991–1009
Wlancthegn	None	1017–1029
Blacman	None	1044–1046
Eadwine	None	1050–1053
Othulf	None	1065–1066
Frethegest	None	1080–1083
Osfrith	Os - 1	979–985
Osfrith	Os - 2	991–997
Sæwine	Sæ - 1	1038–1042
Sæwine	Sæ - 2	1044–1053
Wulfstan	Wulf - 1	973–975
Wulfgeat	Wulf - 2	991–1003
Wulfnoth	Wulf - 3	1017–1044
Wulfstan	Wulf - 4	1029–1040
Wulfnoth	Wulf - 5	1048–1053
Wulfric	Wulf - 6	1044–1046

Table 4.27. Name Sequences of the Warwick Mint

Moneyer Name	Name Sequence	Activity Range
Ælfsige	Ælf - 1	1044–1046
Ælfric	Ælf - 2	1083–1086
Æthelstan	Æthel - 1	997–1003
Æthelric	Æthel - 2	1003–1009
Æthelwine	Æthel - 3	1017–1023
Æthelstan	Æthel - 4	1053–1056

Table 4.27 ***continued***

Moneyer Name	Name Sequence	Activity Range
Æthelstan	Æthel - 5	1059–1062
Godric	God - 1	1017–1023
Godwine	God - 2	1023–1029
Goda	God - 3	1036–1042
Leofweald	Leof - 1	1009–1016
Leofwine	Leof - 2	1017–1023
Leofing	Leof - 3a	1023–1036
Leofwig	Leof - 3b	1023–1042
Leofwine	Leof - 4	1036–1038
Leofwi	Leof - 5	1040–1042
Leofwine	Leof - 6	1042–1044
Leofric	Leof - 7	1044–1046
Leofing	Leof - 8	1048–1053
Leofric	Leof - 9	1050–1053
Leofing	Leof - 10	1056–1059
Leofing	Leof - 11	1066–1066
Leofric	Leof - 12	1074–1077
Leofing	Leof - 13a	1083–1086
Leofric	Leof - 13b	1083–1086
Beorhtsige	None	997–1003
Hyse	None	1009–1016
Sigeweard	None	1036–1038
Eicefric	None	1044–1046
Theodric	None	1065–1066
Swarting	None	1066–1066
Osmær	Os - 1	975–978
Osmær	Os - 2	979–985
Osmær	Os - 3	991–1003
Thorcetel	Thor - 1	1056–1068
Thorcel	Thor - 2a	1059–1062
Thorstan	Thor - 2b	1059–1062
Thorcel	Thor - 3	1074–1077
Thorcel	Thor - 4	1083–1086
Wulfric	Wulf - 1	1009–1023
Wulfwine	Wulf - 2	1062–1065
Wulfwine	Wulf - 3	1066–1066

Table 4.28. Name Sequences of the Hertford Mint

Moneyer Name	Name Sequence	Activity Range
Deorsige	Deor - 1	1017–1040
Deorsige	Deor - 2	1044–1046
Eadwig	Ead - 1	991–997
Eadwi	Ead - 2	995–997
Godric	God - 1	997–1003
Godman	God - 2	1038–1040
Godman	God - 3a	1044–1048
Godwine	God - 3b	1044–1048
Godwine	God - 4	1059–1065
Leofing	Leof - 1	995–997
Leofing	Leof - 2a	1017–1023
Leofwine	Leof - 2b	1017–1036
Leofric	Leof - 3	1023–1040
Leofing	Leof - 4	1029–1036
Leofred	Leof - 5	1040–1042
Leofing	Leof - 6	1048–1050
Æthelweard	None	991–997
Beorhtlaf	None	991–997
Boiga	None	991–997
Burging	None	991–997
Beornulf	None	995–997
Man	None	1009–1016
Ælfwine	None	1046–1048
Goldwine	None	1046–1048
Pidred	None	1048–1050
Sæmær	Sæ - 1	1044–1046
Sæmær	Sæ - 2	1056–1062
Semær	Sæ - 3	1083–1086
Theodred	Theod - 1	1048–1050
Theodric	Theod - 2	1083–1086
Wilgrip	Wil - 1	1050–1056
Wilgrip	Wil - 2	1059–1066
Wulfmær	Wulf - 1	975–978
Wulfmær	Wulf - 2	979–985
Wulfnoth	Wulf - 3	991–997
Wulfric	Wulf - 4	991–997
Wulfric	Wulf - 5	1003–1023
Wulfric	Wulf - 6	1044–1046
Wulfric	Wulf - 7	1048–1050
Wulfric	Wulf - 8	1053–1056
Wulfric	Wulf - 9	1062–1066

Table 4.29. Name Sequences of the Ilchester Mint

Moneyer Name	Name Sequence	Activity Range
Ægelwig	Ægel - 1	1029–1036
Ægelwine	Ægel - 2	1062–1065
Ægelwine	Ægel - 3	1066–1066
Ægelwine	Ægel - 4	1072–1077
Ælfsige	Ælf - 1	979–991
Ælfric	Ælf - 2	997–1003
Ælfsige	Ælf - 3a	1017–1023
Ælfwine	Ælf - 3b	1017–1029
Ælfnoth	Ælf - 4a	1023–1029
Ælfwine Mus	Ælf - 4b	1023–1029
Ælfwine	Ælf - 5	1066–1068
Ælfweard	Ælf - 6	1077–1080
Ælfweard	Ælf – 7a	1083–1086
Ælfwine	Ælf - 7b	1083–1086
Æthelmær	Æthel - 1a	1017–1023
Æthelwig	Æthel - 1b	1017–1036
Æthelwine	Æthel - 2	1036–1038
Æthelwine	Æthel - 3	1062–1066
Æthelwine	Æthel - 4	1074–1077
Æthelweard	Æthel - 5	1083–1086
Goda	God – 1a	979–985
God	God – 1b	979–1003
Goda	God - 2	991–1003
Godwine	God - 3	1017–1023
Godric	God - 4	1029–1036
Godric	God - 5	1038–1042
Godric	God - 6	1056–1062
Godwine	God - 7	1074–1077
God	God - 8	1083–1086
Leofric	Leof - 1	991–997
Leofsige	Leof - 2	991–1009
Hunewine	None	995–997
Thurulf	None	997–1003
Winas	None	1003–1009
Cæfel	None	1029–1036
Dunbeard	None	1040–1044
Oswig	Os - 1	1017–1023
Osward	Os - 2	1050–1053
Pixsi	Pix - 1	1070–1072
Pixsi	Pix - 2	1077–1080
Wihtsige	None	1077–1080
Wulfhelm	Wulf - 1	985–997
Wulfhelm	Wulf - 2	1017–1023

Table 4.30. Name Sequences of the Bristol Mint

Moneyer Name	Name Sequence	Activity Range
Ægelwine	Ægel - 1	1017–1023
Ægelwine	Ægel - 2	1029–1036
Ægelwine	Ægel - 3	1042–1042
Ælfweard	Ælf - 1	1009–1016
Ælfwine	Ælf - 2	1017–1023
Ælfweard	Ælf - 3	1036–1040
Ælfwig	Ælf - 4a	1042–1044
Ælfwine	Ælf - 4b	1042–1044
Ælfweard	Ælf - 5	1044–1053
Ælfric	Ælf - 6	1053–1056
Ælfwine	Ælf - 7	1056–1066
Ælfric	Ælf - 8	1059–1062
Æthelwine	Æthel - 1	1017–1023
Æthelwine	Æthel - 2	1029–1038
Æthelstan	Æthel - 3a	1040–1044
Æthelwine	Æthel - 3b	1040–1042
Æthelweard	Æthel - 4	1042–1044
Æthelstan	Æthel - 5	1050–1059
Ceorl	Ceorl - 1	1065–1068
Ceorl	Ceorl - 2	1070–1072
Ceorl	Ceorl - 3	1074–1077
Godman	God - 1	1017–1023
Godwine	God - 2	1050–1053
Godwine	God - 3	1059–1065
Leofwine	Leof - 1	1029–1040
Leofwine	Leof - 2	1066–1068
Leofwine	Leof - 3	1072–1080
Lifwine	Leof - 4	1083–1086
Sæwine	None	1036–1042
Beorhtweard	None	1083–1086
Brunstan	None	1083–1086
Brwode	None	1083–1086
Colblac	None	1083–1086
Spegn	None	1083–1086
Wulfwine	Wulf - 1	1017–1023
Wulfstan	Wulf - 2	1029–1036
Wulfwine	Wulf - 3	1036–1042
Wulfnoth	Wulf - 4	1038–1040

Table 4.31. Name Sequences of the Shaftesbury Mint

Moneyer Name	Name Sequence	Activity Range
Ægelwine	Ægel - 1	1017–1023
Ægelric	Ægel - 2	1023–1036
Ægelric	Ægel - 3	1040–1042
Ægelwine	Ægel - 4	1066–1066
Ælfwine	Ælf - 1	997–1003
Ælfwine	Ælf - 2	1009–1023
Ælfric	Ælf - 3	1017–1023
Ælfweard	Ælf - 4	1044–1046
Ælfweard	Ælf - 5	1059–1062
Ælfnoth	Ælf - 6	1066–1066
Ælfnoth	Ælf - 7	1074–1077
Ælfnoth	Ælf - 8	1080–1086
Æthelstan	Æthel - 1	979–991
Æthelwi	Æthel - 2	985–991
Æthelgeard	Æthel - 3	991–997
Æthelwig	Æthel - 4	997–1003
Æthelric	Æthel - 5	1003–1042
Æthelwine	Æthel - 6	1017–1023
Æthelric	Æthel - 7	1062–1066
Æthelwine	Æthel - 8	1066–1066
Cantwine	Cant - 1	1074–1077
Cantwine	Cant - 2	1080–1086
Goda	God - 1	991–1036
Godric	God - 2	1062–1066
Godsbrand	God - 3	1077–1086
Lyfa	Lyf - 1	991–1003
Lyfa	Lyf - 2	1017–1023
Beorhtweald	None	978–979
Beola	None	1017–1029
Wuducoc	None	1053–1056
Sæwine	Sæ - 1	997–1009
Sæwine	Sæ - 2	1017–1023
Wulfric	Wulf - 1	1038–1040
Wulfnoth	Wulf - 2	1040–1042
Wulfric	Wulf - 3	1044–1046
Wulfmær	Wulf - 4a	1048–1050
Wulfric	Wulf - 4b	1048–1062
Wulfmær	Wulf - 5	1066–1066

Table 4.32. Name Sequences of the Derby Mint

Moneyer Name	Name Sequence	Activity Range
Blacman	Blac - 1	1003–1009
Blacman	Blac - 2	1017–1023
Blacman	Blac - 3	1036–1038
Blacman	Blac - 4	1042–1044
Blacman	Blac - 5	1048–1050
Colbeinn	Col - 1	1062–1065
Colrin	Col - 2	1062–1065
Colbein	Col - 3	1068–1070
Froma	From - 1	1044–1046
Froma	From - 2	1048–1062
Froma	From - 3	1065–1066
Godwine	God - 1	997–1003
Godric	God - 2	1038–1042
Godric	God - 3	1044–1046
Godwine	God - 4	1068–1070
Godwine	God - 5	1083–1086
Leofwine	Leof - 1	1050–1053
Leofwine	Leof - 2	1059–1065
Lifwine	Leof - 3	1083–1086
Gunner	None	978–985
Ælfcetel	None	1003–1016
Spatic	None	1046–1048
Dunning	None	1056–1066
Forni	None	1066–1068
Osulf	Os - 1	973–985
Oscar	Os - 2	1009–1016
Osbern	Os - 3	1017–1023
Swerting	Swert - 1	1023–1042
Swerting	Swert - 2	1050–1053
Wulfstan	Wulf - 1	979–985
Wulfstan	Wulf - 2	991–1009
Wulfsige	Wulf - 3	997–1003
Wulfsige	Wulf - 4	1009–1016
Wulfheah	Wulf - 5	1036–1038
Wulfheah	Wulf - 6	1040–1044

Table 4.33. Name Sequences of the Chichester Mint

Moneyer Name	Name Sequence	Activity Range
Ælfwig	Ælf - 1	991–997
Ælfwine	Ælf - 2	991–1003
Ælfwine	Ælf - 3	1009–1016
Ælfric	Ælf - 4	1029–1040
Ælfwine	Ælf - 5	1044–1046
Ælfwine	Ælf - 6	1048–1066
Æthelstan	Æthel - 1	991–997
Æthelhelm	Æthel - 2a	991–1009
Æthelm	Æthel - 2b	997–1023
Æthelhelm	Æthel - 3	1017–1036
Æthelwine	Æthel - 4	1050–1053
Brunman	Brun - 1	1066–1068
Brunman	Brun - 2	1070–1072
Brunman	Brun - 3	1074–1086
Eadnoth	Ead - 1	995–1003
Edwine	Ead - 2	1083–1086
Goda	God - 1a	1038–1040
Godric	God - 1b	1038–1040
Godwine	God - 2	1053–1062
Godwine	God - 3	1066–1066
Godwine	God - 4	1074–1080
Heawulf	Heah - 1	979–985
Heawulf	Heah - 2	1003–1009
Leofwine	Leof - 1a	1017–1038
Leofric	Leof - 1b	1017–1042
Leofwig	Leof - 2	1023–1029
Flodwin	None	973–975
Wunstan	None	985–991
Cynna	None	997–1003
Dunstan	None	1009–1016
Beorhtnoth	None	1017–1023
Ægelm	None	1023–1036
Wulfnoth	Wulf - 1	1017–1023
Wulfric	Wulf - 2	1053–1066

Table 4.34. Name Sequences of the Huntingdon Mint

Moneyer Name	Name Sequence	Activity Range
Ælfric	Ælf - 1	979–985
Ælfric	Ælf - 2	991–1003
Ælfnoth	Ælf - 3	1009–1016
Ælfgar	Ælf - 4	1029–1036
Ælfwine	Ælf - 5	1040–1042
Ælfwine	Ælf - 6	1046–1053
Ælfwine	Ælf - 7	1083–1086
Eadwine	Ead - 1	1003–1009
Eadnoth	Ead - 2	1017–1029
Godric	God - 1a	1017–1023
Godleof	God - 1b	1017–1029
Godric	God - 2	1050–1056
Godwine	God - 3	1053–1065
Godric	God - 4	1059–1062
Godwine	God - 5a	1066–1066
Godric	God - 5b	1066–1070
Godwine	God - 6	1070–1072
Godric	God - 7	1072–1074
Godwine	God - 8	1077–1080
Leofric	Leof - 1	991–997
Leofn	Leof - 2	997–1003
Leofwine	Leof - 3	1059–1062
Osgod	None	995–1009
Æthelstan	None	1003–1023
Sæwine	None	1003–1023
Farthegn	None	1017–1023
Steordine	None	1023–1029
Winsige	None	1023–1029
Ada	None	1029–1036
Ulfcetel	None	1048–1050
Wulfgar	Wulf - 1	979–985
Wulfwine	Wulf - 2	1029–1046
Wulfwi	Wulf - 3	1038–1040
Wulfstan	Wulf - 4	1040–1042
Wulfwig	Wulf - 5	1044–1046

Table 4.35. Name Sequences of the Rochester Mint

Moneyer Name	Name Sequence	Activity Range
Eadelm	Ead - 1	979–985
Eadsige	Ead - 2	991–1003
Eadwine	Ead - 3a	997–1003
Eadweard	Ead - 3b	997–1016
Eadnoth	Ead - 4	1009–1016
Eadwine	Ead - 5	1044–1048
Eadwine	Ead - 6	1053–1056
Eadwine	Ead - 7	1062–1065

Table 4.35 ***continued***

Moneyer Name	Name Sequence	Activity Range
Godwine	God - 1	1009–1040
Godwine	God - 2	1042–1048
Godwine	God - 3	1053–1056
Leofric	Leof - 1	985–997
Leofric	Leof - 2	1023–1029
Leofwine	Leof - 3	1056–1065
Leofstan	Leof - 4a	1066–1066
Leofwine	Leof - 4b	1066–1066
Leofwine	Leof - 5	1074–1077
Leofwine	Leof - 6a	1083–1086
Lifstan	Leof - 6b	1083–1086
Lifwinehorn	Leof - 6c	1083–1086
Osfrith	None	991–991
Beorhtmær	None	991–997
Brun	None	991–997
Goldwine	None	991–1003
Ælfheah	None	1009–1038
Sideman	Side - 1	973–978
Sideman	Side - 2a	979–985
Sidewine	Side - 2b	979–997
Sidewine	Side - 3	1017–1023
Wulfred	Wulf - 1	1009–1016
Wulfric	Wulf - 2	1029–1036
Wulfric	Wulf - 3	1046–1048

Table 4.36. Name Sequences of the Bath Mint

Moneyer Name	Name Sequence	Activity Range
Ægelmær	Ægel - 1	1040–1042
Ægelmær	Ægel - 2	1044–1046
Ægelmær	Ægel - 3	1050–1053
Ægelmie	Ægel - 4	1083–1086
Ælfric	Ælf - 1	997–1036
Ælfweald	Ælf - 2	1003–1029
Ælfwine	Ælf - 3	1023–1036
Ælfwig	Ælf - 4	1036–1038
Æthelric	Æthel - 1a	979–1029
Æthelsige	Æthel - 1b	979–985
Æthelsige	Æthel - 2	991–997
Æthelstan	Æthel - 3	1003–1036
Æthelwine	Æthel - 4	1029–1036
Æthelmær	Æthel - 5	1036–1053
Æthelmær	Æthel - 6	1083–1086
Godric	God - 1	1050–1062
Godsbrand	God - 2	1083–1086
Brihferth	None	975–978
Wynstan	None	991–1003
Hildsige	None	991–1016
Eadstan	None	997–1003
Ælhær	None	1038–1040
Leofwine	None	1040–1042
Urlwine	None	1059–1065
Osmær	Os - 1	1053–1065
Osmær	Os - 2	1074–1077
Osmær	Os - 3	1083–1086
Wædel	Wæd - 1	1036–1046
Wædel	Wæd - 2	1048–1050

Table 4.37. Name Sequences of the Cricklade Mint

Moneyer Name	Name Sequence	Activity Range
Ægelwine	Ægel - 1	1023–1029
Ægelwi	Ægel - 2	1046–1048
Ægelwine	Ægel - 3	1050–1056
Ægelwi	Ægel - 4	1056–1059
Ægelwine	Ægel - 5	1062–1065
Ælfwine	Ælf - 1	1009–1036
Ælfwine	Ælf - 2	1038–1040
Ælfwine	Ælf - 3	1042–1046
Ælfwine	Ælf - 4	1083–1086
Æthelstan	Æthel - 1	979–985
Æthelwine	Æthel - 2	995–1003
Æthelsige	Æthel - 3	1003–1016
Æthelwine	Æthel - 4	1017–1042
Æthelwig	Æthel - 5	1056–1059
Goda	God - 1	979–985
Godman	God - 2a	1017–1023
Godwine	God - 2b	1017–1029
Leofgod	Leof - 1	997–1003
Leofing	Leof - 2	1029–1036
Leofred	Leof - 3	1053–1062
Leofred	Leof - 4	1065–1066
Leofred	Leof - 5	1068–1070
Leofred	Leof - 6	1072–1077
Beorhtmær	None	1003–1009

Table 4.37 ***continued***

Moneyer Name	Name Sequence	Activity Range
Toca	None	1017–1023
Wulfheah	Wulf - 1	1029–1036
Wulfstan	Wulf - 2	1074–1077
Wulfstan	Wulf - 3	1080–1083

Table 4.38. Name Sequences of the Hastings Mint

Moneyer Name	Name Sequence	Activity Range
Ælfweard	Ælf - 1	1017–1042
Ælfwine	Ælf - 2a	1029–1036
Ælfred	Ælf - 2b	1029–1038
Brid	Brid - 1	1029–1040
Brid	Brid - 2	1042–1062
Colswegen	Col - 1	1062–1068
Kolsveinn	Col - 2	1066–1068
Dunning	Dun - 1	1053–1066
Dunic	Dun - 2	1066–1068
Dunic	Dun - 3	1074–1077
Dunic	Dun - 4	1083–1086
Eadstan	Ead - 1	991–997
Eadsige	Ead - 2	1003–1009
Eadsige	Ead - 3	1023–1029
Eadwine	Ead - 4	1036–1038
Leofa	Leof - 1	997–1009
Leofing	Leof - 2	1038–1040
Leofwine	Leof - 3	1040–1042
Leofwine	Leof - 4	1046–1048
Leofwine	Leof - 5	1050–1053
Lyua	None	997–1003
Æthelsige	None	1017–1029
Etsige	None	1023–1029
Theodred	None	1059–1066
Diodred	None	1066–1068
Cipinc	None	1083–1086
Wulfnoth	Wulf - 1	1029–1036
Wulfric	Wulf - 2	1056–1062

Table 4.39. Name Sequences of the Nottingham Mint

Moneyer Name	Name Sequence	Activity Range
Forni	For - 1	1053–1065
Forman	For - 2	1062–1065
Forni	For - 3	1066–1066
Forni	For - 4	1068–1074
Halfdene	Half - 1	1042–1044
Halfdene	Half - 2	1048–1053
Leofstan	Leof - 1a	1040–1042
Leofsige	Leof - 1b	1040–1044
Leofsige	Leof - 2	1046–1050
Manna	Man - 1	1066–1066
Man	Man - 2a	1070–1072
Manna	Man - 2b	1070–1074
Man	Man - 3a	1083–1086
Manna	Man - 3b	1083–1086
Blacman	None	1017–1053
Bruning	None	1023–1029
Sægrim	None	1036–1042
Alhmund	None	1048–1050
Snoter	None	1048–1050
Fulnoth	None	1050–1053
Arngrim	None	1062–1065
Ætcer	None	1083–1086
Osweald	Os - 1	991–997
Osweald	Os - 2	1003–1029
Wulfnoth	Wulf - 1	1040–1042
Wulfnoth	Wulf - 2	1050–1053
Wulfnoth	Wulf - 3	1059–1062

Table 4.40. Name Sequences of the Salisbury Mint

Moneyer Name	Name Sequence	Activity Range
Ælfnoth	Ælf - 1	1009–1029
Ælfred	Ælf - 2	1017–1023
Ælfwine	Ælf - 3	1023–1029
Ælfred	Ælf - 4	1029–1040
Ælfweald	Ælf - 5	1046–1050
Godwine	God - 1	1003–1042
Godric	God - 2a	1044–1046
Godwine	God - 2b	1044–1050
Godric	God - 3	1056–1062
Godric	God - 4	1074–1077

Table 4.40 *continued*

Moneyer Name	Name Sequence	Activity Range
Godric	God - 5	1080–1083
Godwine	God - 6	1083–1086
Goldus	Gold - 1	1003–1036
Goldstan	Gold - 2	1036–1038
Leofweald	Leof - 1	1017–1023
Leofstan	Leof - 2	1023–1029
Leofstan	Leof - 3	1038–1042
Siboda	None	1065–1066
Esbern	None	1083–1086
Osbern	None	1083–1086
Sæwine	Sæ - 1	1003–1016
Sæman	Sæ - 2	1009–1023
Sæbeorht	Sæ - 3	1065–1066
Winestan	Wine - 1	1017–1029
Winestan	Wine - 2	1036–1044
Wineman	Wine - 3	1040–1048

Table 4.41. Name Sequences of the Wareham Mint

Moneyer Name	Name Sequence	Activity Range
Ægelric	Ægel - 1	1066–1068
Ægelric	Ægel - 2	1072–1080
Ægelric	Ægel - 3	1083–1086
Ælfgar	Ælf - 1a	991–997
Ælfsige	Ælf - 1b	991–1003
Ælfgar	Ælf - 2	1009–1016
Æthelric	Æthel - 1	997–1003
Æthelric	Æthel - 2	1077–1080
Beorhtric	Beorht - 1a	985–997
Beorhtsige	Beorht - 1b	985–997
Beorn	Beorn - 1	1059–1062
Beorn	Beorn - 2	1074–1077
Godwine	God - 1	1074–1080
Godwine	God - 2	1083–1086
Oda	None	1017–1023
Sideman	Side - 1	1038–1042
Sideman	Side - 2	1044–1048
Sideman	Side - 3	1050–1068
Sideman	Side - 4	1070–1072
Sideloc	Side - 5	1083–1086
Wulfric	Wulf - 1	979–985
Wulfric	Wulf - 2	997–1003
Wulfsige	Wulf - 3	1059–1062

Table 4.42. Name Sequences of the Maldon Mint

Moneyer Name	Name Sequence	Activity Range
Ælfwine	Ælf - 1	991–997
Ælfwine	Ælf - 2	1017–1029
Ælford	Ælf - 3a	1083–1086
Ælfwine	Ælf - 3b	1083–1086
Æthelwine	Æthel - 1	995–997
Æthelwine	Æthel - 2	1003–1023
Dægniht	Dæg - 1	1048–1053
Dægniht	Dæg - 2	1042–1044
Dæg	Dæg - 3	1044–1046
Godwine	God - 1	1017–1023
Godhere	God - 2	1023–1029
Godric	God - 3a	1053–1062
Godwine	God - 3b	1053–1065
Godwine	God - 4	1066–1066
Leofwig	Leof - 1a	991–997
Leofwine	Leof - 1b	991–997
Leofwine	Leof - 2	1023–1029
Leofsunu	Leof - 3	1083–1086
Toca	None	997–1003
Ceolnoth	None	1017–1029
Swetric	None	1056–1059

Table 4.43. Name Sequences of the Malmesbury Mint

Moneyer Name	Name Sequence	Activity Range
Beorhtstan	Beorht - 1	1017–1023
Beorhtnoth	Beorht - 2	1023–1029
Beorhtwine	Beorht - 3	1044–1048
Beorhtwi	Beorht - 4a	1059–1062
Beorhtwig	Beorht - 4b	1059–1062
Beorht	Beorht - 5a	1062–1065
Beorhtwine	Beorht - 5b	1062–1066
Beorhtwig	Beorht - 6	1066–1066
Beorhtwine	Beorht - 7	1068–1070
Beorhtwine	Beorht - 8	1072–1077
Ealdred	Eald - 1	985–1003
Ealdred	Eald - 2	1009–1009
Ealdwig	Eald - 3	1050–1056

Table 4.43 *continued*

Moneyer Name	Name Sequence	Activity Range
Ealdwine	Eald - 4	1056–1059
Godman	God - 1	1038–1040
Godsbrand	God - 2	1083–1086
Huna	Hun - 1	1023–1044
Huna	Hun - 2	1048–1050
Leofgæt	None	997–1003
Seweard	None	1083–1086

Table 4.44. Name Sequences of the Totnes Mint

Moneyer Name	Name Sequence	Activity Range
Ælfstan	Ælf - 1	991–1003
Ælfwine	Ælf - 2	1023–1029
Beorhtwine	Beorht - 1	991–997
Beorhtfrith	Beorht - 2	1003–1009
Farmann	Far - 1	1036–1038
Farmann	Far - 2	1040–1042
Godwine	God - 1	991–1009
Goda	God - 2	1009–1016
Hunewine	Hune - 1	985–991
Huneman	Hune - 2	1009–1016
Winestan	None	975–978
Man	None	978–997
Dodda	None	979–997
Leofgar	None	1017–1023
Thorgod	None	1017–1023
Sæwine	None	1023–1029
Wulfgar	Wulf - 1	985–991
Wulfmær	Wulf - 2	997–1003
Wulfweard	Wulf - 3	1023–1029

Table 4.45. Name Sequences of the Barnstaple Mint

Moneyer Name	Name Sequence	Activity Range
Ælfhelm	Ælf - 1	979–985
Ælfsige	Ælf - 2	991–1003
Ælfgar	Ælf - 3	1017–1036
Ælfgar	Ælf - 4	1038–1040
Ælfric	Ælf - 5	1044–1046
Ælfric	Ælf - 6	1053–1062
Æthelric	Æthel - 1	1003–1009
Æthelmær	Æthel - 2	1044–1046

Moneyer Name	Name Sequence	Activity Range
Beorhtulf	Beorht - 1a	979–985
Beorhtsige	Beorht - 1b	979–1009
Beorhtsige	Beorht - 2	1017–1023
Bryhsige	Byrh - 1	985–1003
Byrhsie	Byrh - 2	1009–1023
Huna	None	997–1009
Ata	None	1017–1023
Leofwine	None	1068–1070
Sæweard	Sæ - 1	1077–1080
Sæweard	Sæ - 2	1083–1086

Table 4.46. Name Sequences of the Dorchester Mint

Moneyer Name	Name Sequence	Activity Range
Blacman	Blac - 1	1042–1044
Blacman	Blac - 2	1053–1056
Blacman	Blac - 3	1059–1065
Blacman	Blac - 4	1066–1066
Godwine	God - 1	1038–1042
Godwin	God - 2	1074–1077
Hwætman	Hwæt - 1	1036–1042
Hwateman	Hwæt - 2	1050–1053
Alfred	None	979–985
Swet	None	1017–1036
Æthelric	None	1036–1038
Ægelric	None	1040–1042
Ottarr	Ot - 1	1070–1072
Oter	Ot - 2	1074–1086
Ottarr	Ot - 3	1077–1080
Ottarr	Ot - 4	1083–1086
Wulfnoth	Wulf - 1	991–1016
Wulfsige	Wulf - 2	1017–1023

Table 4.47. Name Sequences of the Romney Mint

Moneyer Name	Name Sequence	Activity Range
Æthelwine	Æthel - 1	997–1009
Æthelric	Æthel - 2	1023–1029
Æthelstan	Æthel - 3	1048–1050
Godman	God - 1	1009–1016
Godric	God - 2a	1023–1029
Godwine	God - 2b	1023–1029
Godman	God - 3	1029–1036

Table 4.47 *continued*

Moneyer Name	Name Sequence	Activity Range
Leofwine	Leof - 1	997–1003
Leofwine	Leof - 2	1017–1023
Eardnoth	None	1017–1023
Eadmær	None	1038–1040
Ælfmær	None	1074–1080
Pindei	None	1083–1086
Wulfnoth	Wulf - 1	1009–1040
Wulfwig	Wulf - 2	1036–1038
Wulfmær	Wulf - 3	1042–1044
Wulfmær	Wulf - 4	1046–1068
Wulfmær	Wulf - 5	1083–1086

Table 4.48. Name Sequences of the Stafford Mint

Moneyer Name	Name Sequence	Activity Range
Ælfweald	Ælf - 1	978–985
Ælfweald	Ælf - 2	991–997
Ælfweald	Ælf - 3	1009–1016
Ælfric	Ælf - 4	1017–1029
Ælfric	Ælf - 5	1038–1040
Ælfric	Ælf - 6	1050–1053
Godric	God - 1	1003–1016
Godwine	God - 2	1065–1066
Godwine	God - 3	1068–1070
Godric	God - 4a	1083–1086
Godwine	God - 4b	1083–1086
Ægenulf	None	997–1003
Scot	None	997–1003
Fierlf	None	1023–1029
Ecrie	None	1029–1036
Coling	None	1059–1062
Wulfnoth	None	1068–1070
Leofwine	None	1074–1077

Table 4.49. Name Sequences of the Tamworth Mint

Moneyer Name	Name Sequence	Activity Range
Ælfgar	Ælf - 1	991–997
Ælfgar	Ælf - 2	1003–1009
Bruning	Brun - 1	1048–1053
Bruning	Brun - 2	1059–1066
Bruning	Brun - 3	1083–1086
Coling	Col - 1	1056–1062
Coling	Col - 2	1065–1066
Coling	Col - 3	1068–1070
Coling	Col - 4	1083–1086
Leofwine	Leof - 1	978–979
Leofnoth	Leof - 2	1036–1038
Deorwulf	None	973–978
Wine	None	979–985
Fastolf	None	991–997
Ægelwine	None	1050–1053
Æthelwine	None	1050–1053
Beorhtwine	None	1068–1070

Table 4.50. Name Sequences of the Lympne Mint

Moneyer Name	Name Sequence	Activity Range
Godric	God - 1	997–1003
Godric	God - 2	1023–1036
Leofwine	Leof - 1	973–975
Leofweald	Leof - 2	975–978
Leofwine	Leof - 3a	979–985
Leofric	Leof - 3b	979–997
Leofwine	Leof - 4	1017–1023
Ælfweald	None	973–975
Æthelstan	None	973–978
Beorhtric	None	975–978
Eatstan	None	985–991
Eadward	None	991–997
Iohan	None	1017–1023
Wine	Wine - 1	975–978
Wine	Wine - 2	979–985

Table 4.51. Name Sequences of the Steyning Mint

Moneyer Name	Name Sequence	Activity Range
Deorman	Deor - 1	1059–1066
Deorman	Deor - 2	1068–1070
Deorman	Deor - 3	1072–1074
Deorman	Deor - 4	1083–1086
Frithwine	Frith - 1	1029–1040
Frithi	Frith - 2	1040–1042
Frithwine	Frith - 3	1046–1048
Goldwine	Gold - 1	1050–1053
Goldwine	Gold - 2	1059–1066

Table 4.51 ***continued***

Moneyer Name	Name Sequence	Activity Range
Widia	None	1023–1036
Thorbeorn	None	1083–1086
Wulfric	Wulf - 1	1042–1044
Wulfgæt	Wulf - 2a	1048–1053
Wulfric	Wulf - 2b	1048–1059
Wulfric	Wulf - 3	1065–1066

Table 4.52. Name Sequences of the Taunton Mint

Moneyer Name	Name Sequence	Activity Range
Ælfsige	Ælf - 1	1017–1023
Ælfwine	Ælf - 2	1074–1080
Ælfwine	Ælf - 3	1083–1086
Beorhtstan	Beorht - 1	1017–1023
Beorhtric	Beorht - 2	1053–1062
Beorhtric	Beorht - 3	1066–1066
Beorhtric	Beorht - 4	1070–1074
Boiga	Boiga - 1	1040–1044
Boiga	Boiga - 2	1046–1050
Eadric	Ead - 1	1009–1023
Eadric	Ead - 2	1036–1038
Eadric	Ead - 3	1040–1042
Leofwine	Leof - 1	997–1003
Leofwine	Leof - 2	1038–1040
Gillecrist	None	1042–1044

Table 4.53. Name Sequences of the Bridport Mint

Moneyer Name	Name Sequence	Activity Range
Ælfweard	Ælf - 1	1009–1016
Ælfweald	Ælf - 2	1023–1029
Ælfric	Ælf - 3	1083–1086
Beorhtwi	Beorht - 1a	1083–1086
Beorhtwig	Beorht - 1b	1083–1086
Beorhtwine	Beorht - 1c	1083–1086
Hwætman	Hwæt - 1	1036–1038
Hwætman	Hwæt - 2	1040–1042
Hwætman	Hwæt - 3	1048–1050
Hwætman	Hwæt - 4	1065–1066
Thatman	Hwæt - 5	1074–1077
Wine	None	979–985
Eadnoth	None	985–1003
Godric	None	991–997

Table 4.54. Name Sequences of the Lydford Mint

Moneyer Name	Name Sequence	Activity Range
Ælfstan	Ælf - 1	997–1003
Ælfric	Ælf - 2	1036–1038
Ælfwine	Ælf - 3	1038–1042
Ælfric	Ælf - 4	1042–1044
Ælfric	Ælf - 5	1048–1050
Godwine	God - 1	979–991
Goda	God - 2	991–1016
Godwine	God - 3	995–997
Godric	God - 4	1009–1023
Æthelred	None	975–985
Brun	None	997–1023
Sæwine	None	1017–1029
Eadwine	None	1029–1036
Wicing	None	1029–1036

Table 4.55. Name Sequences of the Southampton Mint

Moneyer Name	Name Sequence	Activity Range
Ælfsige	Ælf - 1a	1017–1023
Ælfweard	Ælf - 1b	1017–1023
Æthelweard	Æthel - 1	979–985
Æthelnoth	Æthel - 2	997–1003
Æthelsige	Æthel - 3	1003–1009
Isegod	Ise - 1	979–985
Isegod	Ise - 2	991–997
Eadwine	None	975–978
Landbeorht	None	975–978
Godman	None	991–997
Spileman	None	997–1003
Seolca	None	1009–1016
Leofwine	None	1017–1023
Siboda	None	1017–1023

Table 4.56. Name Sequences of the Guildford Mint

Moneyer Name	Name Sequence	Activity Range
Ælfweard	Ælf - 1	975–978
Ælfweald	Ælf - 2	1029–1036
Ælfric	Ælf - 3	1059–1065
Blacman	Blac - 1	1029–1040
Blacman	Blac - 2	1050–1062
Duncild	Dun - 1a	997–1003

Table 4.56 *continued*

Moneyer Name	Name Sequence	Activity Range
Dunstan	Dun - 1b	997–1003
Leofweald	Leof - 1	991–1003
Leofweald	Leof - 2	1065–1066
Smeawine	None	1017–1023
Godwine	None	1062–1065
Seric	Se - 1	1074–1077
Seric	Se - 2	1083–1086

Table 4.57. Name Sequences of the Buckingham Mint

Moneyer Name	Name Sequence	Activity Range
Ælfwig	Ælf - 1	997–1003
Ælfweard	Ælf - 2	1017–1023
Leofric	Leof - 1	1017–1029
Leofwine	Leof - 2	1038–1040
Leofwine	Leof - 3	1046–1048
Leofwine	Leof - 4	1050–1053
Sibwine	None	991–997
Beorhtwine	None	1036–1038
Theodred	None	1056–1059
Æthelstan	None	1059–1062
Tunulf	Tun - 1	975–978
Tunulf	Tun - 2	991–997

Table 4.58. Name Sequences of the Winchcombe Mint

Moneyer Name	Name Sequence	Activity Range
Ælfnoth	Ælf - 1	973–975
Ælfhelm	Ælf - 2a	997–1003
Ælfgar	Ælf - 2b	997–1009
Goldwine	Gold - 1	1048–1053
Goldwine	Gold - 2	1059–1062
Goldwine	Gold - 3	1066–1066
Goldwine	Gold - 4	1074–1077
Goldwine	Gold - 5	1083–1086
Godleof	None	995–997
Æthelman	None	1017–1023
Drowa	None	1017–1029
Draca	None	1040–1042

Table 4.59. Name Sequences of the Axbridge Mint

Moneyer Name	Name Sequence	Activity Range
Ælfsige	Ælf - 1	973–975
Ælfric	Ælf - 2	1017–1023
Golda	Gold - 1a	1040–1042
Goldcyta	Gold - 1b	1040–1042
Leofwine	Leof - 1	1029–1036
Leofric	Leof - 2	1036–1038
Leofwine	Leof - 3	1040–1042
Hunewine	None	1017–1023
Goda	None	1023–1029

Table 4.60. Name Sequences of the Langport Mint

Moneyer Name	Name Sequence	Activity Range
Ælfwi	Ælf - 1	1017–1023
Ælfweard	Ælf - 2	1036–1038
Æthelwine	Æthel - 1	1017–1038
Æthelwine	Æthel - 2	1050–1053
Godwine	God - 1	1017–1023
Goda	God - 2	1029–1036
Eadric	None	1023–1029
Dunbeard	None	1040–1042
Eilwine	None	1050–1053

Table 4.61. Name Sequences of the Sudbury Mint

Moneyer Name	Name Sequence	Activity Range
Folcwine	Folc - 1	1053–1056
Folcwine	Folc - 2	1059–1065
Folcwine	Folc - 3	1068–1070
Branting	None	1009–1023
Mansige	None	1017–1023
Sperling	None	1017–1023
Æthelmær	None	1023–1029
Wulfric	Wulf - 1	1077–1080
Wulfric	Wulf - 2	1083–1086

Table 4.62. Name Sequences of the Aylesbury Mint

Moneyer Name	Name Sequence	Activity Range
Ælfgar	Ælf - 1	991–997
Ælf	Ælf - 2	1017–1023
Leofstan	Leof - 1	991–997
Leofwine	Leof - 2	1044–1048
Æthelwine	None	1017–1023
Edward	None	1017–1023
Wulfred	Wulf - 1	1053–1056
Wulfred	Wulf - 2	1059–1062

Table 4.63. Name Sequences of the Sandwich Mint

Moneyer Name	Name Sequence	Activity Range
Ælfgeat	Ælf - 1	1074–1080
Ælfheah	Ælf - 2a	1083–1086
Ælfgeat	Ælf - 2b	1083–1086
Godric	God - 1	1062–1065
Godwine	God - 2	1083–1086
Leofwine	Leof - 1	1044–1056
Leofwine	Leof - 2	1059–1062

Table 4.64. Name Sequences of the Watchet Mint

Moneyer Name	Name Sequence	Activity Range
Godcild	God - 1	1017–1044
Godcild	God - 2	1053–1056
Hunewine	None	997–1023
Sæweard	None	1029–1036
Sigeric	Sige - 1	979–997
Sigewulf	Sige - 2	1077–1080
Sigewulf	Sige - 3	1083–1086

Table 4.65. Name Sequences of the Gothaburh Mint

Moneyer Name	Name Sequence	Activity Range
Goda	None	1009–1016
Carla	None	1017–1023
Leofmær	None	1036–1042
Ælfweard	None	1040–1042
Wulfmær	Wulf - 1	997–1009
Wulfmær	Wulf - 2	1017–1023

Table 4.66. Name Sequences of the Warminster Mint

Moneyer Name	Name Sequence	Activity Range
Ælfweald	None	997–1003
Godwine	None	1009–1016
Beorhtric	None	1029–1036
Winegod	None	1029–1036
Wulfstan	Wulf - 1	1036–1038
Wulfstan	Wulf - 2	1048–1050

Table 4.67. Name Sequences of the Cadbury Mint

Moneyer Name	Name Sequence	Activity Range
Ælfwine	Ælf - 1	1009–1016
Ælfhelm	Ælf - 2	1017–1023
Goda	None	1009–1016
Winas	None	1009–1016
Wulfhelm	None	1009–1016

Table 4.68. Name Sequences of the Crewkerne Mint

Moneyer Name	Name Sequence	Activity Range
Beorhtwig	Beorht - 1	1029–1036
Beorhtric	Beorht - 2	1036–1038
Winas	Win - 1	997–1003
Winas	Win - 2	1017–1023
Winas	Win - 3	1029–1036

Table 4.69. Name Sequences of the Bedwin Mint

Moneyer Name	Name Sequence	Activity Range
Cild	Cild - 1	1044–1053
Cild	Cild - 2	1059–1062
Cild	Cild - 3	1065–1066
Cild	Cild - 4	1066–1068

Table 4.70. Name Sequences of the Bruton Mint

Moneyer Name	Name Sequence	Activity Range
Ælfhelm	Ælf - 1a	1017–1036
Ælfwine	Ælf - 1b	1017–1023
Godric	God - 1	1036–1038
Godric	God - 2	1040–1046

Table 4.71. Name Sequences of the Cissbury Mint

Moneyer Name	Name Sequence	Activity Range
Ceolnoth	Ceol - 1	991–997
Ceolnoth	Ceol - 2	1009–1016
Godwine	None	1009–1016
Leofwine	None	1017–1023

Table 4.72. Name Sequences of the Bury St Edmunds Mint

Moneyer Name	Name Sequence	Activity Range
Morcere	Mor - 1	1048–1056
Morcere	Mor - 2	1059–1065
Godwine	None	1070–1072

Table 4.73. Name Sequences of the Newport Pagnell Mint

Moneyer Name	Name Sequence	Activity Range
Sæwen	None	1059–1062
Sigeweard	Sige - 1	1050–1053
Sigered	Sige - 2	1053–1056

Table 4.74. Name Sequences of the Torksey Mint

Moneyer Name	Name Sequence	Activity Range
Leofnoth	None	1017–1023
Thorcetel	Thor - 1	975–991
Thorcetel	Thor - 2	1009–1029

Table 4.75. Name Sequences of the Berkeley Mint

Moneyer Name	Name Sequence	Activity Range
Edgar	Ed - 1	1046–1048
Edgar	Ed - 2	1053–1056

Table 4.76. Name Sequences of the Dernt Mint

Moneyer Name	Name Sequence	Activity Range
Wulfgar	Wulf - 1	1048–1050
Wulfsige	Wulf - 2	1059–1062

Table 4.77. Name Sequences of the Marlborough Mint

Moneyer Name	Name Sequence	Activity Range
Cild	Cild - 1	1070–1080
Cild	Cild - 2	1083–1086

5

Moneyer Grouping Patterns in Anglo-Saxon Mints

Moneyers Operating in Groups within the London Mint

A review of the activity periods of the moneyers within the London mint reveals a consistent pattern of moneyers beginning and ending activity together. This means that at regular intervals in the coinage production cycles multiple moneyers, generally three to six, begin operation together. In many instances, these moneyers also stop production with the same coinage. Occasionally, multiple moneyers will begin together and most of the moneyers stop but one will continue to the next coinage or beyond. Many of the moneyer names that are associated with the group that stops after one or two coinages appear later in the coinage record, having apparently skipped one or two coinage types. It is likely that most of the moneyers did not mint coins as a full-time occupation. As discussed in chapter one, moneyers were also the local exchange point for foreign currency when traders came from the Continent. They also held other positions within many of the towns, prominent offices in some instances, especially in the period after this study. However, since the moneyers were likely not the individuals hammering the coins themselves, with workmen doing the actual manual labour, having their name on the coinage for every coinage would not seemingly have hindered their other activities. Therefore, it seems likely that other mechanisms beyond this just being a part-time job were in play. Potential ramifications of this are discussed in detail below in chapter six. The primary aim of this chapter is to demonstrate that these groups of moneyers working together were evident throughout all the major mint locations in the period 973 to 1086.

For example, each of the primary name sequences in the London mint contain multiple groups of moneyers seemingly acting in concert with one another over several spans of time. What is also evident is that the pattern of these groupings within each name sequence parallel similar periods of grouping in the other name sequences and in the general population of London's moneyers overall. So moneyers of the [Leof-] sequence, for example, are operating in groups at the same time and in the same manner as moneyers of the other sequences. And moneyers that are not directly associated with any of the primary protothemes are doing the same. Further, this pattern of grouping that is found in London is also evident in many of the other major mints, meaning that the coordination of the groups of moneyers acting together at specific points in time seems to encompass the whole of late Anglo-Saxon England to a remarkable extent. Some of these examples beyond London are illustrated below. An analysis of each of the primary name sequences from London, as defined in chapter three above, and the grouping pattern within each can be found below. Then these name sequences will be combined to illustrate the overall pattern the groupings make within the London mint.

The tables provide groups of moneyers that began operation together. Only those periods with multiple moneyers beginning at the same time are included. In the graphs, all of the moneyer periods of activity from the given name element are included but those groups of moneyers that began together are demarked with a bracket ([–). Those moneyers that begin and end, or operated within one extra coinage, together are enclosed in double brackets ([–]). For example, in looking at the moneyers with the [Ælf-] prototheme, there are several instances of groups of moneyers beginning and ending operation together [Table 5.1]. Four moneyers began operation within the mint during the First Hand type (979–985) of Æthelred II: Ælfgar, Ælfstan, Ælfweald, and Ælfwine.[1] Only one of these, Ælfgar, produced coins of the Second Hand type (985–991) and Crux type (991–997) immediately afterwards. Since Ælfgar operated in two coinages after the other three and while in Table 5.1 these four are grouped together, in Figure 5.1 only the first three are enclosed in double brackets [Figure 5.1]. An alternative example are the three new moneyers from the [Ælf-] sequence which began in 985: Ælfgæt, Ælfnoth, and Ælfweard.[2] Ælfgæt and Ælfnoth stopped activity in 997, with Ælfweard continuing to 1003. Since Ælfweard is only active for one coinage beyond the other two, all three are grouped together in both Table 5.1 and Figure 5.1. Also, in 1023, five moneyers began operation together but only two of them stopped at the same time, with the other three covering the succeeding three coinage issues. These five moneyers are depicted as one large group in Table 5.1 but separated into two groups in Figure 5.1: Ælfgæt (1023–1029), Ælfgar (1023–1029), Ælfweard (1023–1036), Ælfred (1023–1038), and Ælfric (1023–1042).[3] Tables [Tables 5.2–5.7] and figures [Figures 5.2–5.7] outlining these groups for each of the dominant name sequences in London: [Ælf-], [Æthel-], [Beorht-], [Ead-], [God-], [Leof-], and [Wulf-] follow.

1 SM1.London.xix–xxii.
2 SM1.London.xxiii–xxv.
3 SM1.London.xxxix–xliii.

Table 5.1. Groups of Moneyers in the [Ælf-] sequence of London

Moneyer Name	Activity Range
Ælfstan	979–985
Ælfweald	979–985
Ælfwine	979–985
Ælfgar	979–997
Ælfgæt	985–997
Ælfnoth	985–997
Ælfweard	985–1003
Ælfstan	991–997
Ælfwig	991–997
Ælfric	991–1003
Ælfwine	991–1038
Ælfgæt	1009–1016
Ælfnoth	1009–1016
Ælfric	1009–1016
Ælfsige	1009–1016
Ælfweard	1009–1016
Ælf	1017–1023
Ælfstan	1017–1036
Ælfgæt	1023–1029
Ælfgar	1023–1029
Ælfweard	1023–1036
Ælfred	1023–1038
Ælfric	1023–1042
Ælfnoth	1036–1038
Ælfweald	1036–1038
Ælfred	1040–1042
Ælfweard	1040–1046
Ælfwine	1040–1056
Ælfgar	1044–1048
Ælfred	1044–1062
Ælf	1048–1050
Ælfgæt	1048–1050
Ælfstan	1048–1050
Ælfweald	1048–1050
Ælfgar	1050–1053
Ælfsige	1050–1053
Ælfwig	1053–1056
Ælfweard	1053–1066
Ælfwine	1066–1070
Ælfsige	1066–1072

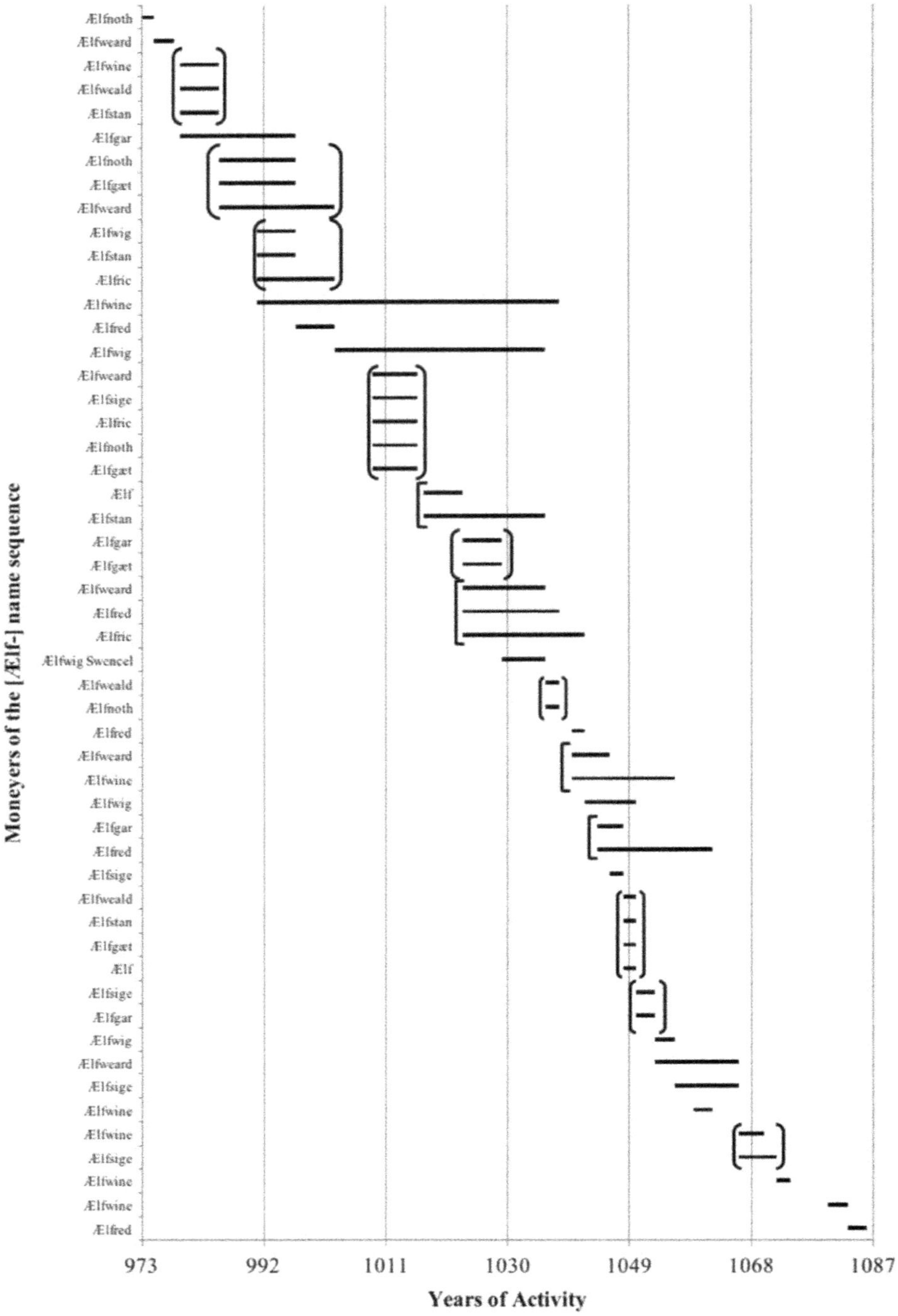

Figure 5.1. Moneyer groupings of the [Ælf-] sequence in London.

Table 5.2. Groups of Moneyers in the [Æthel-] sequence of London

Moneyer Name	Activity Range
Æthelsige	973–975
Æthelstan	973–978
Æthelweald	973–979
Æthelred	973–997
Æthelweard	979–985
Æthelstan	979–985
Æthelwine	991–997
Æthelweard	991–1029
Æthelfrith	997–1003
Æthelric	997–1029
Æthelmær	1003–1009
Æthelwine	1003–1036
Æthelnoth	1009–1016
Æthelred	1009–1016
Æthelwig	1009–1016
Æthelman	1009–1023
Æthelbeorht	1023–1029
Æthelgæt	1023–1029
Æthelnoth	1023–1029
Æthelwig	1023–1036
Æthelwine	1040–1042
Æthelweard	1040–1044
Æthelgar	1044–1046
Æthelman	1044–1046
Æthelric	1044–1046
Æthelwig	1044–1050
Æthelwig	1062–1065
Æthelwine	1062–1065

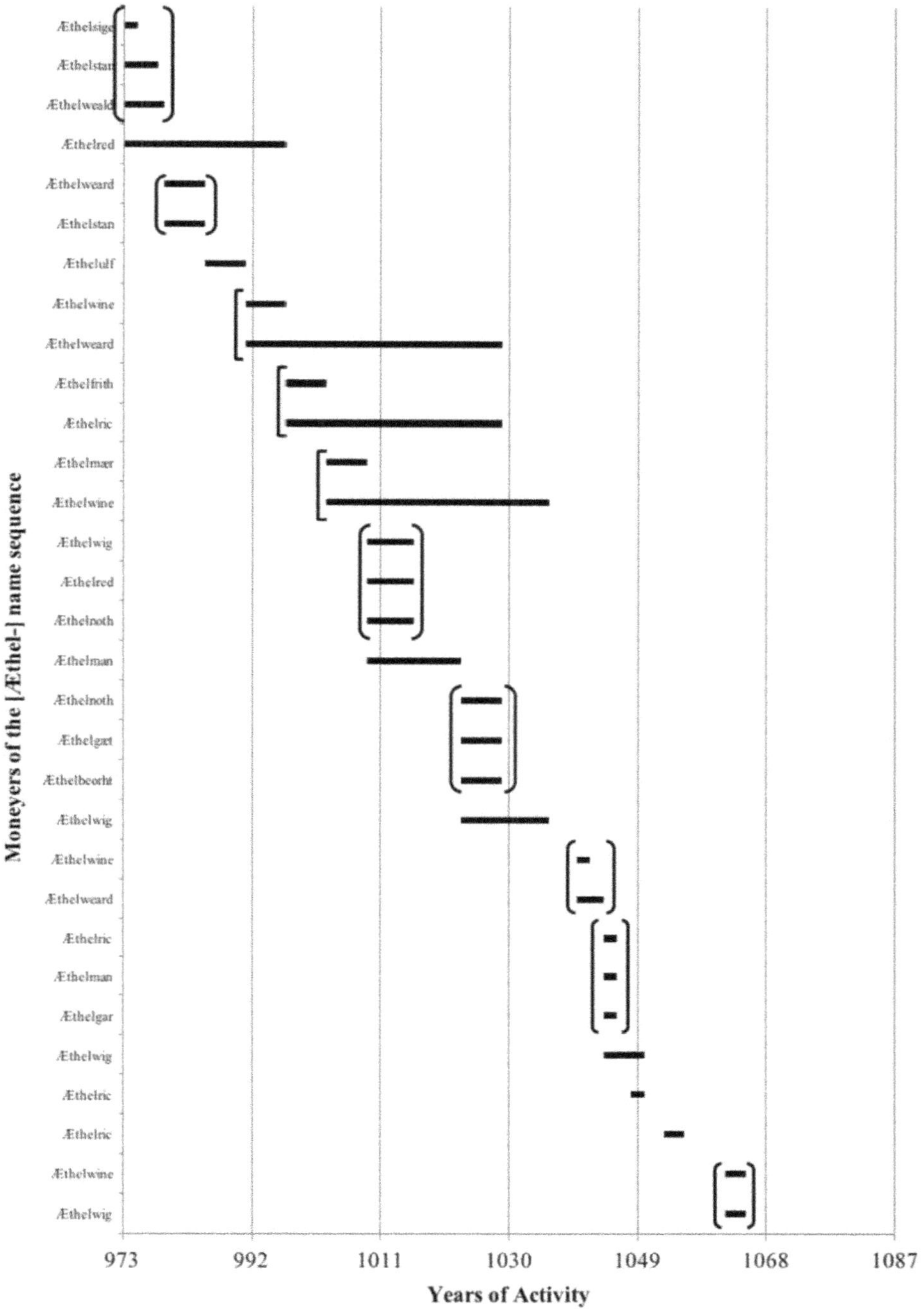

Figure 5.2. Moneyer groupings of the [Æthel-] sequence in London.

Table 5.3. Groups of Moneyers in the [Beorht-] sequence of London

Moneyer Name	Activity Range
Beorhtmær	1009-1016
Beorhtfrith	1009-1023
Beorhtweald	1009-1023
Beorhtnoth	1009-1036
Beorhtmær	1044-1046
Beorhtræd	1044-1056
Beorhtsige	1050-1053
Beorhtwine	1050-1056
Beorhtmær	1074-1077
Beorhtric	1074-1077

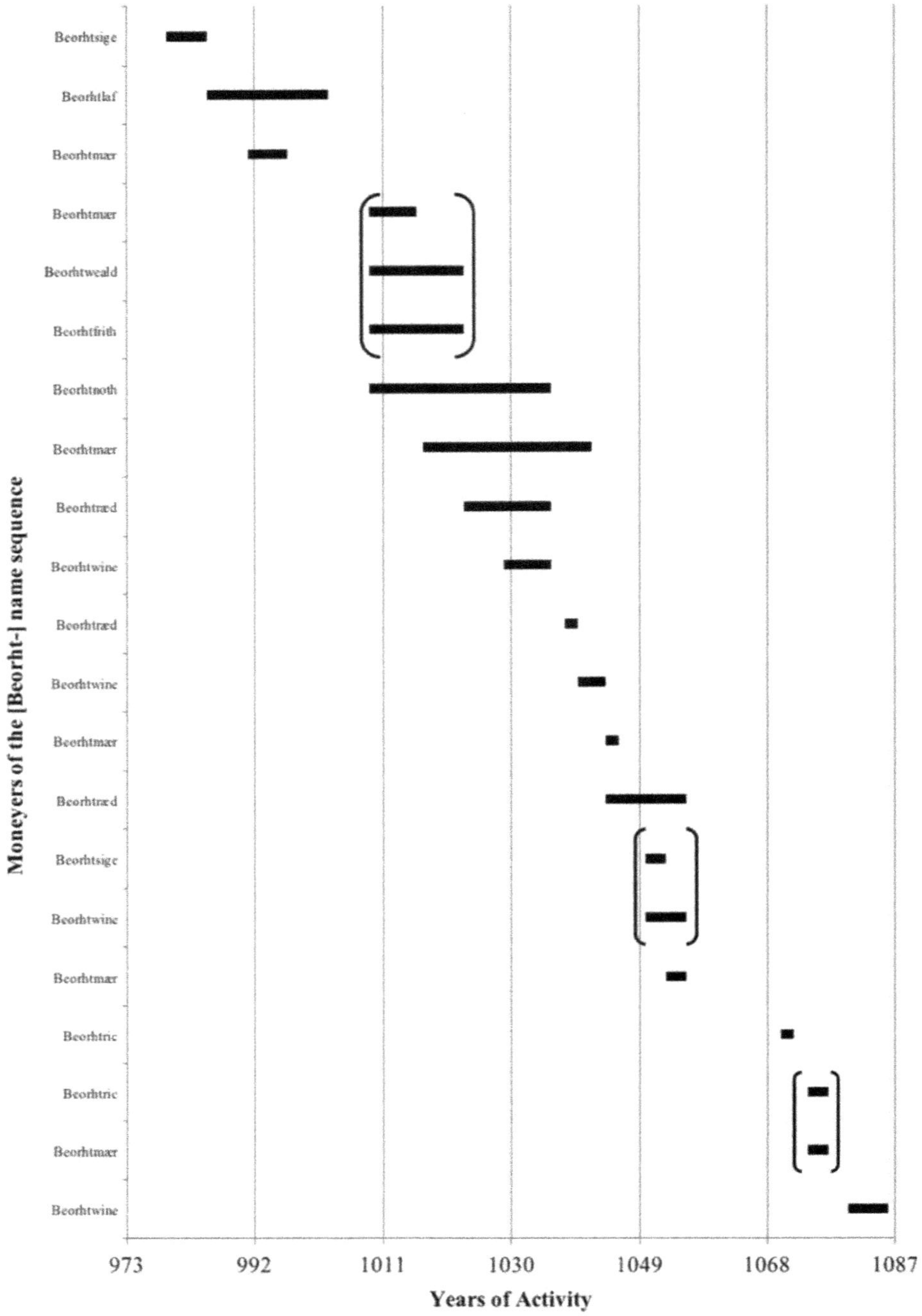

Figure 5.3. Moneyer groupings of the [Beorht-] sequence in London.

Table 5.4. Groups of Moneyers in the [Ead-] sequence of London

Moneyer Name	Activity Range
Eadweald	979–985
Eadhelm	979–991
Eadnoth	985–991
Eadsige	985–991
Eadwi	985–991
Eadwig	985–997
Eadmund	985–1036
Eadwine	985–1040
Eadweard	995–997
Eadwi	995–997
Eadsige	995–1029
Eadgar	1003–1009
Eadwig	1003–1029
Eadweard	1003–1036
Eadsme	1009–1016
Eadwi	1009–1016
Eadric	1009–1048
Eadnoth	1017–1023
Eadgar	1017–1029
Eadhelm	1023–1029
Eadwulf	1023–1036
Eadred	1023–1038
Eadwi	1044–1046
Eadwine	1044–1056
Eadweald	1048–1050
Eadwig	1048–1059
Eadmund	1050–1053
Eadsige	1050–1053
Eadred	1050–1056
Eadric	1053–1056
Eadweald	1053–1056
Eadgar	1059–1062
Eadwine	1059–1077
Eadgar	1065–1066
Eadric	1065–1066

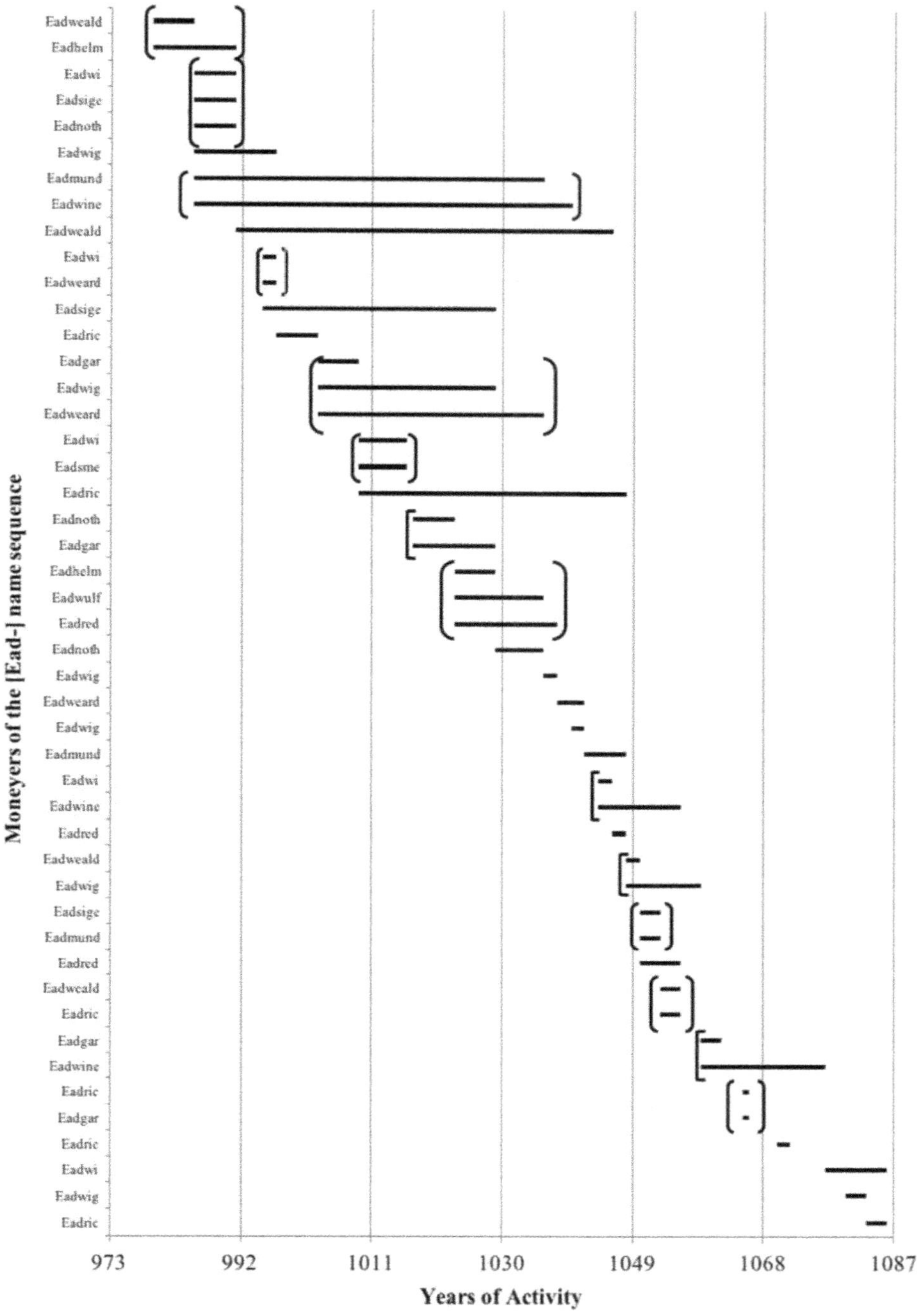

Figure 5.4. Moneyer groupings of the [Ead-] sequence in London.

Table 5.5. Groups of Moneyers in the [God-] sequence of London

Moneyer Name	Activity Range
God	979–985
Godric	979–985
Goda	979–997
Godwine	979–1062
Godhere	991–997
Godric	991–1040
God	995–997
Godra	995–997
Godhere	1003–1036
Goda	1003–1038
God	1029–1036
Goding	1029–1036
Godwine Stew	1036–1038
Godsige	1036–1040
Goda	1040–1042
Godric Calic	1040–1042
Godman	1044–1046
Godsunu	1044–1053
Godwig	1046–1050
Godric	1046–1077
Godhere	1053–1056
Godman	1053–1056
Godwig	1053–1056
Godric	1083–1086
Godwine	1083–1086

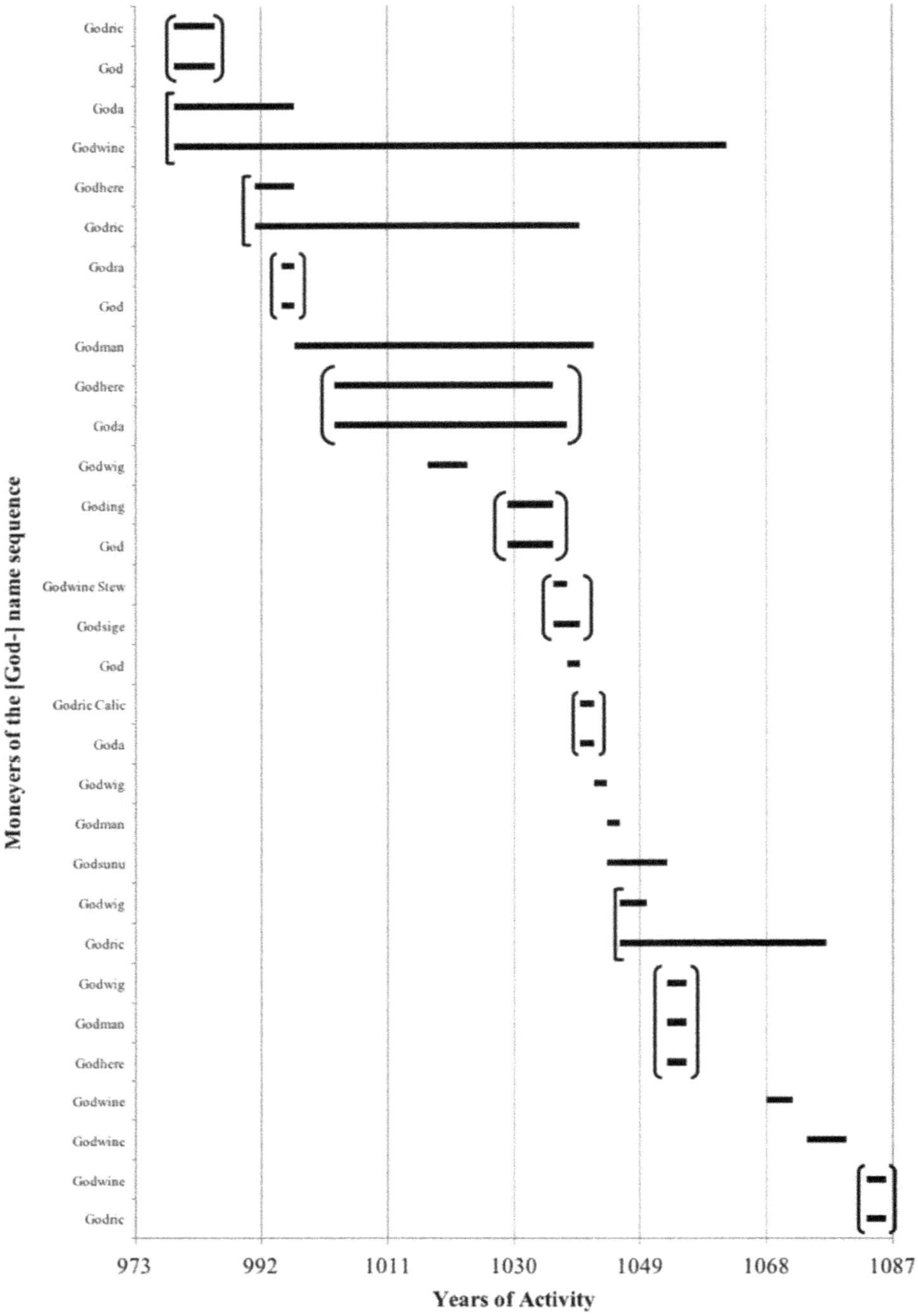

Figure 5.5. Moneyer groupings in the [God-] sequence in London.

Table 5.6. Groups of Moneyers in the [Leof-] sequence of London

Moneyer Name	Activity Range
Leofric	979–985
Leofstan	979–1003
Leofing	991–1042
Leofred	991–1056
Leofric	991–1046
Leofheah	1009–1016
Leofnoth	1009–1016
Leofwig	1009–1036
Leofstan	1009–1046
Leofsige	1017–1029
Leofweard	1017–1036
Leofgar	1023–1029
Leofmær	1023–1029
Leofman	1023–1029
Leofing	1046–1053
Leofwine	1046–1059
Leofnoth	1048–1050
Leofwig	1048–1050
Leofæg	1056–1059
Leofing	1056–1062

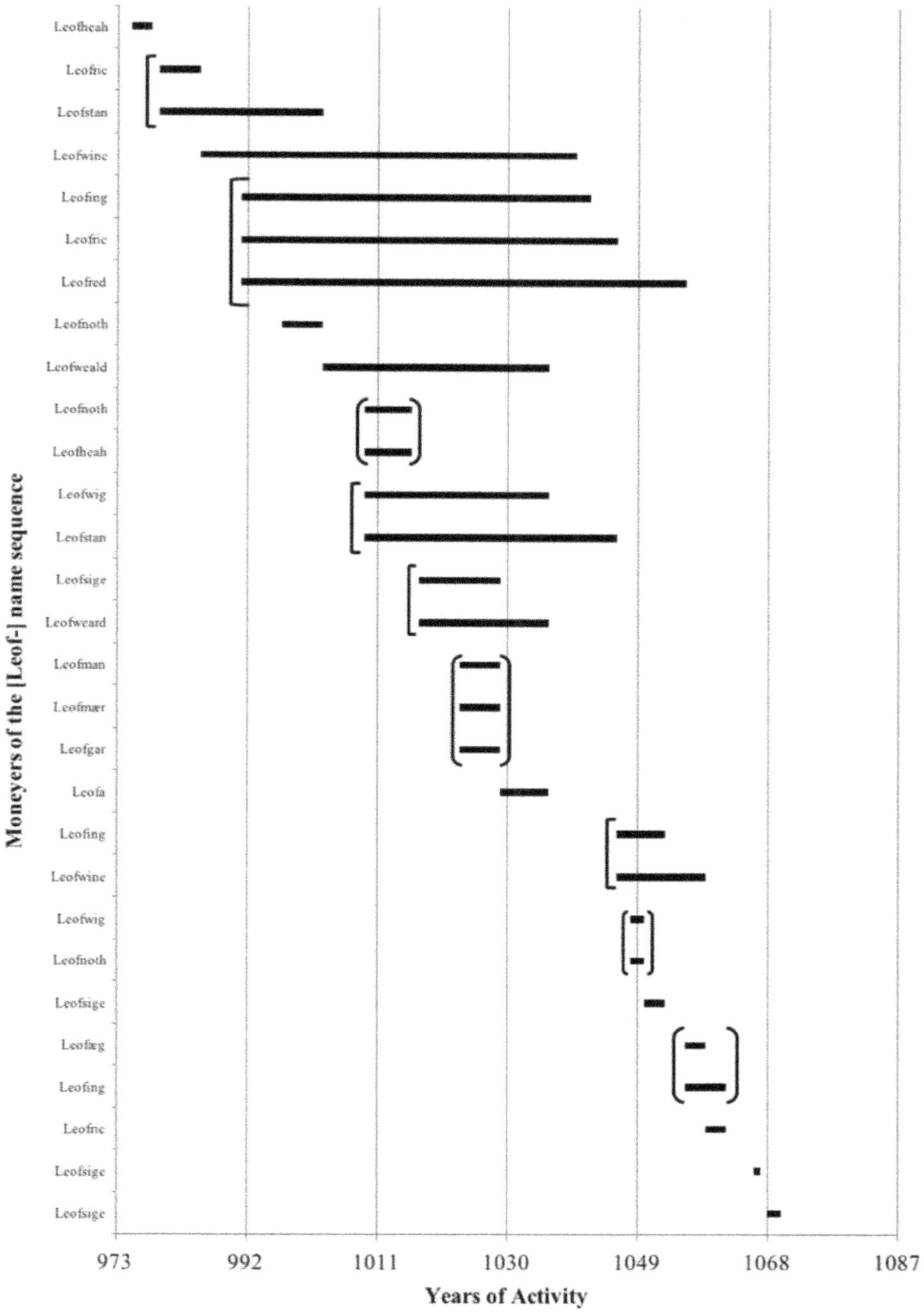

Figure 5.6. Moneyer groupings in the [Leof-] sequence in London.

Table 5.7. Groups of Moneyers in the [Wulf-] sequence of London

Moneyer Name	Activity Range
Wulfmær	979–991
Wulfric	979–991
Wulfstan	979–1029
Wulfgar	991–997
Wulfwine	991–1040
Wulfsige	997–1003
Wulfric	997–1036
Wulfgar	1003–1009
Wulfred	1003–1036
Wulfsige	1017–1023
Wulfweard	1017–1023
Wulfnoth	1017–1029
Wulfgar	1017–1038
Wulf	1038–1040
Wulfsige	1038–1042
Wulfstan	1038–1044
Wulfgar	1040–1042
Wulfred	1040–1042
Wulfgar	1042–1044
Wulfric	1042–1044
Wulfwine	1042–1059
Wulfsige	1044–1046
Wulfred	1044–1053
Wulfsic	1046–1048
Wulfric	1046–1050
Wulfsige	1048–1050
Wulfwig	1048–1050
Wulfcrdd	1050–1053
Wulfweard	1050–1053
Wulfric	1053–1059
Wulfgar	1053–1066
Wulfnoth	1056–1059
Wulfred	1056–1059
Wulfsi	1062–1065
Wulfsige	1062–1066
Wulfweard	1062–1066
Wulfie	1072–1074
Wulfric	1072–1074

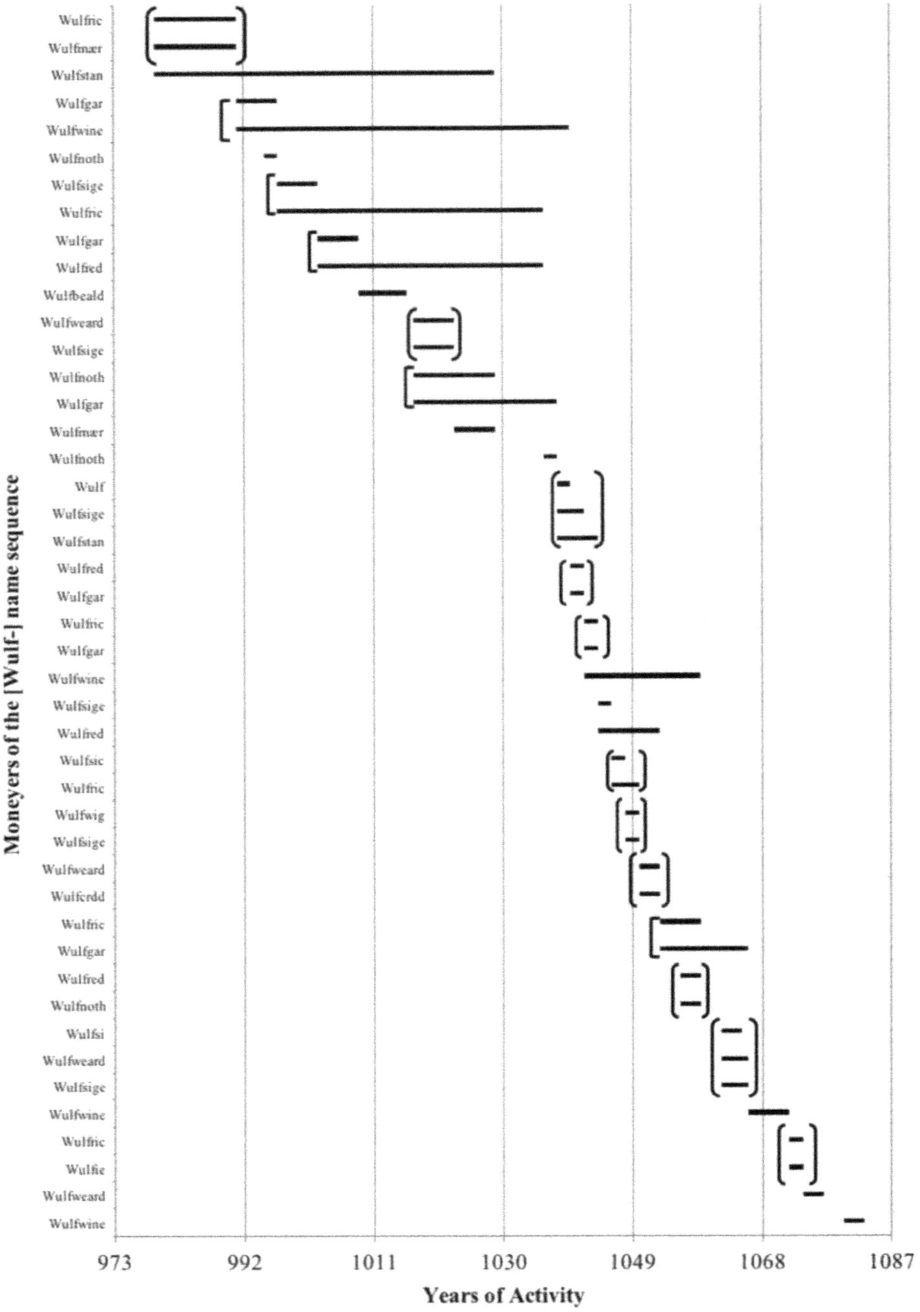

Figure 5.7. Moneyer groupings in the [Wulf-] sequence in London.

The 'Stair-Step' Pattern of Moneyer Grouping

These patterns of grouping are also evident in the visualisation of the London mint as a whole, not only within these specific name sequences. The image that is revealed when reviewing just the pattern associated with the groups of moneyers starting and stopping together gives the impression of a cross-section of a stairway. Figure 5.8 and Figure 5.9 provide a combined visualisation of the top seven name sequences and the complete London mint. Because of the number of records involved, only the graphical representation is present. For a full listing of the moneyers in question the London section of the *MED* is useful for comparative purposes. If the top seven name sequences are combined into one graph, the pattern of groups of moneyers beginning and ending together can be seen to cover each of them collectively [Figure 5.8]. Further, when looking at all 425 periods of moneyer

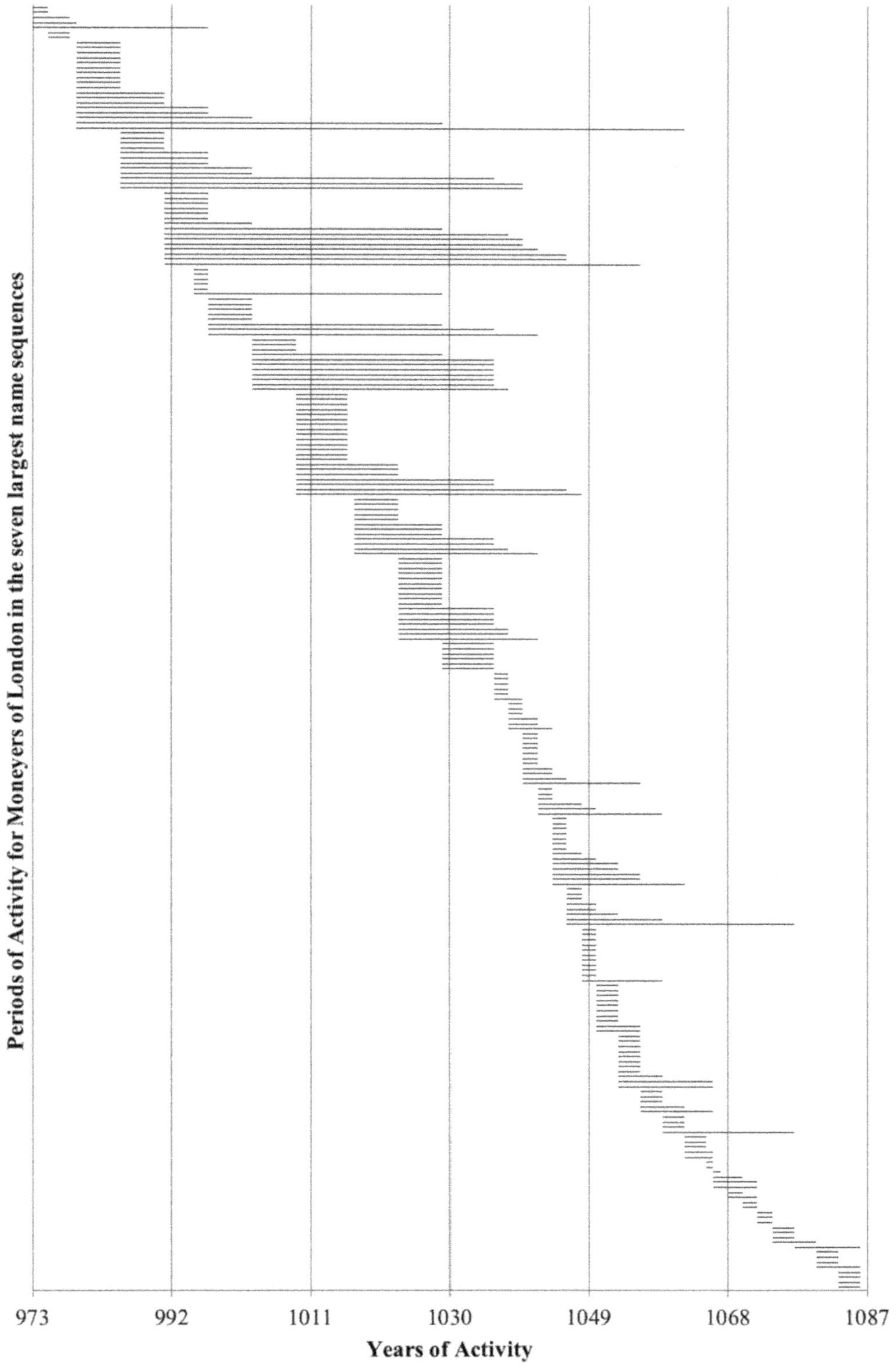

Figure 5.8. Operational years of London moneyers from the seven largest name sequences.

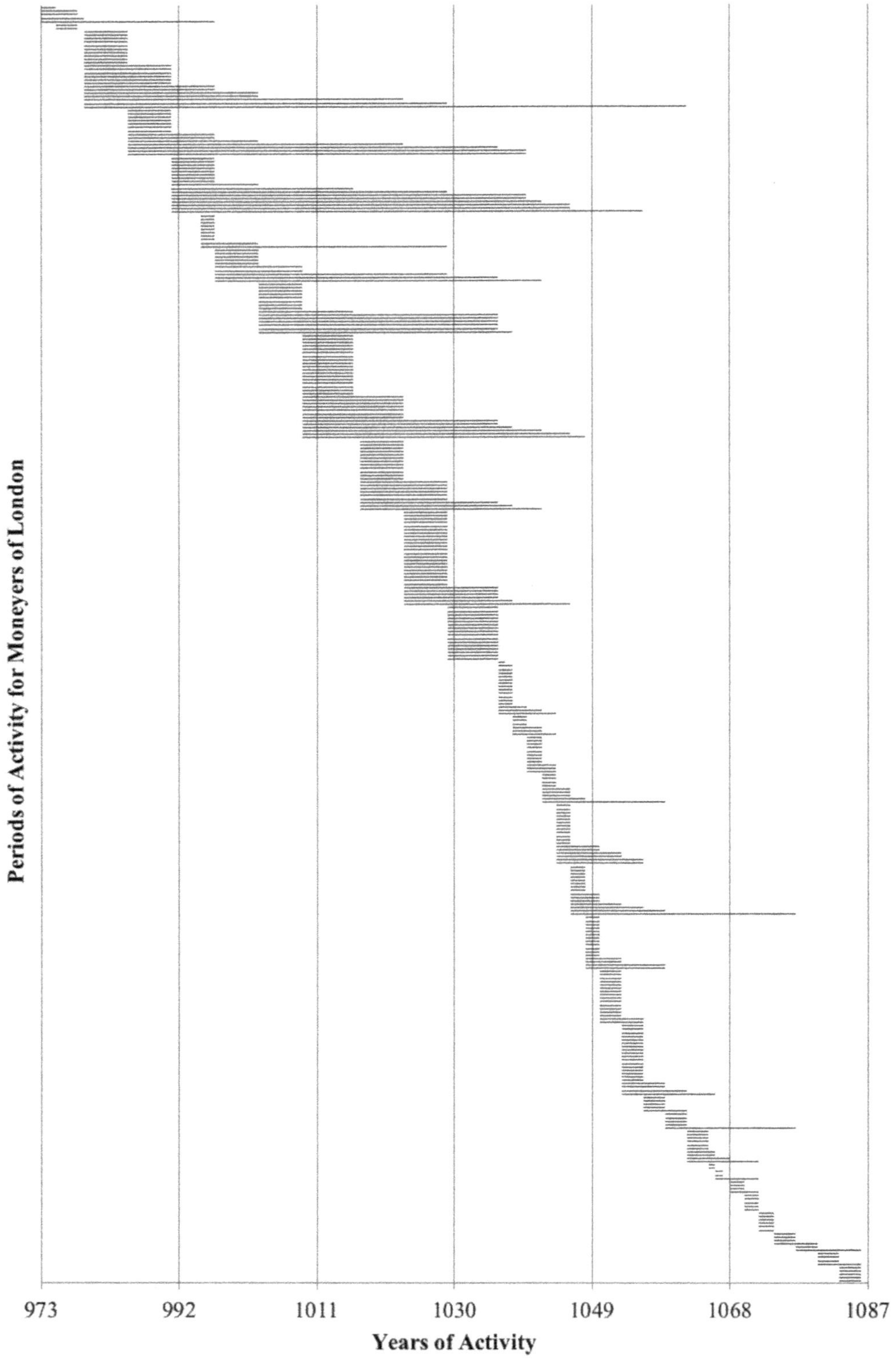

Figure 5.9. Operational years of all moneyers in London.

activity in London [Figure 5.9] we can see that the pattern of groups of moneyers carries forward throughout the entire period of 973 to 1086. The visual representations of the top seven name sequences and the entire mint are nearly identical, and are illustrative of most of the major mints and several of the larger minor mints detailed below. The distinct separation between the activity ranges for moneyers before and after 1036 can also clearly be seen in these representations, with the bands being noticeably longer in the former, while the pattern maintains itself in smaller increments in the latter half. A visualisation of the patterns from York, Lincoln, and Winchester [Figures 5.10–5.12] are also included to demonstrate the similarities in operation periods for the largest mints. The clear 'stair-step' pattern of moneyer grouping is evident in each. A more exact breakdown, with the corresponding moneyer names, can be found below and in the supplemental material. What is also evident, especially in London, where

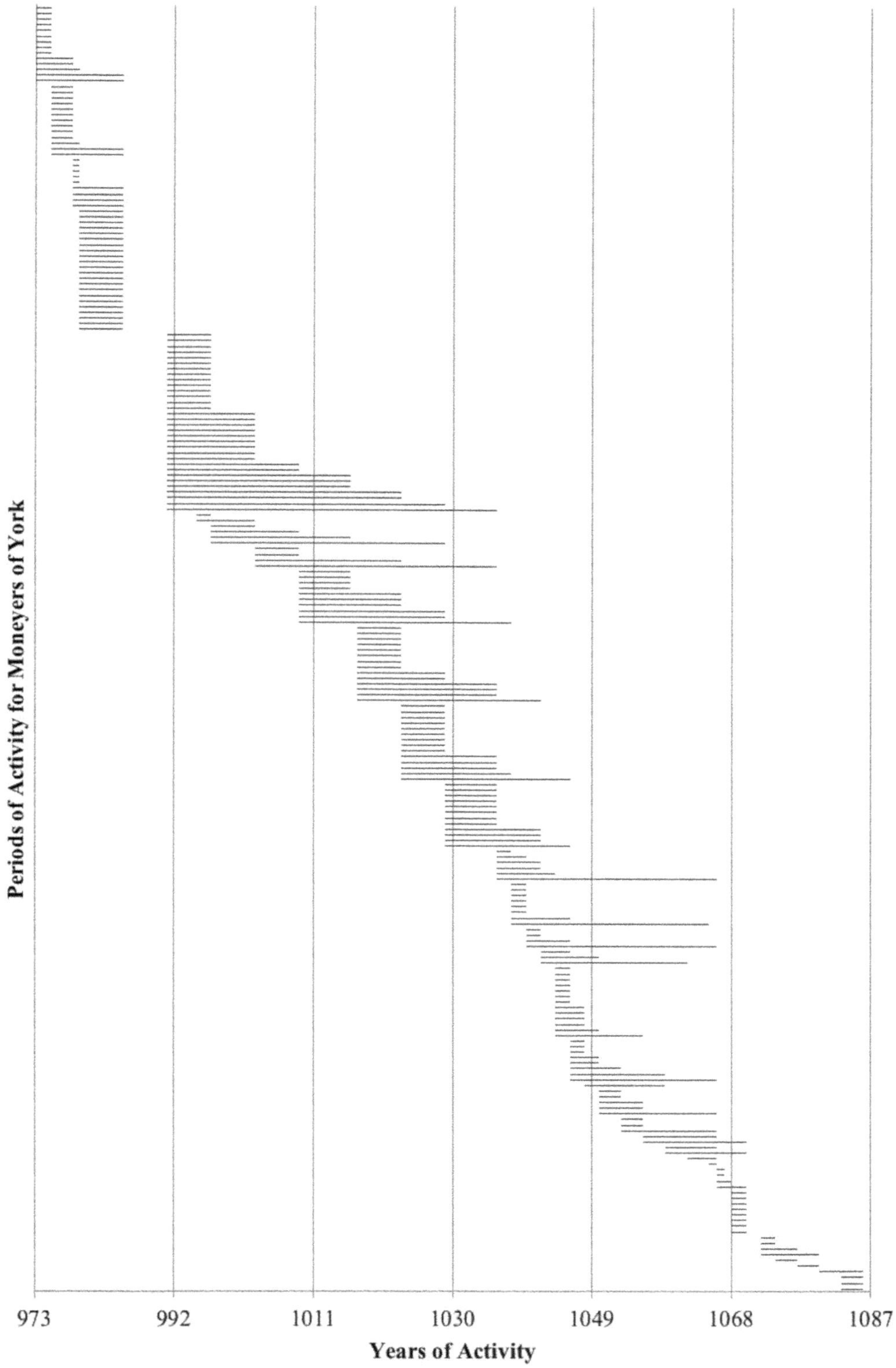

Figure 5.10. Operational years of all moneyers in York.

this is more common, is that there are several moneyer periods of activity that extend far beyond the average of 10.5 years pre-1036 and 4 years post-1036, as discussed in chapters three and four. This could be an indication of 'brand-name' moneyers operating under a single name for extended periods of time, or more likely, moneyers of the same name within the same family operating at consecutive periods. This may also explain the lack of grouping in the first periods of activity in the Gloucester mint as detailed below. If there were moneyers acting under one specific name for an extended period of time then the pattern may have existed but not be discernable. A possible support for this position is that in many of the instances where there are moneyers operating for extended periods of time the immediately succeeding groups of moneyers appear to be smaller than at other intervals in the study period. For example, if looking at the extremely long periods of activity for Godwine (979–1062), who was part of an

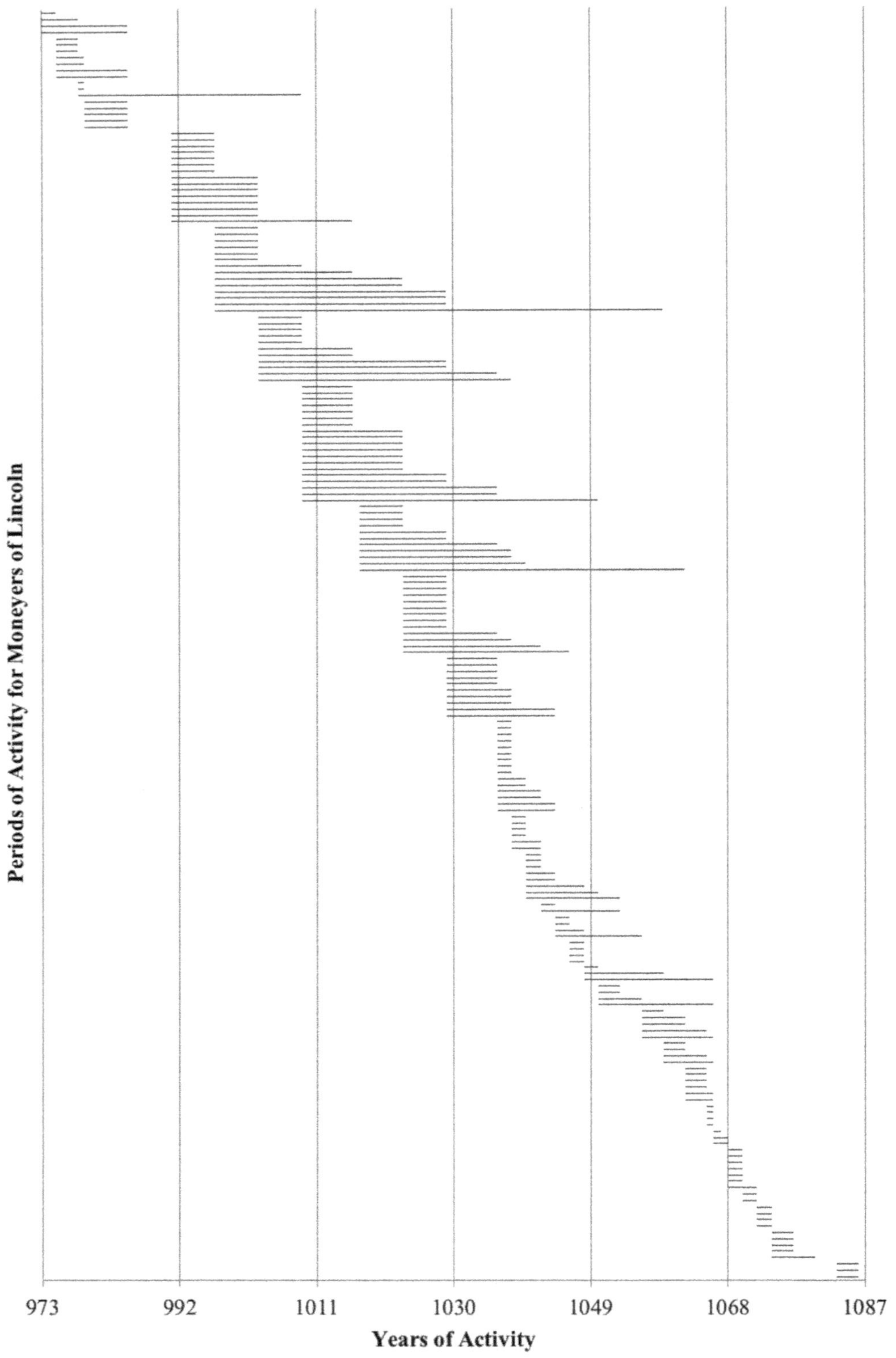

Figure 5.11. Operational years of all moneyers in Lincoln.

original grouping of four moneyers, we can see that the next eight groupings consisted of only two moneyers each, before jumping back up to four in 1053, which is close to the end of the continuous span of Godwine moneyers. This could indicate that there were new moneyers added at these intervals who operated under the Godwine name. Breaking the sequence of Godwines into the corresponding groupings would provide each grouping with three, which is more in line with the other name sequences and mints.

Graphs illustrating this stair-step structure for all of the mints can be found in the fourth set of downloadable supplemental materials accompanying this book. The mints are arranged from high to low volume and include all of the major mints as well as some of the minor mints. The patterns outlined above exist to some extent in all the major mints and in a limited capacity within many of the minor ones. It is important to point out here that each of the minor mints, excepting those in Wales and those

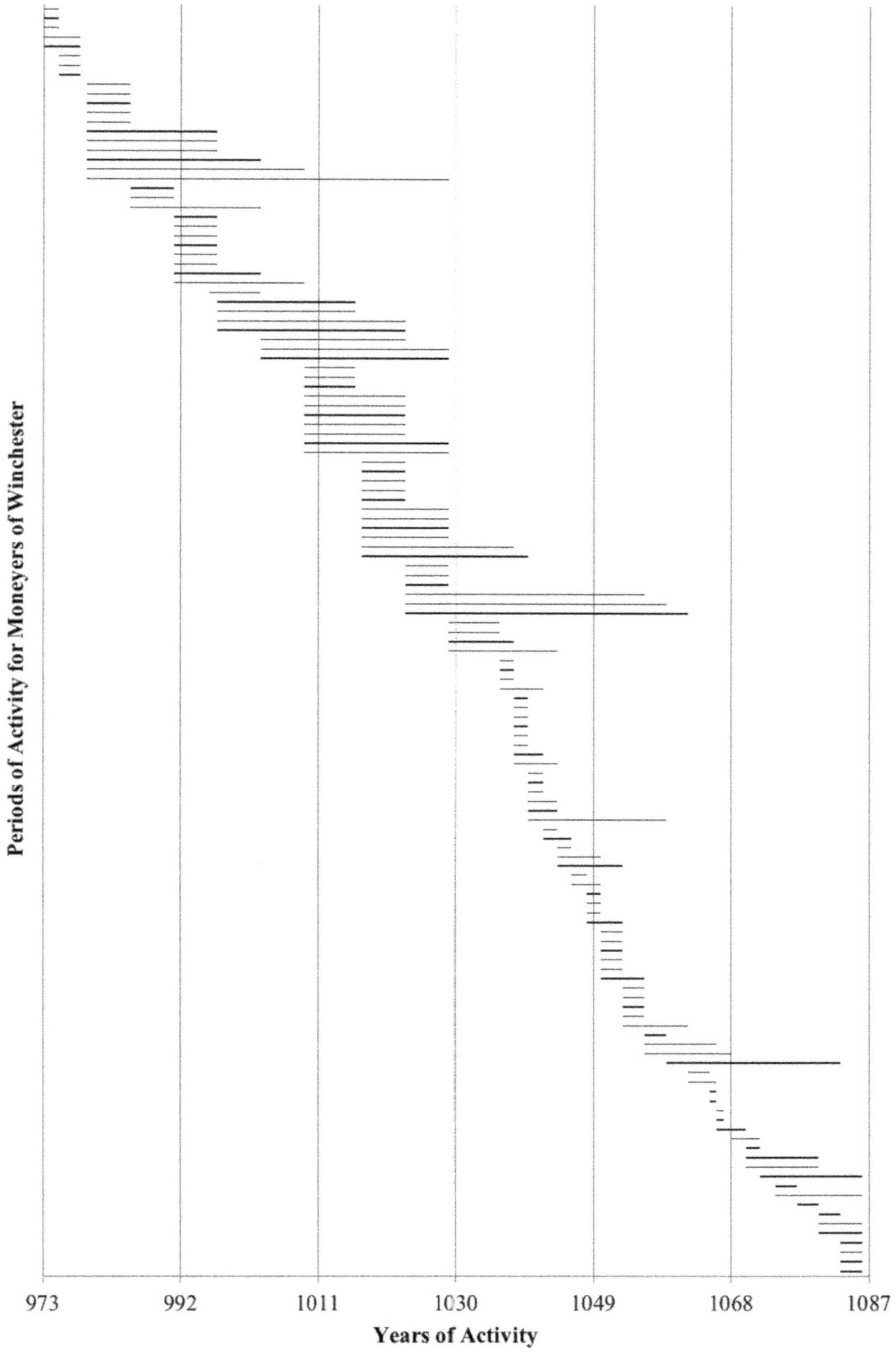

Figure 5.12. Operational years of all moneyers in Winchester.

few outliers that are only active in the last coinage of William I, are geographically close to a major mint and typically within a royal county with a major mint [Table 5.8]. There are some exceptions to this. For example, Buckinghamshire, which is surrounded closely by several counties with major mints, has no major mint of its own. The mint at Niwan is not included in the table because its location is not known.

Table 5.8. Major and Minor Mints by Historic County

County	Major Mints	Minor Mints	
Bedfordshire	Bedford	None	
Berkshire	Wallingford	None	
Buckinghamshire	None	Aylesbury	Newport Pagnell
		Buckingham	
Cambridgeshire	Cambridge	None	
Cheshire	Chester	None	
Cornwall	None	Gothaburh	
Derbyshire	Derby	None	
Devon	Exeter	Barnstaple	Lydford
		Launceston	Totnes
Dorset	None	Bridport	Twynham
		Dorchester	Wareham
Durham	None	Durham	
Essex	Colchester	Horndon	Sudbury
		Maldon	
Gloucestershire	Gloucester	Berkeley	
	Bristol	Winchcombe	
Hampshire	Winchester	Southampton	
Herefordshire	Hereford	None	
Hertfordshire	Hertford	None	
Huntingdonshire	Huntingdon	None	
Kent	Canterbury	Hythe	Romney
	Dover	Lympne	Sandwich
		Rochester	
Lancashire	None	Cuer	
Leicestershire	Leicester	None	
Lincolnshire	Lincoln	Caistor	Torksey
		Horncastle	
Norfolk	Norwich	Wilton (EA)	
Northampton	Northampton	Peterborough	
Nottinghamshire	None	Newark	Nottingham
Oxfordshire	Oxford	None	
Rutland	Stamford	None	
Shropshire	Shrewsbury	None	
Somerset	Ilchester	Axbridge	Langport
		Bath	Petherton
		Bruton	Stes
		Cadbury	Taunton
		Crewkerne	Watchet
		Frome	
Staffordshire	None	Stafford	Tamworth

Table 5.8 ***continued***

County	Major Mints	Minor Mints
Suffolk	Ipswich Thetford	Bury St Edmunds Dernt
Surrey	None	Guildford
Sussex	Chichester Lewes	Cissbury Pevensey Hastings Steyning
Warwickshire	Warwick	None
Wiltshire	Shaftesbury Wilton	Bedwin Milbourne Port Cricklade Salisbury Malmesbury Warminster Marlborough
Worcestershire	Worcester	Droitwich
		Pershore
Yorkshire	York	None
Wales	None	Cardiff St Davids Rhuddlan

6

Organisational Structure of Late Anglo-Saxon Mints

Introduction

In chapter three, it was illustrated that certain name elements appear to have operated at nearly all the major late Anglo-Saxon mints for an extended period of time. Further, the moneyer names themselves seemed to be concentrated within just a few groups of protothemes. The implication of this, considering Anglo-Saxon naming patterns and the regularity of the name structures, is that the moneyers with similar names operating over long periods of time were related, and that these families dominated the minting records for the study period. What is also evident, based upon the grouping patterns outlined in chapter five above, is that these families operated in groups, both within their own dynasty and in conjunction with other families. But, what is not immediately clear from this analysis is that some, in fact many, of those groups of moneyers beginning and ending together seem to have done so more than once over the period of the mints activity. There are examples of these groups beginning and ending together, taking a period of time outside of the coinage record, and then returning en masse to appear on a later coinage. The regularity of this process seems to indicate a very complex level of coordination, not only within the confines of an individual family, but within multiple families working in conjunction with one another. This cycle of rotation indicates that there are considerations beyond simply the passing of the moneyer office from ancestor to progeny. There were considerations of time, periods of activity, and coordination with other families that were part of the process of movement from one member of a family to another within a mint. While the groupings of the families is of paramount importance to the underlying structure of the mints, and the security of the family's monopoly on the coinage production process, this rotational cycle indicates a widespread, almost corporate, undertaking in the Anglo-Saxon minting machine.

Moneyer Rotation Cycles

Different generations within a name sequence might have shifted authority or responsibility for the coinage among themselves over time. This distinct 'cycle of responsibility' [Figure 6.1] points directly to an administrative concept that would have been revolutionary for its time.

Nearly all of the most numerous sequences have periods of relatively large numbers of moneyers with the same forename element working concurrently within the London mints only to have them all replaced by others from the same group for an immediately succeeding coinage minting. Interestingly, of the four largest name sequences in London ([Ælf-], [Ead-], [Leof-], and [Wulf-]) there does seem to be a pattern apparent in the visual representation of each sequence's moneyer periods of activity [Figures 6.2–6.5]. The periods of like-named groupings seem to be similar for each one. In the [Ælf-] sequence the shift in moneyer groupings during the periods around 979, 997, 1016, and 1040 are apparent. These same periods, roughly, see similar shifts in moneyer groupings in the [Ead-], [Leof-], and [Wulf-] name sequences as well.

For each of these name sequences, there is a group of moneyers, typically comprised of between three and six individuals, associated with a couple of coinage issues before being completely replaced by another group of three to six moneyers with the same name element. The uniformity in this practice seems to indicate a set pattern associated either with the political events or some other internal structure. The fact that the install-replace-install cycle is so regular between all of the largest groups, and some of the other three main name sequences ([Æthel-], [Beorht-], and [God-]), indicates some level of cooperation or joint decision-making between the various mints within London and the various families.

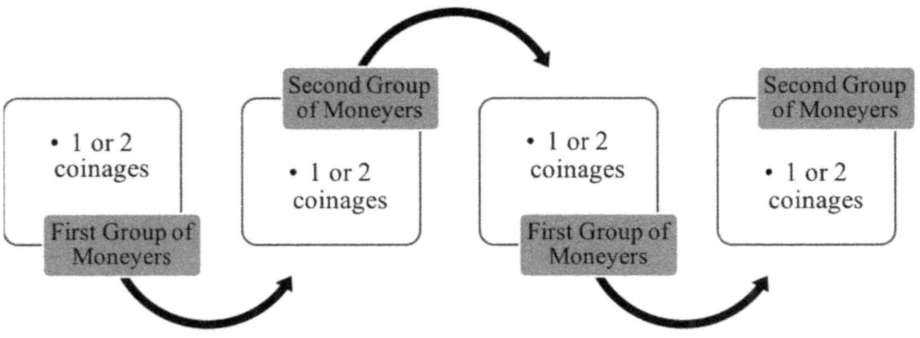

Figure 6.1. The Moneyer Rotation Pattern.

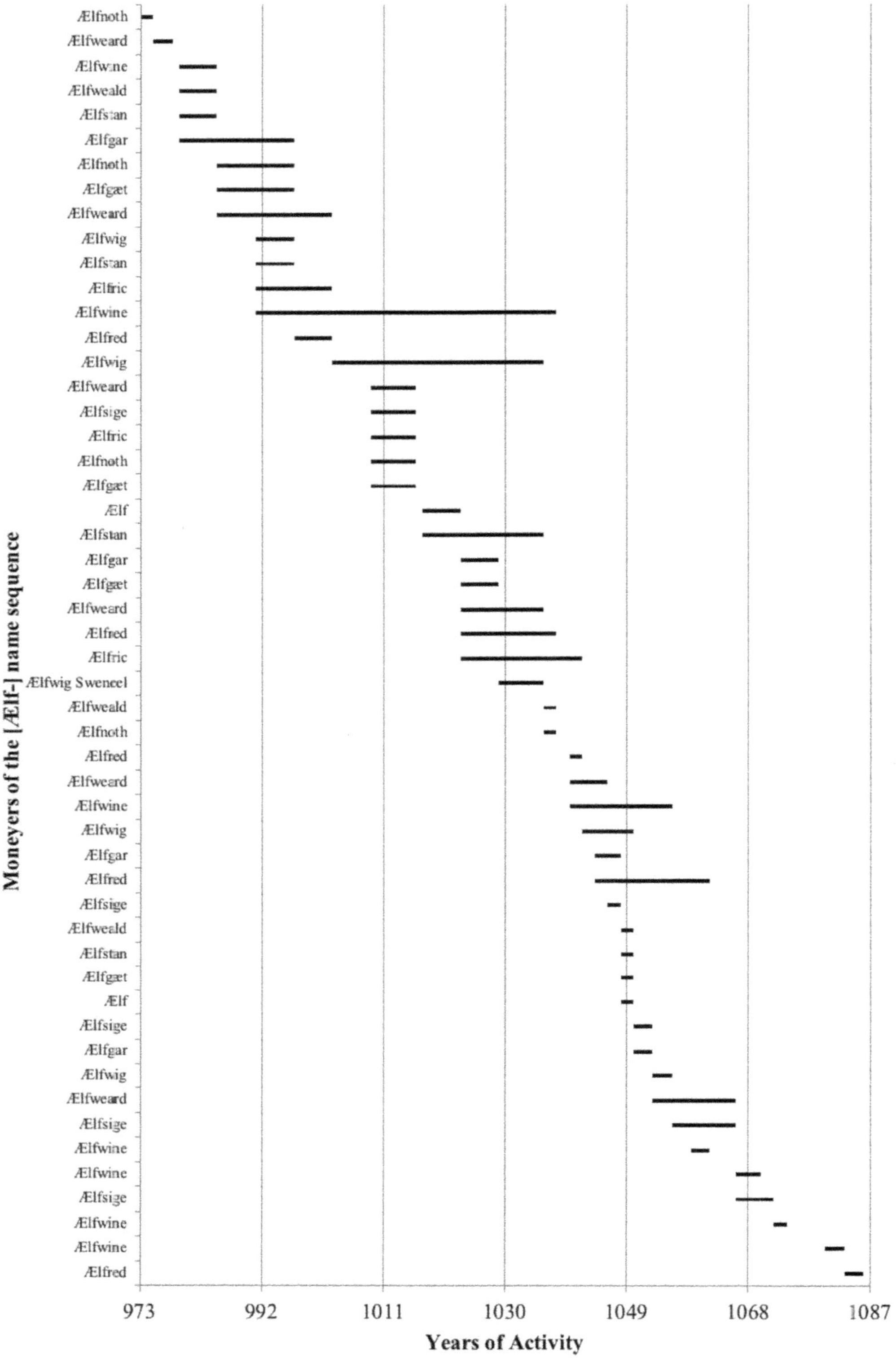

Figure 6.2. Operational years of London moneyers in the [Ælf-] name sequence.

This would seem to imply an internal structure that included rules and regulations beyond the simple idea of one man controlling a certain number of minters and being responsible for the coinage. For there to have been a set pattern of wholesale replacement of the moneyers responsible for the coinage lends itself to the idea of a guild-like structure of regulatory control beyond royal control. A search of the extant laws indicates that there are no instances of the crown having mandated this mass shifting of responsibility.[1] Therefore, it would appear that the moneyers, working in concert, established a process by which certain members of their community maintained responsibility for the coinage over a set period of time (typically one to three coinages, or around five to 15 years) before switching the primary position

[1] <http://www.earlyenglishlaws.ac.uk/laws/>.

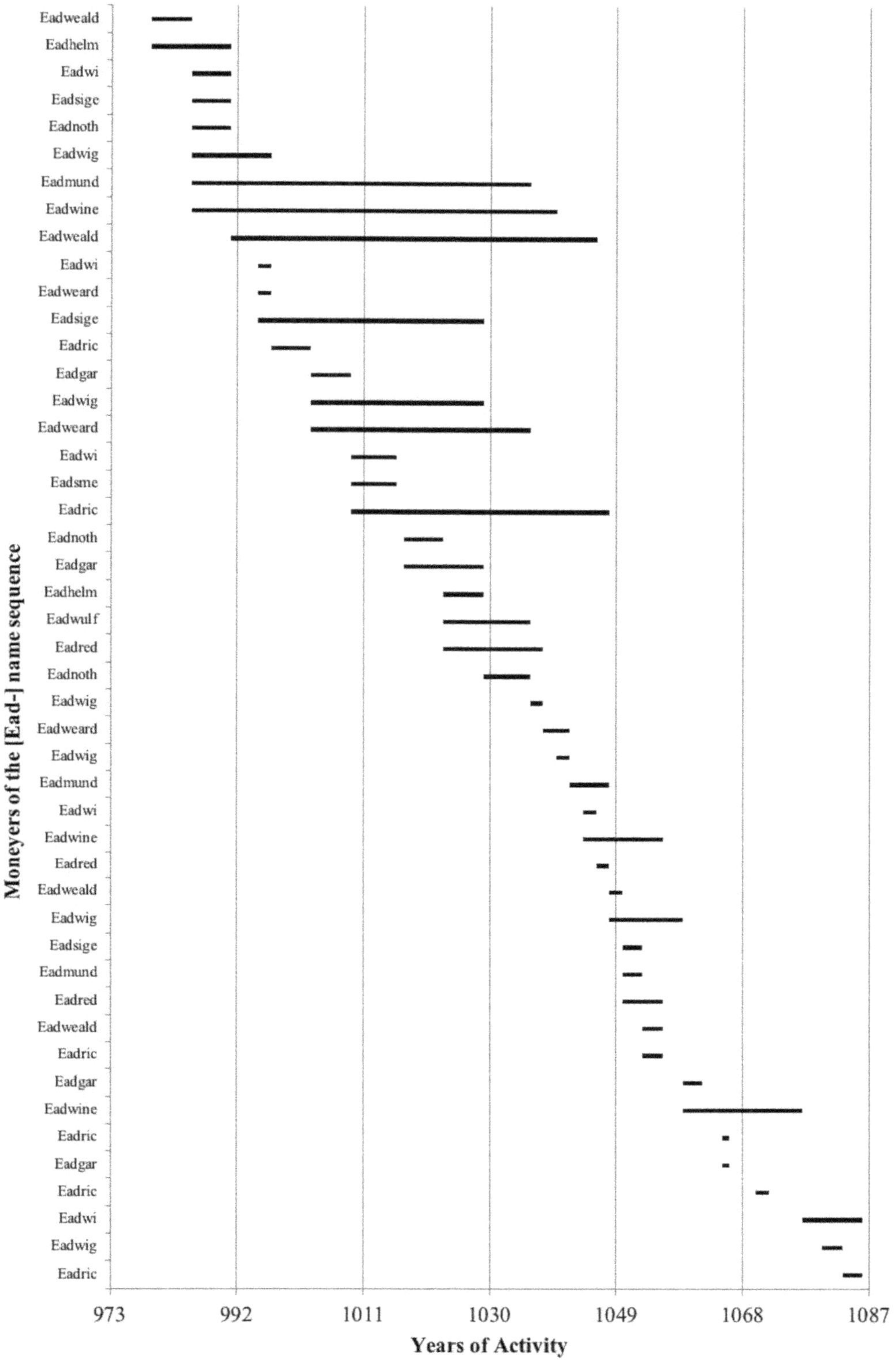

Figure 6.3. Operational years of London moneyers in the [Ead-] name sequence.

out to someone else from their family group. This period of operation and activity shifted after 1036. The overall average for a moneyer's single instance of activity before 1036 was 10.5 years. After 1036, this average dropped substantially to only 4 years. This seems to indicate that even though the regularity of coinage reissuance increased, the limitations on moneyer activity remained attached to the coinages themselves, and not to any specific period of time. If a moneyer was obligated to only one to three coinage series, then it did not matter if the individual series was for two years or seven.

This was not limited to just intra-familial groupings. In reviewing the activity of each moneyer in London for the period 973 to 1086, a wider picture of this rotational practice can be gleaned.[2] What can also be gathered from

[2] Supplemental Material 3 (SM3) – London Moneyer Activity Chart.

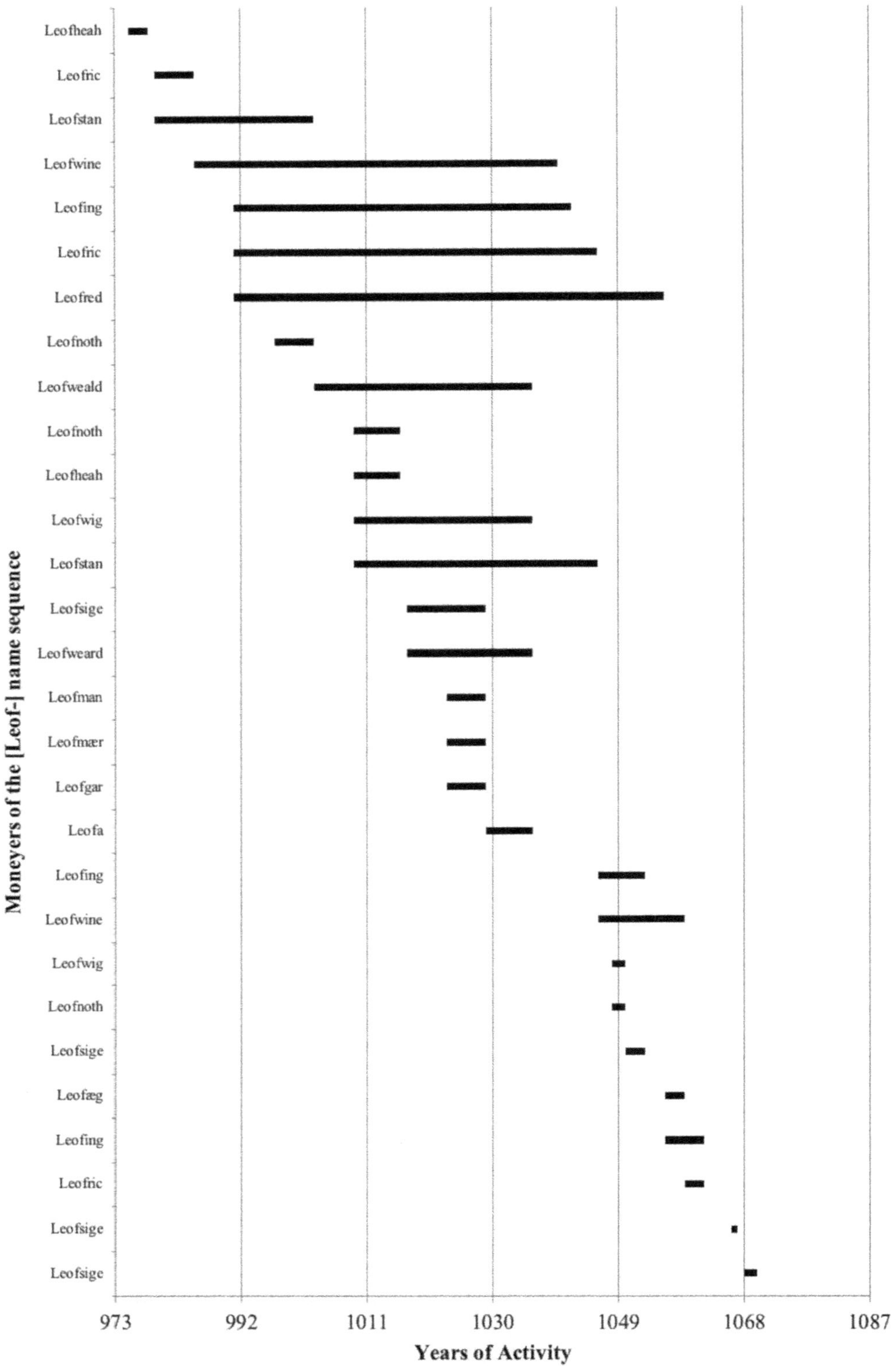

Figure 6.4. Operational years of London moneyers in the [Leof-] name sequence.

this is an example of the cycle possibly crossing familial boundaries and working in conjunction with several of the larger name sequences, which would likely not be the case if this were only a familial phenomenon. For example, in 979, for Æthelred II's First Hand type, moneyers Ælfstan, Ælfwine, God, and Leofric begin minting.[3] These four are only present for this type and are not in the coinage record for the Second Hand type beginning in 985. Eadsige and Eadwi are only documented for the Second Hand type (985–991).[4] In 991, the Crux type sees a return of the three of the first four (Ælfstan, Ælfwine, and Leofric) after an

[3] SM3.C1; SM3.C3; SM3.C9; SM3.C11.

[4] SM3.D3; SM3.D4.

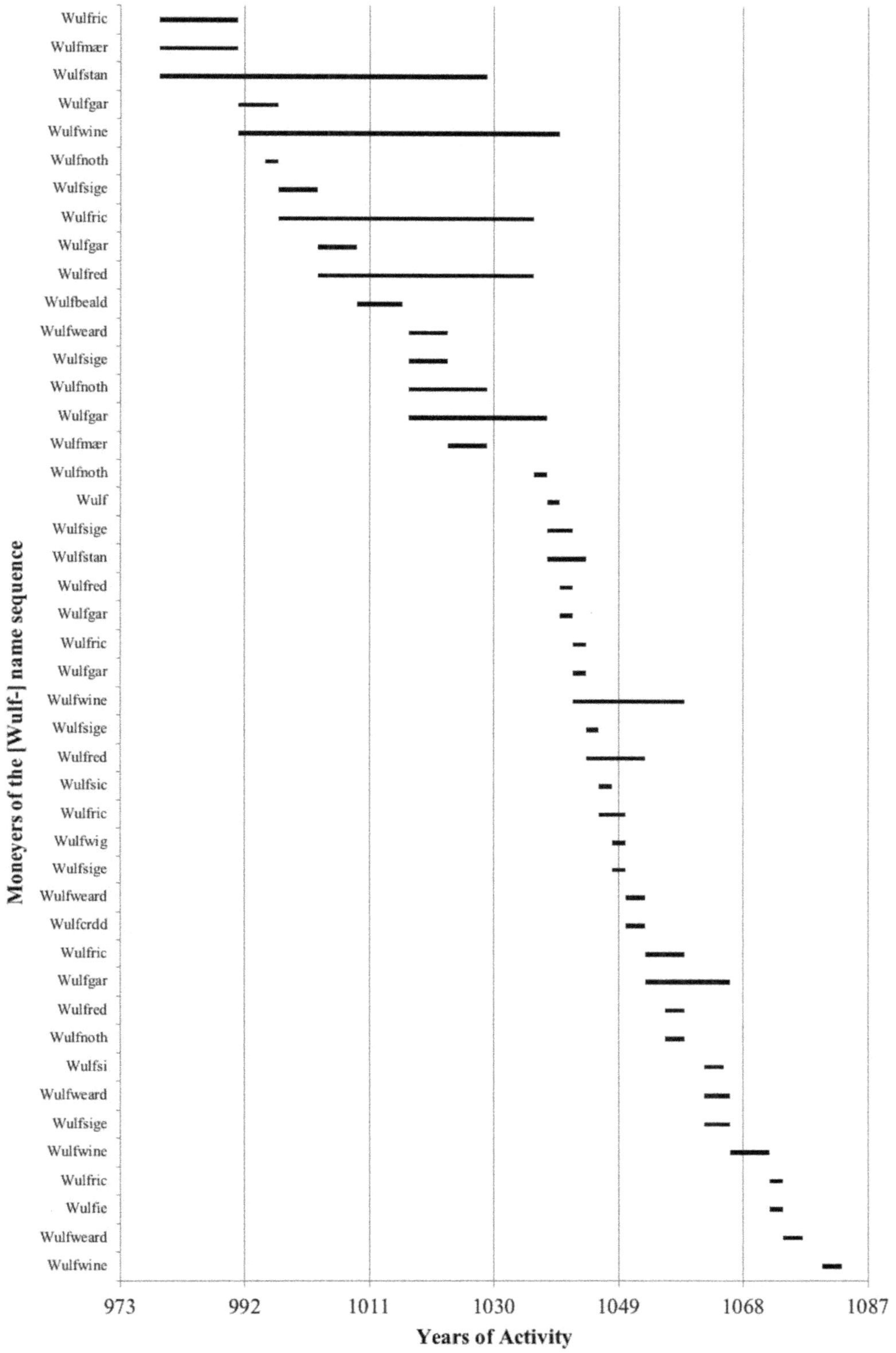

Figure 6.5. Operational years of London moneyers in the [Wulf-] name sequence.

absence.[5] God does not return at this point but does so in 995 for the Small Crux/Transition Crux type, along with Eadsige and Eadwi.[6] These six moneyers seem to have alternated activity within the mint.

If this is indeed what occurred, then the implication is that there was a process in place with mutual participation from nearly all parties, at least the primary name sequences which comprised over two-thirds of the total number of moneyers within London. Not only mutual participation but also clear processes and guidelines were in place to accommodate this patterned shift. This could explain why certain names appear quite often in the coinage record but with seemingly incongruous action. When placed within

[5] SM3.E1; SM3.E15; SM3.E20.
[6] SM3.F5; SM3.F10; SM3.F4.

this formula, that seemingly sporadic activity is placed within the context of a larger mechanism. This explains, generally, why there could have been an Ælfsige operating in London from 1046 to 1048, from 1050 to 1053, from 1056 to 1066 and again, skipping Harold II's Pax type (1066), from 1066 to 1072.[7] Obviously, this pattern recognition is not necessarily designed to address individual moneyers, as each of these Ælfsiges could have been a separate and distinct individual. But the placement of each within one of the groupings of moneyers that was installed, replaced, and then potentially reinstalled is striking.

When this is compared with the other dominant name sequences, similar cyclical name placements are also evident. There is an Eadmund in the [Ead-] sequence from 985 to 1036, from 1042 to 1048, and from 1050 to 1053.[8] Similar patterns emerge when reviewing several other names on both the [Ælf-] (Ælfgar, Ælfsige, Ælfweard, Ælfred) and [Ead-] (Eadgar, Eadric, Eadsige, Eadwig) name sequences, as well as the [Beorht-] (Beorhtmær, Beorhtwine), [God-] (Godric, Godhere), [Leof-] (Leofred, Leofsige), and [Wulf-] (Wulfstan, Wulfric, Wulfnoth) sequences. Each of the primary name sequences have multiple instances of moneyers operating at non-contiguous intervals over several coinage issues. Many of these are seemingly in concert with members of other name sequences like those noted above.

For example, in reviewing the moneyers Theodred and Deorman, there appears to be some correlation between the activities of these moneyers with one another. Theodred is active over two distinct periods before the first Deorman, from 985 to 991 and from 1003 to 1009.[9] From 1009 to 1016, Deorman is first noted in the coinage record.[10] This is followed by a return of Theodred from 1023 to 1029.[11] Deorman is again active from 1036 to 1038 and Theodred returns for the period 1042 to 1046.[12] Deorman is active in two periods, from 1048 to 1050 in the first instance and then again from 1056 to 1059.[13] These placements are grouped with other moneyers acting in concert, but these are significant because of the later importance of the Deorman line in the post-Conquest London moneyers.[14] Could the first Norman-era Deorman, who is thought by Nightingale to be the grandson of the last pre-Conquest moneyer of the same name, be the result of the crossing of these two name sequences?[15]

Considering that the son of the later Deorman was also a moneyer and was named Theodric, which preceded a sequence of Deorman/Theodric moneyers in London, it seems very plausible that this could be the case.[16] The operational years of these first two progenitors are too close together for there to have been likely direct familial connection, at least paternally, but the merging of these two families at a later stage due to the potential close working relationship of the moneyer groups may help fill some of the gaps in the knowledge of how these few families became dynastically powerful through the Norman Conquest. Both the [Theod-] and [Deor-] name sequences are rare in the Anglo-Saxon era. The [Theod-] sequence only appears in Hertford, Lincoln, and London. The [Deor-] element is more widespread, appearing in six other mints outside of London: Chester, Colchester, Hertford, Steyning, and Thetford. It is worth noting here that the overlap in Hertford between the two sequences corresponds not only in place but in time, with a Theodred active in Hertford from 1048 to 1050 and a Deorsige active there from 1017 to 1040 and 1044 to 1046.[17]

Considering Hertford's proximity to London and Southwark, and the high number of moneyers with the same name that were active in that mint concurrently with periods of activity to the south, an argument for Hertford being something of an extended surrogate, or satellite, mint similar to Southwark could potentially be constructed. Boiga, which is a name that saw relatively widespread usage (active at 11 mints) but is absent from London, is active for the Crux type (991–997) in both Hertford and Southwark.[18] The [Burg-] name element, which only appears in a few mints, is present in Hertford, as well as London and Southwark.[19] Similarly, Beorhtlaf, an unusual construct, is present only in Hertford, London, and Southwark, and all within close temporal proximity.[20] Considering this, the single Crux type coin recorded to a moneyer Beorhtlaf with indeterminate mint epigraphy, because of coin damage, could reasonably be attributed to this individual.[21]

Theories and Possible Causes of this Rotation Cycle

The exposition of the moneyers in London and Southwark, as well as the review of the remaining 97 minting locations between 973 and 1086 in chapter four, directly supports two theories, with a few possible causes related directly to the 'Cycle of Rotation' outlined above. First, it was common for mints to organise moneyers into groups between 973 and 1086. This was maintained within family groups and is evident across putative familial boundaries. Groups of moneyers would begin and end operation together at nearly uniform intervals across multiple locations simultaneously. And second, there was widespread rotation within those groups of moneyers operating together between 973 and 1086. A group of moneyers would begin operation, stop, be replaced by another group for a period of time, then

7 SM3.R1; SM3.T3; SM3.V6; SM3.AA2.
8 SM3.D15; SM3.P7; SM3.T8.
9 SM3.D7; SM3.H7.
10 SM3.I11.
11 SM3.K21.
12 SM3.M7; SM3.P6.
13 SM3.S8; SM3.V1.
14 P. Nightingale, 1982, 'Some London Moneyers and Reflections on the Organization of English Mints in the Eleventh and Twelfth Centuries', *NC* 142, 34–50.
15 Nightingale, 1982, 35-6.
16 Nightingale, 1982, 36.
17 SM1.Hertford.xxix; SM1.Hertford.vii–viii.
18 SM1.Hertford.v; SM1.Southwark.xxv.
19 SM1.Hertford.vi; SM1.London.cxlix; SM1.Southwark.xxviii.
20 SM1.Hertford.iii; SM1.London.cvi; SM1.Southwark.xxii.
21 SM1.Indeterminate.xxxi.

return to operation together. This occurred in nearly every location with enough extant source material to map the operative years of the moneyer group. The first potential cause of these grouping and rotational patterns is that they were developed as an internal mechanism by the moneyers to maintain family stability and control over their craft. Possibly in conjunction with this or as a motivation for the changes, these patterns may have developed as a direct response to royal imposition that sought to limit the authority of individual moneyers or families of moneyers which would have been influential and wealthy as the makers of the king's coinage. These royal restrictions may have also sought to maintain guidelines on the regulation of coinage in concordance with other reforms that were possibly initiated in the 970s.

It is certainly the case that the internal structure existed. It is also the case that there was a large coinage reform in the early 970s. Although this reform is not explicitly mentioned in the written record, it is suggested by the numismatic evidence. And it is clear that within two generations of this reform the patterns of grouping and rotation were widespread in Anglo-Saxon England. It is not a great logical leap to assume that the regulations that were introduced by Edgar's coinage reform might have included other restrictions on the moneyers, or that Æthelred II might have introduced such restrictions early in his reign.[22]

These theories and possible causes lead to the overriding conclusion that the moneyers of late Anglo-Saxon England, likely in direct response to royal authority which sought to impose upon their monopoly of the minting of the king's coinage, created an internal structure that resulted in groups of moneyers operating together before allowing another member of their dynasty, in conjunction with other minting families, to take over and carry forward for a set period of time. This temporary replacement resulted in a pattern of rotation through which the individual, within the realms of feasibility with regard to extant material evidence, can be witnessed to act as moneyer, withdraw from the role, and then take up the role again at a future time, typically enduring for one or two coinage issues in each instance. Indeed, the coinage laws of Æthelred II, which are commonly seen as symbolic rather than actual because of the apparent lack of enforcement with regards to the number of moneyers present at any one time within a given mint, could potentially be misunderstood and the catalyst for this organisation.[23] What if the stipulation *[e]t ut monetarii pauciores sint quam antea fuerint: in omni summo portu sint tres monetarii, et in omni alio portu sit unus monetarius* referred to the physical mints, not just the minting towns?[24] If each of the families in London, for example, operated their own mint house within the city then the grouping pattern, which most often included three moneyers within a single name sequence working at any one time, might reveal the beginnings of royal imposition on the minting practice. The rotation pattern that follows from these groups of moneyers acting in concert may have been the result of this new regulation from the king, heretofore thought to have been impotent in practice. If true, this explains the shift to the grouping pattern in the early part of Æthelred II's reign and the rotational aspects of moneyer activity that followed. The groups of three or four moneyers from each of the primary name sequences in London and the other large mints make sense within this context. That there are groups of two to three moneyers in many of the smaller mints operating at the same time from different family groups also fits this pattern. If only one member of each family is active at any specific coinage, then it stands to reason that they would be operating at the same time as single members from other groups. So, the concept of three moneyers from any single family per minting house within the largest mints and single moneyers from a family in the smaller mints makes sense within this context. The fact that there are groups of four moneyers in the coinage record on occasion from a single family can be explained as one leaving during the period of one coinage while another takes over, perhaps due to illness or death.

Since the pattern of grouping is widespread from the coinage record beginning immediately after the Reform Coinage, and the patterns of rotation manifest themselves within two generations of the grouping pattern, it further appears that the overall administrative structure of Anglo-Saxon England was sufficiently complex to support this level of organisation.[25] Not only this, but the fact that the moneyers were able to organise themselves in such a fashion and maintain this structure indicates a level of workforce organisation that is much more complex than expected for this period in history. This organisation indicates that this near-autonomous group of individuals, men who withstood both the Danish and Norman Conquests, established a sort of unionised labour centuries before trade and craft guilds established themselves in England.

The most significant result of this, regardless of the actual cause, is the rotation pattern in the placement of the moneyers. Expanding on the examples above provide further confirmation of how this mechanism worked in the late Anglo-Saxon period. Reviewing how six moneyers of London alternated position in the coinage record can elucidate this point and provides the potential for further review [Figure 6.6]. In 979, for Æthelred II's First Hand type, moneyers Ælfstan, Ælfwine, God, and Leofric begin minting.[26] These four are only present for this type and are not in the coinage record for the Second Hand type beginning in 985. But, with the Second Hand type an Eadsige and Eadwi begin and are only documented on this coinage.[27] In 991, the Crux type sees a return of the three of the first four (Ælfstan, Ælfwine, and Leofric) after an

[22] Screen, 2007, 154.
[23] IV Æthelred 5–9.3, Liebermann, 234–6.
[24] IV Æthelred 9, Liebermann, 236.
[25] Molyneaux, 2015, 120.
[26] SM3.C1; SM3.C3; SM3.C9; SM3.C11.
[27] SM3.D3; SM3.D4.

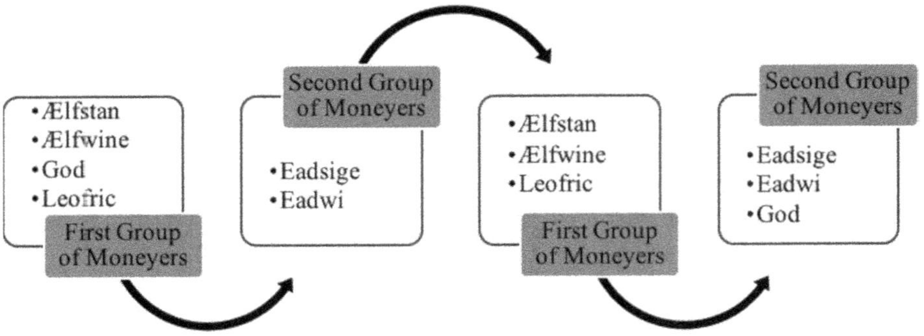

Figure 6.6. Moneyers of London in the Rotation Pattern.

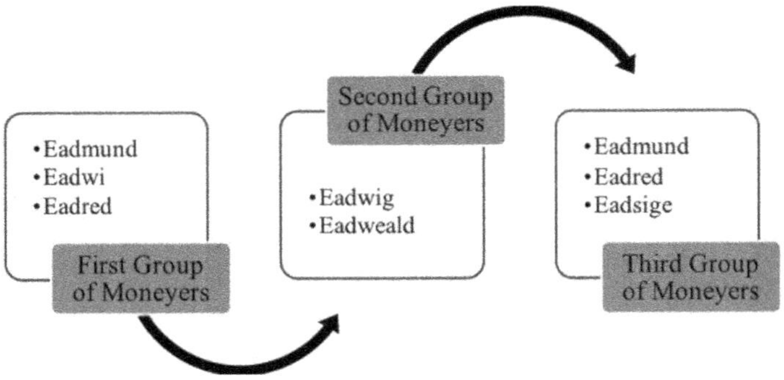

Figure 6.7. Some London [Ead-] moneyers in the Rotation Pattern.

absence.[28] God does not return at this point but does so in 995 for the Small Crux/Transition Crux type, along with Eadsige and Eadwi.[29]

A simple pattern of rotation is illustrated in the example above, but more complicated patterns did exist. Between the internal rotation of moneyers within specific dynasties and the cross-linking of those dynasties with other familial groups, an intricate web of moneyer placements is woven.

Taking the [Ead-] sequence from London during the later reign of Edward the Confessor as a starting point, an image of such a web can be developed. This example begins with an Eadmund, who was active from 1042 to 1048 and again from 1050 to 1053. During his first period of activity an Eadwi (1044–1046) and an Eadred (1046–1048) were active. In 1048 two [Ead-] moneyers began together: Eadwig (1048–1059) and Eadweald (1048–1050). There are arguments for and against including the 'wi' ending names with both 'wig' and 'wine', but since both exist in the record simultaneously within London, they are kept separate.[30] Then, in 1050, three [Ead-] moneyers started operation, including the second period of Eadmund, as well as the return of Eadred (1050–1056) and an Eadsige (1050–1053). These placements can be illustrated in the rotation pattern [Figure 6.7], but this does not give a complete picture of what was occurring.

Table 6.1 provides a more accurate illustration of what was actually occurring with these [Ead-] sequence moneyers during this period [Table 6.1]. While there are clear breaks and moneyers did return after these periods of inactivity, it is not as clear as some of the other examples.

A similar, but not quite as convoluted, arrangement of some [Ælf-] sequence moneyers in London from the same period can be drawn [Figure 6.8 & Table 6.2]. Ælfgar began in 1044 and was joined in 1046 by Ælfsige before both stopped activity in 1048. Four moneyers began together in 1048, with all stopping in 1050: Ælf, Ælfgæt, Ælfstan, and Ælfweald. From 1050 to 1053, both Ælfgar and Ælfsige return. These two are replaced by two other [Ælf-] sequence moneyers in 1053: Ælfwig (1053–1056) and Ælfweard (1053–1066).

The separation of the various groups within this name sequence is more in line with the visual placements within the rotation pattern. But that is still not the overarching picture in this scenario.

In order to see how this complicated system of grouping and rotation really worked, elements of these two name sequences, as well as moneyers from other groups, are placed into similar representations [Figure 6.9 & Table 6.3]. In cross-grouping members of both the [Ælf-] and [Ead-] sequences, and including moneyers from the [Æthel-], [Bur-], [Deor-], and [Ea-] sequences, a truer picture of what was taking place within the minting apparatus of Anglo-Saxon England can be realised. Two groups of three moneyers appear to work together, stop working, rotate with the other group of three, and then begin again in sequence with no shifts or separation.

[28] SM3.E1; SM3.E15; SM3.E20.
[29] SM3.F5; SM3.F10; SM3.F4.
[30] B. H. I. H. Stewart and C. E. Blunt, 1978, 'The Droitwich Mint and *BMC* Type XIV of Edward the Confessor', *BNJ* 48, 52–8 at 54.

Table 6.1. Some London [Ead-] Moneyer Placements by Coinage Type

Pacx	Radiate Crown	Trefoil- Quad.	Short Cross	Expanding Cross	Pointed Helmet	Sovereign/ Eagles
Eadmund (1042–1048)			Eadwig (1048–1059)			
	Eadwi (1044–1046)	Eadred (1046–1048)	Eadweald (1048–1050)	Eadred (1050–1056)		
				Eadmund (1050–1053)		
				Eadsige (1050–1053)		

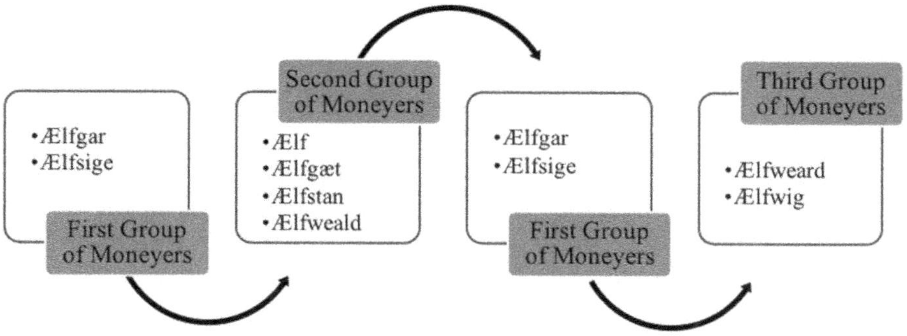

Figure 6.8. Some London [Ælf-] moneyers in the Rotation Cycle.

Table 6.2. Some London [Ælf-] Moneyer Placements by Coinage Type

Radiate Crown	Trefoil- Quad.	Short Cross	Expanding Cross	Pointed Helmet	Sovereign/ Eagles	Hammer Cross
Ælfgar (1044–1048)		Ælf (1048–1050)	Ælfgar (1050–1053)	Ælfweard (1053–1066)		
	Ælfsige (1046–1048)	Ælfgæt (1048–1050)	Ælfsige (1050–1053)	Ælfwig (1053–1056)		
		Ælfstan (1048–1050)				
		Ælfweald (1048–1050)				

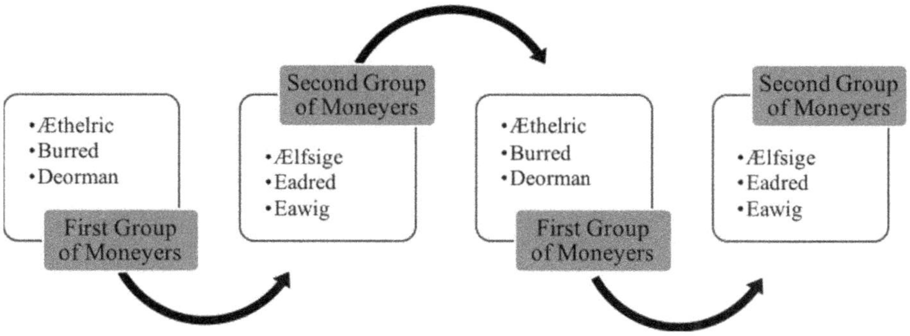

Figure 6.9. Some London moneyers in the Rotation Pattern.

And, as can be seen in Table 6.3, this is much closer to what actually occurred than the illustrations of just the [Ead-] and [Ælf-] sequences above convey when taken alone.

Outside of Burred and Eadred, who both carried forward for one additional coinage after the other two stopped activity in their second iterations, there is almost complete uniformity in the rotation of these six moneyers over four consecutive periods. It is possible that Burred and Eadred were needed for an additional coinage due to

Table 6.3. Some London Moneyer Placements by Coinage Type

<table>
<tr><th>Radiate Crown</th><th>Trefoil- Quad.</th><th>Short Cross</th><th>Expanding Cross</th><th>Pointed Helmet</th></tr>
<tr><td>Æthelric (1044–1046)</td><td>Ælfsige (1046–1048)</td><td colspan="2">Burred (1048–1053)</td><td></td></tr>
<tr><td>Burred (1044–1046)</td><td>Eadred (1046–1048)</td><td>Æthelric (1048–1050)</td><td colspan="2">Eadred (1050–1056)</td></tr>
<tr><td>Deorman (1044–1046)</td><td>Eawig (1046–1048)</td><td>Deorman (1048–1050)</td><td>Ælfsige (1050–1053)</td><td rowspan="2"></td></tr>
<tr><td colspan="3"></td><td>Eawig (1050–1053)</td></tr>
</table>

higher demand or potentially the death or unavailability of another moneyer. Æthelric, Burred, and Deorman began together in 1044 and operated until 1046. Likewise, Ælfsige, Eadred, and Eawig started just after the first three in 1046 and stopped together in 1048. In 1048, Æthelric, Burred, and Deorman return, with Burred carrying forward to 1053 while Æthelric and Deorman cease activity in 1050. Ælfsige, Eadred, and Eawig all return in 1050, with Ælfsige and Eawig stopping in 1053, and Eadred operating for one additional coinage after the end of Burred's tenure.

A review of the major and mint mints will determine if these patterns that are evident within the London mint are also apparent in other parts of Anglo-Saxon England. The first of these sections addresses the largest of the mints outside of London and, as illustrated in chapter five above, do maintain a lot of similarities to it with regard to familial continuity and the pattern of groups of moneyers beginning and ending operation together. If these rotational patterns are also evident then this becomes more than a local anomaly, as much as London can be considered a local concept in regard to late Anglo-Saxon England.

Major Mints Summary

Most of the major mints in operation within England from 973 to 1086 demonstrate both the grouping and rotational patterns, as outlined below [Table 6.4]. All 32 of these mints were in operation for the majority of the study period, many with only one or two breaks in the coinage record. All of these mints had over 30 moneyers, or at least 30 distinct periods of moneyer activity, in operation for their functioning years. Because of the size of these mints, individually and collectively, specific case studies from each mint are addressed instead of a comprehensive detailing of all moneyer activity. These case studies constitute typically the largest, or near-largest, continuous sequences within the mints.

At Lincoln, there are multiple instances of rotation both before and after 1036. Winchester illustrates the pattern of groups of moneyers beginning together, with some ending and others moving forward before being replaced in a rotational alternating sequence. The operational years of the moneyers in Exeter illustrate a nearly uniform pattern of grouping throughout the entire period of this study. There are multiple points at which groups of moneyers begin operation together, stop, and are replaced by a completely new group of moneyers, then are replaced in turn again. The Chester mint also has examples of rotation.[31] A Deorlaf alternates with an Æthelmod over four consecutive coinages. Deorlaf is active for the Last Small Cross type (978–979) and then again for the Second Hand type (985–991). Æthelmod was active during the First Hand type (979–985) and then the Crux type (991–997). There is also an Æthelnoth in Chester operating in rotation with some of the [Leof-] moneyers from 997–1003, 1009–1023, and 1029–1036.[32] Later, in this same mint, there seems to be a rotation between Fargrim and the [Leof-] sequence. Fargrim is active from 1040 to 1042, 1044 to 1046, and 1050 to 1053.[33]

In Canterbury the rotational aspects of the mint are possibly apparent from the earliest records. Heahwulf and a combination of Wulfwine and Wulfwig seem to alternate placement between the periods 979–985, 985–1003, and 1003–1009.[34] In the later period, the [Wulf-] sequence again evidently alternates placement with another group of moneyers, in this instance, the [Man-] sequence. This series of exchanges is complex and does include quite a bit of overlap among the individual moneyers, but the general trend seems to indicate that there are points where one group ended minting while the other began and vice versa.

For example, in looking solely at the post-1036 period, there are 14 [Wulf-] sequence moneyers operating over various periods in Canterbury.[35] When compared to the eight [Man-] sequence moneyers operating from 1042 to 1077, there is an ongoing pattern of replacement occurring where one or more moneyers from one of these sequences is absent the coinage record for a period of time before returning in exchange for the other undergoing a similar period of absence.[36]

The less active name sequences also demonstrate continuity and rotation at Norwich. Hringwulf and Rægenulf are active together in contrast to Ælfric and Ælfwine for at least two placements.[37] Folcard and Leofing are grouped

[31] Metcalf, 1998, 207; R. H. M. Dolley and E. J. E. Pirie, 1964, 'The repercussions on Chester's prosperity of the Viking descent on Cheshire in 980', *BNJ* 33, 39–44 at 43. The mint at Chester was very active prior to Edgar's reform but saw a decline in productivity following the Scandinavian invasion of 980.

[32] SM1.Chester.xxi; SM1.Chester.xxiii; SM1.Chester.xxv.

[33] SM1.Chester.l–lii.

[34] SM1.Canterbury.xliii–xliv; SM1.Canterbury.lxxvi–lxxix.

[35] SM1.Canterbury.lxxxiii–xcvi.

[36] SM1.Canterbury.lvi–lxii.

[37] SM1.Norwich.xlii–xlv; SM1.Norwich.lxxii–lxxiii; SM1.Norwich.iii; SM1.Norwich.viii–ix.

Table 6.4. Grouping and Rotation Patterns in the Major Mints

Mint	Volume	Grouping	Pre-1036	Post-1036	Multiple Sequences	Rotation	Pre-1036	Post-1036	Multiple Sequences
York	High	X	X	X	X	X	X	X	X
Lincoln	High	X	X	X	X	X	X	X	X
Winchester	High	X	X	X	X	X	X	X	X
Exeter	High	X	X	X	X	X	X	X	X
Thetford	High	X	X	X	X	X	X	X	X
Stamford	High	X	X	X	X	X	X	X	X
Chester	High	X	X	X	X	X	X	X	X
Canterbury	High	X	X	X	X	X	X	X	X
Norwich	High	X	X	X	X	X	X	X	X
Oxford	High	X	X	X	X	X	X	X	X
Cambridge	High	X	X	X	X	X	–	X	X
Shrewsbury	High	X	X	X	X	X	X	X	X
Gloucester	High	S	X	X	X	S	X	X	X
Wallingford	High	X	X	X	X	X	–	X	X
Worcester	High	X	X	X	X	S	X	X	–
Lewes	High	X	X	X	X	X	X	X	X
Bedford	High	X	X	X	X	X	X	X	X
Colchester	High	X	X	X	X	X	X	X	X
Ipswich	High	X	X	X	X	X	X	X	X
Dover	High	X	X	X	X	X	X	X	X
Hereford	High	X	X	X	X	–	–	–	–
Wilton	High	S	X	–	X	–	–	–	–
Northampton	High	X	X	X	X	X	X	X	X
Leicester	High	X	X	X	X	X	X	X	X
Warwick	High	X	X	X	X	X	–	X	X
Hertford	High	S	X	X	X	–	–	–	–
Ilchester	High	X	X	X	X	X	X	–	X
Bristol	High	X	X	X	X	X	X	X	X
Shaftesbury	High	S	X	–	X	X	X	X	X
Derby	High	S	X	–	X	X	X	X	X
Chichester	High	S	X	–	X	S	–	X	X
Huntingdon	High	X	X	–	X	X	–	X	–

together in contrast to Swerting.[38] In Oxford, there appears to be consistent rotation between the [God-] and [Wulf-] sequences throughout the period 973 to 1086. The [Æthel-] and [Beorht-] sequences display a similar pattern, although not with the same consistency.

In Cambridge, the first Godwine was active in the mint from 991 to 997.[39] This name reappears in the coinage record from 1017 to 1023, and may be the same individual, but seems unlikely considering the next series of active periods.[40] In 1036, the first Wulfwine is recorded and is active until 1040.[41] In 1040, Godwine is active for Harthcnut's Arm and Sceptre type (1040–1042).[42] Wulfwine returns for Edward the Confessor's Expanding Cross type (1050–1053).[43] He is followed immediately by Godwine, who is active from 1053 to 1059.[44] Godwine is in turn followed immediately by Wulfwine, active from 1059 to 1062.[45] And in 1062, Godwine is once again active through 1065, with a brief resurgence for Harold II's Pax type in 1066.[46]

[38] SM1.Norwich.xxvi–xxvii; SM1.Norwich.xlix–l; SM1.Norwich.lxxvi–lxxvii.
[39] SM1.Cambridge.xxxiv.
[40] SM1.Cambridge.xxxv.
[41] SM1.Cambridge.lxiii.
[42] SM1.Cambridge.xxxvi.
[43] SM1.Cambridge.lxiv.
[44] SM1.Cambridge.xxxvii.
[45] SM1.Cambridge.lxv.
[46] SM1.Cambridge.xxxviii–xxxix.

Shrewsbury has a regular pattern of grouping as well as regular alternation in the position of moneyer, primarily among the members of the primary sequences. A rotational cycle between several moneyers also appears in the coinage record of Gloucester. There is a sustained alternation between the moneyer Wulfgæt and two others, Orderic and Sigelac. Wulfgeat is active in four periods: 1053–1062, 1066, 1070–1072, and 1083–1086.[47] Orderic and Sigelac are active together from 1056 to 1059.[48] Sigelac is also active from 1062 to 1066, while Orderic is active again for 1066–1070.[49] In Wallingford, there is a pattern of grouping throughout the mint's history and some rotation, primarily between the [Beorht-] moneyers and members of the less frequent sequences. The mint at Lewes contains multiple examples of cross-sequence rotation, especially between the [Ead-] and [Leof-] sequences from as early as Æthelred II's reign to the end of Edward the Confessor's rule.

In some mints the rotational aspect is not as clear. For example, in Bedford in the post-1036 period, there are groupings of [Wulf-] and [God-] moneyers on multiple occasions that rotate with groupings of [Swet-] and [Ulf-] moneyers. For instance, there is a Swet in operation from 1038–1042 and 1048–1053, and an Ulfcetel active from 1042–1044 and 1048–1050.[50] Then Godwine, Wulfmær, and Wulfwig are active from 1050 to 1053.[51] Ulfcetel returns in 1053 and is active until 1056.[52] Then he is no longer present in the coinage record. In 1056, the final Swet is once again in the record, remaining until 1059.[53] Also beginning in 1056 are Godric, another (or the same) Godwine, and possibly the returning Wulfwig.[54] Godwine and Wulfwig began and ended at the same time in each instance, while Swet and Ulfcetel alternated position with some overlapping of the other two.

And in some, the longevity of particular sequences results in rotation being between that primary sequence and multiple other name groups. Because of the longevity of the [Wulf-] sequence, the rotation cycles that are present in Colchester are often intermingled with these moneyers. There appear to be instances of alternation between the [Wulf-] sequence and the [Beorht-], [Brun-], and [Deor-] sequences. For the [Beorht-] sequence, there is a Beorhtric that operated over four distinct periods in opposition to [Wulf-] moneyers: 1046–1059, 1062–1065, 1066, and 1068–1070.[55] The [Brun-] sequence consists of three moneyers operating over five periods: Brunman (1017–1023), Brunhuse (1044–1048, 1050–1056, and 1059–1065), and Brunnus (1050–1053).[56] The [Deor-] sequence includes two variant spellings from the epigraphy and is the latest temporally of those that alternate with the [Wulf-] sequence: Deorman (1050–1053 and 1059–1062), Dorman (1077–1080), and Dirman (1083–1086).[57] A Druman (1074–1077) is also active at this time and is possibly another variation, but the difference is sufficiently profound to maintain it outside of the sequence specifically.[58]

Ipswich provides an example of a group that repeats. The group that began in 979 included Branting, Leofman, and Leofric. These three appear together again in 1017. This occurs later in the record as well with Bruning and Leofweald being active together on two instances, the first period ending in 1056 and the second for the period 1059–1065.[59] Along with this repetitive grouping which continues in the pattern throughout the study period at Ipswich, the primary name sequence, [Leof-], maintains a consistent presence throughout. There are 10 name sequences at Ipswich with two or more moneyers present from 973 to 1086. These sequences comprise all but 11 of the moneyer records for the mint, or just over 80 per cent. Of these, the [Leof-] sequence alone constitutes over a third, with 17 records. This provides a high level of generational regularity and continuity for the mint.

The mint at Warwick has a consistent pattern of grouping and several instances of rotation. One such instance is the alternating placement of Leofing and Thorcel in the post-1036 period. A Leofing was active from 1048 to 1053 and again from 1056 to 1059.[60] He was followed by Thorcel in 1059, who carried forward until 1062.[61] In 1066, Leofing was active for Harold II's Pax type.[62] Thorcel was again active afterwards from 1074 to 1077, then again from 1083 to 1086, when he was joined by Leofing.[63] These moneyers were active in alternating coinage issues, with some gaps, possibly due to absences in the coinage record, but only active together for William I's Paxs type (1083–1086).

The rotational aspects of the moneyer placements within Bristol seem a bit clearer than in some other mints. There is alternating placement with Ælfweard (1009–1016, 1036–1040, and 1044–1053) and Æthelwine (1017–1023, 1029–1038, and 1040–1042).[64] A more compact rotation occurs later with Ceorl (1065–1068, 1070–1072, and 1074–1077) and Leofwine (1066–1068, 1072–1080, and 1083–1086).[65] Inter-sequence rotation and continuation is also heavily present within Bristol. Multiple [Ælf-] moneyers seem to rotate in conjunction with the Ælfweard/Æthelwine rotation outlined above as well as the [God-] and [Wulf-] sequences.

47 SM1.Gloucester.l–liii.
48 SM1.Gloucester.xxxvii; SM1.Gloucester.xlii.
49 SM1.Gloucester.xli; SM1.Gloucester.xxxviii.
50 SM1.Bedford.xliv–xlv; SM1.Bedford.xlvii–xlviii.
51 SM1.Bedford.xxiii; SM1.Bedford.l; SM1.Bedford.liv.
52 SM1.Bedford.xlix.
53 SM1.Bedford.xlvi.
54 SM1.Bedford.xxi; SM1.Bedford.xxiv; SM1.Bedford.lv.
55 SM1.Colchester.vi–ix.
56 SM1.Colchester.x–xiv.
57 SM1.Colchester.xv–xviii.
58 SM1.Colchester.xix.
59 SM1.Ipswich.xvii–xviii; SM1.Ipswich.xli-xlii.
60 SM1.Warwick.xv–xvi.
61 SM1.Warwick.xxxv.
62 SM1.Warwick.xvii.
63 SM1.Warwick.xxxvi–xxxvii; SM1.Warwick.xviii.
64 SM1.Bristol.vi–viii; SM1.Bristol.xvi–xviii.
65 SM1.Bristol.xxii–xxiv; SM1.Bristol.xxx–xxxii.

In Derby, there does seem to be a cyclical pattern evident between the sequences [Blac-], [God-], and [Wulf-]. Intermixed with these primary sequence rotations, there is also evidence of the smaller sequences of [From-], [Os-], and [Swert-] taking part in limited rotation. However, because the mint is relatively small and is dominated by the three largest sequences (16 of 36 moneyers belong to these groups), the sequential pattern for these smaller mints does not carry forward to sufficient generations to confirm this pattern.

Chichester has limited moneyer rotation, but there does seem to be some level of alternating between Godwine and Brunman, before they are grouped late in the period. Godwine is active over three periods: 1053–1062, 1066, and 1074–1080.[66] Brunman is in the mint at three closely separated periods: 1066–1068, 1070–1072, and 1074–1086.[67] Outside of this specific example, however, there does not seem to be substantial evidence of a rotational cycle in place at the mint of Chichester.

From Æthelred II to Edward the Confessor's reign in Rochester, there is evidence of rotation between the [Ead-], [God-], and [Wulf-] sequences. Godwine was active from 1009 to 1040, from 1042 to 1048, and from 1053 to 1056.[68] Eadwine also had three periods of activity: 1044–1048, 1053–1056, and 1062–1065.[69] Wulfric was operating in Rochester from 1029 to 1036 and 1046 to 1048.[70]

There were 32 major mints (outside of London/Southwark) operating at some period between 973 and 1086. Each of these mints is recorded through extant coinage as active for the majority of this period and is thus categorised as 'high-volume'. 26 of these mints (79 per cent) had clear grouping patterns, and of these, only one mint, Huntingdon, did not exhibit this pattern in both the pre- and post-1036 periods. The remaining seven major mints had limited evidence of grouping, and within this group, the majority (57 per cent) only had this grouping pattern before 1036.

None of the major mints operated without some indication of this grouping pattern and a sizeable margin (85 per cent) display this pattern across the entire period of the study. It is notable here that there are no instances of this pattern transitioning from a period of no grouping to grouping after 1036. The only possible exception to this is Gloucester, which only has limited evidence of grouping at all and definitely did not have this pattern in place in the early reign of Æthelred II. There are five mints that did have the pattern in place before 1036 but not after. Only one of these, Huntingdon, had clear evidence of the pattern. The remaining four only had limited evidence, which could be explained by gaps in the coinage record or possibly the consolidation of the mint under one dominating name sequence, as described in the Huntingdon section above.

The rotational pattern is a bit more diverse than the grouping pattern but the evidence still supports substantial widespread practice. The pattern is clearly evident in the same number of mints (26), but there are three mints with no evidence of rotation: Hereford, Hertford, and Wilton. Of these, both Hertford and Wilton were among those with limited evidence of grouping. The remaining four mints demonstrate limited rotation patterns, without substantial support from the coinage record beyond a few instances.

Within those mints with either clear or limited rotational placement among the moneyers, the vast majority (77 per cent) had some evidence of this pattern both before and after 1036. Only one mint, Ilchester, demonstrated the pattern before 1036 and not after. Several (Cambridge, Chichester, Huntingdon, Wallingford, and Warwick) only seem to have adopted this pattern of rotation after 1036. Two of the mints, Huntingdon and Worcester, show some rotation, with the latter being limited in its evidence, but only within the confines of a single name sequence, thereby allowing for the possibility of this being a family practice instead of an administrative one.

The major mints consistently exhibited patterns of moneyers beginning and ending operation in groups, often in a rotational cycle with members of other common name sequences. Within the major mints, 100 per cent displayed either very clear grouping patterns or limited evidence of grouping. Of these, nearly 85 per cent illustrated this pattern before and after 1036. Similarly, although not quite as absolute, 91 per cent of these mints had either clear rotational aspects to their moneyer placement or did so to a limited extent. Of those with rotation, 80 per cent operated in this fashion before and after 1036.

Minor Mints Summary

Many of the minor mints, those which have either coinage records that do not extend over the majority of the period 973 to 1086 or which have only a few moneyers operating during the period, still provide opportunities to see the cycle of replacement in action [Table 6.5]. Some, however, because of the scarcity of the extant source material, do not lend themselves directly to this analysis but are still important for comparison purposes as many do illustrate the continuity of the name sequences over the Danish and Norman Conquests. The mints are categorised as low-volume if the overall coinage issue production covers less than 50 per cent of the period 973 to 1086. The chapters above address the data from these mints, outlining specific instances of name sequence progression and possible cycles of replacement.

There were 64 minor mints active at some point in the period 973 to 1086. Less than one-third can be categorised as high-volume. This means that over two-thirds (45

[66] SM1.Chichester.xxv–xxvii.
[67] SM1.Chichester.xiv–xvi.
[68] SM1.Rochester.xii–xiv.
[69] SM1.Rochester.ix–xi.
[70] SM1.Rochester.xxxi–xxxii.

Table 6.5. Grouping and Rotation Patterns in the Minor Mints

Mint	Volume	Grouping	Pre-1036	Post-1036	Multiple Sequences	Rotation	Pre-1036	Post-1036	Multiple Sequences
Rochester	High	S	X	X	X	X	X	X	X
Bath	High	X	X	X	X	X	X	X	X
Cricklade	High	X	X	X	X	X	X	X	X
Hastings	High	X	X	X	X	S	X	X	X
Nottingham	High	X	–	X	X	X	–	X	X
Salisbury	High	X	X	X	X	X	X	X	X
Wareham	High	X	X	X	X	X	X	X	X
Maldon	High	X	X	X	X	X	X	X	X
Malmesbury	High	–	–	–	–	X	–	X	–
Totnes	Low	X	X	–	X	X	X	–	X
Barnstaple	High	X	X	X	X	X	X	X	X
Dorchester	High	–	–	–	–	X	–	X	X
Romney	High	S	X	–	X	S	X	–	X
Stafford	High	S	X	–	X	S	X	X	–
Tamworth	High	X	X	X	X	S	–	X	X
Lympne	Low	X	X	–	X	X	X	–	X
Steyning	Low	–	–	–	–	–	–	–	–
Taunton	High	S	X	X	X	X	X	X	X
Bridport	High	–	–	–	–	–	–	–	–
Lydford	High	–	–	–	–	–	–	–	–
Southampton	Low	X	X	–	X	–	–	–	–
Guildford	High	S	X	–	X	S	X	X	X
Buckingham	High	S	X	–	X	–	–	–	–
Winchcombe	High	S	X	–	X	–	–	–	–
Axbridge	Low	S	X	X	X	–	–	–	–
Langport	Low	S	X	–	X	X	X	X	X
Sudbury	Low	S	X	–	X	–	–	–	–
Aylesbury	Low	X	X	–	X	–	–	–	–
Sandwich	Low	–	–	–	–	S	–	X	X
Watchet	Low	–	–	–	–	–	–	–	–
Gothaburh	Low	–	–	–	–	–	–	–	–
Warminster	Low	–	–	–	–	–	–	–	–
Cadbury	Low	–	–	–	–	–	–	–	–
Crewkerne	Low	–	–	–	–	–	–	–	–
Bedwin	Low	–	–	–	–	–	–	–	–
Bruton	Low	–	–	–	–	–	–	–	–
Cissbury	Low	–	–	–	–	–	–	–	–
Bury St Eds	Low	–	–	–	–	–	–	–	–
Launceston	Low	–	–	–	–	–	–	–	–
Milbourne Pt	Low	–	–	–	–	–	–	–	–
Newport Pgnl	Low	–	–	–	–	–	–	–	–
Torksey	Low	–	–	–	–	–	–	–	–
Berkeley	Low	–	–	–	–	–	–	–	–
Dernt	Low	–	–	–	–	–	–	–	–
Droitwich	Low	–	–	–	–	–	–	–	–
Hythe	Low	–	–	–	–	–	–	–	–

Table 6.5 ***continued***

Mint	Volume	Grouping	Pre-1036	Post-1036	Multiple Sequences	Rotation	Pre-1036	Post-1036	Multiple Sequences
Marlborough	Low	–	–	–	–	–	–	–	–
Niwan	Low	–	–	–	–	–	–	–	–
Caistor	Low	–	–	–	–	–	–	–	–
Cardiff	Low	–	–	–	–	–	–	–	–
Cuer	Low	–	–	–	–	–	–	–	–
Durham	Low	–	–	–	–	–	–	–	–
Frome	Low	–	–	–	–	–	–	–	–
Horncastle	Low	–	–	–	–	–	–	–	–
Horndon	Low	–	–	–	–	–	–	–	–
Newark	Low	–	–	–	–	–	–	–	–
Pershore	Low	–	–	–	–	–	–	–	–
Peterborough	Low	–	–	–	–	–	–	–	–
Petherton	Low	–	–	–	–	–	–	–	–
Pevensey	Low	–	–	–	–	–	–	–	–
Rhuddlan	Low	–	–	–	–	–	–	–	–
St Davids	Low	–	–	–	–	–	–	–	–
Stes	Low	–	–	–	–	–	–	–	–
Twynham	Low	–	–	–	–	–	–	–	–

of 64) of the mints in this category do not have extant coins for over 50 per cent of the coinage issues produced from this period. Of this majority, only four had a clear grouping pattern: Aylesbury, Lympne, Southampton, and Totnes. A further three demonstrate limited evidence of grouping: Axbridge, Langport, and Sudbury. In these seven instances, all but one, Axbridge, was exclusive to the pre-1036 period. The apparent presence of a rotation between moneyers, either across name sequences or within family continuities, is even more sparse in these low-volume mints, with only three, Langport, Lympne, and Totnes, showing this pattern and one additional mint, Sandwich, illustrating rotation in a limited capacity. There is more disparity among these four mints regarding temporal placement of the rotations. Lympne and Totnes both exhibit the rotational pattern before 1036, Sandwich only after 1036, and Langport has evidence of rotation from both before and after 1036.

In contrast to the low-volume mints, as expected based on the evidence presented in previous chapters, the high-volume minor mints only contain four instances of no grouping patterns: Bridport, Dorchester, Lydford, and Malmesbury. There are nine mints that show clear patterns of grouping: Barnstaple, Bath, Cricklade, Hastings, Maldon, Nottingham, Tamworth, Salisbury, and Wareham. And, there are six with only limited evidence of a grouping pattern: Buckingham, Guildford, Romney, Stafford, Taunton, and Winchcombe. Of the nine mints with a clear pattern, all but one, Nottingham, demonstrate this pattern both before and after 1036. Those with limited evidence are almost exclusively so before 1036, with the exception of Taunton.

Similarly, there are only four instances of these mints not conveying evidence of a rotational pattern: Bridport, Buckingham, Lydford, and Winchcombe. Of the 15 other high-volume minor mints, 10 have clear patterns of rotation: Barnstaple, Bath, Cricklade, Dorchester, Maldon, Malmesbury, Nottingham, Salisbury, Taunton, and Wareham. The remaining five, Guildford, Hastings, Romney, Stafford, and Tamworth, have limited examples of rotation. And again, the majority (10 of 15) demonstrate this rotational pattern before and after 1036.

Therefore, the minor mints with sufficient extant source material to complete a picture of production encapsulating over half of the period between 973 and 1086 seem to support the idea of widespread grouping and a process of internal rotation within the office of moneyer. Those mints with only one or two recorded moneyers, who were likely itinerant operators from other mints, cannot provide sufficient support for the argument but, likewise, cannot, because of the dearth of information, take away from the hypothesis, even if they skew the overall percentages of the low-volume minor mints collectively.

In reviewing the data from the high-volume minor mints a clearer picture of the grouping and rotational patterns in operation within the late Anglo-Saxon mints is produced. Within these mints, the grouping pattern exists, in full or with limited examples, 78.9 per cent of the time. Of these 15 mints, 60 per cent have evidence of the pattern both before and after 1036, illustrating a continuity in the process over the entire spectrum of this study. The same level of consistency (nearly 80 per cent) exists when reviewing the rotation of moneyers within the minor mints, with an even higher instance of regularity for the pre- to post-1036 eras (66.7 per cent).

In addressing specific instances of grouping and rotation within the minor mints several examples are available. Bath, for instance, is a mint that illustrates the cycle of replacement within the smaller coin production operations. The average activity of each of the moneyers in Bath seems somewhat out of place when compared with the overall average, however, as there are several moneyers whose names are present in the coinage record for extended periods of time. Of course, each of these moneyers could be separate individuals with the same name consisting of overlapping periods of activity, but by and large, this was not a normal practice. As shown in multiple examples above, those of the same name sequences would typically rotate in and out of office over time, making regular breaks in the coinage record apparent. Having five moneyers that operated for periods greater than 25 years is highly irregular in a mint this size.

The operational years of the moneyers at Cricklade depict the pattern of grouping and periodic replacement that is prevalent in most of the major mints and many of the minor mints with sufficient coinage records. Ægelwine begins operation in 1023 and is active until 1029, when he, along with Godwine, is replaced by two new moneyers: Leofing (1029–1036) and Wulfheah (1029–1036).[71] Again, after 1036, there is a disruption in the pattern of groupings and a marked decline in the average period of activity for each moneyer, but there are several cyclical moneyer placements. Ægelwine appears in the record two more times, in 1050–1059 and 1062–1065.[72] In an alternating pattern with these placements is a Leofred, who was active from 1053 to 1062, and again in a disjointed period of activity covering 1065–1066, 1068–1070, and 1072–1077.[73] Also intermixed with the Ægelwine moneyers is an Ægelwi, who was active 1046–1048 and 1056–1059.[74] This could be the same moneyer with a variant spelling but could also be an Ægelwig or just an individual with a different spelling of the name itself. As it is concurrent with Ægelwine and is distinct on the coin epigraphy, this moneyer has been treated separately. These apparent cyclical placements within the office of moneyer, between Ægelwine and Leofred in particular, fit with the pattern observed in the larger mints and point to a more concrete system of governance and self-regulation within the mint at Cricklade.

The rotation of moneyers is also evident in Nottingham. There are also a couple of places in the coinage record where moneyers seem to swap places, notably between Leofsige and Halfdene as well as Forni and Manna. From 1040 to 1044, Leofsige was a moneyer of Nottingham.[75] Halfdene began in the second coinage of this period, the Pacx type (1042–1044).[76] Then, Leofsige begins again in 1046 and is active until 1050, followed in the same way again by Halfdene beginning in the second coinage in 1048 and continuing to 1053.[77]

The exchange between Forni and Manna is more widespread and convoluted in that there are several apparent breaks in the coinage record for both moneyers. In addition, Man, the possible variant spelling of Manna, is also documented separately within the coinage epigraphy. The first documentation of Forni is from 1053 to 1065, again in 1066, and for the period 1068 to 1074.[78] In parallel to this, Manna is recorded as active in 1066, and again in the periods 1070–1074 and 1083–1086.[79] A moneyer named Man was also active from 1070 to 1072 and, like Manna, from 1083 to 1086.[80] This may be the same individual, but since the epigraphy on the coinages are distinct, they are treated as separate individuals for this study.

There are several cases of generational placements within different name sequences at the mint at Salisbury. The [Sæ-] sequence is present to the end of Edward the Confessor's reign.[81] A Godric was active in the periods 1044–1046, 1056–1062, 1074–1077, and 1080–1083, alternating with Godwine and moneyers of the [Ælf-] and [Sæ-] sequences.[82] This alternation between the various name sequences supports the idea of this being a more systemic organisational structure than merely internal family dynamics.

Overall, the grouping patterns and rotational aspects of the mint at Salisbury support the idea of a widespread organisation within the mint that spread beyond familial boundaries and required a system of overarching authority mandating who would be hammered into the coins at a given point in time.

Wareham illustrates grouping in the first period of minting with no rotational aspects outside of two long-separated periods of activity between the [Wulf-] and [Æthel-] sequences, which indicate that this process was likely not in place during the period prior to 1036 for this mint. However, in the second period of activity (from 1038 onwards) there does seem to be a regular rotation between three separate name sequences throughout this five-decade span. A similar situation exists in Maldon, with the alternating placement of moneyers from the [Ælf-], [God-], and [Leof-] name sequences throughout its minting history. This possibly supports the prospect of there being a cycle of rotation and coordination between family groups over long periods of time.

[71] SM1.Cricklade.iii; SM1.Cricklade.xx; SM1.Cricklade.xxvi.
[72] SM1.Cricklade.iv–v.
[73] SM1.Cricklade.xxi–xxiv.
[74] SM1.Cricklade.i–ii.
[75] SM1.Nottingham.xiii.
[76] SM1.Nottingham.xi.
[77] SM1.Nottingham.xiv; SM1.Nottingham.xii.
[78] SM1.Nottingham.vii–ix.
[79] SM1.Nottingham.xviii–xx.
[80] SM1.Nottingham.xvi–xvii.
[81] SM1.Salisbury.xx.
[82] SM1.Salisbury.vii–x.

This is also true in Malmesbury, where there is an alternation over several coinages between Beorhtwig and Beorhtwine. After Beorhtwig disappears from the record in 1062, a Beorhtwine begins and operates until Edward the Confessor's last coinage, the Pyramids type (1065–1066).[83] Then, Beorhtwig is again active for Harold II's Pax type (1066).[84] This is immediately followed by Beorhtwine being once again active in three of William I's coinages for the periods 1068–1070 and 1072–1077.[85] The rotation between the two [Beorht-] moneyers fits with the cyclical pattern demonstrated at many of the large mints and several of the smaller ones. Malmesbury provides a good illustration of the pattern on a small scale in the post-1036 era, where tenures were shorter overall, yet patterns still existed.

In Dorchester, beginning in 1036 with the placement of Hwætman (1036–1042), and following with the placement of Godwine (1038–1042) and Blacman (1042–1044), there is a period where three moneyers cycle from one to the other in succession.[86] Hwætman appears again from 1050 to 1053.[87] Blacman returns to the coinage record in a broken series: 1053–1056, 1059–1065, and 1066 (Harold II's Pax type).[88] Both Hwætman and Blacman also appear in mint records of close geographic proximity, the former in Bridport and the latter in Wareham.[89] A Godwin is in the coinage record for 1074–1077 and could be the same previously listed Godwine, just in a post-Norman Conquest variant, or another [God-] moneyer from the same sequence or family.[90]

Even in instances where the pattern is less clear, there are still indications of organised groupings and possibly rotation in coinage production. For example, the gaps in each of the moneyers' activity in Stafford may indicate simply absences in the coinage record. But, since they are seemingly uniform (each moneyer operating for one coinage, then absent, then active again), it could also point to cyclical activity. Paired with the information from the other mints, an argument for this being the case more so than not is evident, especially in light of the commonality of the pattern elsewhere. And in Taunton, where the process seems to have existed and then disappeared in favour of two name sequences. There are three name sequences in operation from 997 to 1050 with placement-absence-placement activity that may point to a rotational cycle: [Boiga-], [Ead-], and [Leof-]. These three sequences are seemingly dominant throughout this period, with three other moneyers operating outside of these groups: Beorhtstan (1017–1023), Ælfsige (1017–1023), and Gillecrist (1042–1044).[91]

After the last Boiga in 1050, there is a shift in the operational aspect of the mint. From 1053 to 1074 the only moneyer recorded in the coins of Taunton was Beorhtric, who was active over three separate periods during this time.[92] After Beorhtric, an Ælfwine was active for two periods coving 1074 to 1086.[93] This break from the old cycle is not necessarily atypical for a small mint. But, the two moneyers that took over immediately following this break belong to sequences that were contemporaneously active in the midst of the previous cycles.

Could this potentially point to a collective effort by Beorhtstan and Ælfsige to jointly secure the minting rights in Taunton for their dynasties? Obviously, this is just conjecture and is not supported by any written documentation, but the pattern that is so widespread elsewhere and seems to take place here could support such a conclusion. Regardless, Taunton, as a minor mint, gives positive support for the idea of a rotational cycle at least being partially active during this period.

The first three moneyers in Langport are Godwine (1017–1023), Ælfwi (1017–1023), and Æthelwine (1017–1038).[94] As occurs often in the larger mints, two of these moneyers stop together while the third continues. A Goda is then recorded from 1029 to 1036, followed by an Ælfweard for Harold I's Jewel Cross type (1036–1038).[95] Another Æthelwine is then in the coinage record from 1050 to 1053.[96] Taken alone, this does not support the cycle of replacement or grouping pattern that is so prevalent in the larger mints, but, when paired with those patterns elsewhere, this does seem to indicate an overall structure of grouping moneyers and then rotating them within their family sequences, in conjunction with other sequences. Almost half of the minor mints have only five or less periods of moneyer activity. This makes analysis of these mints difficult in that there is generally not enough extant source material to make a determination as to whether these mints had grouping or rotation, as is illustrated in Table 2.2.b below. However, most of these very low-volume mints were geographically close to major mints and could have been overflow, or satellite, mints operated for short periods by moneyers from those locations. Regardless of this, the absence of records for these mints necessitates that they can not overly affect the ultimate results of this study, namely that there was systemic and widespread grouping and rotation among the major mints and most of the high-volume minor mints.

[83] SM1.Malmesbury.viii.
[84] SM1.Malmesbury.vi.
[85] SM1.Malmesbury.ix–x.
[86] SM1.Dorchester.x; SM1.Dorchester.ix; SM1.Dorchester.iv.
[87] SM1.Dorchester.xi.
[88] SM1.Dorchester.v–vii.
[89] L. Keen, 1984, 'The Towns of Dorset', in J. Haslam, ed., *Anglo-Saxon Towns in Southern England*, Chichester, 203–47 at 241.
[90] SM1.Dorchester.viii.
[91] SM1.Taunton.vii; SM1.Taunton.i; SM1.Taunton.xiii.
[92] SM1.Taunton.iv–vi.
[93] SM1.Taunton.ii–iii.
[94] SM1.Langport.ix; SM1.Langport.i; SM1.Langport.iii.
[95] SM1.Langport.viii; SM1.Langport.ii.
[96] SM1.Langport.iii.

7

Conclusions, Limitations, and Future Implications

Introduction

This project began as an attempt to illustrate continuity in late Anglo-Saxon England through the creation of a prosopography of the moneyers that were active from Edgar's coinage reform of *c*. 973 and the Domesday survey of 1086. The research revealed problems with this somewhat simplistic initial aim, primarily the limitation of the source material in the realisation of a full prosopography of the moneyers. Considering that coins have a finite amount of information on them and that there is a lack of written sources about the moneyers, there are limitations in the ability to identify individuals working at multiple minting locations. So, the project changed. Instead of seeking to establish that continuity existed, this research builds on those notions of continuity by looking at a specific group of people and determining whether or not that group's continuity, and the internal structures of their practice, supports the idea of a complex Anglo-Saxon 'state' in the tenth and eleventh centuries. Therefore, instead of creating a prosopography of the moneyers, a preparatory to a prosopography was created, undertaking all of the steps that are possible within the constraints of the source material.

The result of this is a study that further defines an important group from medieval England, the moneyers, and demonstrates how that group operated in the late Anglo-Saxon kingdom and how its operation supports both the concept of a complicated government and the idea of a 'state' in England during the tenth and eleventh centuries. This is important because the discovery of complicated administrative structures within late Anglo-Saxon England urban societies, seemingly independent of direct continental influence, indicates that the English systems were perhaps more complex than their contemporaries elsewhere in Europe. Also, in looking at how one social group interacted with itself within the confines of a controlled working environment provides a broader picture of how Anglo-Saxon society as a whole might have operated. If the moneyers were sufficiently capable of organising the internal structure of the mints on a national scale, one that conformed to royal demands for uniformity in design and regionally specific purity and weight, it is possible that other segments of society did likewise. In having a point of reference for one such segment, the idea of a complicated Anglo-Saxon society, which was sufficiently advanced to support the concept of a complex government, is realised more fully.

The creation of the *Moneyers of England Database, 973–1086* provides this single point of reference for the moneyers. It includes nearly all of the extant numismatic evidence known for this period. Consisting of information collected from 28,576 individual coins that were minted in 99 geographic locations, the database has uses beyond those illustrated within the present text and can be used by other historians, numismatists, and linguists. The database can be used to look into economic and social history, minting activity, and onomastic trends, just to name a few options. For the present study, the database has been used to provide support for an interesting system of mint administration that compliments the idea of a complex government during the late Anglo-Saxon period.

Findings

This book began by addressing the status of the moneyer. From Ruding's early work on Domesday, expanded upon by Hawkins and Drummond Robertson, outlining the potential privileges of the moneyers, to more definitive assertions from Stewart and Roffe that the moneyers were of the thegn or burgess class, the question of the moneyers' status has been determined by extrapolation from limited extant material. Ruding outlined the points in Domesday that pointed to the special status of the moneyer group in 1840.[1] Edward Hawkins compiled a detailed list of the moneyers and descriptions of the different coinages produced in England in 1841, utilising Ruding's findings as a starting point in his own interpretation of the coinages.[2] Drummond Robertson, in 1885, referred to Ruding's descriptions as too vague and sought to solidify the standing of later moneyers through the use of the Pipe Rolls, noting that several moneyers were also Bailiffs in Gloucester in the thirteenth century.[3] Drummond Robertson also indicated that the reforms of Henry II in 1180 likely introduced a 'superior rank' of moneyer than would have been available before Domesday.[4] This work rejects that claim because the organisation evident in the mints, as well as the apparent regularity in family control of the minting practice, indicates that there was complex administration in place prior to the Norman Conquest. The minting structures that were in place nearly a century before 1066 were still in place over a century later when Henry II undertook his reforms.

Recent scholarship already acknowledges that Anglo-Saxon minting practices continued virtually unchanged through the Norman Conquest and the reigns of the first Norman kings. In the modern era, Ruding's list of moneyer characteristics has seen continued support

[1] Ruding, 1840, 49.
[2] Hawkins, 1841.
[3] Drummond Robertson, 1885, 210.
[4] Drummond Robertson, 1885, 212.

generally. The idea of the moneyers as being part of a special, thegnly class, for example, has been espoused by several historians. Loyn noted in 1981 that the names found in coin epigraphy parallel name patterns associated with thegns.[5] Nightingale produced a lineage of a twelfth century London moneyer, Deorman, highlighting the high social status he and his descendants held within the city.[6] Scholarship has continued to acknowledge the special status of the moneyers with some studies seeking to correlate the names on the coins with the written records of the time. Stewart set out to connect a moneyer to a recorded thegn from a corresponding charter.[7] In Stewart's 1988 work, for the late Anglo-Saxon era he focused upon the moneyer Hunewine, a moneyer of Totnes, who had a long career and at some point was appointed a thegn, or *minister*, by Æthelred II.[8] Roffe, in 2007, noted that the classifications given within Domesday, those outlined nearly two centuries before by Ruding, indicated that the moneyers held thegnly status.[9] Biddle also pointed out that the Norman moneyers held burgess status and landholder rights and that this status could have predated the Conquest.[10] In 2012, Allen compiled a list of those moneyers that could be identified as aldermen or burgesses in the twelfth century, utilising Domesday, the Pipe Rolls, and the works of other scholars.[11] Research on the moneyers continue to describe them in generally the same way: these men were important, they had some rights and privileges, they may have been thegns or royal agents of some sort, they operated alone, or at least individually controlled a mint-place, they may have operated within the confines of a family structure, and we know they existed because we find their names on the coinages that they produced. That is how they have been described to a greater or lesser degree in most work on the coinage for nearly two centuries.[12] Through the accumulation of epigraphic evidence, this research shows that Stewart and Roffe were likely correct in that the moneyers were of thegnly class and often named as *ministri* on charters. Stewart's work on Hunewine within the charters point to a very high correlation between moneyers and *ministrii*. Future work on this model using the *MED* should produce further confirmation of this.

From what is known generally about the moneyers, theories can be, and have been, made about family dynamics within the craft. These theories, most prominent in the works of Nightingale and Tsurushima, are based on hypothetical models associated with the naming patterns of late Anglo-Saxon England and the prevalence of repeating protothemes on the surviving coinage. The idea of fathers or grandfathers passing their craft to their descendants is not new but one that has only been addressed in a limited capacity at a small minority of locales. No previous study of the putative familial relationships of the moneyers has ever been conducted on the scale of that contained herein. The prevailing conclusion from the analysis for every mint is that the vast majority of the moneyers taking part in the activity of the mints and sharing the same prototheme were part of a single family. It would appear that more often than not, a moneyer was part of a family of moneyers.

The moneyers also worked within a complicated minting system that was centrally controlled but regionally operated. But, even with this regional differentiation in the form of die production and distribution, there was uniformity in action for all mints from Edgar's reform to Domesday. Analysis of the internal structure of the mints indicates that the minting structure in late Anglo-Saxon England was advanced and complex. Recurrent patterns in the organisation and rotation of moneyers indicates that the operation of the mints was uniform for the entire country throughout the period from Edgar's Coinage Reform to Domesday. Campbell points to how the minting system was utilised as a means of geld collection and public works as support for an Anglo-Saxon state.[13] He notes that the ability to maintain a widespread and uniform coinage is 'comparably [as] important' as a strong monarch's ability to maintain peace.[14] Campbell points to the coinage and minting system as evidence for the sophistication of the state and posits that economic success goes hand in hand with the ability to successfully maintain roads and bridges, which must have been organised through the public execution of power.[15] Campbell's argument was that these complex administrative structures first began to appear as early as Alfred the Great, but Molyneaux's more recent examination concludes that Edgar and Æthelred II installed administrative structures from the late tenth century. It is Molyneaux's conclusion which stands up to scrutiny when compared with the mint structure analysis undertaken in chapters five and six.[16] As the operating groupings and rotational placements did not take place until after Edgar's Reform and into the early coinages of Æthelred II, it appears that the necessity for complexity in the administration of the mints was not needed before the early 970s. As it appears the changes were made out of some form of necessity, it suggests that there was outside imposition, likely from royal decree, on the mints that prompted these shifts in organisation. Since the organisation that resulted is complex and apparently operated uniformly on a nearly national scale, the imposition that they sought to address must also have been uniform and wide ranging, implying that there was a shift in the manner in which the mints were regulated and governed in the late tenth century. The mints and the

[5] Loyn, 1991, 125.
[6] Nightingale, 1982.
[7] Stewart, 1988.
[8] Stewart, 1988, 167.
[9] Roffe, 2007, 121–22; Roffe, 2012, 217–8.
[10] Biddle, 1976, 402, 421, 443–4.
[11] Allen, 2012a, 5–8.
[12] Naismith, 2017a, 240–3. Naismith outlines the moneyers as being of a special class, likely not in the same circles as other high-ranking officials. He utilises Biddle's survey of the Winton Domesday, Nightingale's account of Deorman of London, and the laws of the late Anglo-Saxon kings to outline the general status of the moneyers.

[13] Campbell, 1995, 52.
[14] Campbell, 1995, 53–4.
[15] Campbell, 1995, 54; idem, 2000, 7–8, 32–3, 160, and 181.
[16] Campbell, 1995, 44; Molyneaux, 2015, 1–9.

organisation of the moneyers were indicators of advanced administrative complexity in England supporting the idea of a late Anglo-Saxon 'state'.

The mints were organised on a national level with a complex internal structure. The book addresses this structure and the gap in knowledge about the moneyers. These men acted as agents of the king and controlled the periodic change of the coinage. They were not within the working classes of peasants, farmers, fishermen, or traditional trade merchants. From the evidence available, they also did not seem to belong to the upper aristocracy. And yet, what scant documentation is available outlines these men as prominent officials within the town, being trustworthy, wealthy, and powerful, and probably of the thegnly or burgess class. Evidence from Domesday, charters, die-links, and the coins that the moneyers produced point to a group of individuals that held high social status but operated largely outside of the circles of ecclesiastic officials, royal agents, and the large land holding aristocracy, making their classification difficult, even if they shared some common privileges attributed to those other important groups.

Prior to the present work, if one wished to study the moneyers directly from multiple locations or over an extended period of time, then multiple coin cabinets, museum collections, catalogues, and online databases needed to be studied in order to begin the formation of even a basic picture of these men. The *Moneyers of England Database* represents a significant advance on this state of affairs, by consolidating epigraphic information collected from all accessible extant coinage for the period from Edgar's reform to the Domesday survey. The database itself, which is included as a downloadable excel file, documents 3,646 named moneyers, derived from 28,576 individual coins produced at 99 geographic locations. This database therefore affords a single point of reference for these individuals, providing a means of studying a group of urban inhabitants from a historical, onomastic, or numismatic perspective, that has not been available previously for England or for any early medieval region.

This work outlines two new theories regarding the activity of the moneyers and the potential internal structures of the mints they operated. The first is that the moneyers who worked in the largest mints, and among many of the smaller mints as well, repeatedly started and ended their work as a unit. For reasons explained in chapter five, this seems to have occurred not only within individual families of moneyers, but also across multiple families, thereby implying coordination between kin-groups. The second theory, outlined in chapter six, is that those groups of moneyers would rotate activity within the mints. A group of moneyers would begin operation, produce coins for one or two coinages, then stop and be replaced by another group, which would then itself produce one or two coinages before stopping and being replaced by that first group, or a group from the same families. This rotation seemingly occurred in most of the largest mints and consisted, like the groupings in general, of coordination between multiple families.

This rotation cycle remained even when the average period of coinage renewal decreased after 1036. The implication here is that the rotation was dependent upon the coinage issuance and not the interval of time associated with that production. The conclusion reached as to the cause is that this was a response to potential royal decree that sought to impose a sort of term limit on any specific moneyer to forestall their individual accumulation of wealth or authority. The moneyers, in response to this imposition, which likely occurred in conjunction with Edgar's coinage reform or shortly thereafter, created a system by which they could retain control of the minting apparatus by rotating with other members of their family and did so in conjunction with other families of moneyers. This perhaps indicates that these men, who were likely members of the thegnly or burgess class, some of whom can be identified in charters as *ministri*, as detailed in chapter two, were acting not only as agents of the king but in a protectionist fashion as well, seeking to solidify their hold on the mints.

These theories provide additional contributions to the understanding of this group and its place in society. Even in periods where the aristocracy was removed or replaced, these men, with a specialist skillset, were able to maintain hereditary control of the office that remained unhindered by the political events of the day. The scale of this study also supports the conclusions reached in other studies of specific mints on the familial connection of the moneyers. The theories of moneyers operating in set groups and then rotating that placement grants a picture of complex internal structure that was widespread and regular throughout the late Anglo-Saxon period. They point to a nearly autonomous group operating its craft in a corporate format before craft guilds outlining specific working guidelines were evident in England. These theories also potentially point to an organised labour movement in response to outside intervention. Possible royal decree seeking to limit the authority of these families was met with organised resistance in the form of the rotation cycle. While the grouping and rotation patterns are prevalent throughout the mints and are significantly placed within each of the primary name sequences, the overarching dynamics of the practice can only truly be appreciated when viewed in conjunction with multiple name sequences operating in concert. The fact that patterns such as this occurred simultaneously so often in so many locations supports the idea that this was definitively organised and implemented on a national scale.

Limitations of the Research

As with many studies that rely predominantly upon material evidence, there are some limitations in regard to the conclusions reached. The most obvious limitation is the lack of written source material directly substantiating the claims made herein regarding the conclusions reached. There are no extant laws or charters that outline regulations on the moneyers' periods of activity during the latter stages of Edgar's reign or the early period of Æthelred II. But an absence of written evidence is a familiar problem in numismatic scholarship. There is after all no single textual source which outlines the monetary reforms that took place in the early 970s; and yet we know that Edgar mandated that all the coins would be minted in a uniform fashion with the mint and moneyer name on the reverse because they exist as such. We do not know what else may have been involved in this reformation at a more administrative level. It therefore seems possible that the organisation of the mints was also affected by these reforms. Mints seem to have been specifically structured in such a way as to protect the groups of families of moneyers over prolonged periods of time. Whether that protection was in response to royal imposition will likely never be absolutely known.

That said, since the organisation does seem to occur in parallel with the reform of the coinage itself, it appears that they must be linked in some fashion. Taking the steps to implement such a complicated system of placement, removal, and replacement across multiple groups must have been prompted by necessity. This text supports the idea of that necessity being in the form of royal regulation and the imposition of that authority to potentially limit the accumulation of influence and wealth among a non-noble class. The crown, not necessarily being able to wholly forestall the monopoly that the moneyers held on the production of the coinage, sought to limit their hold on the system by imposing what were effectively term limits on the men in charge of the mints. Those men, seeing a threat to their prosperity, organised themselves dynastically and in conjunction with other familial groups of likeminded peoples to counter this royal action. This organisation would likely have prevented non-family members from maintaining a strong presence in the craft and may explain why there are sporadic unaffiliated names acting over short periods of time across England. This was collective workforce action on a national scale. The moneyers, who were themselves a tool of royal authority with limited agency, gained semi-autonomous power through internal organisation.

A further limitation is potential absences within the coinage record. The instances where the patterns do not fit or are absent altogether could be due to either a shift that was specific to the mint in question or because the coinage for that particular area is not available. This creates some level of uncertainty with regards to the conclusions. In those rare instances, it is concluded that points in which there is an inexplicable break in the pattern or where there is not enough evidence to support it directly is due to an absence of material instead of an absence of practice. For example, in Canterbury there were 20 distinct periods of activity for moneyers with the [Wulf-] prototheme and 11 with the [Leof-] prototheme.[17] The [Wulf-] sequence was active in the mint from 985 to 1086 and the [Leof-] sequence was active from 979 to 1065. But for each of these there is no moneyer recorded for Edward the Confessor's Pacx type (1042–1044) even though it was produced at the mint. The Pacx type was produced by Ælfred, Cetel, Gildewine, and Manna so it seems likely that a moneyer from two of the largest groups active at the mint during this time would also have produced this coinage.[18] This break in the pattern seems to indicate a lack of surviving source material rather than a distinct differentiation in the practice.

Future Implications

Further scholarship on this model is possible. Most of the mints that are briefly analysed within this study could be extrapolated upon and addressed in more detail, perhaps in studies of their own. The material held within the *Moneyers of England Database, 973–1086* can be expanded upon to include records earlier or later to form a more complete picture of how this phenomenon came into existence within England and progressed to the eventual consolidation of minting in London. The methodology utilised for the creation of the database can be ported to other geographic locations and time periods. Further research on the onomastic structures of the names within the database, or research into specific families, can be conducted utilising the database material. The coinage record documented in the downloadable supplemental materials accompanying the book could be used to study production patterns within the mints greatly benefiting numismatists. Analysing periods of activity for the mints, the number of moneyers active, and the survival rates of the coinage produced would undoubtedly reveal interesting findings.

The material source-base of this study can be replicated in other regions or temporal periods to see if parallel developments took place elsewhere. There are many research questions that can be surmised from the conclusions contained here. Potential future research can address any number of comparative questions. For example, can analysis of the material culture of tenth- and eleventh-century Europe demonstrate continuity and stability within the socio-economic frameworks of populations from different political arenas? Can the early example of labour organisation in England be used as a model of comparison with the underlying economic development of other medieval kingdoms? Was the system of stability within the unique confines of the minting system in England replicated on the Continent? Do the early economic developments in late Anglo-Saxon England lead the way for similar institutions in Capetian France or the Holy Roman Empire during the same period? Might these patterns of organisation illustrate a wider phenomenon that redefines the development of urban labour in western Europe, precipitating the eventual creation of the market economy and influencing the

[17] See Supplemental Materials 4: Name Sequences of the Canterbury Mint.

[18] SM1.Canterbury.vii.15; SM1.Canterbury.xxiv.7; SM1.Canterbury.xxxii.19–21; SM1.Canterbury.lvi.1.

nation-state? These questions represent just a sampling of the potential expansions stemming from the conclusions.

Final Thoughts

Considering the limitations associated with the source material and the lack of written documentation for the moneyers in general, the production of a working database addressing all the known moneyers and mint locations for the period 973 to 1086 represents a substantial body of work and contribution to the knowledge of the late Anglo-Saxon period. The discovery of patterns associated with the minters' apparent periods of activity and the rotational aspect of those patterns indicates a sophisticated level of labour organisation in England. The moneyers organised themselves into groups, both along familial lines and in conjunction with other family groups, that would operate for a set period of time, then withdraw in favour of another member of their kin-group, before returning to activity at a later date. This notable shift in the way the moneyers maintained control of their mints was perhaps in response to the monetary reform of Edgar in the early 970s or further reorganisation in the early reign of Æthelred II. It would appear that royal decree sought to limit the authority, and the accompanying accumulation of wealth, of these men and limited the amount of consecutive coinage issues under which they could operate. This new method of internal organisation allowed for observation of the crown's regulation while keeping control of the mints within the hands of the family, thus maintaining the wealth and status to which many of these families had grown accustomed. The overriding conclusion is that the late tenth century witnessed the collective and widespread organisation of mint workers, potentially in order to maintain a certain level of autonomy and control over their craft. After all, the bearer of the name on the coin was held responsible if the coinage proved light, of insufficient purity, or was otherwise minted outside of the king's directives. It stands to reason that the benefits that accompany this responsibility would be worth protecting.

Bibliography

Primary Sources

Unpublished Material

The British Museum, Department of Coins and Medals

Anglo-Saxon Series

Edgar, Trays 1–3

Edward (the Martyr), Trays 1–4

Æthelred II, Trays 1–57

Cnut, Trays 1–35

Harold I, Trays 1–13

Harthacnut, Trays 1–4

Edward (the Confessor), Trays 1–84

Harold II, Trays 1–8

Norman Series

William I, Trays 1–31

Printed Material

Acta Sanctorum

I. Carnadet, ed., 1866, *Acta Sanctorum quotquot toto orbe coluntur, vel a catholicis scriptoribus celebrantur ex latinis et grœcis, aliarumque gentium antiquis monumentis, Maii tomus sextus quo continentur dies XXV, XXVI, XXVII et XXVIII*, Paris and Rome.

The Anglo-Saxon Chronicle

D. Whitelock, with D. C. Douglas and S. I. Tucker, eds., 1961, *The Anglo-Saxon Chronicle*, London.

Anglo-Saxon Charters

P. H. Sawyer, ed., 1968, *Anglo-Saxon Charters: an Annotated List and Bibliography*, London.

Chartularium Ecclesiae Wigorniensis

T. Hearne, ed., 1723, *Hemingi Chartularium Ecclesiae Wigorniensis*, Volume 1, Oxford.

Codex Diplomaticus Aevi Saxonici

J. M. Kemble, ed., 1839–48, *Codex Diplomaticus Aevi Saxonici*, London.

De Miraculis Sancti Ædmundi, by Abbot Samson

T. Arnold, ed., 2012, *Memorials of St. Edmund's Abbey*, Volume 1, London, 107–208.

Domesday Book

H. Ellis, ed., 1816, *Libri censualis vocati Domesday Book, additamenta ex codic antiquiss: Exon Domesday, Inquisitio Eliensis, Liber Winton, Boldon Book*, London.

M. Biddle, ed., 1976, *Winchester in the Early Middle Ages, an edition and discussion of the Winton Domesday*, Oxford.

A. Williams and R. W. H. Erskine, eds., 1987, *Great Domesday Book, Library Edition: Facsimile, translations, maps, indices*, London.

A. Williams and G. H. Martin, eds., 2012, *Domesday Book: A Complete Translation*, London.

Edictum Rothari

K. F. Drew, ed., 1973, *The Lombard Laws*, Philadelphia.

Gesta pontificum Anglorum

M. Winterbottom, ed., 2007, *The History of the English Bishops, Volume One: Text and Translation*, Oxford.

II Æthelstan 13.1–14.2, III Edgar 8–8.3, III Æthelred 8–8.2, IV Æthelred 5–9.3, II Cnut 79

F. Liebermann, ed., 1883, *Die Gesetze der Angelsachsen. Herausgegeben im Auftrage der Savigny-Stiftung*, Halle.

D. Whitelock, ed., 1953, *English Historical Documents, Volume One: c.500–1042*, New York.

D. C. Douglas, ed., 1953, *English Historical Documents, Volume Two: 1042–1189*, New York.

The Collection of Anglo-Saxon and Earlier Hammered Coins, Formed by the late Captain 'Peter' Arnot, Catalogue, 1995, Buckland Dix & Wood Auctioneers and Valuers, London.

Websites and Online Resources

The Corpus of Early Medieval Coin Finds and Sylloge of Coins of the British Isles at the Fitzwilliam Museum: http://www-cm.fitzwilliam.cam.ac.uk/dept/coins/emc

Corpus Inscriptionum Latinarum: http://cil.bbaw.de/index.html

Early English Laws: http://www.earlyenglishlaws.ac.uk

English Hammered Coinage, the private collection of Timothy D. Cook: http://www.englishhammered.com

The Making of Charlemagne's Europe: http://charlemagneseurope.ac.uk

The Oxford English Dictionary Online: http://www.oed.com

People of Medieval Scotland, 1093–1314: http://www.poms.ac.uk

The Portable Antiquities Scheme of the British Museum: http://finds.org.uk/database

The Prosopography of Anglo-Saxon England: http://www.pase.ac.uk

Unit for Prosopographical Research, Linacre College, Oxford: http://prosopography.modhist.ox.ac.uk

Secondary Sources

Allen, M., 2003, *The Durham Mint*, London.

Allen, M., 2004, 'Medieval English Die-Output', *BNJ* 74, 29–49.

Allen, M., 2006, 'The Volume of the English Currency, c.973–1158', in B. Cook and G. Williams, eds., *Coinage and History in the North Sea World, c. AD 500–1250*, Leiden, 487–523.

Allen, M., 2012a, *Mints and Money in Medieval England*, Cambridge.

Allen, M., 2012b 'The mints and moneyers of England and Wales, 1066–1158', *BNJ* 82, 54–120.

Andrew, W. J., 1901, 'A Numismatic History of the Reign of Henry I. (1100–1135)', *NC* 1 (Fourth Series), 1–502.

Andrew, W. J., 1929, 'Stockbridge, an Anglo-Saxon Mint', *BNJ* 20, 49–61.

Astill, G. G., 1991, 'Towns and town hierarchies in Anglo-Saxon England', *Oxford Journal of Archaeology* 10, 95–117.

Astill, G. G., 2006, 'Community, Identity and the later Anglo-Saxon Town: the case of southern England', in A. Reynolds, W. Davies, and G. Halsall, eds., *People and Space in the Middle Ages, Turnhout*, 233–54.

Baker, J., S. Brookes, and A. Reynolds, eds., 2013, *Landscapes of Defense in Early Medieval Europe*, Turnhout.

Bates, D., 2016, *William the Conqueror*, New Haven.

Baxter, S., 2007, *The Earls of Mercia: Lordship and Power in Late Anglo-Saxon England*, Oxford.

Baxter, S., 2009, 'The limits of the late Anglo-Saxon state', in W. Pohl and V. Wieser, eds., *Der frühmittelalterliche Staat – europäische Perspektiven*, Vienna, 503–14.

Baxter, S., and J. Blair, 2006, 'Land tenure and royal patronage in the early English kingdom: a model and a case study', *Anglo-Norman Studies* 28, 19–46.

Beeaff, D. E., 1978, 'Aelfraed and Haranfot: Anglo-Saxon Personal Names', *History Today* 28, 688–90.

Biddle, M., ed., 1976, *Winchester in the Early Middle Ages*, Oxford.

Biddle, M., 2012, *Winchester Studies 8: The Winchester Mint and Coins and Related Finds from the Excavations of 1961–71*, Oxford.

Björkman, E., 1910, *Nordische Personennamen In England In Alt-Und Frühmittel-Englischer Zeit*, Halle.

Blackburn, M. A. S., 1974, 'The Mint of Watchet', *BNJ* 44, 13–38.

Blackburn, M. A. S., 1990, 'Coinage and Currency Under Henry I: A Review', in M. Chibnall, ed., *Anglo-Norman Studies XIII. Proceedings of the Battle* Conference, Woodbridge, 49–82.

Blackburn, M. A. S., 1996, 'Mints, burhs, and the Grately code, cap. 14.2', in D. Hill and A. R. Rumble, eds., *The Defence of Wessex: the Burghal Hidage and Anglo-Saxon Fortifications*, Manchester, 160–75.

Blackburn, M. A. S., 2000, 'Metheltun not Medeshamstede: an Anglo-Saxon mint at Melton Mowbray rather than Peterborough Abbey', *BNJ* 70, 143–5.

Blackburn, M. A. S., 2007, 'Crosses and conversion: the iconography of the coinage of Viking York ca. 900' in K. L. Jolly, C. E. Karkov, and S. L. Keefer, eds., *Cross and Culture in Anglo-Saxon England: Studies in Honor of George Hardin Brown*, Morgantown, 172–200.

Blackburn, M. A. S., S. Keynes, and T. R. Volk, 1985, *Anglo-Saxon Coins*, Cambridge.

Blackburn, M. A. S., and R. H. M. Dolley, 1986, *Anglo-Saxon Monetary History: Essays in Memory of Michael Dolley*, Leicester.

Blackburn, M. A. S., and C. S. S. Lyon, 1986, 'Regional die-production in Cnut's Quatrefoil issue', in M. Blackburn, 1986, *Anglo-Saxon Monetary History: Essays in Memory of Michael Dolley*, Leicester, 223–72.

Blackburn, M. A. S., and D. N. Dumville, 1998, *Kings, Currency, and Alliances*, Rochester.

Blanchard, I., 2001, *Mining, Metallurgy and Minting in the Middle Ages, Volume 1: Asiatic supremacy, 425–1125*, Stuttgart.

Blanchard, M. E., 2019, "A new perspective on family strategy in tenth- and eleventh-century England: ealdorman status and the Church," *Historical Research* 92, 1–23.

Blunt, C. E., 1960, 'The Anglo-Saxon Coinage and the Historian', *Medieval Archaeology* 4, 1–15.

Blunt, C. E., 1974, 'The Coinage of Æthelstan, 924–939: A Survey', *BNJ* 42, 35–158.

Blunt, C. E., and B. H. I. H. Stewart, 1978, 'The Droitwich Mint and BMC Type XIV of Edward the Confessor', *BNJ* 48, 52–8.

Bolton, J., 2004, 'What is money? What is a money economy? When did a money economy emerge in medieval England?', in D. S. Wood, ed., *Medieval Money Matters*, Oxford, 1–15.

Bolton, J., 2012, *Money in the Medieval English Economy, 973–1489*, Manchester.

Bolton, T., 2009, *The Empire of Cnut the Great: Conquest and Consolidation of Power in Northern Europe in the Early Eleventh Century*, Leiden.

Bolton, T., 2017, *Cnut the Great*, New Haven.

Brand, J. D., 1984, *Periodic Change of Type in the Anglo-Saxon and Norman Periods*, Rochester.

Brooke, C. E., 1910, 'Mr Parsons' arrangement of the coin types of Aethelred II. A criticism', *NC* 10 (Fourth Series), 370–80.

Brooke, C. E., 1916, *A Catalogue of English Coins in the British Museum: the Norman Kings*, 2 vols., London.

Brooke, C. N. L., B. H. I. H. Stewart, J. G. Pollard, and T. R. Volk, eds., 1983, *Studies in Numismatic Method presented to Philip Grierson*, Cambridge.

Brooke, G. C., 1929, 'Quando moneta vertebatur: the change of coin types in the eleventh century; its bearing on mules and overstrikes', *BNJ* 20, 105–16.

Brooke, G. C., 1931, 'The Medieval Moneyers', *BNJ* 21, 59–66.

Brooke, G. C., 1950, *English Coins*, 3rd Edition, London.

Butler, V. J., and R. H. M. Dolley, 1960, 'Two Die-Links Relative to the Anglo-Saxon Mint at Northampton', *BNJ* 30, 54–6.

Buttrey, T. V., 1993, 'Calculating Ancient Coin Production: Facts and Fantasies', *NC* 153, 335–51.

Buttrey, T. V., 1994, 'Calculating Ancient Coin Production II: Why it cannot be done', *NC* 154, 341–52.

Campbell, J., 1984, 'Some Twelfth-Century Views of the Anglo-Saxon Past', *Peritia* 3, 131–50.

Campbell, J., 1986, *Essays in Anglo-Saxon History*, London.

Campbell, J., 1987, 'Some agents and agencies of the late Anglo-Saxon state', in J. C. Holt, ed., *Domesday Studies: Papers Read at the Novocentenary Conference of the Royal Historical Society and the Institute of British Geographers, Winchester, 1986*, Woodbridge, 201–18.

Campbell, J., 1995, 'The Late Anglo-Saxon State: A Maximal View', *Proceedings of the British Academy* 87, 39–65.

Campbell, J., 2000, *The Anglo-Saxon State*, London.

Carcassone, C., and T. Hackens, eds., 1981, *Statistics and Numismatics*, Strasbourg.

Carlyon-Britton, P. W. P., 1902, 'Bedwin and Marlborough and the Moneyer Cilda', *NC* 2, 20–5.

Carlyon-Britton, P. W. P., 1905a, 'A Numismatic History of the Reigns of William I and II (1066–1100)', *BNJ* 2, 87–184.

Carlyon-Britton, P. W. P., 1905b, 'Eadward the Confessor and his coins', *NC* 5 (Fourth Series), 179–205.

Carlyon-Britton, P. W. P., 1906, 'Cornish Numismatics', *BNJ* 8, 107–16.

Carlyon-Britton, P. W. P., 1909, 'A Numismatic History of the Reigns of William I and II (1066–1100), Part II', *BNJ* 6, 147–76.

Carlyon-Britton, P. W. P., 1921, 'The chronological sequence of the types of Eadweard the Martyr and Æthelræd II', *BNJ* 16, 5–31.

Carroll, J., and D. Parsons, 2007, *Anglo-Saxon Mint Names: Part 1: Axbridge to Hythe*, Volume 1, Nottingham.

Carson, R. A. G., 1949, 'The Mint of Thetford', *NC* 6, 189–236.

Carson, R. A. G., 1976, 'A history of the Royal Numismatic Society', *NC* 16 (Seventh Series), xii–xv.

Carter, G. F., 1981, 'Comparison of Methods for Calculating the Total Number of Dies from Die-Link Statistics', in C. Carcassone and T. Hackens, eds., *Statistics and Numismatics*, Strasbourg, 204–13.

Chadwick, H. M., 1905, *Studies on Anglo-Saxon Institutions*, Cambridge.

Challis, C. E., 1978, *The Tudor coinage*, Manchester.

Challis, C. E., ed., 1992, *A New History of the Royal Mint*, Cambridge.

Chibnall, M., ed., 1990, *Anglo-Norman Studies XIII. Proceedings of the Battle Conference*, Woodbridge.

Christie, N., and H. Herold, eds., 2016, *Fortified Settlements in Early Medieval Europe: Defended Communities of the 8th–10th Centuries*, Oxford.

Clark, C., 1995, 'Clark's First Three Laws of Applied Anthroponymics', in P. Jackson, ed., *Words, Names, and History: Selected Writings of Cecily Clark*, Suffolk, 77–83.

Clarke, W. N., and D. Symons, 2007, 'The Mint of Aylesbury', *BNJ* 77, 173–90.

Colman, F., 1989, 'Neutralization: On Characterizing Distinctions between Old English Proper Names and Common Nouns', *Leeds Studies in English* 20, 249–70.

Colman, F., 1990, 'Numismatics, Names and Neutralisations', *Transactions of the Philological Society* 88, 59–96.

Colman, F., 1992, *Money Talks: Reconstructing Old English: Trends in Linguistics - Studies and Monographs* 56, New York.

Colman, F., 2014, *The Grammar of Names in Anglo-Saxon England: The Linguistics and Culture of the Old English Onomasticon*, Oxford.

Cook, B., and G. Williams, eds., 2006, *Coinage and History in the North Sea World, c. AD 500–1250*, Leiden.

Corbett, W. J., 1900, 'The Tribal Hidage', *Transactions of the Royal Historical Society* 14, 187–230.

Crummy, P., 1981, 'Aspects of Anglo-Saxon and Norman Colchester', in *Colchester Archaeological Reports*, London, 1–91.

Crump, C. G., and C. Johnson, 1902, 'Notes on "A Numismatic History of the Reign of Henry I" by W. J. Andrew', *NC* 2 (Fourth Series), 372–77.

Daunt, M., 1955, 'A Philological and Topographical note on Cissbury', *BNJ* 28, 281–2.

De Callataÿ, F., 1995, 'Calculating Ancient Coin Production: Seeking A Balance', *NC* 155, 289–311.

De Moor, T., 2009, 'The Silent Revolution: A New Perspective on the Emergence of Commons, Guilds and Other Forms of Corporate Collective Action in Western Europe', in J. Lucassen, T. De Moor, and J. L. van Zanden, eds., *The Return of the Guilds, International Review of Social History, Supplement* 16, 179–212.

Dolley, R. H. M., 1955a, 'Three Late Anglo-Saxon Notes', *BNJ* 28, 88–105.

Dolley, R. H. M., 1955b, 'Two Anglo-Saxon Notes', *BNJ* 28, 499–508.

Dolley, R. H. M., 1956, 'The Shaftesbury hoard of pence of Æthelræd II', *NC* 16 Sixth Series, 267–80.

Dolley, R. H. M., 1958a, *Some Reflections on Hildebrand Type A of Aethelraed II*, Stockholm.

Dolley, R. H. M., 1958b, 'Three More Late Saxon Notes', *BNJ* 29, 51–60.

Dolley, R. H. M., 1959, 'The Earliest Penny of the Bruton Mint', *BNJ* 19, 183–5.

Dolley, R. H. M., 1960, 'A New Late Saxon Mint in Suffolk', *NCirc* 68, 236.

Dolley, R. H. M., 1961, 'A Note on the Anglo-Saxon Mint at Reading', *BNJ* 30, 70–5.

Dolley, R. H. M., 1962, 'Two Anglo-Saxon Notes', *BNJ* 31, 53–6.

Dolley, R. H. M., 1966, 'Further Southampton/Winchester Die-Links in the Reign of Æthelræd II', *BNJ* 35, 25–33.

Dolley, R. H. M., 1970, *Anglo-Saxon Pennies*, London.

Dolley, R. H. M., 1978, 'An Introduction to the Coinage of Æthelred II', in D. Hill, ed., *Ethelred the Unready: Papers from the Millenary Conference*, Oxford, 115–33.

Dolley, R. H. M., 1979, 'Roger of Wendover's Date for Eadgar's Coinage Reform', *BNJ* 49, 1–11.

Dolley, R. H. M., and F. E. Jones, 1955, 'The Mints "ÆT GOTHABYRIG" and "ÆT SITH(M)ESTEBYRIG"', *BNJ* 28, 270–82.

Dolley, R. H. M., and G. van der Meer, 1958, 'A Group of Anglo-Saxon Pence at Sudeley Castle', *NC* 18 (Sixth Series), 123–29.

Dolley, R. H. M., and D. M. Metcalf, 1961, 'The Reform of the English Coinage under Eadgar', in R. H. M. Dolley, ed., *Anglo-Saxon Coins: Studies Presented to F. M. Stenton on the Occasion of his 80th Birthday, 17 May 1960*, London, 136–68.

Dolley, R. H. M., and E. J. E. Pirie, 1964, 'The repercussions on Chester's prosperity of the Viking descent on Cheshire in 980', *BNJ* 33, 39–44.

Dolley, R. H. M., D. J. Elliott and F. E. Jones, 1965, 'The Buckingham Mint', *BNJ* 34, 46–52.

Dolley, R. H. M, and T. Talvio, 1977, 'The Regional Pattern of Die-Cutting Exhibited by the First Hand pennies of Aethelraed II Preserved in the British Museum', *BNJ* 47, 53–65.

Douglas, D. C., 1964, *William the Conqueror: the Norman Impact upon England*, Berkeley.

Drummond Robertson, J., 1885, 'The Status of the Anglo-Norman Moneyer', *NC* 5 (Third Series), 209–12.

Dumas, E., 1868, *Notes sur l'émission en France des monnaies décimales de bronze (1852-1865)*, Paris.

Eaglen, R. J., 1999, 'The mint of Huntingdon', *BNJ* 69, 47–145.

Ellis, H., 1836, 'Letter from Sir H. Ellis', in Proceedings of the Numismatic Society, 1837–8, London, 97–9.

Ellis, H., 1837, 'Note on Ruding's Annals', *Transactions of the Numismatic Society, The Numismatic Journal*, Vol. 2, 252–5 at 253.

Elmore Jones, F., 1960, 'The Mint of Axbridge', *BNJ* 30, 61–9.

Elmore Jones, F., 1962, 'The Mysterious Mint of 'Dernt'', *BNJ* 31, 66–8.

Elmore Jones, F., 1970, 'Southampton/Winchester die-links in Canute's Quatrefoil type', *BNJ* 39, 6–11.

Esty, W. W., 1986, 'Estimation of the Size of a Coinage: a Survey and Comparison of Methods', *NC* 146, 185–215.

Esty, W. W., 2006, 'How to estimate the original number of dies and the coverage of a sample', *NC* 166, 359–64.

Fellows Jensen, G., 1968, *Scandinavian Personal Names in Lincolnshire and Yorkshire*, Copenhagen.

Fleming, R., 1991, *Kings and Lords in Conquest England*, Cambridge.

Foot, S., 2011, *Æthelstan: the First King of England*, New Haven.

Forssner, T., 1916, *Continental-Germanic Personal Names in England in Old and Middle English Times*, Uppsala.

Gannon, A., 2003, *The Iconography of Early Anglo-Saxon Coinage: Sixth to Eighth Centuries*, Oxford.

Garipzanov, I., 1999, 'The Image of Authority in Carolingian Coinage: the image of a ruler and Roman imperial tradition', *Early Medieval Europe* 8, 197–218.

Garipzanov, I., 2016, 'Regensburg, Wandalgarius and the novi denarii: Charlemagne's monetary reform revisited', *Early Medieval Europe* 24, 58–73.

Gillingham, J., 1989, "The Most Precious Jewel in the English Crown': levels of Danegeld and heregeld in the early eleventh century', *EHR* 104, 373–84.

Golding, B., 1994, *Conquest and Colonisation: The Normans in Britain, 1066–1100*, New York.

Green, J. A., 1981, 'The Last Century of Danegeld', *EHR* 96, 241–58.

Green, J. A., 2017, Forging the Kingdom: Power in English Society, 973–1189, Cambridge.

Grierson, P., 1962, 'The President's Address: Numismatics and the historian', *NC* 2, i–xiv.

Grierson, P., 1975, *Numismatics*, Oxford.

Grierson, P., 1979, 'The Volume of Anglo-Saxon Coinage', in *Dark Age Numismatics: Selected Studies*, London, 153–60.

Grierson, P., 1987, 'The Monetary System under William I', in A. Williams, ed., *Domesday Book Studies*, London, 75–9.

Grierson, P., and M. A. S. Blackburn, 1986, *Medieval European Coinage, Volume 1: The Early Middle Ages (5th–10th centuries)*, Cambridge.

Grinsell, L. V., 1973, *The Bath Mint, an Historical Outline*, Oxford.

Harvey, S., 2014, *Domesday: Book of Judgement*, Oxford.

Haslam, J., 1984, *Anglo-Saxon Towns in Southern England*, Chichester.

Haslam, J., 2011, 'Daws Castle, Somerset, and Civil Defence Measures in Southern and Midland England in the Ninth to Eleventh Centuries', *Archaeological Journal* 168, 195–226.

Hawkins, E., 1841, *The Silver Coins of England Arranged and Described with Remarks on British Money, Previous to the Saxon Dynasties*, London.

Hawkins, E., 1887, *The Silver Coins of England Arranged and Described with Remarks on British Money, Previous to the Saxon Dynasties*, Second Edition, London.

Head, B. V., 1867, 'An account of the hoard of Anglo-Saxon coins found at Chancton Farm, Sussex', *NC* 7, 63–126.

Herlihy, D., 1985, *Medieval Households*, Cambridge.

Hendy, M. F., 1985, *Studies in the Byzantine Monetary Economy, c. 300–1450*, Cambridge.

Hendy, M. F., 1988, 'From Public to Private: The Western Barbarian Coinages as a Mirror of the Disintegration of Late Roman State Structures', *Viator* 19, 29–78.

Hildebrand, B. E., 1846, *Anglosachsiska Mynt i Svenska Kongliga Myntkabinettet*, Stockholm.

Hildebrand, B. E., 1881, *Anglosachsiska Mynt i Svenska Kongliga Myntkabinettet*, 2nd Edition, Stockholm.

Hill, D., 1981, *An Atlas of Anglo-Saxon England*, Oxford.

Hill, F., 1948, *Medieval Lincoln*, Cambridge.

Holt, J. C., ed., 1987, *Domesday Studies: Papers Read at the Novocentenary Conference of the Royal Historical Society and the Institute of British Geographers, Winchester, 1986*, Woodbridge.

Hudson, J., 2012, *The Oxford History of the Laws of England*, Volume 2, Oxford.

Insley, C., 2002, 'Where did all the charters go? Anglo-Saxon charters and the new politics of the eleventh century', *ANS* 24, 109–27.

Johanek, P., 2000, 'Merchants, Markets and Towns', in T. Reuter, ed., *The New Cambridge Medieval History*, vol. III, Cambridge, 64–94.

John, E., 1996, *Reassessing Anglo-Saxon England*, Manchester.

Jonsson, K., 1987a, *The New Era*, London.

Jonsson, K., 1987b, *Viking-Age Hoards and Late Anglo-Saxon Coins: A Study in Honour of Bror Emil Hildebrand's Anglosachsiska mynt*, Stockholm.

Jonsson, K., 2006, 'The Pre-Reform Coinage of Edgar – the Legacy of the Anglo-Saxon Kingdoms', in B. Cook and G. Williams, eds., *Coinage and History in the North Sea World, c. AD 500–1250*, Leiden, 325–46.

Jonsson, K., ed., 1990, *Studies in Late Anglo-Saxon Coinage in Memory of Bror Emil Hildebrand*, Stockholm.

Kapelle, W. E., 1979, *The Norman Conquest of the North: The Region and Its Transformation, 1000–1135*, Chapel Hill.

Keats-Rohan, K. S. B., 2007, 'Biography, Identity and Names: Understanding the Pursuit of the Individual in Prosopography' in K. S. B. Keats-Rohan, ed., *Prosopography Approaches and Applications, A Handbook*, Oxford, 139–82.

Keats-Rohan, K. S. B., ed., 2007, *Prosopography Approaches and Applications. A Handbook*, Oxford.

Keder, N., 1708, *Nummorum in Hibernia antequam haec insula sub Henrico II. Angliae rege Anglici facta sit juris cusorum indagatio; Accessit catalogus nummorum Anglo-Saxonicor. & Anglo-Danicor. Musei Kederiani*, Leipzig.

Keen, L., 1984, 'The Towns of Dorset', in J. Haslam, ed., *Anglo-Saxon Towns in Southern England, Chichester*, 203–47.

Keene, D., 1995, 'London in the Early Middle Ages 600–1300', *The London Journal* 20, 9–21.

Keene, D., 2000, 'London from the post-Roman period to 1300', in D. M. Palliser, ed., *The Cambridge Urban History of Britain, Cambridge*, 187–216.

Keene, D., 2004, 'Towns and the growth of trade', in D. E. Luscombe and J. S. C. Riley-Smith, eds., *The New Cambridge Medieval History*, vol. IV, Cambridge, 47–85.

Keynes, S., 1990, 'Royal Government and the Written Word in Late Anglo-Saxon England', in R. McKitterick, ed., *The Uses of Literacy in Medieval Europe*, Cambridge, 226–57.

Keynes, S., 2008, 'Edgar, rex admirabilis', in D. Scragg, ed., *Edgar, King of the English, 959–975: New Interpretations*, Manchester, 3–59.

Keynes, S., 2013a, 'Church councils, royal assemblies, and Anglo-Saxon royal diplomas', in G. R. Owen-Crocker and B. W. Schneider, eds., *Kingship, Legislation and Power in Anglo-Saxon England*, Woodbridge, 1–182.

Keynes, S., 2013b, 'Cynethryth', in M. Lapidge, ed., *The Wiley-Blackwell Encyclopedia of Anglo-Saxon England*, 133.

Keynes, S., 2013c, 'Wulfstan I', in M. Lapidge, ed., *The Wiley-Blackwell Encyclopedia of Anglo-Saxon England*, 513.

Keynes, S., 2014, 'Shire' in M. Lapidge, J. Blair, S. Keynes, and D. Scragg, eds., *The Wiley-Blackwell Encyclopedia of Anglo-Saxon England*, Chichester, 434–5.

Keynes, S., and R. Naismith, 2011, 'The Agnus Dei pennies of King Æthelred the Unready', *ASE* 40, 175–223.

Kinsey, R. S., 1960, 'Anglo-Saxon Law and Practice Relating to Mints and Moneyers', *BNJ* 29, 12–50.

Kokeritz, H., 1939, *Notes on the Pre-Conquest Personal Names of Domesday Book*, Uppsala.

Latouche, R., 1961, *The Birth of the Western Economy: Economic Aspects of the Dark Ages*, London.

Lawson, M. K., 1984, 'The collection of Danegeld and Heregeld in the reigns of Æthelred II and Cnut', *EHR* 99, 721–38.

Lawson, M. K., 1989, "Those stories look true': levels of taxation in the reigns of Æthelred II and Cnut', *EHR* 104, 385–406.

Lawson, M. K., 1990, 'Danegeld and Heregeld Once More', *EHR* 105, 951–61.

Lear, F. S., 1950, 'Treason and Related Offenses in the Anglo-Saxon Dooms', *Rice Institute Pamphlet - Rice University Studies* 37, Houston, 1–20.

Lopez, R. S., 1953, 'An Aristocracy of Money in the Early Middle Ages', *Speculum* 28, 1–43.

Lopez, R. S., 1986, 'Continuità e adattamento nel medio evo: Un millenio di storia delle associazioni di monetieri nell'Europa meridionalle' in *The Shape of Medieval Monetary History*, London, 74–117.

Loyn, H. R., 1961a, 'The origin and early development of the Saxon borough with special reference to Cricklade', *Wiltshire Archaeological Magazine* 58, 7–15.

Loyn, H. R., 1961b, 'Boroughs and Mints, A.D. 900–1066', in R. H. M. Dolley, ed., *Anglo-Saxon Coins: Studies Presented to F. M. Stenton on the Occasion of his 80th Birthday, 17 May 1960*, London, 122–135.

Loyn, H. R., 1984, *The Governance of Anglo-Saxon England, 500–1087*, Stanford.

Loyn, H. R., 1991, *Anglo–Saxon England and the Norman Conquest*, Second Edition, London.

Loyn, H. R., 1992, *Society and Peoples: Studies in the History of England and Wales, c. 600–1200*, London.

Lyon, C. S. S., 1962, 'Two Notes on the 'Last Small Cross' Type of Æthelræd II', *BNJ* 31, 49–52.

Lyon, C. S. S., 1976, 'Some Problems in Interpreting Anglo-Saxon Coinage', *ASE* 5, 173–224.

Lyon, C. S. S., 1998, 'Die-cutting in the Last Small Cross issue of c. 1009–1017 and some problematic East Anglian dies and die-links', *BNJ* 68, 21–41.

Lyon, C. S. S., 2003, 'Anglo-Saxon numismatics', *BNJ* 73, 58–75.

Lyon, C. S. S., 2016, *The Lyon Collection of Anglo-Saxon Coins* (*Sylloge of Coins of the British Isles* 68), Oxford.

Magdalino, P., 2003, 'Prosopography and Byzantine Identity' in A. Cameron, ed., *Fifty Years of Prosopography: The Later Roman Empire, Byzantium and Beyond*, Oxford, 41–56.

Mahany, C., and D. Roffe, 1983, 'Stamford: The Development of an Anglo-Scandinavian Borough', *ANS* 5, 197–219.

Mathisen, R. W., 2007, 'Where are all the PDBs?: The Creation of Prosopographical Databases for the Ancient and Medieval Worlds', in K. S. B. Keats-Rohan, ed.,

Prosopography Approaches and Applications, A Handbook, Oxford, 95–126.

Metcalf, D. M., 1980, 'Continuity and Change in English Monetary History', *BNJ* 50, 20–49.

Metcalf, D. M., 1986, 'The taxation of moneyers under Edward the Confessor and in 1086', in *Domesday Studies: Papers read at the Novocentenary Conference of the Royal Historical Society and the Institute of British Geographers, Winchester, 1986*, Woodbridge, 279–93.

Metcalf, D. M., 1987, 'A penny life will give you all the facts', *NC* 147, 184–8.

Metcalf, D. M., 1998, *An Atlas of Anglo-Saxon and Norman Coin Finds, C.973–1086*, London.

Metcalf, D. M. and J. P. Northover, 1986, 'Interpreting the alloy of the later Anglo-Saxon coinage', *BNJ* 56, 35–63.

Metcalf, D. M. and J. P. Northover, 2002, 'Sporadic debasement in the English coinage, c.1009–1052', *NC* 162, 217–36.

Molyneaux, G., 2015, *The Formation of the English Kingdom in the Tenth Century*, Oxford.

Mossop, H. R., 1970, *The Lincoln Mint, c. 890–1279*, Newcastle.

Montagu, H., 1891, 'The Anglo-Saxon Mints of Chester and Leicester', *NC* 11, 12–24.

Naismith, R., 2012a, *Money and Power in Anglo-Saxon England: the Southern English Kingdoms, 757–865*, Cambridge.

Naismith, R., 2012b, 'Kings, crisis and coinage reforms in the mid-eighth century', *Early Medieval Europe* 20, 291–332.

Naismith, R., 2013a, 'The English monetary economy, c. 973–1100: the contribution of single-finds', *EcHR* 66, 198–225.

Naismith, R., 2013b, 'London and its mint c. 880–1066: a preliminary survey', *BNJ* 83, 44–74.

Naismith, R., 2014a, 'Prelude to Reform: Tenth-Century English Coinage in Perspective', in R. Naismith, M. Allen, and E. Screen, eds., *Early Medieval Monetary History, Studies in Memory of Mark Blackburn*, Farnham, 39–84.

Naismith, R., 2014b, 'The social significance of monetization in the early Middle Ages', *Past & Present* 223, 3–39.

Naismith, R., 2015, 'Spending Power: Money and Power Relations in Early Medieval Europe', *Uppsala University Coin Cabinet Working Papers* 16, Uppsala.

Naismith, R., 2016, 'The coinage of Æthelred II: a new evaluation', *English Studies* 97, 117–39.

Naismith, R., 2017a, *Medieval European Coinage, Vol. 8: Britain and Ireland c. 400–1066*, Cambridge.

Naismith, R., 2017b, 'The Historian and Anglo-Saxon Coinage: The Case of Late Anglo-Saxon England', in R. Naismith and D. A. Woodman, eds., *Writing, Kingship and Power in Anglo-Saxon England*, Cambridge, 162–80.

Nightingale, P., 1982, 'Some London Moneyers and Reflections on the Organization of English Mints in the Eleventh and Twelfth Centuries', *NC* 142, 34–50.

Nordman, C. A., 1921, *Anglo-Saxon Coins Found in Finland*, Helsingfors.

North, J. J., 1980, *English Hammered Coinage, Volume I: Early Anglo-Saxon to Henry III c. 600–1272*, London.

Ogilvie, S., 2014, 'The Economics of Guilds', *The Journal of Economic Perspectives* 28, 169–92.

Packe, A. E., 1893, 'The Coinage of the Norman Kings', *NC* 13, 129–45.

Pagan, H., 1990, 'The coinage of Harold II', in K. Jonsson, ed., *Studies in Late Anglo-Saxon Coinage in Memory of Bror Emil Hildebrand*, Stockholm, 179–205.

Pagan, H., 2008, 'The Pre-Reform Coinage of Edgar', in D. Scragg, ed., *Edgar, King of the English, 959–975: New Interpretations*, Manchester, 192–208.

Pagan, H., 2011, 'The Paxs type of Edward the Confessor', *BNJ* 81, 9–106.

Page, W., ed., 1925, *A History of the County of Buckingham: Volume 3*, London.

Page, W., G. Proby, and S. Inskip Ladds, eds., 1932, *A History of the County of Huntingdon: Volume 2*, London.

Palliser, D. M., ed.,, 2000, *The Cambridge Urban History of Britain*, Cambridge.

Palliser, D. M., 2014, *Medieval York: 600–1540*, Oxford.

Parsons, H. A., 1910a, 'The coin types of Aethelred II', *NC* 10 (Fourth Series), 251–90.

Parsons, H. A., 1910b, 'Mr G. C. Brooke on "the coin types of Aethelred II." A reply', *NC* 10 (Fourth Series), 381–7.

Peirce, I. G., 2002, *Swords of the Viking Age*, Woodbridge.

Pelteret, D. E., 2007, 'Should One Include Unnamed Persons in a Prosopographical Study?' in K. S. B. Keats-Rohan, ed., *Prosopography Approaches and Applications, A Handbook*, Oxford, 183–96.

Petersson, H. B. A., 1969, *Anglo-Saxon Currency: King Edgar's Reform to the Norman Conquest*, Lund.

Pinner, R., 2015, *The Cult of St Edmund in Medieval East Anglia*, Woodbridge.

Pratt, D., 2010, 'Written Law and the Communication of Authority in Tenth-Century England', in D. Rollason,

C. Leyser, and H. Williams, eds., *England and the Continent in the Tenth Century: Studies in Honour of Wilhelm Levison (1876–1947)*, Turnhout, 331–50.

Redin, M. A., 1919, *Studies on Uncompounded Personal Names in Old English*, Uppsala.

Reynolds, A., 2013, 'Archaeological Correlates for Anglo-Saxon Military Activity in Comparative Perspective' in Baker et al, *Landscapes of Defense in Early Medieval Europe*, Turnhout, 1–38.

Reynolds, S., 1984, *Kingdoms and Communities in Western Europe*, Oxford.

Reynolds, S., 1985, 'What do we mean by "Anglo-Saxon" and "Anglo-Saxons"?', *Journal of British Studies* 24, 395–414.

Reuter, T., 1998, 'Debating the "feudal revolution"', in J. L. Nelson, ed., 2006, *Medieval Polities and Modern Mentalities*, Cambridge, 72–88.

Roach, L., 2013a, *Kingship and Consent in Anglo-Saxon England, 871–978: Assemblies and the State in the Early Middle Ages*, Cambridge.

Roach, L., 2013b, 'Law Codes and Legal Norms in Later Anglo-Saxon England', *Historical Research* 86, 465–86.

Roach, L., 2016, *Æthelred the Unready*, New Haven.

Robertson, A. J., ed., 1956, *Anglo-Saxon Charters*, Cambridge.

Roffe, D., 2007, *Decoding Domesday*, Woodbridge.

Roffe, D., ed., 2012, *The English and their Legacy, 900–1200: Essays in Honour of Ann Williams*, Woodbridge.

Romaneix, G., 2008, 'Les privilèges des monnayers du Serment de France aux XIIIe et XIVe siècles', in Y. Benhima, ed., *Actes des congrès nationaux des sociétés historiques et scientifiques*, 88–99.

Rosser, G., 1988, 'The Anglo-Saxon Gilds', in J. Blair, ed., *Minsters and Parish Churches: The Local Church in Transition, 950–1200*, Oxford, 31–43.

Round, J. H., 1903, 'The Colchester Mint in Norman Times', *EHR* 18, 305–15.

Ruding, R., 1817, *Annals of the Coinage of Britain and its Dependencies: from the earliest period of authentic history to the reign of Victoria, Volume I*, First Edition, London.

Ruding, R., 1840, *Annals of the Coinage of Britain and its Dependencies: from the earliest period of authentic history to the reign of Victoria, Volume I*, Third Edition, London.

Russo, D., 1998, *Town Origins and Development in Early England, c.400–950 A.D.*, Westport.

S., R., 1837–8, 'An Attempt to Locate Some Coins of Unappropriated Mints, in Ruding from Domesday, and the New Topographical Dictionary', *TNJ* 2, 45–51.

Sawyer, P. H., 1965, 'The wealth of England in the eleventh century', *Transactions of the Royal Historical Society* (Fifth Series) 15, 145–64.

Sawyer, P. H., 2013, *The Wealth of Anglo-Saxon England*, Oxford.

Screen, E., 2007, 'Anglo-Saxon Law and Numismatics: A Reassessment in Light of Patrick Wormald's The Making of English Law', *BNJ* 77, 150–172.

Seaby, P., 1955, 'The Sequence of Anglo-Saxon Coin Types, 1030–50', *BNJ* 28, 112–46.

Searle, W. G., 1897, *Onomasticon Anglo-Saxonicum, A List of Anglo-Saxon Proper Names from Bede to that of King John*, Cambridge.

Shaw, P., 2008, 'Orthographic Standardization and Seventh- and Eighth-Century Coin Inscriptions', in T. Abramson, ed., *Two Decades of Discovery: Studies in Early Medieval Coinage*, 97–112.

Shortt, H. D. S., 1948, 'The Mints of Wiltshire: From Eadgar to Henry III', *Archaeological Journal* 104, 112–32.

Smart, V., 1968, 'Moneyers of the late Anglo-Saxon Coinage, 973–1016', in *Commentationes de Nummis Saeculorum IX-XI in Suecia Repertis*, Volume II, Stockholm, 193–276.

Smart, V., 1975, Corrections to Hildebrand's Corpus of Anglo-Saxon Moneyers: from Cnut to Edward the Confessor', *ASE* 4, 155–70.

Smart, V., 1981, *Cumulative index of Volumes 1–20, in Sylloge of Coins of the British Isles*, London.

Smart, V., 1987a, 'Moneyers of the late Anglo-Saxon coinage: the Danish Dynasty', *ASE* 16, 233–308.

Smart, V., 1987b, 'Moneyers of the late Anglo-Saxon Coinage, 973–1016', in *Commentationes de Nummis Saeculorum IX-XI in Suecia Repertis*, Volume II, Stockholm, 193–276.

Smart, V., 2012, 'The Names of the Moneyers of the Winchester Mint' in M. Biddle, ed., *Winchester Studies 8: The Winchester Mint and Coins and Related Finds from the Excavations of 1961–71*, Oxford, 66–78.

Smythe, D. C., 2007, '"A Whiter Shade of Pale": Issues and Possibilities in Prosopography', in K. S. B. Keats-Rohan, ed., *Prosopography Approaches and Applications, A Handbook*, Oxford, 127–37.

Spufford, P., 1983, 'Mint organisation in the Burgundian Netherlands in the fifteenth century', in C. N. L. Brooke, B. H. I. H. Stewart, J. G. Pollard, and T. R. Volk, eds., *Studies in Numismatic Method presented to Philip Grierson*, Cambridge, 239–62.

Spufford, P., 1988, *Money and Its Use in Medieval Europe*, Cambridge.

Stafford, P., 1978, 'Historical implications of the regional production of dies under Ethelred II', *BNJ* 48, 35–51.

Stafford, P., 1982, 'The laws of Cnut and the history of Anglo-Saxon royal promises', *ASE* 10, 173–90.

Stenton, F. M., 1970, 'Lindsey and Its Kings', in D. M. Stenton, ed., *Preparatory to Anglo-Saxon England: The Collected Papers of Frank Merry Stenton*, Oxford, 127–35.

Stenton, F. M., 1971, *Anglo-Saxon England*, 3rd Edition, Oxford.

Stewart, B. H. I. H., 1971, 'The Early Coins of Ethered II's Crux Issue with Right-facing Bust', *NC* 11 (Seventh Series), 237–42.

Stewart, B. H. I. H., 1975, 'Reflections on some Wessex mints and their moneyers', *NC* 15, 219–29.

Stewart, B. H. I. H., 1988, '*Ministri* and *Monetarii*', in *Revue numismatique*, 6e série - Tome 30, année, 166–75.

Stewart, B. H. I. H., 1990, 'Coinage and Recoinage after Edgar's Reform', in K. Jonsson, ed., *Studies in Late Anglo-Saxon Coinage in Memory of Bror Emil Hildebrand*, Stockholm, 455–85.

Stewart, B. H. I. H., 1992, 'The English and Norman Mints, c.600–1158', in C. E. Challis, ed., *A New History of the Royal Mint*, Cambridge, 1–82.

Stewart, B. H. I. H., 1998, 'Moneyers in the Written Records', in M. A. S. Blackburn and D. N. Dumville, eds., *Kings, Currency, and Alliances: History and Coinage of Southern England in the Ninth Century*, Woodbridge, 151–3.

Symons, D. J., 2006, 'The Moneyers of the Worcester Mint, 1066–1158: Some Thoughts and Comments', in B. Cook, ed., *Coinage and History in the North Sea World, c. AD 500–1250*, Leiden, 545–88.

Symonds, H., 1922, 'Bridport as an Anglo-Saxon Mint', *NC* 5, 144–5.

Thomas, H., 2008, *The Norman Conquest: England after William the Conqueror*, Plymouth.

Thornton, D. E., 2003, *Kings, Chronologies, and Geneologies: Studies in the Political History of Early Medieval Ireland and Wales*, Oxford.

Thorpe, B., 1840, *Ancient Laws and Institutes of England*, Ghent.

Tsurushima, H., 2012, 'The Moneyers of Kent in the Long Eleventh Century', in D. Roffe, ed., *The English and Their Legacy, 900–1200: Essays in Honour of Ann Williams*, Woodbridge, 33–59.

Verboven, K., M. Carlier, and J. Dumolyn, 2007, 'A Short Manual to the Art of Prosopography', in K. S. B. Keats-Rohan, ed., *Prosopography Approaches and Applications. A Handbook*, Oxford, 35–70.

von Feilitzen, O., 1937, *The Pre-Conquest Personal Names of Domesday Book*, Uppsala.

Wainwright, F. T., 1942, 'North-west Mercia A.D. 871–924', *Transactions of the Historical Society of Lancashire and Cheshire* 94, 3–53.

Wallace, L., 2015, *The Origin of Roman London*, Cambridge.

Wareham, A., 2012, 'Fiscal policies and the institution of a tax state in Anglo-Saxon England within a comparative context', *EcHR* 65, 910–31.

Wells, W. C., 1934, 'The Stamford and Peterborough Mints', *BNJ* 6, 35–77.

Wickham, C., 2009, *The Inheritance of Rome: a History of Europe from 400 to 1000*, London.

Williams, A., 1999, *Kingship and Government in Pre-Conquest England, c. 500–1066*, New York.

Williams, A., 2008, *The World Before Domesday: The English Aristocracy, 900–1066*, London.

Williams, G., 2013a, 'Military and Non-Military Functions of the Anglo-Saxon Burh, c. 878–978', in Baker et al, *Landscapes of Defense in Early Medieval Europe*, Turnhout, 129–64.

Williams, G., 2013b, 'Coins and kingship', in G. R. Owen-Crocker and B. W. Schneider, eds., *Royal Authority in Anglo-Saxon England*, Oxford, 37–61.

Williams, T. J. T., 2012, 'The mint at Wallingford: an introduction to the corpus', *Yorkshire Numismatist* 4, 141–57.

Woolf, H. B., 1939, *The Old Germanic Principles of Name-Giving*, Baltimore.

Wormald, P., 1994, 'Engla Lond: The Making of an Allegiance', *Journal of Historical Sociology* 7, 1–24.

Wormald, P., 1999, *Making of English Law: King Alfred to the Twelfth Century, Legislation and its Limits*, Volume 1, Oxford.

Yarrow, S., 2006, *Saints and their Communities: Miracle Stories in Twelfth-Century England*, Oxford.

Yorke, B., 1990, *Kings and Kingdoms of Early Anglo-Saxon England*, London.

Appendix 1

The Moneyers of England Database, 973–1086

The information within the *Moneyers of England Database, 973–1086* is organised below in a readily accessible and referenceable format. The raw data can be downloaded as part of the supplemental materials available with the book. The database is formatted to include:

- Two tables of general information regarding the number of records within each mint:
  - An alphabetical listing of the mints, along with the number of Moneyer periods of activity and the number of associated coinage records.
  - A listing of the mints arranged in descending order by the number of periods of Moneyer activity.
- A series of nine maps geographically placing the mints active at some point during the reign of each of the monarchs that issued coins during the 113-year period from Edgar's coinage reform of *c*.973 to the Domesday survey of 1086. The mint locations are numerically labelled on the corresponding map and listed on the immediately successive page. County boundaries are on the historic county model (pre-1972).
- A gazetteer of the ninety-nine minting locations with full listings of Moneyer names and their ranges of activity in tabular and graphical representations (graphs included in the electronic download material).

Table A1. Alphabetical List of Mints and Data

Mint	Periods of Moneyer Activity	Coinage Records
Axbridge	9	16
Aylesbury	8	18
Barnstaple	18	68
Bath	29	305
Bedford	57	210
Bedwin	4	14
Berkeley	2	3
Bridport	14	28
Bristol	38	226
Bruton	4	32
Buckingham	12	19
Bury St Edmunds	3	16
Cadbury	5	14
Caistor	1	3
Cambridge	65	386
Canterbury	97	1035
Cardiff	1	1
Chester	101	942
Chichester	35	269
Cissbury	4	28
Colchester	57	244
Crewkerne	5	13
Cricklade	28	79

Table A1 ***continued***

Mint	Periods of Moneyer Activity	Coinage Records
Cuer	1	2
Derby	36	155
Dernt	2	4
Dorchester	18	77
Dover	52	388
Droitwich	2	2
Durham	1	2
Exeter	119	741
Frome	1	2
Gloucester	63	363
Gothaburh	6	25
Guildford	13	52
Hastings	28	347
Hereford	51	205
Hertford	41	171
Horncastle	1	1
Horndon	1	1
Huntingdon	35	208
Hythe	2	5
Ilchester	43	284
Ipswich	57	345
Langport	9	27
Launceston	3	7
Leicester	43	191
Lewes	61	446
Lincoln	211	2969
London	424	5292
Lydford	14	106
Lympne	15	53
Maldon	21	86
Malmesbury	20	67
Marlborough	2	8
Milbourne Port	3	7
Newark	1	4
Newport Pagnell	3	5
Niwan	2	4
Northampton	46	260
Norwich	90	637
Nottingham	27	129
Oxford	80	534
Pershore	1	1
Peterborough	1	1

Table A1 ***continued***

Mint	Periods of Moneyer Activity	Coinage Records
Petherton	1	1
Pevensey	1	2
Rhuddlan	1	2
Rochester	32	172
Romney	18	87
Salisbury	26	213
Sandwich	7	28
Shaftesbury	38	198
Shrewsbury	64	254
Southampton	14	65
Southwark	68	375
St Davids	1	3
Stafford	18	69
Stamford	113	1218
Stes	1	2
Steyning	15	124
Sudbury	9	26
Tamworth	17	37
Taunton	15	52
Thetford	116	1053
Torksey	3	13
Totnes	19	137
Twynham	1	1
Wallingford	63	344
Wareham	23	89
Warminster	6	11
Warwick	42	134
Watchet	7	55
Wilton	49	257
Wilton (East Anglia)	1	1
Winchcombe	12	32
Winchester	152	1666
Worcester	62	193
York	237	3291
Sub-total	**3499**	**28388**
Indeterminate Mint	147	188
Total	**3646**	**28576**

Table A2. Mints by Periods of Moneyer Activity

Mint	Periods of Moneyer Activity	Coinage Records
London	424	5292
York	237	3291
Lincoln	211	2969
Winchester	152	1666
Exeter	119	741
Thetford	116	1053
Stamford	113	1218
Chester	101	942
Canterbury	97	1035
Norwich	90	637
Oxford	80	534
Southwark	68	375
Cambridge	65	386
Shrewsbury	64	254
Gloucester	63	363
Wallingford	63	344
Worcester	62	193
Lewes	61	446
Bedford	57	210
Colchester	57	244
Ipswich	57	345
Dover	52	388
Hereford	51	205
Wilton	49	257
Northampton	46	260
Ilchester	43	284
Leicester	43	191
Warwick	42	134
Hertford	41	171
Bristol	38	226
Shaftesbury	38	198
Derby	36	155
Chichester	35	269
Huntingdon	35	208
Rochester	32	172
Bath	29	305
Cricklade	28	79
Hastings	28	347
Nottingham	27	129
Salisbury	26	213
Wareham	23	89
Maldon	21	86

Table A2 ***continued***

Mint	Periods of Moneyer Activity	Coinage Records
Malmesbury	20	67
Totnes	19	137
Barnstaple	18	68
Dorchester	18	77
Romney	18	87
Stafford	18	69
Tamworth	17	37
Lympne	15	53
Steyning	15	124
Taunton	15	52
Bridport	14	28
Lydford	14	106
Southampton	14	65
Guildford	13	52
Buckingham	12	19
Winchcombe	12	32
Axbridge	9	16
Langport	9	27
Sudbury	9	26
Aylesbury	8	18
Sandwich	7	28
Watchet	7	55
Gothaburh	6	25
Warminster	6	11
Cadbury	5	14
Crewkerne	5	13
Bedwin	4	14
Bruton	4	32
Cissbury	4	28
Bury St Edmunds	3	16
Launceston	3	7
Milbourne Port	3	7
Newport Pagnell	3	5
Torksey	3	13
Berkeley	2	3
Dernt	2	4
Droitwich	2	2
Hythe	2	5
Marlborough	2	8
Niwan	2	4
Caistor	1	3
Cardiff	1	1

Table A2 ***continued***

Mint	Periods of Moneyer Activity	Coinage Records
Cuer	1	2
Durham	1	2
Frome	1	2
Horncastle	1	1
Horndon	1	1
Newark	1	4
Pershore	1	1
Peterborough	1	1
Petherton	1	1
Pevensey	1	2
Rhuddlan	1	2
St Davids	1	3
Stes	1	2
Twynham	1	1
Wilton (East Anglia)	1	1
Sub-total	**3499**	**28388**
Indeterminate Mint	147	188
Total	**3646**	**28576**

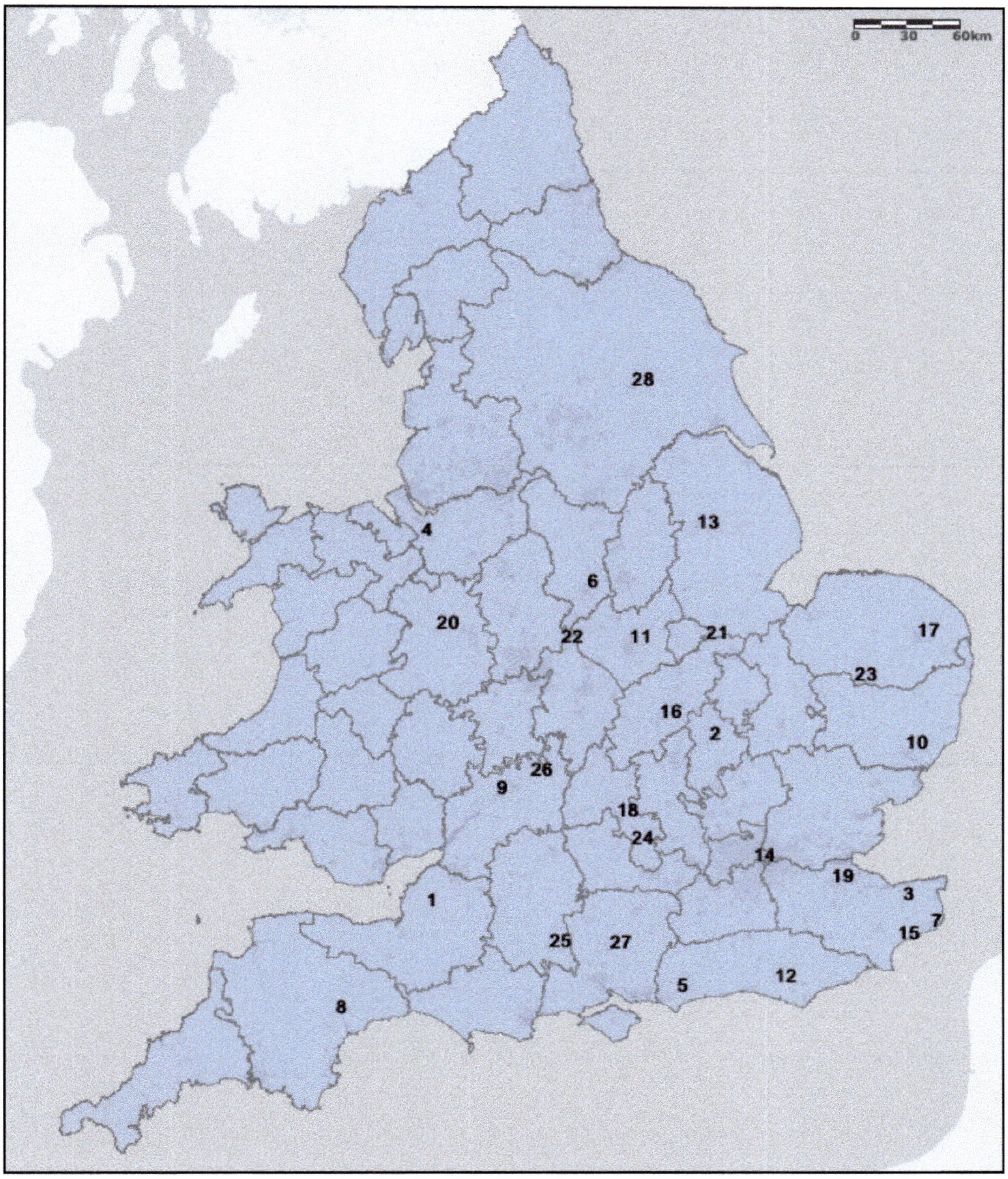

Map 1. Mints active in the reign of Edgar (from 973 to 975)

1. Axbridge
2. Bedford
3. Canterbury
4. Chester
5. Chichester
6. Derby
7. Dover
8. Exeter
9. Gloucester
10. Ipswich
11. Leicester
12. Lewes
13. Lincoln
14. London
15. Lympne

    Niwan (unknown)

16. Northampton
17. Norwich
18. Oxford
19. Rochester
20. Shrewsbury
21. Stamford
22. Tamworth
23. Thetford
24. Wallingford
25. Wilton
26. Winchcombe
27. Winchester
28. York

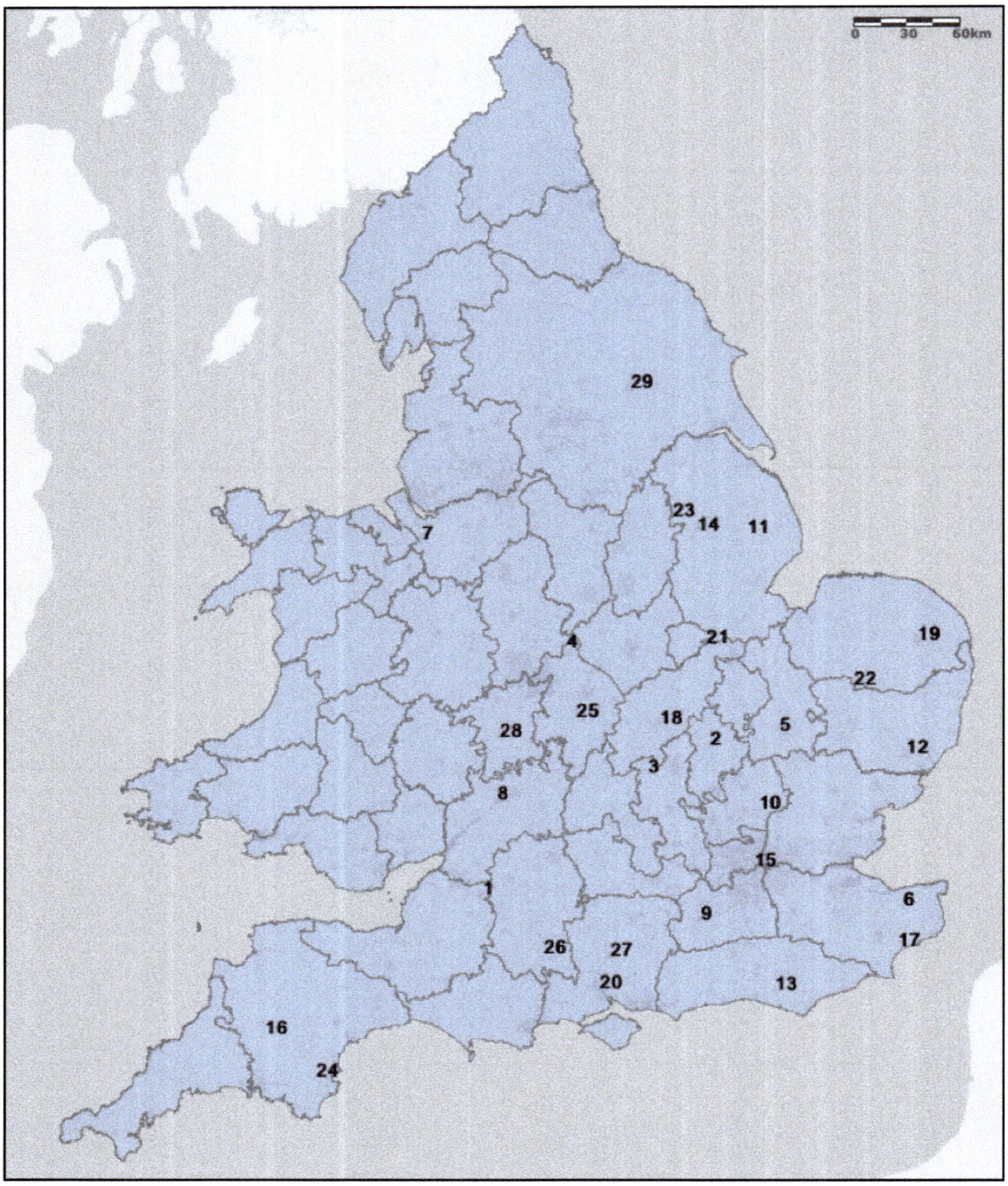

Map 2. Mints active in the reign of Edward the Martyr (975–978)

1. Bath
2. Bedford
3. Buckingham
4. Caistor
5. Cambridge
6. Canterbury
7. Chester
8. Gloucester
9. Guildford
10. Hertford
11. Horncastle
12. Ipswich
13. Lewes
14. Lincoln
15. London
16. Lydford
17. Lympne
18. Northampton
19. Norwich
20. Southampton
21. Stamford
22. Thetford
23. Torksey
24. Totnes
25. Warwick
26. Wilton
27. Winchester
28. Worcester
29. York

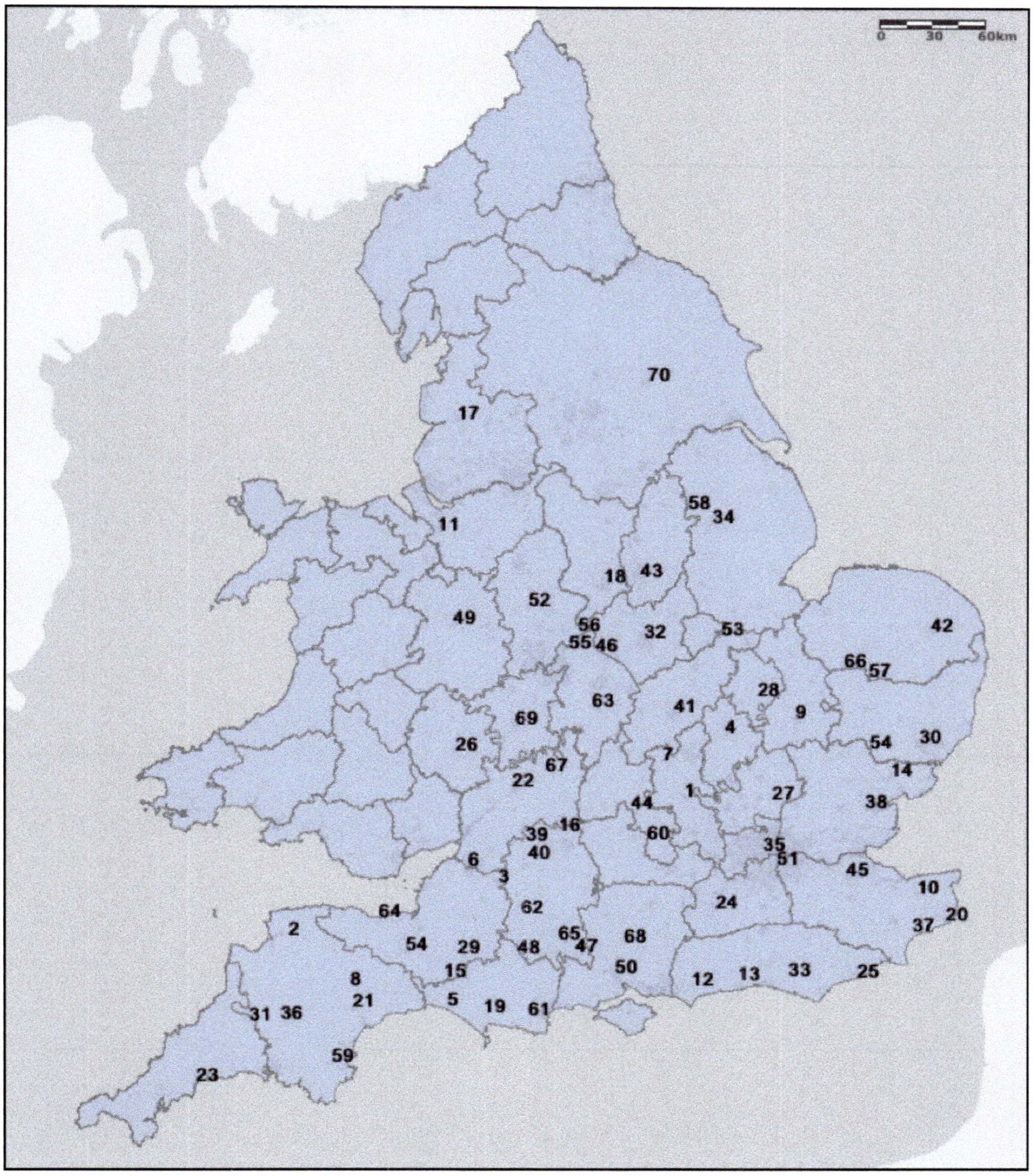

Map 3. Mints active in the reign of Æthelred II (978–1016)

1. Aylesbury
2. Barnstaple
3. Bath
4. Bedford
5. Bridport
6. Bristol
7. Buckingham
8. Cadbury
9. Cambridge
10. Canterbury
11. Chester
12. Chichester
13. Cissbury
14. Colchester
15. Crewkerne
16. Cricklade
17. Cuer
18. Derby
19. Dorchester
20. Dover
21. Exeter
22. Gloucester
23. Gothaburh
24. Guildford
25. Hastings
26. Hereford
27. Hertford
28. Huntingdon
29. Ilchester
30. Ipswich
31. Launceston
32. Leicester
33. Lewes
34. Lincoln
35. London
36. Lydford
37. Lympne
38. Maldon
39. Malmesbury
40. Milbourne Port
    Niwan (unknown)
41. Northampton
42. Norwich
43. Nottingham
44. Oxford
45. Rochester
46. Romney
47. Salisbury
48. Shaftesbury
49. Shrewsbury
50. Southampton
51. Southwark
52. Stafford
53. Stamford
54. Sudbury
55. Tamworth
56. Taunton
57. Thetford
58. Torksey
59. Totnes
60. Wallingford
61. Wareham
62. Warminster
63. Warwick
64. Watchet
65. Wilton
66. Wilton (EA)
67. Winchcombe
68. Winchester
69. Worcester
70. York

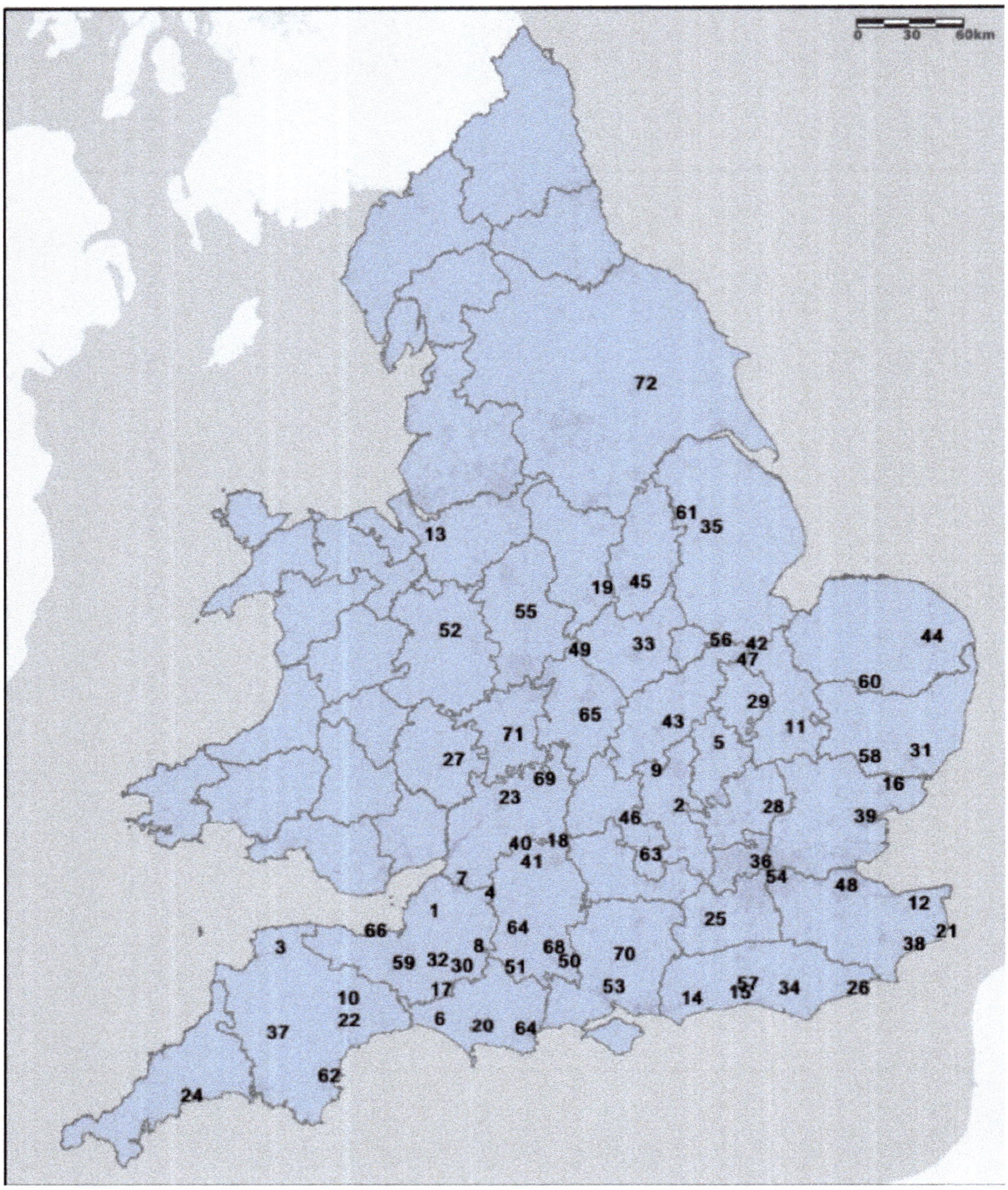

Map 4. Mints active in the reign of Cnut (1016–1035/6)

1. Axbridge
2. Aylesbury
3. Barnstaple
4. Bath
5. Bedford
6. Bridport
7. Bristol
8. Bruton
9. Buckingham
10. Cadbury
11. Cambridge
12. Canterbury
13. Chester
14. Chichester
15. Cissbury
16. Colchester
17. Crewkerne
18. Cricklade
19. Derby
20. Dorchester
21. Dover
22. Exeter
23. Gloucester
24. Gothaburh
25. Guildford
26. Hastings
27. Hereford
28. Hertford
29. Huntingdon
30. Ilchester
31. Ipswich
32. Langport
33. Leicester
34. Lewes
35. Lincoln
36. London
37. Lydford
38. Lympne
39. Maldon
40. Malmesbury
41. Milbourne Port
42. Newark
43. Northampton
44. Norwich
45. Nottingham
46. Oxford
47. Peterborough
48. Rochester
49. Romney
50. Salisbury
51. Shaftesbury
52. Shrewsbury
53. Southampton
54. Southwark
55. Stafford
56. Stamford
57. Steyning
58. Sudbury
59. Taunton
60. Thetford
61. Torksey
62. Totnes
63. Wallingford
64. Wareham
65. Warminster
66. Warwick
67. Watchet
68. Wilton
69. Winchcombe
70. Winchester
71. Worcester
72. York

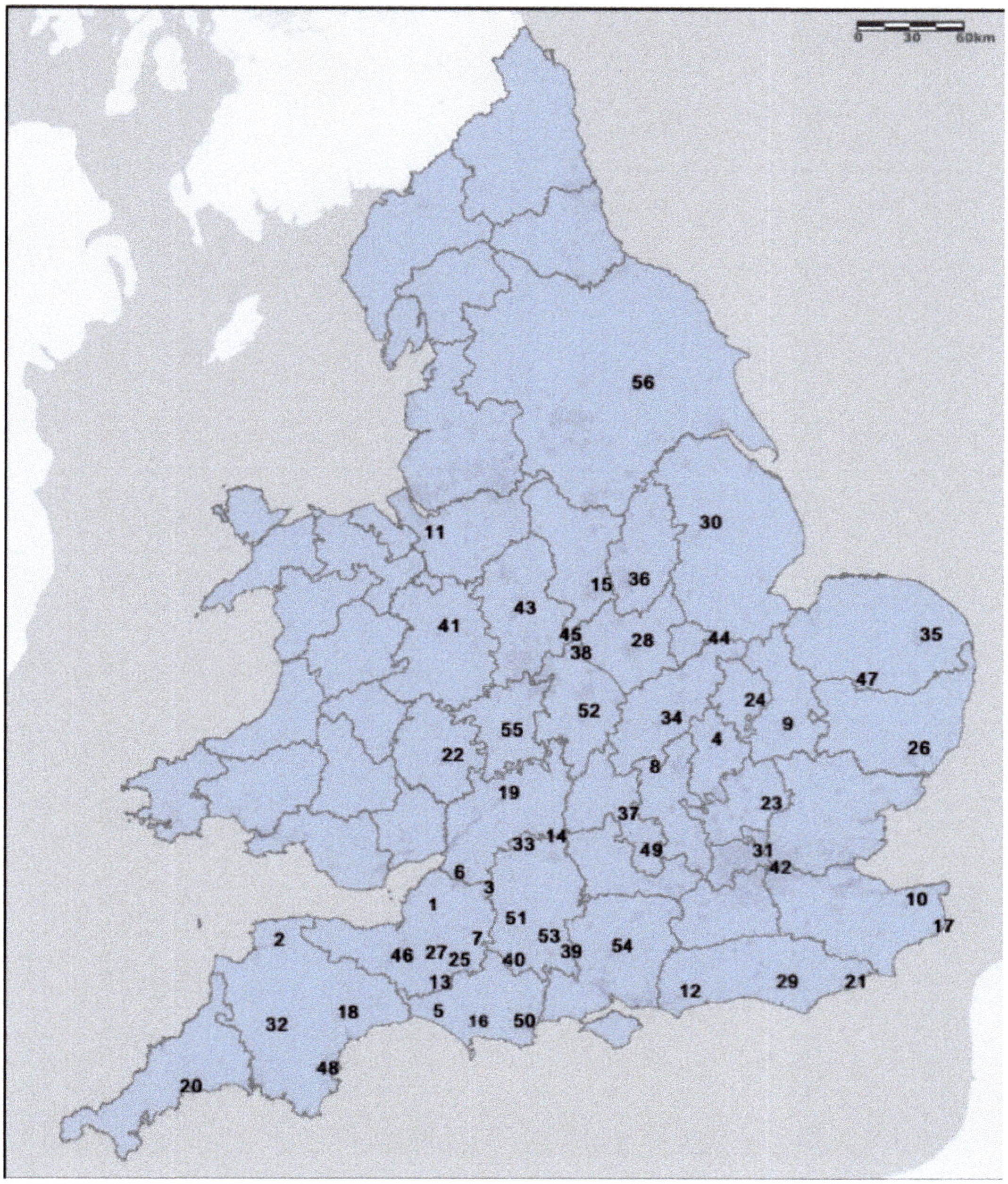

Map 5. Mints active in the reign of Harold I (1035–1040)

1. Axbridge
2. Barnstaple
3. Bath
4. Bedford
5. Bridport
6. Bristol
7. Bruton
8. Buckingham
9. Cambridge
10. Canterbury
11. Chester
12. Chichester
13. Crewkerne
14. Cricklade
15. Derby
16. Dorchester
17. Dover
18. Exeter
19. Gloucester
20. Gothaburh
21. Hastings
22. Hereford
23. Hertford
24. Huntingdon
25. Ilchester
26. Ipswich
27. Langport
28. Leicester
29. Lewes
30. Lincoln
31. London
32. Lydford
33. Malmesbury
34. Northampton
35. Norwich
36. Nottingham
37. Oxford
38. Romney
39. Salisbury
40. Shaftesbury
41. Shrewsbury
42. Southwark
43. Stafford
44. Stamford
45. Tamworth
46. Taunton
47. Thetford
48. Totnes
49. Wallingford
50. Wareham
51. Warminster
52. Warwick
53. Wilton
54. Winchester
55. Worcester
56. York

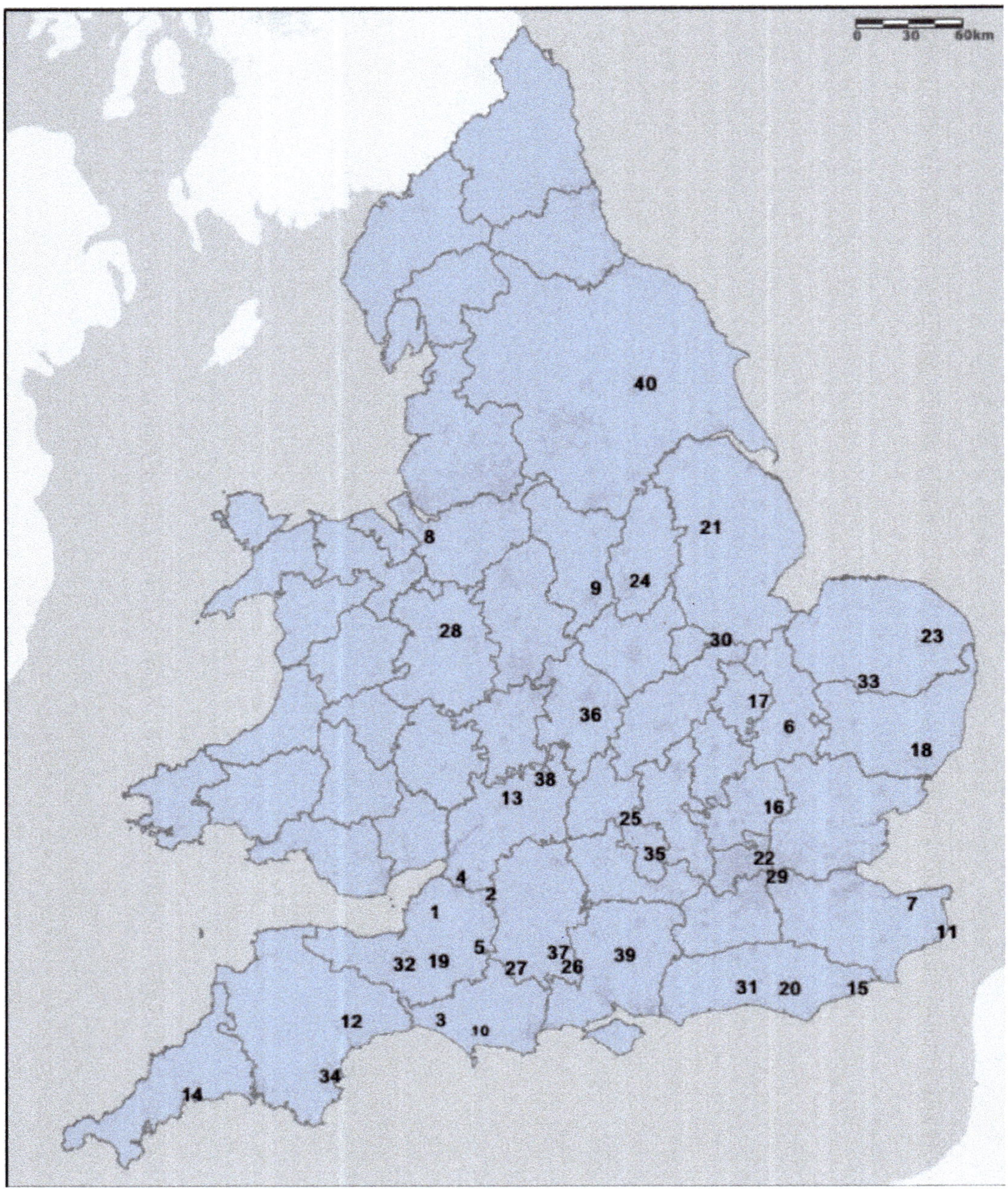

Map 6. Mints active in the reign of Harthacnut (1040–1042)

1. Axbridge
2. Bath
3. Bridport
4. Bristol
5. Bruton
6. Cambridge
7. Canterbury
8. Chester
9. Derby
10. Dorchester
11. Dover
12. Exeter
13. Gloucester
14. Gothaburh
15. Hastings
16. Hertford
17. Huntingdon
18. Ipswich
19. Langport
20. Lewes
21. Lincoln
22. London
23. Norwich
24. Nottingham
25. Oxford
26. Salisbury
27. Shaftesbury
28. Shrewsbury
29. Southwark
30. Stamford
31. Steyning
32. Taunton
33. Thetford
34. Totnes
35. Wallingford
36. Warwick
37. Wilton
38. Winchcombe
39. Winchester
40. York

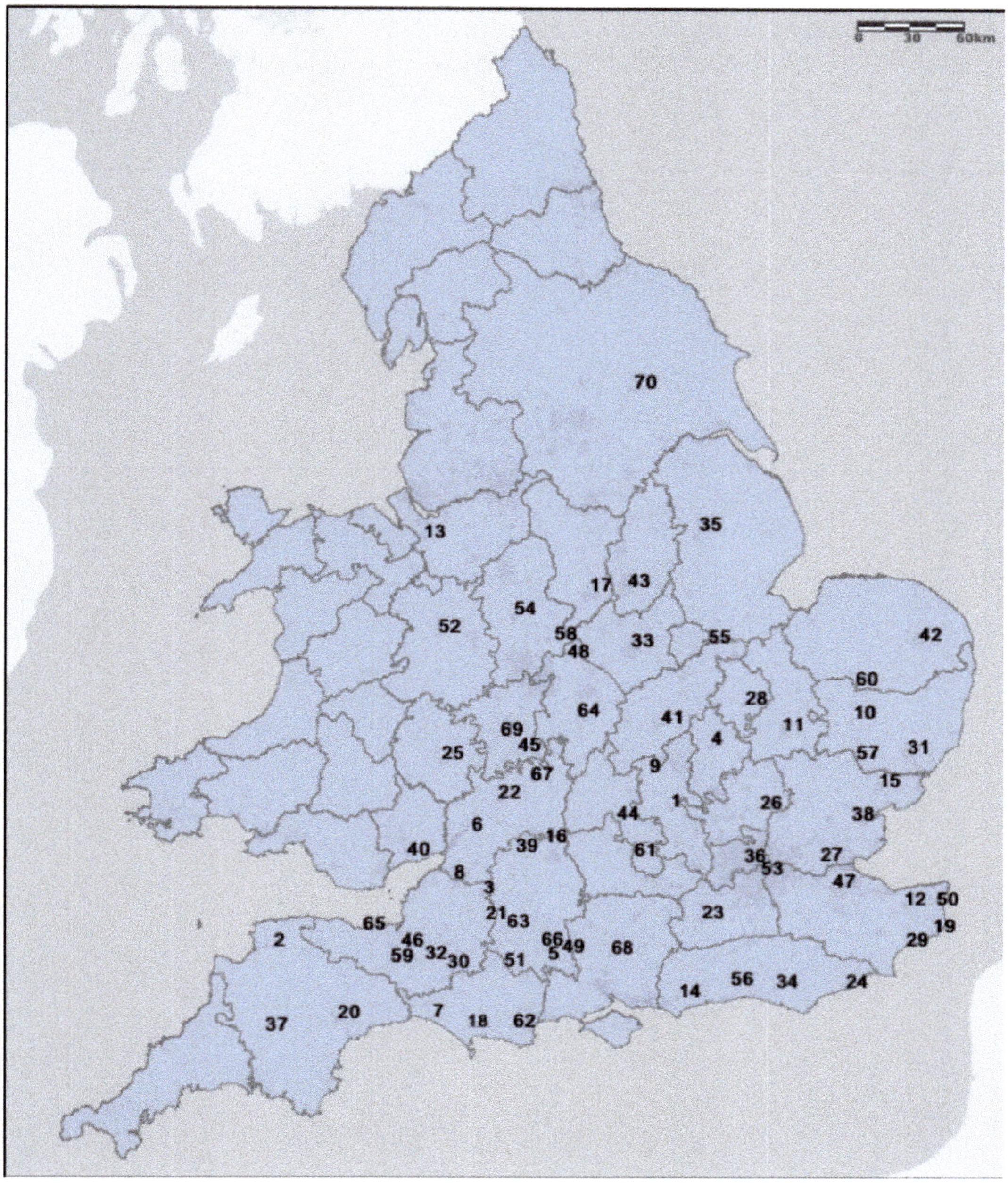

Map 7. Mints active in the reign of Edward the Confessor (1042–1066)

1. Aylesbury
2. Barnstaple
3. Bath
4. Bedford
5. Bedwin
6. Berkeley
7. Bridport
8. Bristol
9. Buckingham
10. Bury St Edmunds
11. Cambridge
12. Canterbury
13. Chester
14. Chichester
15. Colchester
16. Cricklade
17. Derby

Dernt (unknown)

18. Dorchester
19. Dover
20. Exeter
21. Frome
22. Gloucester
23. Guildford
24. Hastings
25. Hereford
26. Hertford
27. Horndon
28. Huntingdon
29. Hythe
30. Ilchester
31. Ipswich
32. Langport
33. Leicester
34. Lewes
35. Lincoln
36. London
37. Lydford
38. Maldon
39. Malmesbury
40. Newport
41. Northampton
42. Norwich
43. Nottingham
44. Oxford
45. Pershore
46. Petherton
47. Rochester
48. Romney
49. Salisbury
50. Sandwich
51. Shaftesbury
52. Shrewsbury
53. Southwark
54. Stafford
55. Stamford

Stes (unknown)

56. Steyning
57. Sudbury
58. Tamworth
59. Taunton
60. Thetford
61. Wallingford
62. Wareham
63. Warminster
64. Warwick
65. Watchet
66. Wilton
67. Winchcombe
68. Winchester
69. Worcester
70. York

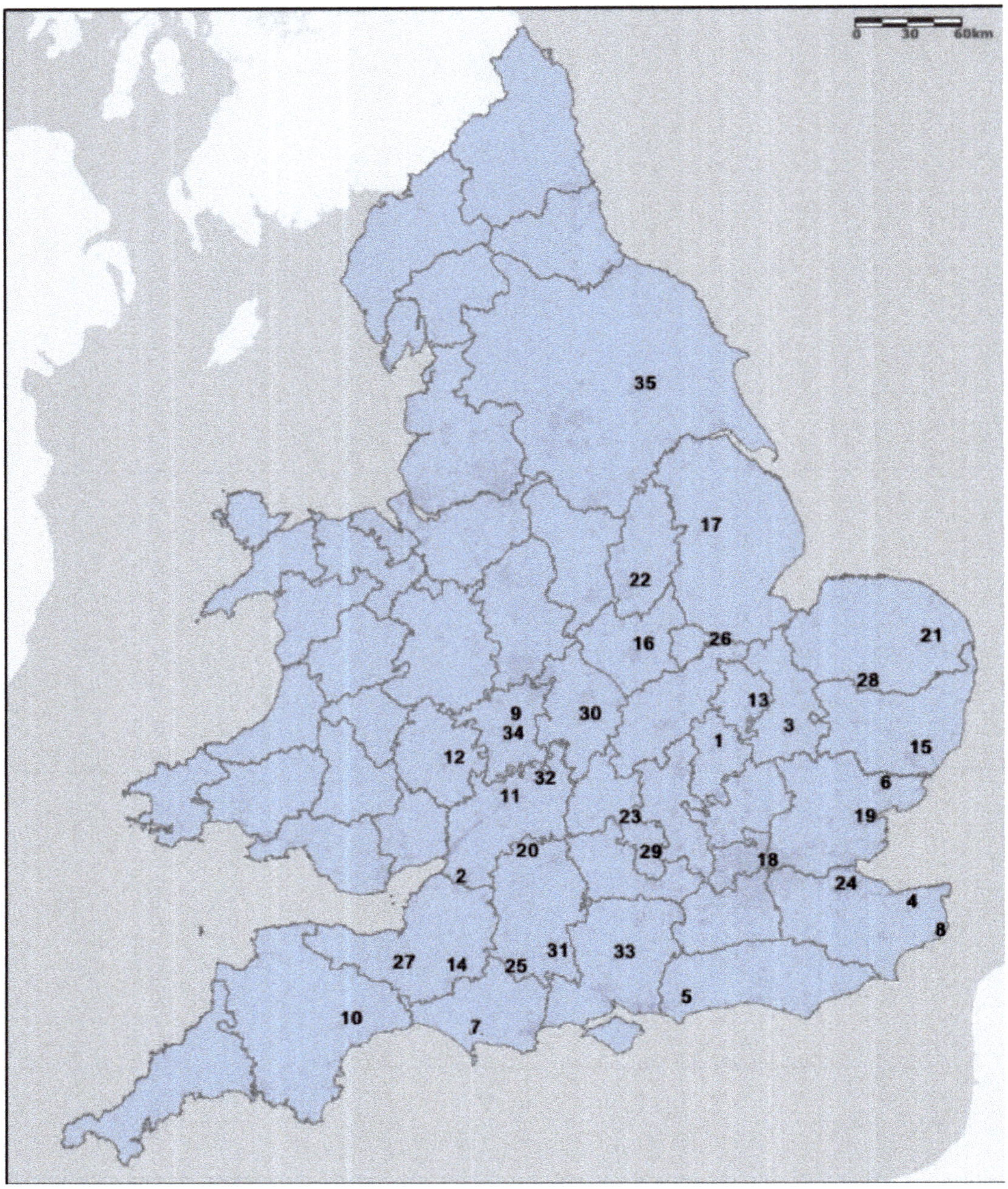

Map 8. Mints active in the reign of Harold II (1066)

1. Bedford
2. Bristol
3. Cambridge
4. Canterbury
5. Chichester
6. Colchester
7. Dorchester
8. Dover
9. Droitwich
10. Exeter
11. Gloucester
12. Hereford
13. Huntingdon
14. Ilchester
15. Ipswich
16. Leicester
17. Lincoln
18. London
19. Maldon
20. Malmesbury
21. Norwich
22. Nottingham
23. Oxford
24. Rochester
25. Shaftesbury
26. Stamford
27. Taunton
28. Thetford
29. Wallingford
30. Warwick
31. Wilton
32. Winchcombe
33. Winchester
34. Worcester
35. York

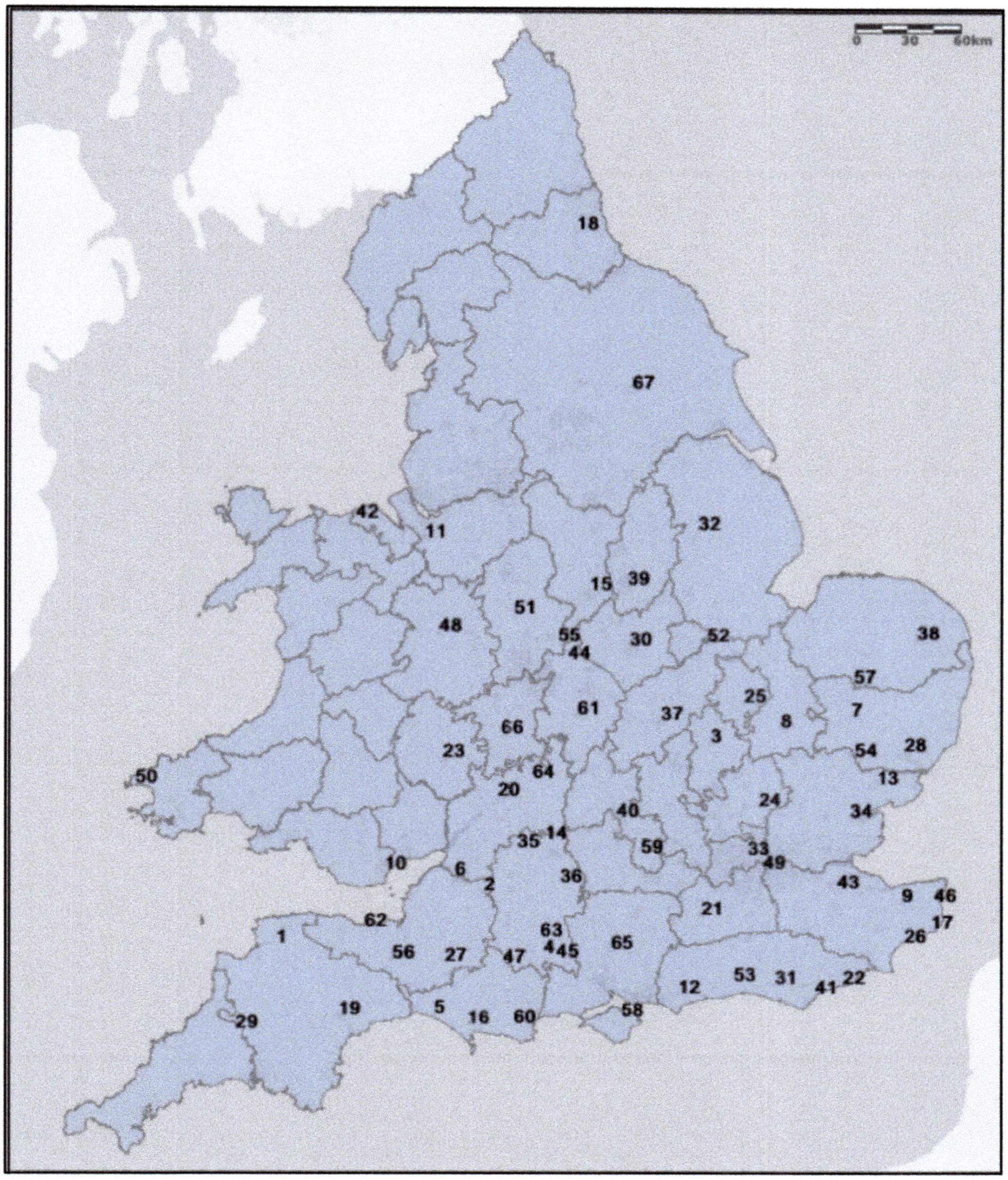

Map 9. Mints active in the reign of William I (1066–1087)

1.	Barnstaple	18.	Durham	35.	Maldon	52.	Stamford
2.	Bath	19.	Exeter	36.	Marlborough	53.	Steyning
3.	Bedford	20.	Gloucester	37.	Northampton	54.	Sudbury
4.	Bedwin	21.	Guildford	38.	Norwich	55.	Tamworth
5.	Bridport	22.	Hastings	39.	Nottingham	56.	Taunton
6.	Bristol	23.	Hereford	40.	Oxford	57.	Thetford
7.	Bury St Edmunds	24.	Hertford	41.	Pevensey	58.	Twynham
8.	Cambridge	25.	Huntingdon	42.	Rhuddlan	59.	Wallingford
9.	Canterbury	26.	Hythe	43.	Rochester	60.	Wareham
10.	Cardiff	27.	Ilchester	44.	Romney	61.	Warwick
11.	Chester	28.	Ipswich	45.	Salisbury	62.	Watchet
12.	Chichester	29.	Launceston	46.	Sandwich	63.	Wilton
13.	Colchester	30.	Leicester	47.	Shaftesbury	64.	Winchcombe
14.	Cricklade	31.	Lewes	48.	Shrewsbury	65.	Winchester
15.	Derby	32.	Lincoln	49.	Southwark	66.	Worcester
16.	Dorchester	33.	London	50.	St Davids	67.	York
17.	Dover	34.	Malmesbury	51.	Stafford		

Axbridge

Moneyer	Activity Range
Ælfsige	973–975
Ælfric	1017–1023
Hunewine	1017–1023
Goda	1023–1029
Leofwine	1029–1036
Leofric	1036–1038
Golda	1040–1042
Goldcyta	1040–1042
Leofwine	1040–1042

Aylesbury

Moneyer	Activity Range
Ælfgar	991–997
Leofstan	991–997
Ælf	1017–1023
Æthelwine	1017–1023
Edward	1017–1023
Leofwine	1044–1048
Wulfred	1053–1056
Wulfred	1059–1062

Barnstaple

Moneyer	Activity Range
Ælfhelm	979–985
Beorhtulf	979–985
Beorhtsige	979–1009
Bryhsige	985–1003
Ælfsige	991–1003
Huna	997–1009
Æthelric	1003–1009
Byrhsie	1009–1023
Beorhtsige	1017–1023
Ata	1017–1023
Ælfgar	1017–1036
Ælfgar	1038–1040
Ælfric	1044–1046
Æthelmær	1044–1046
Ælfric	1053–1062
Leofwine	1068–1070
Sæweard	1077–1080
Sæweard	1083–1086

Bath

Moneyer	Activity Range
Brihferth	975–978
Æthelsige	979–985
Æthelric	979–1029
Æthelsige	991–997
Wynstan	991–1003
Hildsige	991–1016
Eadstan	997–1003
Ælfric	997–1036
Ælfweald	1003–1029
Æthelstan	1003–1036
Ælfwine	1023–1036
Æthelwine	1029–1036
Ælfwig	1036–1038
Wædel	1036–1046
Æthelmær	1036–1053
Ælhær	1038–1040
Ægelmær	1040–1042
Leofwine	1040–1042
Ægelmær	1044–1046
Wædel	1048–1050
Ægelmær	1050–1053
Godric	1050–1062
Osmær	1053–1065
Urlwine	1059–1065
Osmær	1074–1077
Ægelmie	1083–1086
Æthelmær	1083–1086
Godsbrand	1083–1086
Osmær	1083–1086

Bedford

Moneyer	Activity Range
Grim	973–978
Baldric	975–979
Ælfstan	975–985
Bealdwulf	978–979
Byrnwine	978–979
Beorhtwine	979–985
Oswi	979–985
Oswig	991–997
Ælfstan	991–1003
Leofnoth	991–1003
Ælfwig	997–1003
Gunni	997–1003
Deorwine	997–1009

Bedford

Moneyer	Activity Range
Leofing	1009–1016
Godric	1009–1023
Leofwine	1009–1036
Æthelgeat	1017–1023
Godwine	1017–1023
Leofsige	1017–1023
Æthelman	1023–1040
Ægelman	1029–1036
Swet	1029–1036
Leofthegn	1036–1040
Ægelman	1038–1040
Leofwine	1038–1040
Swet	1038–1042
Ulfcetel	1042–1044
Æthelman	1042–1048
Godcild	1044–1046
Ulfcetel	1048–1050
Swet	1048–1053
Ælmon	1050–1053
Æthelman	1050–1053
Godwine	1050–1053
Wulfmær	1050–1053
Wulfwig	1050–1053
Ælfman	1050–1056
Sigod	1053–1056
Ulfcetel	1053–1056
Wulfwi	1053–1056
Godric	1056–1059
Swet	1056–1059
Godwine	1056–1062
Wulfwig	1056–1062
Wulfwi	1059–1059
Leofthegn	1059–1065
Sigod	1059–1066
Wulfwine	1062–1065
Beorhtric	1066–1066
Wulfwi	1066–1066
Wulfwig	1066–1066
Sibrand	1066–1070
Sigod	1068–1077
Beorht	1074–1077
Sibrand	1074–1077
Sibrand	1083–1086
Sigebrand	1083–1086

Bedwin

Moneyer	Activity Range
Cild	1044–1053
Cild	1059–1062
Cild	1065–1066
Cild	1066–1068

Berkeley

Moneyer	Activity Range
Edgar	1046–1048
Edgar	1053–1056

Bridport

Moneyer	Activity Range
Wine	979–985
Eadnoth	985–1003
Godric	991–997
Ælfweard	1009–1016
Ælfweald	1023–1029
Hwætman	1036–1038
Hwætman	1040–1042
Hwætman	1048–1050
Hwætman	1065–1066
Thatman	1074–1077
Ælfric	1083–1086
Beorhtwi	1083–1086
Beorhtwig	1083–1086
Beorhtwine	1083–1086

Bristol

Moneyer	Activity Range
Ælfweard	1009–1016
Ægelwine	1017–1023
Ælfwine	1017–1023
Æthelwine	1017–1023
Godman	1017–1023
Wulfwine	1017–1023
Ægelwine	1029–1036
Wulfstan	1029–1036
Æthelwine	1029–1038
Leofwine	1029–1040
Ælfweard	1036–1040
Sæwine	1036–1042
Wulfwine	1036–1042
Wulfnoth	1038–1040

Bristol

Moneyer	Activity Range
Æthelwine	1040–1042
Æthelstan	1040–1044
Ægelwine	1042–1042
Ælfwig	1042–1044
Ælfwine	1042–1044
Æthelweard	1042–1044
Ælfweard	1044–1053
Godwine	1050–1053
Æthelstan	1050–1059
Ælfric	1053–1056
Ælfwine	1056–1066
Ælfric	1059–1062
Godwine	1059–1065
Ceorl	1065–1068
Leofwine	1066–1068
Ceorl	1070–1072
Leofwine	1072–1080
Ceorl	1074–1077
Lifwine	1083–1086
Beorhtweard	1083–1086
Brunstan	1083–1086
Brwode	1083–1086
Colblac	1083–1086
Spegn	1083–1086

Bruton

Moneyer	Activity Range
Ælfwine	1017–1023
Ælfhelm	1017–1036
Godric	1036–1038
Godric	1040–1046

Buckingham

Moneyer	Activity Range
Tunulf	975–978
Sibwine	991–997
Tunulf	991–997
Ælfwig	997–1003
Ælfweard	1017–1023
Leofric	1017–1029
Beorhtwine	1036–1038
Leofwine	1038–1040
Leofwine	1046–1048
Leofwine	1050–1053

Buckingham

Moneyer	Activity Range
Theodred	1056–1059
Æthelstan	1059–1062

Bury St Edmunds

Moneyer	Activity Range
Morcere	1048–1056
Morcere	1059–1065
Godwine	1070–1072

Cadbury

Moneyer	Activity Range
Ælfwine	1009–1016
Goda	1009–1016
Winas	1009–1016
Wulfhelm	1009–1016
Ælfhelm	1017–1023

Caistor

Moneyer	Activity Range
Leofman	975–979

Cambridge

Moneyer	Activity Range
Hunstan	975–978
Ælfwine	978–997
Hunstan	979–985
Wilmund	979–985
Eadmund	991–997
Eadric	991–997
Godwine	991–997
Hunstan	991–997
Leofnoth	991–997
Sidewine	991–997
Oscytel	991–997
Wulfgar	991–997
Ælfric	991–1003
Eadwine	991–1003
Godric	997–1003
Wulfsige	997–1029
Cniht	1003–1023
Leofsige	1003–1029
Ælfric	1009–1016
Clern	1009–1016

Cambridge

Moneyer	Activity Range
Ælfwi	1009–1023
Ælfwig	1009–1023
Eadric	1017–1023
Godwine	1017–1023
Stængrim	1017–1023
Ada	1017–1029
Ornost	1017–1029
Ælfwine	1023–1029
Grim	1023–1029
Eadwine	1023–1036
Ælfwig	1029–1042
Eadwacer	1036–1038
Osgeat	1036–1038
Wulfwine	1036–1040
Ælfwi	1038–1040
Stircere	1038–1040
Eadwine	1040–1042
Godwine	1040–1042
Wulfmær	1040–1042
Godsunu	1040–1046
Eadstan	1044–1046
Eadweard	1044–1046
Eadstan	1048–1050
Eadweard	1048–1065
Ælfwine	1050–1053
Godsunu	1050–1053
Wulfwine	1050–1053
Ælfwig	1050–1059
Ælfwi	1053–1059
Godwine	1053–1059
Sæcoll	1056–1065
Sægolf	1059–1062
Wulfwig	1059–1062
Wulfwine	1059–1062
Godwine	1062–1065
Wibearn	1062–1065
Godlamb	1062–1066
Godwine	1066–1066
Beorhtric	1066–1066
Wulfwi	1066–1066
Godric	1066–1068
Othbeorn	1072–1074
Ægelmie	1074–1077
Alfcil	1083–1086
Ulfcytel	1083–1086

Canterbury

Moneyer	Activity Range
Boiga	973–975
Garwig	973–975
Wine	973–985
Ælfstan	975–978
Æthelstan	975–978
Boiga	978–991
Heahwulf	979–985
Leofing	979–997
Leofric	979–1009
Eadweald	979–1023
Leofstan	979–1023
Wulfwine	985–991
Goldwine	991–997
Dudda	991–997
Wulfwig	991–1003
Godwine	991–1016
Wulfwi	995–997
Ælfred	997–1003
Heahwulf	1003–1009
Godman	1003–1016
Godric	1003–1029
Ulf	1009–1016
Wulfstan	1009–1029
Ælfred	1009–1036
Leofnoth	1009–1040
Winred	1017–1023
Leofwine	1017–1038
Wynhere	1017–1038
Winedæg	1017–1038
Eadwine	1023–1029
Godman	1023–1029
Wulfwig	1023–1040
Godwine	1029–1036
Winred	1029–1036
Wulfwine	1029–1036
Ælfric	1029–1038
Beorhtræd	1029–1038
Leofwig	1029–1038
Leofing	1036–1038
Wulfric	1036–1038
Cetel	1036–1044
Ælfred	1036–1062
Gildewine	1036–1065
Leofstan	1038–1040
Wulfwine	1038–1040

Canterbury

Moneyer	Activity Range
Leofwine	1040–1042
Caldwine	1040–1042
Windei	1040–1042
Wulfwig Ubi	1040–1042
Manna	1042–1044
Wulfgeat	1044–1046
Leofstan	1044–1062
Rudcarl	1046–1048
Brunman	1046–1050
Man	1046–1056
Leofwine	1046–1065
Eadweard	1046–1068
Goldwine	1048–1050
Manna	1048–1066
Æthelræd	1050–1053
Thorstan	1050–1053
Wulfred	1050–1053
Wulfstan	1050–1056
Eadmær	1053–1056
Godwine	1053–1056
Wulfnoth	1053–1056
Wulfgeat	1053–1059
Stanherd	1059–1059
Ælfric	1059–1062
Æthelwine	1059–1062
Æceread	1059–1062
Wulfwine	1059–1062
Man	1059–1065
Ælfwine	1062–1065
Ædric	1062–1065
Wulfweard	1062–1065
Ælfweard	1062–1066
Sigered	1062–1066
Sired	1062–1066
Ælfwine	1066–1066
Eadwine	1066–1066
Man	1066–1066
Manna	1066–1068
Wulfred	1066–1068
Man	1068–1077
Goldwine	1070–1072
Wulfric	1072–1077
Manna	1074–1077
Ælfred	1074–1080
Godric	1080–1086

Canterbury

Moneyer	Activity Range
Ælfred	1083–1086
Beorhtweald	1083–1086
Burnoth	1083–1086
Pinedi	1083–1086
Simær	1083–1086
Wulfbold	1083–1086
Wulfric	1083–1086

Cardiff

Moneyer	Activity Range
Sveinn	1083–1086

Chester

Moneyer	Activity Range
Mælsuthain	973–978
Boiga	975–978
Ælfstan	975–985
Deorlaf	978–979
Æthelmod	979–985
Eadric	979–985
Leofman	979–985
Deorlaf	985–991
Wulflaf	991–991
Æthelmod	991–997
Boiga	991–997
Hringwulf	991–997
Sigewine	991–997
Eadric	991–1003
Ælfstan	991–1009
Elemod	995–997
Ælfsige	997–1003
Ælfwine	997–1003
Æthelnoth	997–1003
Oscytel	997–1003
Othulf	997–1003
Swegen	997–1023
Ælfnoth	997–1036
Æthelwine	997–1038
Leofwine	997–1044
Leofnoth	1003–1029
Gunleof	1003–1036
Thorald	1009–1016
Æthelnoth	1009–1023
Ealhsige	1009–1023

Chester

Moneyer	Activity Range
Swarting	1009–1029
Ælfsige	1009–1042
Ælfsi	1017–1023
Ælfweard	1017–1023
Æthelric	1017–1023
Elewine	1017–1023
Godric	1017–1023
Leofa	1017–1023
Leofman	1017–1023
Lific	1017–1023
Macsuthan	1017–1023
Thormod	1017–1023
Godwine	1017–1029
Leofing	1017–1029
Leofwig	1017–1029
Trotan	1017–1029
Leofsige	1017–1036
Ceolnoth	1017–1036
Croc	1017–1042
Snell	1017–1042
Wulfnoth	1023–1029
Æthelnoth	1029–1036
Elewine	1036–1038
Swegen	1036–1038
Leofwig	1036–1040
Swarting	1036–1040
Gillacrist	1036–1042
Leofnoth	1036–1044
Wulfnoth	1038–1040
Colbeinn	1040–1042
Fargrim	1040–1042
Leofing	1040–1042
Bruning	1040–1066
Colthegn	1042–1044
Leofwi	1042–1044
Leofwig	1042–1044
Arngrim	1042–1044
Croc	1044–1046
Fargrim	1044–1046
Colbrand	1044–1059
Ælfsige	1044–1062
Ælfsic	1046–1048
Leofnoth	1046–1048
Ælfwine	1048–1050
Brun	1048–1050

Chester

Moneyer	Activity Range
Leofwine	1048–1053
Huscarl	1048–1066
Ælfsie	1050–1053
Fargrim	1050–1053
Ealhsige	1050–1062
Leofnoth	1050–1066
Ælfgar	1053–1056
Dunstan	1053–1056
Swartcol	1053–1062
Sprot	1056–1059
Wigal	1056–1059
Duninc	1056–1062
Æthelwine	1059–1062
Ordric	1059–1062
Ælfsi	1059–1066
Ælfsige	1065–1066
Ealhsige	1065–1066
Thrond	1065–1066
Ælfsi	1068–1070
Ælfweard	1068–1070
Frithegist	1068–1070
Ælfsi	1083–1086
Lifinc	1083–1086
Lifwine	1083–1086
Sunolf	1083–1086
Unnulf	1083–1086

Chichester

Moneyer	Activity Range
Flodwin	973–975
Heawulf	979–985
Wunstan	985–991
Ælfwig	991–997
Æthelstan	991–997
Ælfwine	991–1003
Æthelhelm	991–1009
Eadnoth	995–1003
Cynna	997–1003
Æthelm	997–1023
Heawulf	1003–1009
Ælfwine	1009–1016
Dunstan	1009–1016
Beorhtnoth	1017–1023

Chichester

Moneyer	Activity Range
Wulfnoth	1017–1023
Æthelhelm	1017–1036
Leofwine	1017–1038
Leofric	1017–1042
Leofwig	1023–1029
Ægelm	1023–1036
Ælfric	1029–1040
Goda	1038–1040
Godric	1038–1040
Ælfwine	1044–1046
Ælfwine	1048–1066
Æthelwine	1050–1053
Godwine	1053–1062
Wulfric	1053–1066
Godwine	1066–1066
Brunman	1066–1068
Brunman	1070–1072
Godwine	1074–1080
Brunman	1074–1086
Edwine	1083–1086

Cissbury

Moneyer	Activity Range
Ceolnoth	991–997
Ceolnoth	1009–1016
Godwine	1009–1016
Leofwine	1017–1023

Colchester

Moneyer	Activity Range
Ælfwine	991–997
Beorhthelm	991–997
Eadwig	991–997
Godwine	991–997
Leofred	991–997
Manwine	991–997
Sweting	991–997
Toca	991–997
Wulfnoth	991–997
Wulfric	991–997
Wulfwine	991–1003
Eadsige	991–1009
Sidwine	995–997
Eadmund	997–1003

Colchester

Moneyer	Activity Range
Godric	997–1003
Leofweald	997–1003
Leofwig	997–1003
Eadsige	1003–1009
Elewine	1009–1016
Wulfred	1009–1016
Eadwine	1009–1023
Godric	1009–1040
Brunman	1017–1023
Ælfwine	1017–1029
Wulfwine	1017–1042
Leofwine	1029–1036
Standre	1044–1046
Brunhuse	1044–1048
Leofweard	1044–1048
Stanmær	1044–1056
Ælfwine	1046–1048
Wulfwine	1046–1048
Beorhtric	1046–1059
Brunnus	1050–1053
Brunhuse	1050–1056
Leofweard	1050–1056
Deorman	1053–1056
Wulfwine	1053–1066
Deorman	1059–1062
Godwine	1059–1062
Goldman	1059–1062
Brunhuse	1059–1065
Beorhtric	1062–1065
Beorhtric	1066–1066
Goldman	1066–1066
Wulfwi	1066–1066
Wulfwig	1066–1066
Goldstan	1066–1070
Beorhtric	1068–1070
Druman	1074–1077
Wulfwine	1074–1077
Dorman	1077–1080
Ælfsi	1083–1086
Dirman	1083–1086
Wulfric	1083–1086
Wulfwine	1083–1086
Wulfweard	1083–1086

Crewkerne

Moneyer	Activity Range
Winas	997–1003
Winas	1017–1023
Beorhtwig	1029–1036
Winas	1029–1036
Beorhtric	1036–1038

Cricklade

Moneyer	Activity Range
Æthelstan	979–985
Goda	979–985
Æthelwine	995–1003
Leofgod	997–1003
Beorhtmær	1003–1009
Æthelsige	1003–1016
Ælfwine	1009–1036
Godman	1017–1023
Toca	1017–1023
Godwine	1017–1029
Æthelwine	1017–1042
Ægelwine	1023–1029
Leofing	1029–1036
Wulfheah	1029–1036
Ælfwine	1038–1040
Ælfwine	1042–1046
Ægelwi	1046–1048
Ægelwine	1050–1056
Leofred	1053–1062
Ægelwi	1056–1059
Æthelwig	1056–1059
Ægelwine	1062–1065
Leofred	1065–1066
Leofred	1068–1070
Leofred	1072–1077
Wulfstan	1074–1077
Wulfstan	1080–1083
Ælfwine	1083–1086

Cuer

Moneyer	Activity Range
Eadstan	979–985

Derby

Moneyer	Activity Range
Osulf	973–985
Gunner	978–985
Wulfstan	979–985
Wulfstan	991–1009
Godwine Wulfsige	997–1003 997–1003
Blacman	1003–1009
Ælfcetel	1003–1016
Oscar	1009–1016
Wulfsige	1009–1016
Blacman	1017–1023
Osbern	1017–1023
Swerting	1023–1042
Blacman	1036–1038
Wulfheah	1036–1038
Godric	1038–1042
Wulfheah	1040–1044
Blacman	1042–1044
Froma	1044–1046
Godric	1044–1046
Spatic	1046–1048
Blacman	1048–1050
Froma	1048–1062
Leofwine	1050–1053
Swerting	1050–1053
Dunning	1056–1066
Leofwine	1059–1065
Colbeinn	1062–1065
Colrin	1062–1065
Froma	1065–1066
Forni	1066–1068
Colbein	1068–1070
Godwine	1068–1070
Godwine	1083–1086
Lifwine	1083–1086

Dernt

Moneyer	Activity Range
Wulfgar	1048–1050
Wulfsige	1059–1062

Dorchester

Moneyer	Activity Range
Alfred	979–985
Wulfnoth	991–1016
Wulfsige	1017–1023
Swet	1017–1036
Æthelric	1036–1038
Hwætman	1036–1042
Godwine	1038–1042
Ægelric	1040–1042
Blacman	1042–1044
Hwateman	1050–1053
Blacman	1053–1056
Blacman	1059–1065
Blacman	1066–1066
Ottarr	1070–1072
Godwin	1074–1077
Oter	1074–1086
Ottarr	1077–1080
Ottarr	1083–1086

Dover

Moneyer	Activity Range
Leofgar	973–975
Osfrith	979–991
Cyneric	991–997
Leofwine	991–997
Godwine	995–1003
Eadsige	997–1003
Wulfstan	997–1003
Leofhyse	997–1009
Cynesige	997–1016
Manning	1003–1023
Godman	1009–1023
Beorhtmær	1009–1023
Leofstan	1017–1023
Wulfsi	1017–1023
Eadsige	1017–1038
Leofwine	1017–1038
Swertafe	1023–1029
Cynesige	1023–1036
Etsige	1023–1036
Ælfstan	1029–1036
Ælfwine	1029–1036
Eadwig	1029–1036
Leofric	1029–1036
Boiga	1029–1042

Dover

Moneyer	Activity Range
Eadwine	1029–1042
Cynestan	1036–1044
Eadsige	1040–1042
Leofwine	1040–1042
Boiga	1044–1046
Eadwine	1044–1046
Etsige	1046–1048
Cynestan	1046–1059
Wynstan	1048–1050
Godwine	1053–1062
Ceolwig	1053–1066
Manwine	1059–1066
Cynestan	1062–1065
Wulfweard	1062–1066
Cynestan	1066–1066
Manwine	1066–1068
Brunman	1070–1072
Manwine	1072–1077
Brunman	1074–1077
Cynestan	1080–1083
Leofric	1080–1086
Eadweard	1083–1086
Godwine	1083–1086
Lifric	1083–1086
Lifwine	1083–1086
Lulfric	1083–1086
Goldwine	1083–1086

Droitwich

Moneyer	Activity Range
Godric	1066–1066
Heathwulf	1066–1066

Durham

Moneyer	Activity Range
Cuthbeorht	1083–1086

Exeter

Moneyer	Activity Range
Ælfstan	973–975
Iohan	973–978
Beorhtfrith	979–985
Byrhfrith	979–985

Exeter

Moneyer	Activity Range
Godwine	979–985
Brun	979–985
Tuna	979–985
Ælfstan	979–997
Beorhtsige	979–997
Luda	979–997
Ælfnoth	979–1016
Byrhsige	985–991
Leofsunu	985–991
Beorhtstan	985–997
Leofric	985–997
Goda	985–1029
Byrhstan	991–997
Eadwine	991–997
Hunwine	991–997
Cetel	991–997
Tuna	991–997
Eadric	991–1003
Ælfric	991–1009
Byrhred	995–997
Wynstan	995–997
Beorhtfrith	996–1003
Beorhtric	997–1003
Byrhtric	997–1003
God	997–1003
Mangod	997–1003
Manna	997–1003
Dunstan	997–1003
Wynsige	997–1003
Man	997–1009
Carla	997–1023
Wulfsige	997–1023
Ælfmær	1003–1009
Eadwine	1003–1009
Dudel	1003–1009
Beorhtstan	1009–1016
Byrhstan	1009–1016
Eadstan	1009–1016
God	1009–1016
Æthelstan	1009–1016
Eatstan	1009–1016
Sæwine	1009–1016
Isegod	1009–1023
Thorgod	1009–1023
Eadmær	1009–1029

Exeter

Moneyer	Activity Range
Godwine	1017–1023
Hunwine	1017–1023
Wine	1017–1023
Wulfric	1017–1023
Wulfsie	1017–1023
Man	1017–1029
Wulfstan	1017–1036
Eadsige	1017–1038
Ælfstan	1023–1029
Dodda	1023–1029
Godberht	1023–1029
Leofwine	1023–1029
Mana	1023–1029
Ealdbeard	1023–1029
Sæwine	1023–1029
Wulfweard	1023–1029
Ælfwine	1023–1036
Scule	1023–1036
Ælfric	1029–1036
Eadsige Ware	1029–1036
Eadwine	1029–1036
Huna	1029–1036
Hunman	1029–1038
Thegnwine	1029–1038
Carla	1036–1038
Hærra	1036–1038
Eadmær	1036–1042
Manleof	1036–1042
Wulfnoth	1036–1042
Leofwine	1038–1046
Ælfstan	1040–1042
Carla	1040–1042
Dodda	1040–1042
Eadwine	1040–1042
Godwine	1040–1042
Hærra	1040–1042
Etsige	1040–1042
Thegnwine	1040–1042
Ifing	1042–1044
Wulfnoth	1042–1044
Eadmær	1044–1046
Ælfwine	1044–1048
Leofing	1046–1048
Wulfmær	1046–1062
Ælfric	1048–1062

Exeter

Moneyer	Activity Range
Eadsige	1050–1053
Eadwig	1050–1053
Hunwine	1050–1053
Sæwulf	1050–1053
Sæwine	1050–1059
Leofing	1053–1065
Leofwine	1059–1062
Wicing	1059–1062
Sæwine	1062–1066
Wulfnoth	1065–1066
Wulfwine	1065–1066
Beorhtric	1066–1066
Leofing	1066–1066
Leofwig	1066–1066
Leofwine	1066–1068
Ælfwine	1068–1072
Spotinc	1070–1074
Sigewine	1072–1074
Wulfwine	1072–1080
Ælfwine	1074–1077
Sæweard	1074–1077
Sæwine	1074–1086
Esmær	1077–1080
Simær	1080–1086
Lifwine	1083–1086

Frome

Moneyer	Activity Range
Beorhtwine	1046–1050

Gloucester

Moneyer	Activity Range
Æthelstan	973–975
Wynsige	973–975
Beorhtstan	975–978
Leofsige	979–991
Wihtsige	985–1003
Godwine	991–1029
Leofsige	997–1029
Sigered	1009–1036
Bolla	1017–1029
Sired	1017–1036
Godric	1017–1042
Leofnoth	1023–1042

Gloucester

Moneyer	Activity Range
Ægelric	1029–1036
Wulfnoth	1029–1038
Æthelric	1029–1042
Wulfred	1036–1038
Ælfsige	1036–1040
Æthelmær	1038–1040
Æleric	1038–1042
Wulfweard	1038–1042
Æthelwulf	1040–1042
Wulfheard	1040–1042
Ælfsige	1042–1044
Wulfwig	1042–1046
Godric	1044–1046
Wulfweard	1044–1046
Ælfsige	1046–1048
Æthelric	1046–1053
Wulfwig	1048–1050
Æwulf	1048–1053
Godric	1048–1056
Leofnoth	1048–1059
Ægelric	1050–1053
Ælfric	1050–1053
Ælfsige	1050–1062
Wulfweard	1050–1062
Æleric	1053–1056
Wulfred	1053–1056
Wulfgæt	1053–1062
Godwine	1056–1059
Eadwig	1056–1059
Ordric	1056–1059
Sigelac	1056–1059
Silac	1056–1059
Æthelric	1056–1062
Leofwine	1056–1065
Seolcwine	1056–1065
Ælfsi	1059–1062
Guolcwine	1059–1062
Beorhtnoth	1059–1065
Sigelac	1062–1066
Silac	1062–1066
Ælfsige	1065–1066
Seolcwine	1066–1066
Wulfgæt	1066–1066
Ordric	1066–1070
Leofwine	1070–1072

Gloucester

Moneyer	Activity Range
Wulfgæt	1070–1072
Leofwine	1074–1077
Beorhtnoth	1083–1086
Silac	1083–1086
Silacwine	1083–1086
Wulfgæt	1083–1086

Gothaburh

Moneyer	Activity Range
Wulfmær	997–1009
Goda	1009–1016
Carla	1017–1023
Wulfmær	1017–1023
Leofmær	1036–1042
Ælfweard	1040–1042

Guildford

Moneyer	Activity Range
Ælfweard	975–978
Leofweald	991–1003
Duncild	997–1003
Dunstan	997–1003
Smeawine	1017–1023
Ælfweald	1029–1036
Blacman	1029–1040
Blacman	1050–1062
Ælfric	1059–1065
Godwine	1062–1065
Leofweald	1065–1066
Seric	1074–1077
Seric	1083–1086

Hastings

Moneyer	Activity Range
Eadstan	991–997
Lyua	997–1003
Leofa	997–1009
Eadsige	1003–1009
Æthelsige	1017–1029
Ælfweard	1017–1042
Eadsige	1023–1029
Etsige	1023–1029
Ælfwine	1029–1036

Hastings

Moneyer	Activity Range
Wulfnoth	1029–1036
Ælfred	1029–1038
Brid	1029–1040
Eadwine	1036–1038
Leofing	1038–1040
Leofwine	1040–1042
Brid	1042–1062
Leofwine	1046–1048
Leofwine	1050–1053
Dunning	1053–1066
Wulfric	1056–1062
Theodred	1059–1066
Colswegen	1062–1068
Kolsveinn	1066–1068
Dunic	1066–1068
Diodred	1066–1068
Dunic	1074–1077
Dunic	1083–1086
Cipinc	1083–1086

Hereford

Moneyer	Activity Range
Ælfstan	979–985
Godman	979–985
Ælfgeat	991–1003
Beorhtstan	991–1003
Leofgar	991–1009
Byrhstan	995–1003
Æthelwi	997–1003
Æthelwig	997–1003
Dilion	997–1003
Eadric	1009–1016
Leofmær	1009–1016
Æthelwig	1009–1038
Leofgar	1017–1029
Eadstan	1017–1036
Wulfsige	1017–1042
Ordric	1017–1046
Etstan	1023–1029
Elewig	1023–1038
Leofnoth	1029–1044
Earnwig	1038–1042
Wulfsige	1044–1046
Wulfstan	1044–1048
Eielric	1046–1048

Hereford

Moneyer	Activity Range
Rædulf	1046–1048
Wulfwi	1046–1048
Eadwig	1048–1056
Leofnoth	1050–1062
Æthelstan	1053–1056
Wulfwine	1053–1056
Ægelric	1056–1059
Eadric	1056–1059
Ælfwig	1056–1062
Ælfric	1059–1062
Eadwi	1059–1062
Earnwig	1059–1062
Ælfwi	1059–1065
Eadric	1065–1066
Earnwig	1065–1066
Ælfwi	1066–1066
Æthelric	1066–1068
Beorhtric	1068–1070
Æcepi	1070–1072
Wulfwine	1070–1072
Beorhtric	1072–1074
Leofstan	1072–1074
Hethwi	1074–1077
Ægelwine	1083–1086
Ælfwi	1083–1086
Æthelwine	1083–1086
Lifstan	1083–1086
Ordwi	1083–1086

Hertford

Moneyer	Activity Range
Wulfmær	975–978
Wulfmær	979–985
Eadwig	991–997
Æthelweard	991–997
Beorhtlaf	991–997
Boiga	991–997
Burging	991–997
Wulfnoth	991–997
Wulfric	991–997
Eadwi	995–997
Leofing	995–997
Beornulf	995–997
Godric	997–1003
Wulfric	1003–1023

Hertford

Moneyer	Activity Range
Man	1009–1016
Leofing	1017–1023
Leofwine	1017–1036
Deorsige	1017–1040
Leofric	1023–1040
Leofing	1029–1036
Godman	1038–1040
Leofred	1040–1042
Deorsige	1044–1046
Sæmær	1044–1046
Wulfric	1044–1046
Godman	1044–1048
Godwine	1044–1048
Ælfwine	1046–1048
Goldwine	1046–1048
Leofing	1048–1050
Pidred	1048–1050
Theodred	1048–1050
Wulfric	1048–1050
Wilgrip	1050–1056
Wulfric	1053–1056
Sæmær	1056–1062
Godwine	1059–1065
Wilgrip	1059–1066
Wulfric	1062–1066
Semær	1083–1086
Theodric	1083–1086

Horncastle

Moneyer	Activity Range
Æthelhelm	975–978

Horndon

Moneyer	Activity Range
Dudinc	1056–1059

Huntingdon

Moneyer	Activity Range
Ælfric	979–985
Wulfgar	979–985
Leofric	991–997
Ælfric	991–1003
Osgod	995–1009

Huntingdon

Moneyer	Activity Range
Leofn	997–1003
Eadwine	1003–1009
Æthelstan	1003–1023
Sæwine	1003–1023
Ælfnoth	1009–1016
Godric	1017–1023
Farthegn	1017–1023
Eadnoth	1017–1029
Godleof	1017–1029
Steordine	1023–1029
Winsige	1023–1029
Ælfgar	1029–1036
Ada	1029–1036
Wulfwine	1029–1046
Wulfwi	1038–1040
Ælfwine	1040–1042
Wulfstan	1040–1042
Wulfwig	1044–1046
Ælfwine	1046–1053
Ulfcetel	1048–1050
Godric	1050–1056
Godwine	1053–1065
Godric	1059–1062
Leofwine	1059–1062
Godwine	1066–1066
Godric	1066–1070
Godwine	1070–1072
Godric	1072–1074
Godwine	1077–1080
Ælfwine	1083–1086

Hythe

Moneyer	Activity Range
Goldwine	1059–1062
Edred	1083–1086

Ilchester

Moneyer	Activity Range
Goda	979–985
Ælfsige	979–991
God	979–1003
Wulfhelm	985–997
Hunewine	991–997
Leofric	991–997

Ilchester

Moneyer	Activity Range
Goda	991–1003
Leofsige	991–1009
Ælfric	997–1003
Thorulf	997–1003
Winas	1003–1009
Ælfsige	1017–1023
Æthelmær	1017–1023
Godwine	1017–1023
Oswig	1017–1023
Wulfhelm	1017–1023
Ælfwine	1017–1029
Æthelwig	1017–1038
Ælfnoth	1023–1029
Ælfwine Mus	1023–1029
Ægelwig	1029–1036
Godric	1029–1036
Cæfel	1029–1036
Æthelwine	1036–1038
Godric	1038–1042
Dunbeard	1040–1044
Osward	1050–1053
Godric	1056–1062
Ægelwine	1062–1065
Æthelwine	1062–1068
Ægelwine	1066–1066
Ælfwine	1066–1068
Pixsi	1070–1072
Æthelwine	1072–1077
Ægelwine	1072–1077
Godwine	1074–1077
Ælfweard	1077–1080
Pixsi	1077–1080
Wihtsige	1077–1080
Ælfweard	1083–1086
Ælfwine	1083–1086
Æthelweard	1083–1086
God	1083–1086

Ipswich

Moneyer	Activity Range
Leofric	973–975
Wilebeart	975–978
Branting	979–985
Leofman	979–985
Leofric	979–985

Ipswich

Moneyer	Activity Range
Osulf	979–985
Rodbert	979–985
Waldfrith	979–985
Wilebeart	979–985
Lytelman	979–1003
Godric	991–997
Godwine	991–997
Leofstan	991–997
Leofsige	991–1023
Æthelbeorht	1003–1009
Godric	1003–1009
Erlewin	1003–1009
Sigeweald	1009–1016
Oda	1009–1023
Leofing	1009–1048
Branting	1017–1023
Leofman	1017–1023
Leofric	1017–1023
Folcard	1017–1023
Eadric	1017–1029
Æthelbeorht	1017–1036
Widfara	1036–1040
Ælfbeorht	1038–1040
Æthelbeorht	1038–1040
Leofric	1040–1042
Leofstan	1040–1046
Bruning	1044–1046
Eadwig	1048–1050
Bruning	1048–1056
Wulfsige	1048–1056
Leofing	1050–1053
Leofweald	1053–1056
Brunman	1056–1066
Bruning	1059–1065
Leofweald	1059–1065
Beorhtric	1059–1065
Ælfwine	1062–1066
Leofstan	1066–1066
Ægelbeorht	1068–1070
Leofstan	1068–1070
Wulfwine	1068–1070
Æthelbeorht	1068–1074
Ægelbeorht	1072–1074
Wulfweard	1074–1077
Leofstan	1074–1080

Ipswich

Moneyer	Activity Range
Ælfwine	1080–1086
Ægelwine	1083–1086
Ælfric	1083–1086
Æthelwine	1083–1086
Lifwine	1083–1086
Spegen	1083–1086
Wulfwine	1083–1086

Langport

Moneyer	Activity Range
Ælfwi	1017–1023
Godwine	1017–1023
Æthelwine	1017–1038
Eadric	1023–1029
Goda	1029–1036
Ælfweard	1036–1038
Dunbeard	1040–1042
Æthelwine	1050–1053
Eilwine	1050–1053

Launceston

Moneyer	Activity Range
Brun	979–985
Sasoti Stefani	1074–1077
Godric	1083–1086

Leicester

Moneyer	Activity Range
Man	973–975
Wulfstan	973–975
Styrcar	979–985
Osfrith	979–985
Dunn	979–991
Ælfric	991–997
Osfrith	991–997
Wulfgeat	991–1003
Thorulf	991–1009
Ælfric	1003–1016
Æthelwig	1009–1036
Ælfwig	1017–1023
Wlancthegn	1017–1029
Wulfnoth	1017–1044
Ægelwine	1023–1029
Ægelwig	1029–1036

Leicester

Moneyer	Activity Range
Godric	1029–1036
Wulfstan	1029–1040
Sæwine	1038–1042
Blacman	1044–1046
Wulfric	1044–1046
Sæwine	1044–1053
Godric	1046–1066
Æthelwig	1048–1050
Wulfnoth	1048–1053
Eadwine	1050–1053
Leofric	1053–1056
Æthelric	1053–1062
Ægelric	1056–1059
Ælfwine	1056–1062
Leofric	1059–1062
Ælfric	1059–1065
Æthelwine	1059–1066
Æthelric	1065–1066
Othulf	1065–1066
Ægelwine	1066–1066
Leofric	1068–1070
Lierie	1068–1070
Ægelwine	1070–1077
Ægelwine	1080–1083
Frethegest	1080–1083
Godric	1083–1086
Lierie	1083–1086

Lewes

Moneyer	Activity Range
Goldstan	973–975
Theodgar	973–985
Seaxberht	975–978
Goldstan	979–985
Leofstan	979–991
Herebreht	985–991
Ælfnoth	991–997
Eadweard	991–997
Osweald	991–997
Wulfstan	991–997
Ælfgar	991–1003
Leofwine	991–1029
Leofnoth	995–1003
Godfrith	997–1003
Hereberht	997–1003
Merewine	997–1009

Lewes

Moneyer	Activity Range
Leofa	1003–1029
Ælfweard	1009–1016
Eadweard	1009–1016
Leofstan	1009–1016
Olaf	1009–1016
Leofnoth	1009–1023
Godfrith	1009–1036
Ælfwine	1017–1023
Godman	1017–1023
Godwig	1017–1023
Ealdred	1017–1023
Coling	1023–1029
Ælfweard	1023–1036
Eadwine	1023–1042
Eadweard	1036–1042
Northman	1036–1046
Godwine	1038–1040
Wulfric	1040–1042
Eadwine	1042–1044
Eadweard	1046–1048
Godric	1046–1048
Leofnoth	1046–1048
Osweald	1046–1048
Osmund	1046–1050
Deoring	1048–1050
Eadwig	1048–1050
Eadwine	1048–1050
Leofman	1048–1050
Leofwig	1048–1050
Leofwine	1048–1053
Ælfsige	1050–1053
Eadweard	1050–1059
Godwine	1050–1066
Osweald	1050–1066
Eadwine	1053–1059
Deoring	1059–1062
Wulfwine	1059–1062
Leofweard	1059–1066
Leofweald	1062–1065
Ælfric	1072–1074
Osweald	1072–1077
Winered	1072–1086
Ælfric	1083–1086
Osweald	1083–1086

Lincoln

Moneyer	Activity Range
Æscman	973–975
Eanwulf	973–978
Grind	973–985
Leofing	973–985
Farthegn	975–978
Leofwig	975–978
Adelaver	975–978
Hafgrim	975–979
Levig	975–979
Goding	975–985
Rodbert	975–985
Grim	978–979
Osfrith	978–979
Swarting	978–1009
Æscman	979–985
Colgrim	979–985
Farthegn	979–985
Theodgeld	979–985
Unbegn	979–985
Cetelbeorn	991–997
Garfin	991–997
Gife	991–997
Grind	991–997
Leofman	991–997
Theodred	991–997
Ulf	991–997
Æscman	991–1003
Colgrim	991–1003
Eadsige	991–1003
Grim	991–1003
Stegenbit	991–1003
Theodgeld	991–1003
Unbegn	991–1003
Æthelnoth	991–1016
Ælfgeat	997–1003
Ælfsige	997–1003
Grimcetel	997–1003
Leofric	997–1003
Oscut	997–1003
Wulfmær	997–1003
Wulfred	997–1003
Wulfric	997–1003
Osmund	997–1009
Rægenweald	997–1016
Dreng	997–1023

Lincoln

Moneyer	Activity Range
Othgrim	997–1023
Osgeat	997–1029
Sumerlida	997–1029
Ulfcetel	997–1029
Osfrith	997–1059
Eadweald	1003–1009
Stegencetel	1003–1009
Theodulf	1003–1009
Wulfgeat	1003–1009
Wulfwine	1003–1009
Cetelbeorn	1003–1016
Boiga	1003–1016
Bruntat	1003–1029
Sunegod	1003–1029
Godwine	1003–1036
Leofing	1003–1038
Æscman	1009–1016
Æthelred	1009–1016
Colswegen	1009–1016
Eadsige	1009–1016
Eamær	1009–1016
Osfram	1009–1016
Thorcetel	1009–1016
Ælfric	1009–1023
Æthelnoth	1009–1023
Leofric	1009–1023
Snelling	1009–1023
Othbeorn	1009–1023
Wulfric	1009–1023
Wulfgrim	1009–1023
Wulfheah	1009–1023
Man	1009–1029
Iustan	1009–1029
Æthelmær	1009–1036
Wulfbeorn	1009–1036
Leofwine	1009–1050
Eadmund	1017–1023
Eadweald	1017–1023
Wulfgeat	1017–1023
Wulfnoth	1017–1023
Aslac	1017–1029
Grimcetel	1017–1029
Crinan	1017–1036
Oslac	1017–1038
Swartebrand	1017–1038

Lincoln

Moneyer	Activity Range
Matathan	1017–1040
Ælfnoth	1017–1042
Godric	1017–1062
Asferth	1023–1029
Goda	1023–1029
Leofman	1023–1029
Leofthegn	1023–1029
Matan	1023–1029
Ægelmær	1023–1029
Eustan	1023–1029
Osfram	1023–1029
Osmund	1023–1029
Wulfwine	1023–1036
Matathan Balluc	1023–1038
Colgrim	1023–1042
Swarting	1023–1046
Godric Spot	1029–1036
Leofa	1029–1036
Cnut	1029–1036
Swart	1029–1036
Wulfric	1029–1036
Beorhtric	1029–1038
Harthacnut	1029–1038
Wedlos	1029–1038
Swafa	1029–1044
Wælræfn	1029–1044
Eadric	1036–1038
Eadwine	1036–1038
Leofric	1036–1038
Leofthegn	1036–1038
Conrin	1036–1038
Hildulf	1036–1038
Pælræfen	1036–1038
Othbeorn	1036–1038
Thorstan	1036–1038
Leofnoth	1036–1040
Wulfgeat	1036–1040
Osmund	1036–1042
Othgrim	1036–1042
Leofwig	1036–1044
Sumerlida	1036–1044
Ælfwici	1038–1040
Æthelnoth	1038–1040
Godwine	1038–1040
Pororie	1038–1040

Lincoln

Moneyer	Activity Range
Wororic	1038–1040
Wulfbeorn	1038–1042
Wulfnoth	1038–1042
Leofing	1040–1042
Othbeorn	1040–1042
Wedlos	1040–1042
Eadmund	1040–1044
Wulfric	1040–1044
Thorgrim	1040–1048
Eadric	1040–1050
Beorhtric	1040–1053
Guthfrith	1042–1044
Ulf	1042–1053
Ælfnoth	1044–1046
Leofnoth	1044–1046
Udd	1044–1046
Wulf	1044–1048
Colgrim	1044–1056
Æthelnoth	1046–1048
Wineman	1046–1048
Wulfgar	1046–1048
Wilgrip	1048–1050
Man	1048–1059
Ælfnoth	1048–1062
Othgrim	1048–1066
Manna	1050–1053
Oslac	1050–1053
Othbeorn	1050–1056
Auti	1050–1066
Manna	1056–1059
Thorcetel	1056–1062
Wulfric	1056–1062
Wulfbeorn	1056–1065
Ulf	1056–1066
Ælfwine	1059–1062
Aslac	1059–1062
Wulfgar	1059–1062
Gife	1059–1065
Oslac	1059–1066
Agmund	1062–1065
Agmund	1062–1065
Eanmund	1062–1065
Leofwine	1062–1065
Eadric	1062–1066
Garfin	1062–1066

Lincoln

Moneyer	Activity Range
Ælfgeat	1065–1066
Ælfmær	1065–1066
Æthelmær	1065–1066
Outti	1065–1066
Swart	1065–1066
Wulfgar	1065–1066
Wulfmær	1066–1066
Garwig	1066–1068
Ginch	1066–1068
Ælfmær	1068–1070
Agmund	1068–1070
Iegner	1068–1070
Othgrim	1068–1070
Siferth	1068–1070
Sifweard	1068–1070
Wulfsige	1068–1070
Gifel	1068–1072
Leofnoth	1070–1072
Sigeweard	1070–1072
Sinferth	1072–1074
Ulf	1072–1074
Unspac	1072–1074
Wulfstan	1072–1074
Wihtric	1074–1077
Sifweard	1074–1077
Sigeferth	1074–1077
Thorstan	1074–1077
Ansthuc	1074–1080
Siferth	1083–1086
Sigeferth	1083–1086
Ulf	1083–1086

London

Moneyer	Activity Range
Ælfnoth	973–975
Æthelsige	973–975
Æthelstan	973–978
Wigfrith	973–978
Æthelweald	973–979
Æthelred	973–997
Ælfweard	975–978
Leofheah	975–978
Wigfend	975–978
Ælfstan	979–985
Ælfweald	979–985

London

Moneyer	Activity Range
Ælfwine	979–985
Æthelweard	979–985
Æthelstan	979–985
Beorhtsige	979–985
Brunsige	979–985
Eadweald	979–985
God	979–985
Godric	979–985
Leofric	979–985
Sibwine	979–985
Winesige	979–985
Beornwulf	979–991
Burnsige	979–991
Cynesige	979–991
Eadhelm	979–991
Wulfmær	979–991
Wulfric	979–991
Ælfgar	979–997
Ealhstan	979–997
Goda	979–997
Leofstan	979–1003
Oscetel	979–1003
Osulf	979–1023
Wulfstan	979–1029
Godwine	979–1062
Æthelulf	985–991
Eadnoth	985–991
Eadsige	985–991
Eadwi	985–991
Ecferth	985–991
Osfrith	985–991
Theodred	985–991
Ælfgæt	985–997
Ælfnoth	985–997
Eadwig	985–997
Sidewine	985–997
Ælfweard	985–1003
Beorhtlaf	985–1003
Sweting	985–1023
Eadmund	985–1036
Eadwine	985–1040
Leofwine	985–1040
Ælfstan	991–997
Ælfwig	991–997
Æthelwine	991–997

London

Moneyer	Activity Range
Beorhtmær	991–997
Deorsige	991–997
Godhere	991–997
Goldwine	991–997
Oda	991–997
Osmund	991–997
Wulfgar	991–997
Ælfric	991–1003
Heahwulf	991–1003
Sibwine	991–1016
Æthelweard	991–1029
Ælfwine	991–1038
Godric	991–1040
Wulfwine	991–1040
Leofing	991–1042
Eadweald	991–1046
Leofric	991–1046
Leofred	991–1056
Ægnulf	995–997
Burnmær	995–997
Eadweard	995–997
Eadwi	995–997
God	995–997
Godra	995–997
Drihtweald	995–997
Wulfnoth	995–997
Swarting	995–1003
Eadsige	995–1029
Ælfred	997–1003
Æthelfrith	997–1003
Deorwulf	997–1003
Eadric	997–1003
Leofnoth	997–1003
Wulfsige	997–1003
Brunstan	997–1009
Toca	997–1009
Æthelric	997–1029
Wulfric	997–1036
Godman	997–1042
Æthelmær	1003–1009
Eadgar	1003–1009
Ealdgar	1003–1009
Blundered	1003–1009
Stithulf	1003–1009
Swartgar	1003–1009

London

Moneyer	Activity Range
Theodred	1003–1009
Wulfgar	1003–1009
Eadwig	1003–1029
Ælfwig	1003–1036
Æthelwine	1003–1036
Eadweard	1003–1036
Godhere	1003–1036
Leofweald	1003–1036
Wulfred	1003–1036
Goda	1003–1038
Ælfgæt	1009–1016
Ælfnoth	1009–1016
Ælfric	1009–1016
Ælfsige	1009–1016
Ælfweard	1009–1016
Æthelnoth	1009–1016
Æthelred	1009–1016
Æthelwig	1009–1016
Beornfrith	1009–1016
Deorman	1009–1016
Eadsme	1009–1016
Eadwi	1009–1016
Goldwine	1009–1016
Leofheah	1009–1016
Leofnoth	1009–1016
Ælman	1009–1016
Sunegod	1009–1016
Oda	1009–1016
Oswald	1009–1016
Oswig	1009–1016
Swegen	1009–1016
Wulfbeald	1009–1016
Æthelman	1009–1023
Beorhtfrith	1009–1023
Beorhtweald	1009–1023
Ealdred	1009–1023
Grim	1009–1023
Eardnoth	1009–1023
Osmund	1009–1023
Beorhtnoth	1009–1036
Leofwig	1009–1036
Brunman	1009–1038
Winesige	1009–1042
Beorhtmær	1009–1042
Leofstan	1009–1046

London

Moneyer	Activity Range
Eadric	1009–1048
Ælf	1017–1023
Brun	1017–1023
Coleman	1017–1023
Deorsige	1017–1023
Eadnoth	1017–1023
Frith	1017–1023
Frithwine	1017–1023
Godwig	1017–1023
Borstig	1017–1023
Holeman	1017–1023
Sigeweard	1017–1023
Wulfsige	1017–1023
Wulfweard	1017–1023
Eadgar	1017–1029
Leofsige	1017–1029
Sigenoth	1017–1029
Winestan	1017–1029
Wulfnoth	1017–1029
Ælfstan	1017–1036
Leofweard	1017–1036
Wulfgar	1017–1038
Ægfrie	1023–1029
Ægelweard	1023–1029
Ælfgæt	1023–1029
Ælfgar	1023–1029
Æthelbeorht	1023–1029
Æthelgæt	1023–1029
Æthelnoth	1023–1029
Brunic	1023–1029
Eadhelm	1023–1029
Etsige	1023–1029
Leofgar	1023–1029
Leofmær	1023–1029
Leofman	1023–1029
Aslac	1023–1029
Dunstan	1023–1029
Gauti	1023–1029
Sæwine	1023–1029
Sigered	1023–1029
Sired	1023–1029
Stithulf	1023–1029
Theodred	1023–1029
Thorcetel	1023–1029
Toca	1023–1029

London

Moneyer	Activity Range
Wulfmær	1023–1029
Ægelwine	1023–1036
Ælfweard	1023–1036
Æthelwig	1023–1036
Beorhtræd	1023–1036
Eadwulf	1023–1036
Ælfred	1023–1038
Eadred	1023–1038
Ælfric	1023–1042
Brungar	1023–1046
Ælfwig Swencel	1029–1036
Beorhtwine	1029–1036
Brunmar	1029–1036
Eadnoth	1029–1036
Frithwine	1029–1036
God	1029–1036
Goding	1029–1036
Grim	1029–1036
Leofa	1029–1036
Enfdici	1029–1036
Swan	1029–1036
Wadweald	1029–1036
Osfrith	1029–1036
Osulf	1029–1036
Sweting	1029–1036
Swetman	1029–1036
Swegen	1029–1036
Oda	1036–1038
Ælfnoth	1036–1038
Ælfweald	1036–1038
Brun	1036–1038
Cyneweald	1036–1038
Cynewig	1036–1038
Deorman	1036–1038
Duding	1036–1038
Eadwig	1036–1038
Godwine Stew	1036–1038
Man	1036–1038
Farmann	1036–1038
Ulfcetel	1036–1038
Widia	1036–1038
Wulfnoth	1036–1038
Godsige	1036–1040
Corf	1036–1042
Goldsige	1036–1044

London

Moneyer	Activity Range
Beorhtræd	1038–1040
God	1038–1040
Wulf	1038–1040
Eadweard	1038–1042
Wulfsige	1038–1042
Wulfstan	1038–1044
Ælfred	1040–1042
Æthelwine	1040–1042
Brun	1040–1042
Brunman	1040–1042
Eadwig	1040–1042
Goda	1040–1042
Godric Calic	1040–1042
Wulfred	1040–1042
Ægelweard	1040–1044
Æthelweard	1040–1044
Beorhtwine	1040–1044
Wulfgar	1040–1044
Ælfweard	1040–1046
Ælfwine	1040–1056
Godwig	1042–1044
Orlaf	1042–1044
Wulfric	1042–1044
Duding	1042–1046
Ealdgar	1042–1046
Theodred	1042–1046
Eadmund	1042–1048
Ælfwig	1042–1050
Wulfwine	1042–1059
Æthelgar	1044–1046
Æthelman	1044–1046
Æthelric	1044–1046
Beorhtmær	1044–1046
Burred	1044–1046
Deorman	1044–1046
Eadwi	1044–1046
Ealdwine	1044–1046
Ealhsige	1044–1046
Eastmær	1044–1046
Godman	1044–1046
Wulfsige	1044–1046
Ælfgar	1044–1048
Æthelwig	1044–1050
Swetman	1044–1050
Godsunu	1044–1053

London

Moneyer	Activity Range
Wulfred	1044–1053
Beorhtræd	1044–1056
Eadwine	1044–1056
Ælfred	1044–1062
Ælfsige	1046–1048
Brunman	1046–1048
Eawig	1046–1048
Eadred	1046–1048
Alric	1046–1048
Sneiman	1046–1048
Wihtred	1046–1048
Uhtred	1046–1048
Wulfsic	1046–1048
Ægelwig	1046–1050
Godwig	1046–1050
Wulfric	1046–1050
Leofing	1046–1053
Goldsige	1046–1056
Leofwine	1046–1059
Godric	1046–1077
Ægelric	1048–1050
Ælf	1048–1050
Ælfgæt	1048–1050
Ælfstan	1048–1050
Ælfweald	1048–1050
Æthelric	1048–1050
Cynemær	1048–1050
Deorman	1048–1050
Durred	1048–1050
Eadweald	1048–1050
Leofnoth	1048–1050
Leofwig	1048–1050
Thor	1048–1050
Thorfrith	1048–1050
Wulfsige	1048–1050
Wulfwig	1048–1050
Burred	1048–1053
Duding	1048–1053
Eadwig	1048–1059
Ealdgar	1048–1059
Ægelred	1050–1053
Ælfgar	1050–1053
Ælfsige	1050–1053
Æwi	1050–1053
Beorhtsige	1050–1053

London

Moneyer	Activity Range
Burgræd	1050–1053
Eawig	1050–1053
Eadmund	1050–1053
Eadsige	1050–1053
Ealdred	1050–1053
Etsige	1050–1053
Leofsige	1050–1053
Bricsige	1050–1053
Spracling	1050–1053
Wulfcrdd	1050–1053
Wulfweard	1050–1053
Beorhtwine	1050–1056
Eadred	1050–1056
Ægelric	1053–1056
Ægelwig	1053–1056
Ægelwine	1053–1056
Ælfwig	1053–1056
Æthelric	1053–1056
Beorhtmær	1053–1056
Brungar	1053–1056
Eadric	1053–1056
Eadweald	1053–1056
Ealdulf	1053–1056
Eastmund	1053–1056
Godhere	1053–1056
Godman	1053–1056
Godwig	1053–1056
Glifwine	1053–1056
Sigered	1053–1056
Sired	1053–1056
Swetman	1053–1056
Ægelweard	1053–1059
Wulfric	1053–1059
Osmund	1053–1062
Ælfweard	1053–1066
Wulfgar	1053–1066
Deorman	1056–1059
Leofæg	1056–1059
Wulfnoth	1056–1059
Wulfred	1056–1059
Leofing	1056–1062
Ælfsige	1056–1066
Ælfwine	1059–1062
Duric	1059–1062
Eadgar	1059–1062

London

Moneyer	Activity Range
Goldwine	1059–1062
Leofric	1059–1062
Eadwine	1059–1077
Ægelwine	1062–1065
Æthelwig	1062–1065
Æthelwine	1062–1065
Eastmund	1062–1065
Wine	1062–1065
Wulfsi	1062–1065
Wulfsige	1062–1066
Wulfweard	1062–1066
Swetman	1062–1068
Ealdgar	1062–1072
Eadgar	1065–1066
Eadric	1065–1066
Leofsige	1066–1066
Osmund	1066–1066
Ælfwine	1066–1070
Ælfsige	1066–1072
Wulfwine	1066–1072
Ægelwine	1068–1070
Leofsige	1068–1070
Idcefis	1068–1070
Godwine	1068–1072
Ægelric	1070–1072
Beorhtric	1070–1072
Eadric	1070–1072
Sibode	1070–1072
Uhtred	1070–1072
Ægelwine	1072–1074
Ælfwine	1072–1074
Colspegen	1072–1074
Blacsunu	1072–1074
Winediec	1072–1074
Wulfie	1072–1074
Wulfric	1072–1074
Beorhtmær	1074–1077
Beorhtric	1074–1077
Wulfweard	1074–1077
Godwine	1074–1080
Manic	1077–1080
Eadwi	1077–1086
Ælfwine	1080–1083
Eadwig	1080–1083
Beriteri	1080–1083

London

Moneyer	Activity Range
Wulfwine	1080–1083
Beorhtwine	1080–1086
Ælfred	1083–1086
Æwi	1083–1086
Brunic	1083–1086
Eadric	1083–1086
Godric	1083–1086
Godwine	1083–1086

Lydford

Moneyer	Activity Range
Æthelred	975–985
Godwine	979–991
Goda	991–1016
Godwine	995–997
Ælfstan	997–1003
Brun	997–1023
Godric	1009–1023
Sæwine	1017–1029
Eadwine	1029–1036
Wicing	1029–1036
Ælfric	1036–1038
Ælfwine	1038–1042
Ælfric	1042–1044
Ælfric	1048–1050

Lympne

Moneyer	Activity Range
Leofwine	973–975
Ælfweald	973–975
Æthelstan	973–978
Leofweald	975–978
Beorhtric	975–978
Wine	975–978
Leofwine	979–985
Wine	979–985
Leofric	979–997
Eatstan	985–991
Eadward	991–997
Godric	997–1003
Leofwine	1017–1023
Iohan	1017–1023
Godric	1023–1036

Maldon

Moneyer	Activity Range
Ælfwine	991–997
Leofwig	991–997
Leofwine	991–997
Æthelwine	995–997
Toca	997–1003
Æthelwine	1003–1023
Godwine	1017–1023
Ælfwine	1017–1029
Ceolnoth	1017–1029
Godhere	1023–1029
Leofwine	1023–1029
Dægniht	1042–1044
Dæg	1044–1046
Dægniht	1048–1053
Godric	1053–1062
Godwine	1053–1065
Swetric	1056–1059
Godwine	1066–1066
Ælford	1083–1086
Ælfwine	1083–1086
Leofsunu	1083–1086

Malmesbury

Moneyer	Activity Range
Ealdred	985–1003
Leofgæt	997–1003
Ealdred	1009–1009
Beorhtstan	1017–1023
Beorhtnoth	1023–1029
Huna	1023–1044
Godman	1038–1040
Beorhtwine	1044–1048
Huna	1048–1050
Ealdwig	1050–1056
Ealdwine	1056–1059
Beorhtwi	1059–1062
Beorhtwig	1059–1062
Beorht	1062–1065
Beorhtwine	1062–1066
Beorhtwig	1066–1066
Beorhtwine	1068–1070
Beorhtwine	1072–1077
Godsbrand	1083–1086
Seweard	1083–1086

Marlborough

Moneyer	Activity Range
Cild	1070–1080
Cild	1083–1086

Milbourne Port

Moneyer	Activity Range
Æthelric	997–1003
Godwine	1023–1029
Swetric	1029–1036

Newark

Moneyer	Activity Range
Leofsige	1023–1029

Newport Pagnell

Moneyer	Activity Range
Sigeweard	1050–1053
Sigered	1053–1056
Sæwen	1059–1062

Niwan

Moneyer	Activity Range
Ingolf	973–985
Æthestan	979–985

Northampton

Moneyer	Activity Range
Mantat	973–975
Baldric	973–975
Eadnoth	973–975
Osweald	973–975
Leofsige	973–978
Cylm	973–978
Cetel	975–978
Mancrent	975–979
Leofsige	979–985
Leofing	979–985
Leofsige	991–997
Leofstan	991–997
Leofwine	991–1003
Bruning	991–1003
Thorcetel	995–997
Æthelnoth	997–1003

Northampton

Moneyer	Activity Range
Leofweald	997–1003
Man	997–1003
Leofgod	997–1009
Wulfric	997–1016
Wulfnoth	1009–1016
Leofweald	1009–1023
Leofwine	1009–1040
Ælfwine	1017–1023
Leofnoth	1017–1029
Godric	1023–1029
Ælfwine	1036–1048
Æthelwine	1038–1040
Godric	1038–1042
Leofwine	1042–1046
Æthelwine	1044–1046
Leofwine	1050–1053
Ælfwine	1050–1062
Leofric	1053–1059
Wulfnoth	1053–1065
Sæwine	1056–1062
Godwine	1065–1066
Leofstan	1065–1066
Sæwine	1065–1066
Swetman	1065–1066
Wulfsi	1065–1066
Swetman	1068–1070
Wulfwine	1070–1072
Sæwine	1070–1080
Sæwig	1074–1077
Sæwine	1083–1086

Norwich

Moneyer	Activity Range
Branting	973–975
Leofing	973–975
Oslac	973–975
Manning	975–997
Osfrith	978–979
Folcard	979–985
Leofing	979–985
Branting	979–991
Swerting	985–991
Æthelwine	991–997
Eadmund	991–997
Folcard	991–997

Norwich

Moneyer	Activity Range
Leofing	991–997
Swerting	995–1003
Ælfwine	997–1003
Leofwine	997–1003
Ælfric	997–1029
Hwætman	997–1029
Leofstan	1003–1009
Edelwine	1003–1009
Eadwacer	1003–1023
Cyneric	1009–1016
Eadwine	1009–1016
Wulfmær	1009–1016
Leofwine	1009–1023
Osweald	1009–1023
Thorstan	1009–1023
Leofric	1009–1029
Man	1009–1040
Eadmund	1017–1023
Godwine	1017–1023
Weimund	1017–1023
Sigeric	1017–1023
Swerting	1017–1023
Hringwulf	1017–1029
Thorfrith	1017–1029
Rægenulf	1017–1036
Manna	1017–1042
Oslac	1023–1029
Ælfrith	1029–1036
Æthelfrith	1029–1036
Ægelferth	1029–1036
Sigeric	1029–1036
Leofwine	1029–1048
Ælfric	1036–1038
Ælfwine	1036–1038
Ælfweald	1036–1040
Hringwulf	1038–1042
Rægenulf	1038–1042
Grim	1040–1042
Leofwig	1040–1044
Man	1040–1046
Osmund	1040–1046
Godwine	1044–1046
Hringwulf	1044–1046
Leofwig	1048–1050
Thorfrith	1048–1062

Norwich

Moneyer	Activity Range
Cynehelm	1050–1053
Leofwine	1050–1056
Thorstan	1050–1066
Godman	1053–1056
Hringwulf	1053–1056
Thorman	1053–1056
Leofric	1056–1062
Wulfsige	1056–1062
Ælfwine	1059–1062
Wulfstan	1059–1062
Leofwine	1059–1065
Eadwine	1062–1065
Godfrith	1062–1065
Wrice	1062–1065
Godwine	1062–1066
Thorgrim	1065–1066
Cyneric	1066–1066
Man	1066–1068
Eadwine	1066–1070
Leofold	1068–1070
Godric	1072–1074
Ælfweald	1074–1077
Eadweald	1074–1077
Godrun	1074–1077
Godric	1080–1086
Eadweald	1083–1086
Godric brd	1083–1086
Godwid	1083–1086
Godwig	1083–1086
Godwine	1083–1086
Howorth	1083–1086
Inhuhe	1083–1086
Ulfcetel	1083–1086

Nottingham

Moneyer	Activity Range
Osweald	991–997
Osweald	1003–1029
Blacman	1017–1053
Bruning	1023–1029
Sægrim	1036–1042
Leofstan	1040–1042
Wulfnoth	1040–1042
Leofsige	1040–1044
Halfdene	1042–1044

Nottingham

Moneyer	Activity Range
Leofsige	1046–1050
Alhmund	1048–1050
Snoter	1048–1050
Halfdene	1048–1053
Fulnoth	1050–1053
Wulfnoth	1050–1053
Forni	1053–1065
Wulfnoth	1059–1062
Forman	1062–1065
Arngrim	1062–1065
Forni	1066–1066
Manna	1066–1066
Forni	1068–1074
Man	1070–1072
Manna	1070–1074
Man	1083–1086
Manna	1083–1086
Ætcer	1083–1086

Oxford

Moneyer	Activity Range
Æthelwine	973–975
Seleweald	973–975
Wulfred	973–978
Goding	979–1003
Eadwig	991–997
Æthelmær	991–1003
Æthelwine	991–1003
Wulfwine	991–1003
Ælfwine	991–1009
Ælfmær	997–1003
Eadwine	997–1003
Leofman	997–1016
Leofwine	1003–1009
Beorhtwine	1003–1023
Coleman	1003–1040
Æthelric	1003–1046
Beorhtnoth	1009–1016
Ælfweald	1009–1036
Godman	1017–1023
Sæwine	1017–1023
Sibwine	1017–1023
Wulfmær	1017–1023
Wulfwig	1017–1023
Ælfwine	1017–1029

Oxford

Moneyer	Activity Range
Eadwig	1017–1036
Wulfwine	1017–1036
Godwine	1017–1042
Leofing	1017–1042
Ægelric	1023–1029
Eadwine	1029–1036
Ælfwine Tosti	1029–1038
Ægelwig	1036–1038
Æthelwine	1036–1038
Lafdensic	1036–1038
Leofwine	1036–1040
Ælfwine	1036–1042
Æthelwig	1036–1066
Æthelmær	1038–1040
Eadwig	1038–1042
Ælfwig	1038–1044
Ægelwine	1040–1042
Æthelwine	1040–1042
Beorhtweald	1042–1053
Ælfwine	1044–1046
Godwine	1044–1050
Heregod	1044–1050
Ægelwig	1046–1048
Ælfwine	1048–1050
Ælfwig	1048–1066
Ælfwi	1050–1053
Æthelwine	1050–1053
Ægelwine	1050–1062
Swetman	1050–1062
Ægelwig	1053–1056
Ælfwine	1053–1056
Eadwine	1053–1059
Beorhtweald	1056–1059
Æthelwine	1056–1062
Æthelric	1059–1062
Beorhtræd	1059–1062
Godwine	1059–1065
Heregod	1059–1066
Wulfwi	1062–1065
Beorhtweald	1062–1066
Wulfwig	1062–1066
Ælfwi	1065–1066
Godwine	1066–1066
Ælfwig	1068–1070
Ælfwine	1068–1070

Oxford

Moneyer	Activity Range
Godwine	1068–1074
Wulfwine	1068–1074
Ægelwine	1070–1074
Heregod	1072–1074
Ælfwine	1074–1077
Agulf	1074–1077
Wulfwine	1077–1080
Heregod	1080–1083
Beorhtræd	1080–1086
Swetman	1083–1086
Wulfwi	1083–1086

Pershore

Moneyer	Activity Range
Wulfric	1059–1062

Peterborough

Moneyer	Activity Range
Leofæg	1017–1023

Petherton

Moneyer	Activity Range
Beorhtric	1044–1046

Pevensey

Moneyer	Activity Range
Ælfheah	1083–1086

Rhuddlan

Moneyer	Activity Range
Ælfwine	1083–1086

Rochester

Moneyer	Activity Range
Sideman	973–978
Eadelm	979–985
Sideman	979–985
Sidewine	979–997
Leofric	985–997
Osfrith	991–991
Beorhtmær	991–997
Brun	991–997

Rochester

Moneyer	Activity Range
Eadsige	991–1003
Goldwine	991–1003
Eadwine	997–1003
Eadweard	997–1016
Eadnoth	1009–1016
Wulfred	1009–1016
Ælfheah	1009–1038
Godwine	1009–1040
Sidewine	1017–1023
Leofric	1023–1029
Wulfric	1029–1036
Godwine	1042–1048
Eadwine	1044–1048
Wulfric	1046–1048
Eadwine	1053–1056
Godwine	1053–1056
Leofwine	1056–1065
Eadwine	1062–1065
Leofstan	1066–1066
Leofwine	1066–1066
Leofwine	1074–1077
Leofwine	1083–1086
Lifstan	1083–1086
Lifwinehorn	1083–1086

Romney

Moneyer	Activity Range
Leofwine	997–1003
Æthelwine	997–1009
Godman	1009–1016
Wulfnoth	1009–1040
Leofwine	1017–1023
Eardnoth	1017–1023
Æthelric	1023–1029
Godric	1023–1029
Godwine	1023–1029
Godman	1029–1036
Wulfwig	1036–1038
Eadmær	1038–1040
Wulfmær	1042–1044
Wulfmær	1046–1068
Æthelstan	1048–1050
Ælfmær	1074–1080
Pindei	1083–1086
Wulfmær	1083–1086

Salisbury

Moneyer	Activity Range
Sæwine	1003–1016
Goldus	1003–1036
Godwine	1003–1042
Sæman	1009–1023
Ælfnoth	1009–1029
Ælfred	1017–1023
Leofweald	1017–1023
Winestan	1017–1029
Ælfwine	1023–1029
Leofstan	1023–1029
Ælfred	1029–1040
Goldstan	1036–1038
Winestan	1036–1044
Leofstan	1038–1042
Wineman	1040–1048
Godric	1044–1046
Godwine	1044–1050
Ælfweald	1046–1050
Godric	1056–1062
Siboda	1065–1066
Sæbeorht	1065–1066
Godric	1074–1077
Godric	1080–1083
Godwine	1083–1086
Esbern	1083–1086
Osbern	1083–1086

Sandwich

Moneyer	Activity Range
Leofwine	1044–1056
Leofwine	1059–1062
Godric	1062–1065
Ælfgeat	1074–1080
Ælfheah	1083–1086
Ælfgeat	1083–1086
Godwine	1083–1086

Shaftesbury

Moneyer	Activity Range
Beorhtweald	978–979
Æthelstan	979–991
Æthelwi	985–991
Æthelgeard	991–997
Lyfa	991–1003

Shaftesbury

Moneyer	Activity Range
Goda	991–1036
Ælfwine	997–1003
Æthelwig	997–1003
Sæwine	997–1009
Æthelric	1003–1042
Ælfwine	1009–1023
Ægelwine	1017–1023
Ælfric	1017–1023
Æthelwine	1017–1023
Lyfa	1017–1023
Sæwine	1017–1023
Beola	1017–1029
Ægelric	1023–1036
Wulfric	1038–1040
Ægelric	1040–1042
Wulfnoth	1040–1042
Ælfweard	1044–1046
Wulfric	1044–1046
Wulfmær	1048–1050
Wulfric	1048–1062
Wuducoc	1053–1056
Ælfweard	1059–1062
Æthelric	1062–1066
Godric	1062–1066
Ægelwine	1066–1066
Ælfnoth	1066–1066
Æthelwine	1066–1066
Wulfmær	1066–1066
Ælfnoth	1074–1077
Cantwine	1074–1077
Godsbrand	1077–1086
Ælfnoth	1080–1086
Cantwine	1080–1086

Shrewsbury

Moneyer	Activity Range
Æthelsige	973–975
Hildic	973–975
Sigeweald	973–975
Ælfric	979–985
Leofhelm	979–985
Ævic	979–985
Martin	991–997
Winesige	991–1003
Brungar	995–1003

Shrewsbury

Moneyer	Activity Range
Ælfheah	997–1003
Leofnoth	997–1003
Leofsige	997–1003
Ordgar	997–1003
Oswald	997–1003
Unspac	997–1009
Eadsige	1003–1009
Ælfstan	1009–1016
Æthelnoth	1009–1016
Sigered	1009–1016
Winesige	1009–1016
Ælfhelm	1017–1023
Crinan	1017–1023
Grim	1017–1023
Wada	1017–1023
Brungar	1017–1036
Eadsige	1017–1036
Godwine	1017–1036
Wulfred	1017–1040
Eadstan	1023–1029
Wulfweard	1023–1036
Leofstan	1023–1042
Wulfgeat	1023–1046
Godhere	1036–1038
Leofwine	1036–1042
Ælfheah	1040–1042
Wulfmær	1040–1042
Wulfmær	1044–1046
Leofwine	1046–1048
Wulfgeat	1048–1053
Wulfmær	1048–1056
Ælfheah	1050–1056
Leofwine	1050–1056
Leofstan	1050–1059
Godsbrand	1050–1066
Ærnwig	1056–1066
Ælfgæt	1059–1062
Ælfheah	1059–1062
Wulfmær	1059–1062
Godwine	1059–1066
Wudeman	1059–1066
Ægelric	1062–1065
Goldwine	1062–1065
Wulfmær	1065–1066
Ægelric	1068–1070

Shrewsbury

Moneyer	Activity Range
Ærnwi	1068–1070
Godsbrand	1068–1070
Ærnwi	1072–1074
Wulfmær	1072–1074
Ærnwine	1074–1077
Sigewine	1074–1077
Lernwi	1077–1080
Ærnwi	1083–1086
Godsbrand	1083–1086
Sægrim	1083–1086

Southampton

Moneyer	Activity Range
Eadwine	975–978
Landbeorht	975–978
Æthelweard	979–985
Isegod	979–985
Isegod	991–997
Godman	991–997
Æthelnoth	997–1003
Spileman	997–1003
Æthelsige	1003–1009
Seolca	1009–1016
Ælfsige	1017–1023
Ælfweard	1017–1023
Leofwine	1017–1023
Siboda	1017–1023

Southwark

Moneyer	Activity Range
Ælfnoth	991–997
Ælfric	991–997
Ælfwig	991–997
Æthelweard	991–997
Beorhthelm	991–997
Beorhtlaf	991–997
Beorhtric	991–997
Eadwig	991–997
Goda	991–997
Godwine	991–997
Leofstan	991–997
Boiga	991–997
Heahwulf	991–997
Tuneman	991–997
Eadwine	991–1003

Southwark

Moneyer	Activity Range
Godric	991–1003
Leofwine	991–1003
Eadwi	995–997
Leofwine	1009–1016
Tuneman	1009–1016
Eadwine	1009–1023
Ælfwine	1009–1036
Ælfsige	1017–1023
Ælfweard	1017–1023
Æthelsige	1017–1023
Æthelwig	1017–1023
Æthelwine	1017–1023
Beorhtmær	1017–1023
Brunman	1017–1023
Eadweard	1017–1023
Leofric	1017–1023
Swegen	1017–1023
Swarting	1017–1023
Wulfric	1017–1023
Wulfstan	1017–1023
Ælfgar	1017–1029
Ælfric	1023–1029
Æthelric	1023–1029
Eadnoth	1023–1029
Godwine	1023–1029
Toca	1023–1029
Leofing	1023–1038
Æthelwig	1029–1036
Leofric	1036–1038
Ælfwine	1038–1040
Æthelwine	1040–1042
Brunræd	1040–1042
Leofric	1040–1042
Ægelwig	1040–1042
Ælfric	1040–1046
Burred	1042–1042
Burgræd	1042–1046
Wulfwine	1042–1046
Leofwine	1046–1050
Ælfwine	1048–1050
Wulfwine	1048–1053
Leofred	1050–1056
Swetman	1053–1056
Osmund	1053–1066
Godman	1056–1059

Southwark

Moneyer	Activity Range
Swetman	1059–1062
Godric	1062–1065
Leofwine	1068–1070
Leofwine	1074–1080
Godric	1080–1086
Ælfdoulf	1083–1086
Lifweard	1083–1086
Osmund	1083–1086

St Davids

Moneyer	Activity Range
Turri	1083–1086

Stafford

Moneyer	Activity Range
Ælfweald	978–985
Ælfweald	991–997
Ægenulf	997–1003
Scot	997–1003
Godric	1003–1016
Ælfweald	1009–1016
Ælfric	1017–1029
Fierlf	1023–1029
Ecrie	1029–1036
Ælfric	1038–1040
Ælfric	1050–1053
Coling	1059–1062
Godwine	1065–1066
Godwine	1068–1070
Wulfnoth	1068–1070
Leofwine	1074–1077
Godric	1083–1086
Godwine	1083–1086

Stamford

Moneyer	Activity Range
Ælfweald	973–978
Cnapa	973–978
Man	973–978
Æscman	973–979
Oge	973–979
Wulfgar	973–991
Wacer	975–978
Wine	975–978
Hild	975–979

Stamford

Moneyer	Activity Range
Iole	975–979
Leofing	975–985
Grim	975–985
Boiga	975–991
Wulfstan	975–991
Godwine	979–985
Leofæg	979–985
Ælfweald	979–991
Æthelfrith	985–991
Ælfgar	991–997
Ælfgeat	991–997
Brun	991–997
Godwine	991–997
Goldwine	991–997
Cristin	991–1003
Swartgar	991–1016
Godleof	991–1023
Ælfweald	995–997
Wulfstan	995–997
Ælfweard	997–1003
Ælfwine	997–1003
Eadwig	997–1003
Ælebeorht	997–1003
Æscwig	997–1016
Godæg	997–1016
Æscea	1003–1009
Æthelberht	1003–1009
Æthelwine	1009–1016
Godelc	1009–1016
Godhere	1009–1016
Osmund	1009–1016
Brunstan	1009–1023
Godric	1009–1023
Swart	1009–1023
Swartebrand	1009–1023
Æscman	1009–1029
Eadwine	1009–1029
Thorstan	1009–1038
Godwine	1009–1042
Leofwine	1009–1042
Ælfwig	1017–1023
Fargrim	1017–1023
Brand	1017–1023
Leofsige	1017–1029
Capelin	1017–1029

Stamford

Moneyer	Activity Range
Ceawlin	1017–1029
Osweald	1017–1029
Eadweard	1017–1036
Morulf	1017–1036
Ælfheah	1023–1029
Æthelstan	1023–1029
Leofing	1023–1029
Leofric	1023–1029
Leofweald	1023–1029
Agisman	1023–1029
Osweard	1023–1038
Thorulf	1023–1044
Leofthegn	1029–1036
Thor	1029–1036
Leofæg	1029–1038
Brunwine	1029–1042
Fargrim	1029–1042
Swart	1029–1042
Godric	1029–1046
Ælfwine	1036–1038
Leofing	1036–1038
Leofric	1036–1066
Arncetel	1038–1040
Harcin	1038–1040
Wilgrip	1038–1042
Ælfheah	1038–1046
Thorstan	1040–1042
Arngrim	1042–1044
Wulfnoth	1042–1044
Godwine	1044–1046
Baldwin	1044–1046
Thorstan	1044–1046
Wilgrip	1044–1048
Eadwine	1046–1048
Harcin	1046–1048
Wulfric	1046–1048
Brunwine	1046–1050
Leofwine	1046–1053
Arnfrith	1046–1056
Fargrim	1048–1053
Ærfra	1048–1053
Harcin	1050–1053
Wulfwine	1050–1053
Godwine	1053–1059
Brunwine	1053–1068

Stamford

Moneyer	Activity Range
Wilgrip	1056–1062
Leofwine	1056–1065
Harcin	1059–1062
Osweard	1059–1066
Swartcol	1062–1066
Godwine	1066–1066
Wulfweard	1066–1066
Leofwine	1066–1070
Ælfnpne	1070–1072
Brunwine	1070–1072
Leofwine	1072–1077
Brunstan	1083–1086
Godelef	1083–1086
Wulfweard	1083–1086

Stes

Moneyer	Activity Range
Beorhtric	1044–1046

Steyning

Moneyer	Activity Range
Widia	1023–1036
Frithwine	1029–1040
Frithi	1040–1042
Wulfric	1042–1044
Frithwine	1046–1048
Wulfgæt	1048–1053
Wulfric	1048–1059
Goldwine	1050–1053
Deorman	1059–1066
Goldwine	1059–1066
Wulfric	1065–1066
Deorman	1068–1070
Deorman	1072–1074
Deorman	1083–1086
Thorbeorn	1083–1086

Sudbury

Moneyer	Activity Range
Branting	1009–1023
Mansige	1017–1023
Sperling	1017–1023
Æthelmær	1023–1029

Sudbury

Moneyer	Activity Range
Folcwine	1053–1056
Folcwine	1059–1065
Folcwine	1068–1070
Wulfric	1077–1080
Wulfric	1083–1086

Tamworth

Moneyer	Activity Range
Deorwulf	973–978
Leofwine	978–979
Wine	979–985
Ælfgar	991–997
Fastolf	991–997
Ælfgar	1003–1009
Leofnoth	1036–1038
Bruning	1048–1053
Ægelwine	1050–1053
Æthelwine	1050–1053
Coling	1056–1062
Bruning	1059–1066
Coling	1065–1066
Coling	1068–1070
Beorhtwine	1068–1070
Bruning	1083–1086
Coling	1083–1086

Taunton

Moneyer	Activity Range
Leofwine	997–1003
Eadric	1009–1023
Ælfsige	1017–1023
Beorhtstan	1017–1023
Eadric	1036–1038
Leofwine	1038–1040
Eadric	1040–1042
Boiga	1040–1044
Gillecrist	1042–1044
Boiga	1046–1050
Beorhtric	1053–1062
Beorhtric	1066–1066
Beorhtric	1070–1074
Ælfwine	1074–1080
Ælfwine	1083–1086

Thetford

Moneyer	Activity Range
Ælfgar	973–975
Sperling	975–978
Leofthegn	978–979
Osfrith	979–985
Eadgar	979–997
Sperling	979–997
Beorhtric	991–997
Eadweard	991–997
Eadwig	991–997
Folcard	991–997
Godman	991–997
Leofwine	991–997
Boiga	991–997
Fugolta	991–997
Osfrith	991–997
Ælfgar	991–1003
Osbeorn	991–1009
Ælfwine	997–1003
Grim	997–1003
Grimcetel	997–1003
Osulf	997–1009
Manna	997–1016
Man	997–1023
Deorwine	1003–1009
Æthelweald	1003–1016
Eadric	1003–1029
Eadwine	1003–1029
Ælfcetel	1009–1016
Ælfgar	1009–1016
Ælfweald	1009–1016
Leofæg	1009–1016
Leofthegn	1009–1016
Fastolf	1009–1016
Palgist	1009–1016
Wulfnoth	1009–1016
Eadwig	1009–1023
Wælgist	1009–1023
Sumerlida	1009–1023
Leofric	1009–1029
Ælfwine	1009–1042
Ælfwig	1017–1023
Beorhtnoth	1017–1023
Deorwine	1017–1023
Godman	1017–1023
Leofwine	1017–1023

Thetford

Moneyer	Activity Range
Ealdred	1017–1023
Sprunt	1017–1023
Stanmær	1017–1023
Osulf	1017–1023
Wulfmær	1017–1023
Brunstan	1017–1044
Leofing	1023–1029
Thorfrith	1023–1029
Tidred	1023–1029
Wineman	1023–1036
Ælfwig	1029–1036
Runstan	1029–1036
Ælfweald	1029–1038
Æthelmær	1036–1038
Leofwine	1036–1050
Ælfwig	1038–1040
Rincolf	1038–1040
Eadric	1038–1046
Godwine	1040–1044
Sægrim	1040–1044
Tidred	1040–1046
Æthelsige	1044–1046
Manna	1044–1046
Ægelsige	1044–1048
Eastmær	1044–1056
Eastmund	1044–1056
Brunstan	1046–1048
Ælfsige	1048–1050
Ælfric	1048–1053
Æthelsige	1048–1053
Leofric	1048–1053
Eadric	1050–1053
Ægelsige	1050–1056
Eadwig	1053–1056
Leofwine	1053–1056
Blachere	1053–1065
Godleof	1053–1065
Thorfrith	1056–1062
Atsere	1056–1065
Sumerlida	1056–1065
Folcard	1059–1062
Godeln	1059–1062
Goelic	1059–1062
Ælfwine	1059–1066
Godric	1059–1066

Thetford

Moneyer	Activity Range
Godwine	1062–1065
Godwig	1065–1066
Godleof	1066–1066
Thorgod	1066–1066
Cynewig	1066–1068
Godwine	1066–1068
God	1066–1072
Cyneric	1066–1077
Beorhtwine	1068–1070
Blacsunu	1068–1070
Goda	1068–1070
Godric	1068–1070
Otbeorn	1068–1070
Godwine	1070–1072
Osbeorn	1070–1072
Eastbeorn	1072–1077
Godric	1072–1080
Folcard	1074–1080
Godred	1074–1080
Ælfwine	1083–1086
Cyneric	1083–1086
Folcard	1083–1086
Goding	1083–1086
Godleof	1083–1086
Godred	1083–1086
Godric	1083–1086

Torksey

Moneyer	Activity Range
Thorcetel	975–991
Thorcetel	1009–1029
Leofnoth	1017–1023

Totnes

Moneyer	Activity Range
Winestan	975–978
Man	978–997
Dodda	979–997
Hunewine	985–991
Wulfgar	985–991
Beorhtwine	991–997
Ælfstan	991–1003
Godwine	991–1009
Wulfmær	997–1003

Totnes

Moneyer	Activity Range
Beorhtfrith	1003–1009
Goda	1009–1016
Huneman	1009–1016
Leofgar	1017–1023
Thorgod	1017–1023
Ælfwine	1023–1029
Sæwine	1023–1029
Wulfweard	1023–1029
Farmann	1036–1038
Farmann	1040–1042

Twynham

Moneyer	Activity Range
Coleman	1080–1083

Wallingford

Moneyer	Activity Range
Wulfstan	973–975
Beorhtric	979–985
Siolf	991–991
Ælfred	991–997
Ælfweard	991–997
Ælfwine	991–997
Leofwine	991–997
Eoda	991–997
Sigewulf	991–997
Ælfric	991–1003
Ælfweald	991–1003
Ælfwig	991–1003
Oda	991–1003
Leofric	995–997
Ælfmær	997–1003
Eadric	997–1003
Man	997–1003
Wulfwine	997–1009
Ælfweard	1003–1009
Eadwig	1003–1009
Ælfric	1009–1016
Leofstan	1009–1016
Wine	1009–1016
Eadwine	1017–1023
Man	1017–1029
Colman	1017–1029
Eadweard	1023–1036

Wallingford

Moneyer	Activity Range
Ælfwine	1023–1042
Æthelwine	1029–1036
Leofwine	1029–1036
Godwine	1029–1036
Ælfwig	1036–1042
Burewine	1036–1042
Æthelric	1038–1040
Eadweard	1038–1042
Wulfwine	1038–1042
Leofwine	1038–1044
Ælfric	1040–1042
Beorhtric	1040–1042
Beorhtwine	1040–1042
Brunwine	1040–1042
Æthelwig	1040–1046
Ægelwig	1042–1044
Eadweard	1044–1046
Beorhtric	1046–1048
Beorhtwine	1046–1050
Ægelwig	1050–1053
Ælfwi	1050–1053
Ælfwine	1050–1053
Beorhtric	1050–1059
Brunwine	1050–1062
Burewine	1053–1056
Beorhtwine	1053–1059
Brand	1053–1065
Burewine	1059–1066
Beorhtmær	1059–1072
Brunwine	1065–1066
Swartlind	1066–1068
Brand	1066–1077
Swarting	1066–1086
Swartwine	1070–1072
Ægelwine	1083–1086
Withman	1083–1086

Wareham

Moneyer	Activity Range
Wulfric	979–985
Beorhtric	985–997
Beorhtsige	985–997
Ælfgar	991–997
Ælfsige	991–1003
Æthelric	997–1003

Wareham

Moneyer	Activity Range
Wulfric	997–1003
Ælfgar	1009–1016
Oda	1017–1023
Sideman	1038–1042
Sideman	1044–1048
Sideman	1050–1068
Beorn	1059–1062
Wulfsige	1059–1062
Ægelric	1066–1068
Sideman	1070–1072
Ægelric	1072–1080
Beorn	1074–1077
Godwine	1074–1080
Æthelric	1077–1080
Ægelric	1083–1086
Godwine	1083–1086
Sideloc	1083–1086

Warminster

Moneyer	Activity Range
Ælfweald	997–1003
Godwine	1009–1016
Beorhtric	1029–1036
Winegod	1029–1036
Wulfstan	1036–1038
Wulfstan	1048–1050

Warwick

Moneyer	Activity Range
Osmær	975–978
Osmær	979–985
Osmær	991–1003
Æthelstan	997–1003
Beorhtsige	997–1003
Æthelric	1003–1009
Leofweald	1009–1016
Hyse	1009–1016
Wulfric	1009–1023
Æthelwine	1017–1023
Godric	1017–1023
Leofwine	1017–1023
Godwine	1023–1029
Leofing	1023–1036
Leofwig	1023–1042
Leofwine	1036–1038

Warwick

Moneyer	Activity Range
Sigeweard	1036–1038
Goda	1036–1042
Leofwi	1040–1042
Leofwine	1042–1044
Ælfsige	1044–1046
Leofric	1044–1046
Eicefric	1044–1046
Leofing	1048–1053
Leofric	1050–1053
Æthelstan	1053–1056
Leofing	1056–1059
Thorcetel	1056–1068
Æthelstan	1059–1062
Thorcel	1059–1062
Thorstan	1059–1062
Wulfwine	1062–1065
Theodric	1065–1066
Leofing	1066–1066
Swarting	1066–1066
Wulfwine	1066–1066
Leofric	1074–1077
Thorcel	1074–1077
Ælfric	1083–1086
Leofing	1083–1086
Leofric	1083–1086
Thorcel	1083–1086

Watchet

Moneyer	Activity Range
Sigeric	979–997
Hunewine	997–1023
Godcild	1017–1044
Sæweard	1029–1036
Godcild	1053–1056
Sigewulf	1077–1080
Sigewulf	1083–1086

Wilton

Moneyer	Activity Range
Ælfsige	973–975
Eadwine	973–975
Leofweald	973–975
Osbeorn	973–975
Boiga	975–979
Eadwine	978–979

Wilton

Moneyer	Activity Range
Wadwine	979–985
Osbeorn	979–985
Sæwine	979–985
Leofweald	991–997
Wulfgar	991–997
Godwine	991–1003
Sæwine	991–1003
Boiga	995–997
Boca	995–997
Leofwine	996–1003
Goldus	997–1003
Winesige	1009–1016
Ælfstan	1017–1040
Æthelstan	1023–1029
Ælfred	1029–1036
Goldstan	1036–1040
Leofing	1038–1040
Ælfwine	1040–1046
Leofing	1042–1048
Ælfstan	1044–1048
Wineman	1044–1048
Ælfwine	1050–1059
Thorcetel	1050–1062
Ælfweald	1050–1066
Swartric	1056–1062
Sæwine	1056–1062
Hærred	1056–1065
Ælfweard	1059–1062
Brixi	1059–1062
Ælfwine	1062–1065
Leofwine	1062–1065
Winus	1062–1066
Centwine	1065–1066
Æthelweald	1066–1066
Opi	1066–1068
Sefar	1068–1070
Godric	1068–1074
Sæware	1070–1072
Sæwine	1072–1077
Ælfwine	1074–1077
Ælfwine	1080–1086
Sæwine	1083–1086
Sefmrol	1083–1086

Wilton (East Anglia)

Moneyer	Activity Range
Pensige	997–1003

Winchombe

Moneyer	Activity Range
Ælfnoth	973–975
Godleof	995–997
Ælfhelm	997–1003
Ælfgar	997–1009
Æthelman	1017–1023
Drowa	1017–1029
Draca	1040–1042
Goldwine	1048–1053
Goldwine	1059–1062
Goldwine	1066–1066
Goldwine	1074–1077
Goldwine	1083–1086

Winchester

Moneyer	Activity Range
Ælfsige	973–975
Marscalc	973–975
Thihtsige	973–975
Rægenweald	973–975
Frithmund	973–978
Rægenulf	973–978
Eatstan	975–978
Mægenfrith	975–978
Wihtsige	975–978
Æthelstan	979–985
Frithmund	979–985
Ingalric	979–985
Rægenulf	979–985
Wulfstan	979–985
Beorhtræd	979–997
Eadsige	979–997
Toca	979–997
Ælfsige	979–1003
Beorhtnoth	979–1003
Beorhtsige	979–1009
Leofweald	979–1029
Æthelweard	985–991
Eadwine	985–991
Beorhtmær	985–1003
Æthelstan	991–997

Winchester

Moneyer	Activity Range
Eadnoth	991–997
Heahwulf	991–997
Herewulf	991–997
Wulfgar	991–997
Wynstan	991–997
Godwine	991–1003
Æthelgar	991–1009
Beorhtweald	996–1003
Ælfweald	997–1016
Godman	997–1016
Wulfnoth	997–1016
Cynna	997–1023
Spileman	997–1023
Seolca	1003–1023
Brunstan	1003–1029
Leofwine	1003–1029
Ælfheah	1009–1016
Ælfmær	1009–1016
Æthelmær	1009–1016
Beorhtric	1009–1016
Beorhtstan	1009–1016
Ælfhelm	1009–1023
Æthelwine	1009–1023
Beorhtnoth	1009–1023
Eadwine	1009–1023
Leofsunu	1009–1023
Ordbeorht	1009–1023
Ælfstan	1009–1029
Oda	1009–1029
Siboda	1009–1029
Ælfsige	1009–1036
Ælfric	1017–1023
Leofstan	1017–1023
Sigegar	1017–1023
Sparafuc	1017–1023
Siwine	1017–1023
Wulfric	1017–1023
Eadweard	1017–1029
Burgweald	1017–1029
Wihtsige	1017–1029
Wine	1017–1029
Æthelric	1017–1038
Wulfnoth	1017–1040
Ælfweald	1023–1029
Ælfwine	1023–1029

Winchester

Moneyer	Activity Range
Beorhtweald	1023–1029
Goda	1023–1029
Godioluwa	1023–1029
Ælfheah	1023–1036
Ladmær	1023–1056
Æthelstan	1023–1059
Godwine	1023–1062
Leofstan	1029–1036
Wynstan	1029–1036
Ægelric	1029–1038
Spileman	1029–1044
Ælfred	1036–1038
Ælfweard	1036–1038
Brunstan	1036–1038
Godman	1036–1038
Godwine Ceoc	1036–1038
Ælfwine	1036–1042
Widia	1036–1042
Ægelwine	1038–1040
Eadwine	1038–1040
Leofstan	1038–1040
Leofwine	1038–1040
Elawine	1038–1040
Spracling	1038–1040
Æthelwig	1038–1042
Siweard	1038–1044
Æthelric	1040–1042
Godwine Ceoc	1040–1042
Wine	1040–1042
Godman	1040–1044
Siwine	1040–1044
Leofing	1040–1059
Ægelwine	1042–1044
Ifing	1042–1046
Widia	1044–1046
Godric	1044–1050
Leofwine	1044–1053
Ælfwine	1044–1072
Æstan	1046–1048
Eadwine	1046–1050
Ælfstan	1048–1050
Eadwig	1048–1050
Ifing	1048–1050
Coll	1048–1050
Loc	1048–1053

Winchester

Moneyer	Activity Range
Ægelwine	1050–1053
Beorhtweald	1050–1053
Eadric	1050–1053
Brand	1050–1053
Wynstan	1050–1053
Widia	1050–1056
Godman	1053–1056
Godwine Ceoc	1053–1056
Godwine Widia	1053–1056
Ertan	1053–1056
Beorhtmær	1053–1062
Æstan	1056–1059
Spracling	1056–1066
Anderboda	1056–1068
Leofweald	1059–1083
Godric	1062–1065
Leofing	1062–1066
Godwine	1065–1066
Heahwulf	1065–1066
Godric	1066–1066
Swerting	1066–1066
Leofwine	1066–1070
Godnoth	1068–1072
Godwine	1070–1072
Anderboda	1070–1080
Leofing	1070–1080
Siweard	1072–1086
Garulf	1074–1077
Godwine	1074–1086
Æstan	1077–1080
Ægstan	1080–1083
Brunic	1080–1086
Lifinc	1080–1086
Æstan	1083–1086
Lifweald	1083–1086
Dimund	1083–1086
Spracling	1083–1086

Worcester

Moneyer	Activity Range
Man	975–978
Man	979–985
Martin	979–985
Sigefrith	991–997
Sigewine	991–997

Worcester

Moneyer	Activity Range
Æthelmær	991–1003
Goda	991–1009
Durant	991–1009
Ælfsige	997–1003
Wulfric	997–1003
Æthelstan	1009–1016
Garwulf	1009–1023
Wulfmær	1017–1023
Goda	1017–1029
Ælfweald	1017–1036
Ælf	1023–1029
God	1023–1029
Leofric	1023–1029
Ælfwine	1023–1036
Æthelwine	1023–1040
Godwine	1029–1036
Leofstan	1029–1046
Leofric	1036–1042
Ægelwine	1038–1040
Æthelwig	1038–1040
Ælfwine	1042–1044
Ælfwine	1046–1048
Godwine	1048–1050
Leofric	1048–1050
Leofstan	1048–1050
Wulfwine	1048–1050
Ælfwine	1050–1053
Leofing	1050–1053
Ealdwine	1050–1053
Æthelric	1053–1056
Garwulf	1053–1056
Wicing	1053–1066
Ægelwine	1056–1062
Leofstan	1056–1062
Æthelwine	1059–1062
Garwulf	1059–1062
Leofric	1059–1062
Ælfwine	1062–1065
Baldric	1062–1065
Eastmær	1062–1065
Heathwulf	1062–1065
Æthelwine	1065–1066
Eastmær	1066–1066
Garwulf	1066–1066
Heathwi	1066–1066

Worcester

Moneyer	Activity Range
Wulfwine	1066–1066
Leofric	1066–1070
Eastmær	1068–1072
Garwulf	1068–1072
Refwine	1068–1072
Ælfweard	1072–1074
Baldric	1072–1074
Ælfgeat	1077–1080
Ælfgærd	1080–1086
Baldric	1083–1086
Eastmær	1083–1086
Sæwine	1083–1086

York

Moneyer	Activity Range
Brentinc	973–975
Fastolf	973–975
Iohan	973–975
Man	973–975
Manna	973–975
Osmund	973–975
Tuma	973–975
Unspac	973–975
Wulfric	973–975
Dunn	973–978
Osulf	973–978
Oscetel	973–979
Isulf	973–985
Oda	973–985
Ælfstan	975–978
Æthelweald	975–978
Beaniene	975–978
Boiga	975–978
Ealhstan	975–978
Gunner	975–978
Gunnulf	975–978
Iustan	975–978
Stirgar	975–978
Surclos	975–978
Winbeald	975–978
Rægenbeald	975–979
Beolan	975–985
Stir	975–985
Arncetel	978–979
Cieolog	978–979

York

Moneyer	Activity Range
Man	978–979
Swerting	978–979
Uri	978–979
Farmann	978–985
Fastolf	978–985
Thorstan	978–985
Tuma	978–985
Ælfstan	979–985
Asbeorn	979–985
Colgrim	979–985
Ellaf	979–985
Fællan	979–985
Frostulf	979–985
Golla	979–985
Herewulf	979–985
Hundulf	979–985
Hwætman	979–985
Oban	979–985
Osulf	979–985
Othgrim	979–985
Scadwine	979–985
Scanig	979–985
Snecol	979–985
Stirgar	979–985
Sunulf	979–985
Thorcetel	979–985
Tumne	979–985
Ulf	979–985
Wineman	979–985
Wulfstan	979–985
Ælfhere	991–997
Beorhtwine	991–997
Golla	991–997
Gunhwæt	991–997
Iole	991–997
Leofman	991–997
Leofwine	991–997
Oge	991–997
Osulf	991–997
Othcetel	991–997
Othulf	991–997
Swertcol	991–997
Swerting	991–997
Thorcetel	991–997
Winterlida	991–997

York

Moneyer	Activity Range
Eadric	991–1003
Frostulf	991–1003
Leofstan	991–1003
Oda	991–1003
Stirgar	991–1003
Sumerlida	991–1003
Sunulf	991–1003
Swert	991–1003
Wengos	991–1003
Hundulf	991–1009
Oban	991–1009
Arnthor	991–1016
Thorstan	991–1016
Wulfsige	991–1016
Othgrim	991–1023
Ulfcetel	991–1023
Cetel	991–1029
Hildulf	991–1036
Arncetel	995–997
Oscetel	995–1003
Theodred	997–1003
Ire	997–1009
Thorulf	997–1016
Beorhtnoth	997–1029
Beorhtwine	1003–1009
Cetelbeorn	1003–1009
Colgrim	1003–1023
Osgot	1003–1036
Deorwulf	1009–1016
Isulf	1009–1016
Leofwine	1009–1016
Sumerlida	1009–1016
Bretecol	1009–1023
Dagfin	1009–1023
Snecol	1009–1023
Ælfstan	1009–1029
Stircol	1009–1029
Wulfstan	1009–1029
Sunulf	1009–1038
Beornnoth	1017–1023
Fastolf	1017–1023
Gunhwæt	1017–1023
Leofwine	1017–1023
Osfrith	1017–1023
Selecol	1017–1023

York

Moneyer	Activity Range
Stirgar	1017–1023
Wulfgrim	1017–1023
Swerting	1017–1029
Toca	1017–1029
Fargrim	1017–1036
Frithcol	1017–1036
Godman	1017–1036
Arncetel	1017–1042
Arnolf	1023–1029
Asgout	1023–1029
Crinan	1023–1029
Grurn	1023–1029
Ire	1023–1029
Oustman	1023–1029
Pitherwine	1023–1029
Surtinc	1023–1029
Withrin	1023–1029
Æthelwine	1023–1036
Farthegn	1023–1036
Wulfnoth	1023–1036
Crucan	1023–1038
Grimulf	1023–1046
Ægelwine	1029–1036
Arngrim	1029–1036
Colgrim	1029–1036
Earngrim	1029–1036
Hrafn	1029–1036
Landfrith	1029–1036
Othan	1029–1036
Ræfen	1029–1036
Othin	1029–1042
Thorgrim	1029–1042
Ucede	1029–1042
Beorn	1029–1046
Duracan	1036–1038
Pitherwine	1036–1040
Stircol	1036–1042
Withrin	1036–1042
Swegen	1036–1044
Scule	1036–1066
Ægelmær	1038–1040
Ælfwine	1038–1040
Æthelmær	1038–1040
Arncill	1038–1040
Goding	1038–1040

York

Moneyer	Activity Range
Godman	1038–1040
Swert	1038–1040
Æthelwine	1038–1046
Ælfhere	1038–1050
Arngrim	1038–1065
Thærdine	1040–1042
Wulfric	1040–1042
Cetel	1040–1046
Ulfcetel	1040–1066
Unolf	1042–1046
Sæfugel	1042–1050
Iole	1042–1062
Egann	1044–1046
Elfere	1044–1046
Gunnulf	1044–1046
Iocil	1044–1046
Iolana	1044–1046
Man	1044–1046
Othen	1044–1046
Othin	1044–1048
Ræfen	1044–1048
Stircol	1044–1048
Thorgrim	1044–1048
Hrafn	1044–1050
Ælfwine	1044–1053
Arncetel	1044–1056
Ælfstan	1046–1048
Io	1046–1048
Iurerel	1046–1048
Wulfwine	1046–1048
Eltan	1046–1050
Iocetel	1046–1050
Coll	1046–1053
Leofnoth	1046–1059
Thor	1046–1066
Iola	1048–1059
Æitel	1050–1053
Etyrcol	1050–1053
Stircol	1050–1056
Winterfugol	1050–1056
Swertcol	1050–1066
Hrafn	1053–1056
Ræfen	1053–1056
Iocetel	1053–1066
Snebeorn	1056–1066

York

Moneyer	Activity Range
Othgrim	1056–1070
Arncetel	1059–1066
Othbeorn	1059–1070
Othulf	1062–1066
Aleof	1065–1066
Leofing	1066–1066
Sutere	1066–1066
Wulf	1066–1068
Roscetel	1066–1070
Althwulf	1068–1070
Arncetel	1068–1070
Harthulf	1068–1070
Inleif	1068–1070
Leofsige	1068–1070
Swertcol	1068–1070
Thor	1068–1070
Ulfcetel	1068–1070
Arthulf	1072–1074
Othgrim	1072–1074
Aleof	1072–1077
Harthulf	1072–1080
Althwulf	1074–1077
Thor	1077–1080
Leifinc	1080–1086
Aleof	1083–1086
Othbeorn	1083–1086
Thor	1083–1086

Indeterminate Mint

Moneyer	Activity Range
Leofing	973–975
Wulfgar	973–975
Ætheln	975–978
Leofwine	975–978
Leofwine	975–979
Grim	978–979
Wilberht	978–979
Edgar	979–985
Goda	979–985
Hild	979–985
Man	979–985
Godwine	979–991
Leofstan	985–991
Beorhtsige	985–997
Ælfwine	991–997

Indeterminate Mint

Moneyer	Activity Range
Beorhtlaf	991–997
Eadsige	991–997
Leofstan	991–997
Stegenbit	991–997
Wulfgar	991–997
Wulfwine	991–997
Leofwine	991–1003
Leofric	991–1016
Alfweald	995–997
Beorhtnoth	995–997
Byrhsige	995–997
Godwine	995–997
Godwine	995–997
Toca	995–997
Wynstan	995–997
Ælfric	997–1003
Godwine	997–1003
Grim	997–1003
Man	997–1003
Ælfgar	997–1009
Godric	997–1016
Osweald	1009–1009
Beorhtmær	1009–1016
Beorhtnoth	1009–1016
Edmund	1009–1016
Coll	1017–1023
Leofing	1017–1023
Leofstan	1017–1023
Ælfgar	1023–1029
Æthelric	1023–1029
Arncetel	1023–1029
Cetel	1023–1029
Elfsige	1023–1029
Godleof	1023–1029
Godwine	1023–1029
Leofric	1023–1029
Leofwine	1023–1029
Oda	1023–1029
Thorstan	1023–1029
Godric	1023–1036
Wulfwine	1023–1036
Ælfwig	1029–1036
Æthestan	1029–1036
Wulfnoth	1029–1036
Ælf	1036–1038

Indeterminate Mint

Moneyer	Activity Range
Ælfstan	1036–1038
Ælfwine	1036–1038
Ælfwine	1036–1038
Æthelmær	1036–1038
Leofing	1036–1038
Wulfweard	1036–1038
Leofwine	1036–1040
Æthelmær	1038–1040
Eadric	1038–1040
Eadwine	1038–1040
Edweard	1038–1040
Leofing	1038–1040
Leofwine	1038–1040
Leofwine	1038–1040
Rader	1038–1040
Sund	1038–1040
Wulfwine	1038–1040
Ælfstan	1040–1042
Ælfwine	1040–1042
Æthelwine	1040–1042
Eadweald	1040–1042
Fargrim	1040–1042
Godric	1040–1042
Leofred	1040–1042
Leofsige	1040–1042
Leofstan	1040–1042
Leofwine	1040–1042
Leofwine	1040–1042
Man	1040–1042
Wulfheah	1040–1042
Wulfstan	1040–1042
Wulfwine	1040–1042
Blacman	1042–1044
Bruning	1042–1044
Brunman	1042–1044
Leofstan	1042–1046
Beorhtred	1044–1046
Wine	1044–1046
Wulfsige	1044–1046
Ælfgar	1046–1048
Elfsie	1046–1048
Godsunu	1046–1048
Lefwine	1046–1048
Leofwine	1046–1048
Tafere	1046–1048

Indeterminate Mint

Moneyer	Activity Range
Wulfwine	1046–1048
Godwine	1046–1050
Ælfred	1048–1050
Ælfsie	1048–1050
Ælfstan	1048–1050
Ælfstan	1048–1050
Ælfwine	1048–1050
Beorhtred	1048–1050
Direme	1048–1050
Dunning	1048–1050
Estan	1048–1050
Godwine	1048–1050
Leofwine	1048–1050
Lific	1048–1050
Lifinc	1048–1050
Lifinc	1048–1050
Liofwine	1048–1050
Wulfgar	1048–1050
Ælfwine	1048–1053
Beorhtric	1050–1053
Beorhtwine	1050–1053
Leofwine	1050–1053
Eilnoth	1056–1059
Godwine	1056–1059
Leofdæg	1056–1059
Alfred	1059–1062
Blachere	1059–1062
Leofred	1059–1062
Leofwine	1059–1062
Ælfric	1062–1065
Dunning	1062–1065
Wulfgeat	1062–1065
Leofweald	1065–1066
Sibwine	1065–1066
Wulfgar	1065–1066
Ælfweald	1066–1066
Beorhtric	1066–1066
Leofwine	1066–1066
Beorhtwig	1068–1070
Leofwine	1080–1083
Ælfwine	1083–1086
Beorhtnoth	1083–1086